LAW AND POLITICS

A CROSS-CULTURAL ENCYCLOPEDIA

ENCYCLOPEDIAS OF THE HUMAN EXPERIENCE

David Levinson, Series Editor

LAW AND POLITICS

A CROSS-CULTURAL ENCYCLOPEDIA

Daniel P. Strouthes

ABC-CLIO
Santa Barbara, California
Denver, Colorado
Oxford, England

Library of Congress Cataloging-in-Publication Data

Strouthes, Daniel.
    Law and politics: a cross-cultural encyclopedia/Daniel Strouthes.
        p.   cm. — (Encyclopedias of the human experience)
    Includes bibliographical references and index.
    1. Law and politics—Encyclopedias.   I. Title.   II. Series.
    K487.P65S77   1995   340'.03'—dc20   95-46014

ISBN 0-87436-777-8 (alk. paper)

02 01 00 99 98 97 96 95   10 9 8 7 6 5 4 3 2 1 (hc)

ABC-CLIO, Inc.
130 Cremona Drive, P.O. Box 1911
Santa Barbara, California 93116-1911

This book is printed on acid-free paper (∞).
Manufactured in the United States of America

Contents

CONTENTS

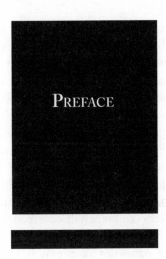

PREFACE

Law and politics are two central features of all human cultures. Politics is about the ways in which power is exercised in a society. Because power is exercised by all members of every society, politics is a cultural universal, that is, it is found in all cultures. Law, because it also deals with the use of power, is a component of politics. But law also encompasses those principles of behavior that the people in a society think are so important that they must not be violated. Is law, like politics, a cultural universal, common to all societies? Some experts have argued that law exists only in technologically advanced societies, particularly those in the West. They associate the law with black robes, thick tomes, wood-paneled court rooms, and juries. When they go to Mongolia, to central Africa, or to Native American communities in northern Quebec and do not see these things, they assume that law does not exist in these places.

But while some societies lack these Western features of law, every society does have social and cultural institutions that we know by the term *law*. All societies have legal authorities (whom we usually call judges) who make deci-

sions in cases of dispute, decisions that are regularly applied (applied the same way in similar situations) and made on the basis of principles that can be stated. Furthermore, these decisions state the rights of one party and the duties of the other in relation to the principle. These principles we know as laws. Every single known language has a word that is synonymous with our English word "law"; only the English word "law" is different, in that it alone refers not only to the principles behind legal decisions but also to legislation, the rules made by legislators.

In short, there is very good behavioral and linguistic evidence that law is universal to all societies. So, if both politics and law are universal, why should we bother to learn about the legal and political systems of societies other than our own? We need to know about legal and political systems for three main reasons.

First, to acquire practical knowledge so that one can participate in the political and legal affairs of one's own society. A good example of this is the training one receives in law school, which is geared toward a knowledge of the law of one society, so that one can practice law. In this type of learning, it is perfectly reasonable to restrict one's focus to the legal or political system of the society in which one will be active, although it is always better to have a wider base of knowledge than that provided by a study of one legal or political system.

Second, to learn about the unique features of an historical event and to draw attention to that which is different about that event. Here too, it is reasonable to have knowledge of only one political or legal system, the one belonging to the society being studied, although for analytical purposes it is always better to have a wider base of knowledge.

Third, to understand the concept of law as a whole from a scientific point of view. With this approach we ask about how law and politics work, what their component parts are, what their functions are, etc., so that we can make generalizations about law and politics across cultures. We want to be able to say, for example, that law always does *x*, or that it always changes in way *y* when a society is exposed to influence *z*.

In order to understand the concepts of law and politics this well, it is necessary to understand them as they are in all of their manifestations. We cannot understand law without understanding law in Morocco, in an American Indian band in Brazil, in a Thai village, etc. If we were to say that we can understand either law or politics by studying just one society's example, it would be like claiming that we could know all about the subject of war by studying the American Revolutionary War. It cannot be done. Not only do other wars occur for completely different reasons, but they have greatly differing tactics, strategies, weapons, and historical developments. Imagine if Norman Schwarzkopf, who led allied military forces in the Persian Gulf War, had had only the strategic and tactical knowledge that could be gained from studying the American Revolutionary War. It would have been a disaster, because he would not have been able to make generalizations about or predict the actions of the enemy.

In the scientific study of law and politics, scholars try to make generalizations and predictions about the fields of law and politics as whole entities as well as their component concepts. One example of how this process works should show this approach clearly. For many decades, if not centuries, it was established as a valid generalization about law that all legal systems made use of the principle of res judicata (Latin for "the thing that has been decided"), the principle that all legal disputes are at some point finally decided, i.e., they cannot be further pursued, by appeal or by any other means, by any of the parties associated with the case. Legal scholars assumed that res judicata is universal to all societies because it was found in every society whose legal system had been studied, and because it

seemed to fulfill a main function of the law—putting disputes to rest forever. This function was assumed to be central to the nature of the law in that it was believed that law existed to put disputes to rest with finality so that the people involved could get on with their lives and with doing the productive work that keeps societies going. In other words, if there was no res judicata in law, why would law exist?

This generalization stood as absolute fact for a long time until the 1980s, when the anthropologist Rebecca French discovered that for civil law cases (cases of private wrongs), the Tibetan legal system does not have res judicata. The reasons for this are discussed in the entry on res judicata. But, for the purposes of scientific enquiry, it is enough to say that the generalization concerning res judicata is false for at least one society, thereby demonstrating it to be not universal to all legal systems. In this manner the science of human behavior advances. Without French's study of Tibetan law, we would be further away from a true knowledge of law as it actually exists in human societies and about the function of law generally. And it is for this reason that law, politics, and any other field of human behavior must be studied across all cultures if we are to arrive at an accurate portrayal.

The goal of this volume is far more modest than to achieve a scientific breakthrough. Rather, it is to provide readers with the definitions and cross-cultural patterns or variations of some of the central concepts of law and politics. In addition, there are some concepts, such as misprision, that are quite uneven in their distribution in the legal systems of the world, and for this reason alone they are of interest and are included here. Each entry provides a definition of the concept and gives some background data that the reader may use to get a firmer understanding of the concept. I have tried to incorporate data from a variety of different societies so that the reader can have a multidimensional view of the manifestations a concept takes in different legal systems. In every entry, my goal has been to provide a precise and accurate definition for an important concept, as well as some concise background detail and discussion, using data gathered from a variety of legal and political systems around the globe. In many entries, I have included an illustrative example of a concept from U.S. law and a contrasting example or examples taken from another legal system or systems so as to make the multicultural approach more clear. I have also where relevant included the text or extracts of text from original legal documents so as to provide readers with a knowledge of how law is practiced in various societies.

Acknowledgments

I would like to thank a number of people for help that I have received in writing this book.

First, I would like to thank my parents for their emotional and financial support. I thank my graduate school advisor, Leopold Pospisil of the Anthropology Department of Yale University, for his wisdom and for a significant portion of the ideas on law and politics that I have used in this book.

I also thank the Micmac people of Eskasoni, Nova Scotia, who with great patience and understanding helped me to learn about their culture and society. I thank them as well for their friendship, which has been of great personal value to me.

Finally, I wish to thank The Jacobs Funds of the Whatcom Museum Society, the Canadian Embassy, and the American Philosophical Society for their financial support of my work with the Micmac in the years 1985 through 1987.

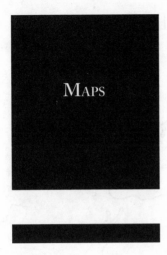

MAPS

The following maps show approximate locations
of the cultures mentioned in the text.

Africa and the Middle East

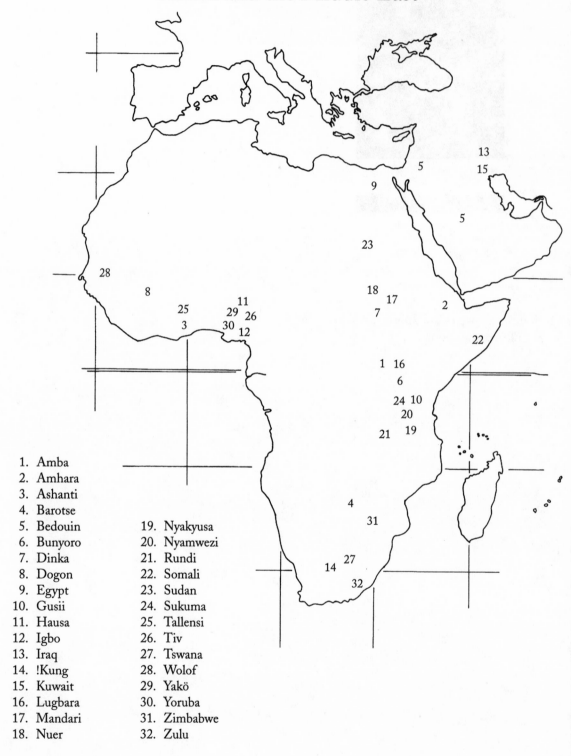

1. Amba
2. Amhara
3. Ashanti
4. Barotse
5. Bedouin
6. Bunyoro
7. Dinka
8. Dogon
9. Egypt
10. Gusii
11. Hausa
12. Igbo
13. Iraq
14. !Kung
15. Kuwait
16. Lugbara
17. Mandari
18. Nuer
19. Nyakyusa
20. Nyamwezi
21. Rundi
22. Somali
23. Sudan
24. Sukuma
25. Tallensi
26. Tiv
27. Tswana
28. Wolof
29. Yakö
30. Yoruba
31. Zimbabwe
32. Zulu

Central and South America

1. Inca
2. Jivaro
3. Tarascans
4. Yaqui
5. Yanomamö

Europe and Asia

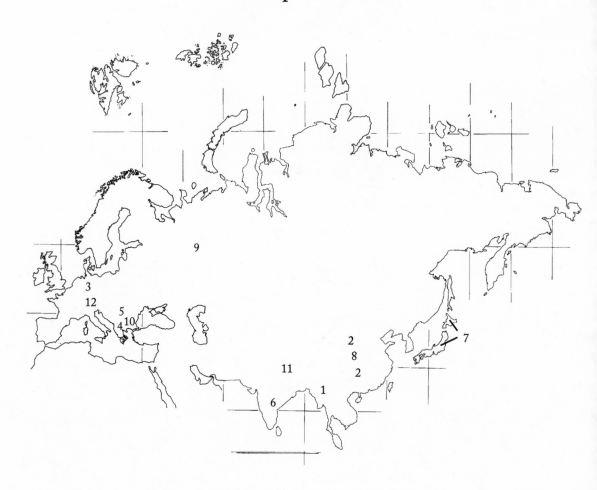

1. Burmese
2. China
3. Germany
4. Greece
5. Hungary
6. India
7. Japan
8. Lolo
9. Russia
10. Sarakatsani
11. Tibetans
12. Tiroleans

North America

1. Cherokee
2. Cheyenne
3. Choctaw
4. Cochiti
5. Cree
6. Crow
7. Iroquois
8. Micmac
9. Naskapi
10. Navajo
11. Nunamiut

Oceania

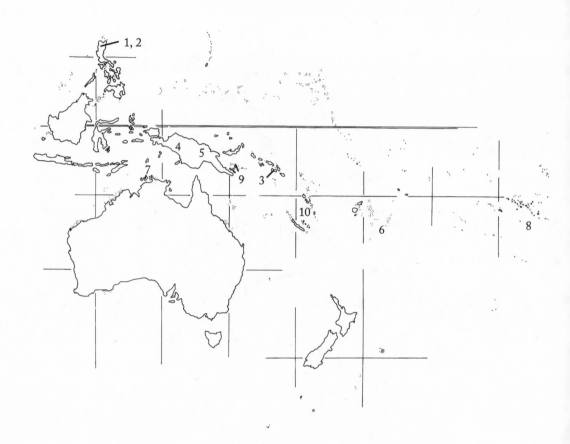

1. Ifugao
2. Kalinga
3. Kaoka
4. Kapauku
5. Tairora
6. Tikopia
7. Tiwi
8. Tongans
9. Trobriands
10. Vanuatu

LAW AND POLITICS
A CROSS-CULTURAL ENCYCLOPEDIA

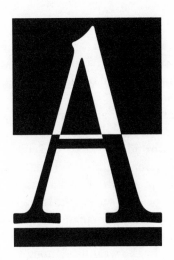

or with detention, or with a fine of not more than three hundred yuan.

If the commission of the offence results in death, the offender shall be punished with imprisonment for a period of not more than five years; if the commission of the offence results in grievous bodily harm, the offender shall be punished with imprisonment for a period of not more than three years.

Article 304. Whoever being bound by law or contract to support, mantain, or protect any helpless person abandons such person or fails to give to such person the support, maintenance, or protection necessary for preservation of life, shall be punished in accordance with the provisions relating to the offence of intentionally causing bodily harm resulting in death or in grievous bodily harm.

Article 305. Whoever commits against any of his lineal ascendants the offence specified in paragraph 1 of the last preceding Article, shall be liable to the punishment prescribed for the offence increased by one-half.

Whoever commits against any of his collateral ascendants the offence specified in paragraph 1 of the last preceding Article, shall be liable to the punishment prescribed for the offence increased by one-third.

If the commission of the offence results in death or grievous bodily harm to the ascendant, the offender shall be punished in accordance with the provisions relating to the offence of intentionally causing bodily harm to an ascendant resulting in death or grievous bodily harm.

The Law Codification Commission. (1919) *The Criminal Code of the Republic of China (Second Revised Draft).*

ABANDONMENT Abandonment occurs when helpless people are left to fend for themselves. In many societies, it is a criminal offense, because leaders and authorities want the people within the society to take care of each other rather than depend upon the government to do so. In other societies, particularly some hunting and gathering societies, abandonment is considered a moral rather than a legal matter. While it is a crime to abandon a child in the United States, most other kinds of abandonment are not considered criminal. In the Republic of China, as shown below, the law makes it a crime to abandon anyone, and increases the penalty for abandoning one's ancestors and relatives in the generations preceding one's own. This law, then, reflects the Confucian tradition's high positive value on helping the older people of one's family (The Law Codification Commission, 1919: 102–103).

Chapter XXV
Abandonment

Article 303. Whoever abandons a helpless person shall be punished with imprisonment for a period of not more than one year,

ACEPHALOUS SOCIETIES Acephalous (or "headless") societies are those that have no common government that rules all of its members. The term was first used explicitly by anthropologists Meyer Fortes and E. E. Evans-Pritchard to refer to segmentary lineage societies. In these societies, lineage segments united when the need arose, such as in time of war or feud, but had no formal leaders who commanded the united segments.

Another type of society that is sometimes called acephalous is a traditional indigenous society that had in the past its own native political and legal structure but then lost it to a conquering colonial power. Such examples are common throughout the world. Here the term *acephalous society* is a misnomer. What happens when the conquering colonists destroy a native political and legal structure is that they replace it with their own or with one that is compliant with their interests. Colonists do not always want to destroy a native leadership or authority, although they almost always wish to dominate the people of the society for their own purposes. Thus, though a band society that has lost its headman as an effective leader may appear on the surface to be acephalous, it is actually the case that the society is being led by the colonists and its legal affairs (or at least the ones that the colonists care about) decided by colonial courts.

See also SEGMENTARY LINEAGE.

Fortes, Meyer, and E. E. Evans-Pritchard, eds. (1940) *African Political Systems*.

ADOPTION

Adoption refers to the dissolution of the legal parent-offspring relationship between parents and their natural offspring and the creation of the legal parent-offspring relationship between that offspring and someone other than his or her natural parents. As such, adoption is a legal fiction; the relationship between adoptive parent(s) and adopted child is not a natural or biological one, but only a legal one.

The reason for adoption in most societies is to acquire an heir. People with some accumulated wealth and with no natural children of their own will adopt a child so as to have someone to inherit their wealth. This pattern can be seen clearly in societies such as the Ifugao of the Philippines and the Micmac Indians of eastern Canada. Among the Ifugao, adoption is practiced only by the wealthy. Among the Micmac, adoption traditionally never existed, and exists today only very rarely. However, foster parentage is quite common and functions to provide for the care of children whose natural parents are incapable of caring for them. Adoption is not practiced because there is virtually no wealth to be inherited, and in the past this was even more true than it is today. Further, foster parentage is considered sufficient for the proper raising of another couple's child, and the idea of changing the name and identity of the foster child, in order to adopt, seems alien to them.

The following legal decision regards an adoption involving Brahmans, the highest caste in India, and is settled according to Hindu law (*The Indian Law Reports, Bombay Series*, 1925: 515-520).

ADOPTION
APPELLATE CIVIL.

Before Sir Norman Macleod, Kt., Chief Justice, and Mr. Justice Crump.

GOVINDPRASAD LALITAPRASAD MISHAR (Original Defendant No. 1), Appellant v. RINDABAI KIX LALITAPRASAD (Original Plaintiff), Respondent.

Hindu law—Adoption—Datta Homan—Brahmins.

The ceremony of *datta homan* is essential to validate an adoption amongst Brahmins unless the adoptive father and son belong to the same *gotra* [lineage].

First appeal against the decision of J. H. Betigeri, First Class Subordinate Judge of Dharwar.

Suit for declaration and possession.

One Lalitaprasad dies in 1911, leaving a widow, Rindabai. Lalitaprasad was a Karoj Brahmin living at Morab, in Dharwar District.

The defendant No. 1, Govindprasad, was in possession of Lalitaprasad's property and claimed to retain it on the ground that he was adopted by Rindabai in February 1913.

In 1919, the plaintiff, Rindabai, sued for a declaration that Govindprasad was not the legally adopted son of the plaintiff's husband; that *datta homan* and adoption ceremony had never taken place.

The Subordinate Judge held that the fact of the adoption of Govindprasad was proved, but that the adoption itself was invalid as the *datta homan* ceremony had not been performed, that ceremony being essential in the case of Kanoj Brahmins governed by the Mitakashara law, where the adoptive father and adopted son belonged to different *gotras*. His observations were as follows:—

"Defendant No. 1 admits in para. 5 of Exhibit 69 that his *gotra* in the genitive line was *barha* and his *gotra* in the adoptive line was *upamanyu*: So the question to be decided in this case is whether *datta homan* ceremony is indispensable or not for the validity of an adoption when the *gotras* of the adopter and the adoptee are different, i.e., *bhinna*. On behalf of defendant No. 1, the case in 4 Mad. H.C.R., page 165, is relied upon. It does lay down that in order to establish a valid adoption in a Brahmin family, proof of the performance of the *datta homan* is not essential. But from the facts of this case, it cannot be clearly made out, whether adopter and the adoptee in it were the same or of different *gotras*. Further the

correctness of the ruling in the above case was questioned in I.L.R. 7 Mad., page 548 wherein the Madras High Court expressed an opinion that amongst Brahmins the ceremony of *datta homan* is an essential element of adoption. All the High Courts are agreed that where the adoptive father and son belong to the same *gotra* the *datta homan* is not necessary, vide I.L.R. 11 Mad., page 5, I.L.R. 6 All, page 276, I.L.R. 24 Born., page 218, 27 Indian Cases, page 39, and I.L.R. 39 Born., page 441. In the judgment of the case in I.L.R. 24 Born., page 218, on page 223 is mentioned an unreported decision of the Bombay High Court decided in 1865 in which it was held that the ceremony of *datta homan* was not essential to the legal validity of an adoption. It is stated there that the parties in the said case belonged to the three regenerate classes. So that case might be one amongst Brahmins or Kshatrias or Vaishyas. Unless that case were shown to be one concerning Brahmins, it cannot help the present defendant No. 1 since it is held by the Madras High Court that *datta homan* is not necessary for the validity of an adoption among Kshatrias, vide I.L.R. 6 Mad., page 20. Besides, I am not bound to follow the above unreported case in view of section 3 of Act XVII of 1875. In the case in 27 Indian Cases, page 39, all the Hindu texts on the subject have been considered and so also the case law till 1914. It is noted there that there is a great diversity of opinion amongst the text-writers as there is absence of uniformity in the judicial decisions of the Indian Courts on this point. Finally the following observation is recorded:— 'In this diversity of judicial opinion, it must concede that the principle that *datta homan* ceremony is essential for the validity of an adoption among Brahmins, still counts a strong body of supporters and that the rationalistic view has not yet finally triumphed over formalism.' The same judgment further observes:— 'Whether the rule (that *datta homan* is necessary among Brahmins) itself will ultimately stand discredited and disappear, it is needless to speculate in this instance (the case then before the High Court being one in which the adoptive father and the son were of the same *gotra*).' According to the observations to be found on page 994 of West and Buhler's Hindu Law, 4th Edition, *datta homan* appears essential for the validity of an adoption among Brahmins, where the adoptive father and son are of different *gotra*. In this state of the authorities, I am not prepared to hold that the time has come to discredit and discard the respectable body of Hindu opinion, in texts and in decided cases, which lays down the *datta homan* is an indispensable requisite for a valid adoption between persons of different *gotras*. I am, therefore, constrained to find that the adoption of defendant No. 1 is not valid, though in fact it took place."

The Subordinate Judge, therefore, passed a decree in favor of the plaintiff declaring the adoption invalid and awarding possession of the property.

The defendant No. 1 appealed to the High Court.

A. G. Desai, for the appellant.
Coyajee, with *R. A. Jahagirdar*, for the respondent.

MACLEOD, C. J.:— The plaintiff sued to obtain a declaration that the first defendant was not the legally adopted son of the plaintiff's husband. The plaintiff disputed the factum of the adoption. That issue was found in the affirmative, but on the issue of whether the adoption was valid, the Court held that the adoption was not valid though in fact it had been made, because the adoptive father and the adopted son were of different *gotra*.

Consequently the *datta homan* was essential to validate the adoption, and in this case it is not disputed that the *datta homan* had not been performed. If we were of opinion that the adoption was valid, it would have been necessary to consider the authorities at some length. But we agree with the judgment in the Court below that in this particular case the *datta homan* was necessary.

The authorities are considered in the latest Edition of Mayne at pp. 205-208, and at the bottom of page 207 the conclusion is as follows: "So far as it is possible to reconcile these conflicting decisions, they seem to point to the conclusion that, among the twice-born classes, the *datta homan* is necessary, unless the adopted boy is of the same *gotra* as his adopter, or unless a usage to the contrary can be established". In *Mahashoya Shosinath Ghose v. Srimati Krishna Soondari Dasi* their Lordships observed:—

"The mode of giving and taking a child in adoption continues to stand on Hindu law and on Hindu usage, and it is perfectly clear that amongst the twice born classes there could have been such adoption by deed, because certain religious ceremonies, the *datta homan* in particular, are in their case requisite."

The question in issue in that appeal was whether there could be in the case of Sudras such a giving and taking as was necessary to satisfy the law, by mere deed, without an actual delivery of the child by the father. Still this dictum of their Lordships may be taken as stating what their Lordships considered at that time was necessary to validate an adoption amongst the twice-born classes.

In this Presidency at any rate the only cases in which an adoption has been recognized as valid without the *datta homan* being performed have been those in which the adoptive father and the adopted son belonged to the same *gotra*. All the authorities on this subject are discussed in *Valnbai v. Gorind Kushinath*, and in *Bal Gangadhar Tilak v.*

Shrinivas Pandit, their Lordships in considering the same question gave their approval to the judgment of Sir Lawrence Jenkins in that case. On a review of the arguments in that judgment it is obvious that the learned chief Justice considered that it was only because there was identity of *gotra* that *datta homan* could be dispensed with. It must be noted, however, that in referring to the decision of the Full Bench of the Madras High Court in *Govindayyar v. Dorasami,* their Lordships in *Bal Gangadhar Tilak v. Shrinivas Pandit* considered that decision as being of value as containing a careful study of the authorities and affirming that the ceremony of *datta homan* was not essential to a valid adoption amongst Brahmins in Southern India. With all due respect it would seem difficult to find from the judgment of the Full Bench that it was decided that the *datta homan* was not essential to any adoption amongst Brahmins. The headnote is as follows:—

> "The ceremony of *datta homan* is not essential to a valid adoption among Brahmins in Southern India when the adoptive father and son belong to the same *gotra.*"

Their Lordships considered whether they should depart from the decision in *V. Singamma v. Vinjamuri Venkatacharlu.* They pointed out that some doubt had been thrown upon the case by the observation of the Judicial Committee in *Mahashoya Shosinath Ghose v. Srimati Krishna Soondari Dasi* that *datta homan* was requisite in the case of Brahmins and referred to the case of *Venkala v. Subhadra,* which was to the same effect. In *V. Singamma v. Vinjamuri Venkatacharlu* the point was not argued on both sides and Jagannatha, who was cited in the case, was no authority in Southern India. Their Lordships concluded that the original texts conveyed the impression that *datta homan* might probably be an essential part of a valid adoption as a general rule, and that in a proper case there was sufficient ground for directing an inquiry as to usage.

Although the general rule might be as indicated above there was reason to think that there were exceptions to it. There was a text of Manu to the effect that if, among several brothers, one has a son, that son was the son of all. To this extent, that *dotta homan* was not essential when the adoptive father and son were of the same *gotra,* they thought they might safely adhere to the decision in *V. Singamma v. Vinjamuri Venkatacharlu.*

The rule, therefore, may be stated in this form. The ceremony of *datta homan* is essential to validate an adoption amongst Brahmins unless the adoptive father and son belong to the same *gotra.* Apart from all the considerations there is this justification for it, that when it is sought to introduce a stranger into a family it is desirable that all the religious ceremonies should be performed so as to ensure the requisite publicity for the adoption. It may be said that there is a tendency in these days towards dispensing with religious ceremonies, but that is no reason why we should seek in this case to depart from what must be recognized as an established rule of Hindu law. The appeal is dismissed with costs.

Barton, Roy F. (1969 [1919]) *Ifugao Law.*

The Indian Law Reports, Bombay Series. (1925) Vol. XLIX. Edited by K. McI. Kemp.

Strouthes, Daniel P. (1994) *Change in the Real Property Law of a Cape Breton Island Micmac Band.*

ADVERSE POSSESSION

Adverse possession is a legal means by which an individual may acquire ownership of a piece of real property by taking possession of the real property for a period of time without interruption, and in full view of the public, including the owner of the property. In United States law, the possession must be open, notorious, hostile to the actual owner, continuous, under claim of right (meaning that the adverse possessor must believe that the property is his or hers, and this is often demonstrated by the payment of property taxes), and exclusive. Adverse possession takes ownership from the original owner and gives it to the possessor. Adverse possession is a part of the law of real property. Not all legal systems recognize adverse possession, and those that do often have different requirements to establish it. In the United States, for example, adverse possession is usually established with a continuous possession of twenty years, although one cannot possess adversely against the federal government, on the idea that it would take the government too much time and expense to patrol its vast landholdings to detect people trying to establish adverse possession. On the other hand, Canada, which has far more land under government ownership, allows adverse possession to run against the federal government, except on federal Indian reserves.

AGE SET

An age set is a group of people of about the same age who are given an age-set name and who go through life with permanent associations with other members of their age set. Age sets typically are groups of males, and are usually formed during or just prior to adolescence. Age-set societies are found around the world, but are especially common in Africa and Melanesia. An age set differs from an age grade in that an age grade is simply a categorical age range, such as "middle age."

A very interesting, and perhaps unique, form of the age set is found among the Nyakyusa people of the Great Rift Valley in Africa. When boys reach the age of ten or eleven years, they begin to live in huts, which they construct themselves, near their village. Though they still go to their mothers' huts to eat their meals, they sleep in their huts and begin to spend a lot of time with other males of the same age. In fact, the boys often visit their mothers in gangs to eat. The Nyakyusa age village continues to grow by attracting area boys when they reach the age of ten or eleven. By the time that the oldest boys in the village reach the age of sixteen, the boys' village stops accepting new members, and the ten-year-old boys must then begin to construct a new village of their own.

As the boys of the village mature and marry, they bring their wives to live with them. Often their daughters marry a man who is of the same age set as their fathers, and so remain in the village. Every generation, the older men give up their leadership and authority to an age set of younger men in a special ritual. The older men also give up the land that they had been farming, so that it will be available for the young men to use. Each of the younger men's villages chooses its own headman, and the two oldest sons of the former chief are installed as chiefs over the whole chiefdom. The chiefdom is then divided in two between the two sons, and the division made permanent when the older chief dies. Thus, about every generation, the number of chiefdoms among the Nyakyusa people doubles; this doubling corresponds to the increasing Nyakyusa population, as well as their geographic expansion. The retiring chief chooses the headmen of the villages and allots land for the use of the younger men who have just come into power.

The age-set villages are further organized by age grades. There are three age grades at any one time: the young men before they reach the position of authority and leadership, the middle-aged men in position of authority and leadership, and the older men who have retired from positions of authority and leadership. The men of the young men's age grade and the men of the

Older Xavante boys in Brazil conduct initiation ceremonies for younger boys. Age sets—groups of people, usually males, of about the same age—are widespread in societies around the world.

middle-aged men's age grade both fight in wars, with the young men in their own units but under the direction of the middle-aged men.

The question as to just why this unusual system of political and social organization developed cannot, of course, ever be fully answered, since it is impossible to go back in time to when the system began. The Nyakyusa themselves say that they developed it to separate a man's wife from his own father, and so to keep them both virtuous by eliminating their opportunities to sleep together; this explanation even has a historical myth to give it support. The more likely reason is that it developed to separate the young men from their fathers' wives, particularly the

young wives. When young men move away from home and into their own village, they have very few chances to see girls or women until they marry, and this is quite a bit later in life. Thus, had they remained near their father's area, they would be tempted to have sexual relations with his younger wives. Furthermore, it is the rule that men inherit their fathers' wives as their own wives after he dies (though men may certainly not marry their own natural mothers). Thus, it is expected among all that there is a natural sexual attraction between sons and their fathers' wives, an attraction that will be the basis of sexual relations in the future. So, the age-set villages probably evolved to keep a man and his fathers' wives apart beginning at the age of boys' puberty, ten to twelve years of age.

The age-set villages have one further function, which may or may not have been intentional in the development of the villages. The villages make alliances between men that cross lines of kinship. In other words, without these villages, men would probably only have social and political alliances with his own kin and with people who marry into his family. The age-set village provides a man with another social network he can utilize in making a more secure life for himself and his family.

Wilson, Monica. (1967 [1949]) "Nyakyusa Age-Villages." In *Comparative Political Systems*, edited by Ronald Cohen and John Middleton, 217-227.

ANARCHY

Anarchy refers to a situation in which there is a complete absence of government; the term comes from the Greek word *anarchia* (without rule). The subject of anarchy has drawn a good deal of attention from social theorists, students of government, and philosophers. However, it is something that can exist only in the minds of people. True anarchy cannot exist for any length of time because whenever leaders and/or authorities are removed, new ones inevitably develop in their place, and this is true of any group of people.

The term *anarchy* is frequently misused by some scholars to refer to societies in which there is no centralized political system and/or no formal political institutions.

ARISTOCRACY

The term *aristocracy* refers to a political system in which power is held by the social elite. *Aristocracy* is derived from the Greek language; the word *aristoi* is the word meaning "best people." The term *aristoi* was probably first used in the Greek middle ages, 1100-700 B.C., and referred to the wealthy city dwellers who were also the ruling class, although the term *aristocracy* itself was not used until centuries later. The aristocrats were the families who came early to the new city and were able to get the best land, that on the plains. They had the money to live in the city, whereas the poorer people were forced by financial constraints to find some open land far from the city. The wealthy people considered themselves the *aristoi*, and often called those poorer folk who lived far away pejorative names, including "dusty-feet" and "sheepskin-wearers."

In modern times, those governments that are known as aristocracies, most of them European, are also governments run by people of wealth or political power who, once having acquired power, consider themselves to be the best people in the society. They frequently consider themselves not only the best suited to rule, but the best people in every sense of the word. Aristocracies are often run by members of the wealthy upper social class or classes, and are therefore in such cases more properly called plutocracies.

Burn, A. R. (1974 [1965]) *The Pelican History of Greece*.

ASSOCIATIONS

An association is an organized group with an absolute membership that is not formed solely on the basis of kinship, descent, residence, or territorial inclusion; it is a group whose members join voluntarily and intentionally. Common examples from our soci-

Members of the British royal family, gathered here following Queen Elizabeth II's coronation in 1953, are hereditary peers, which includes them among the elite in British society.

ety include sororities, fraternities, political parties, social clubs, professional associations, and service organizations (such as the Shriners, the Rotary, etc.). All associations have political impact, whether it is only upon their members in the conduct of the association's business or whether it is by design in the larger community.

Among the Yakö people of Nigeria, associations were an important part of social and political organization. In addition to such things as professional associations (some Yakö men belonged to a fighters' association, others to a hunters' association), the Yakö had an association of priests and an association for ritual and recreational activities to which most boys and

men belonged. But what is perhaps most interesting about the Yakö was that their villages, which were independent of one another, were governed by associations and not by headmen, priests, chiefs, kings, or presidents.

The Yakö traced their descent bilineally. The patriclans were local, but the membership of each of the matriclans was dispersed among a number of villages. The heads of the patriclans usually belonged to an association of leaders in each ward (part of a village). However, they were not the only members, and were actually in a minority. Other members were those with ambition and intelligence who possessed leadership qualities. Though most of the association of ward

Members of the Republican Party celebrate in New Orleans in 1988 as George Bush and Dan Quayle become nominees for the presidency and vice-presidency of the United States. Men and women with similar political views join a party, an example of a voluntary association, that is, a group not based on descent, kinship, or residence.

leaders were older men, some younger men with unusually great abilities were welcomed as members too. Priests were also gladly received into this association. The ward leaders, in short, were the eminent men of the ward. Those who left the ward leaders' association were expected to provide their own successors, and they were fined if they did not do so. It was the members of the ward leaders' association who selected their own leaders from among their ranks.

The ward leaders' association had several means of governing, two of which depended upon the prestige of being a member of the association. If a clan leader wished to join the association, but there was a dispute within the clan or involving the clan leader, the dispute had to be resolved properly before the clan leader could join. More usually, however, the clan leader used the prestige of being a member of the ward leaders' association to give him at least some of the authority he needed to have people within his clan abide by his decisions. A more direct and powerful authority was that which the head of the association had, in the name of the association, over all other men's associations within the ward, including those of the fighters and of the hunters, as well as the age sets of younger men.

However, the ward leaders' association had no control over another men's association within the ward, called the *nkpe*. The *nkpe* was essentially associated with the supernatural, in the form of the Leopard Spirit. Using the Leopard Spirit, the *nkpe* punished those who stole from, or seduced the wives of, its members or anyone else who paid for this protection. The *nkpe* also considered itself a means of thwarting the excess power of the ward leaders' association, a sort of political opposition. The ward leaders' association in turn would admit no prominent *nkpe* members.

The ward leaders' association had, thus, no authority in disputes between wards or disputes between clans in different wards, disputes that could sometimes have severe consequences. The Yakö had developed a townwide association that, though primarily religious in function, also served to resolve such disputes. Many of the members of this association, known as the *Okenga*, were the heads of the various ward leaders' associations and their deputies. As with the ward leaders' association, the members had authority primarily not through any formal authority, but because of the prestige that membership brought to the heads of the ward leaders. Using this prestige, they were able to get many people to abide by their decisions when they otherwise would not have done so.

There was yet another villagewide association, known as the "Body of Men." This association dealt specifically with trespass on farms and the theft of crops. Those who paid the Body of Men a fee received in return detective services to discover the thief, prosecution of the alleged offender before the ward leaders' association or the village priests' association, and the enforcement of any sanctions decided by either of those associations. Payment also guaranteed the protection of the spirit associated with the Body of Men.

A final association that held villagewide legal authority was the council of priests. The Yakö had a large number of religious cults, and the priests of these cults formed an association of their own. To them were brought disputes involving offenses that were either taboo (punished by supernatural forces), such as murder, incest, and abortion, or major offenses that the aforementioned associations could not resolve. The council of priests had at their disposal the reputation of high moral caliber and the power of the supernatural world. Thus, their decisions were often accepted when the decisions of the other associations went unheeded.

In short, the Yakö associations generally constituted weak legal authorities. With the exception of the Body of Men in cases involving crop theft, there was no way to enforce the law through coercion. All of the other associations depended upon the prestige of the authorities, their ability to use supernatural power, or their moral rectitude. Though one or more of these was generally sufficient to resolve a dispute, they were not universally effective. For this reason, the colonial District Native Court fairly quickly was adopted by the Yakö as the quickest and best way to handle most disputes, although associations remained and carried out other tasks.

The Yoruba people, who also live in Nigeria, have a number of different kinds of associations. Many of these are secret, and anyone who reveals to nonmembers the rites and ceremonies of the secret society may face the death penalty. The Yoruba also have trade guilds, which one must join if one wishes to engage in a trade.

Ajisafe, A. K. (1946) *The Laws and Customs of the Yoruba People.*

Forde, Daryll. (1961) "The Governmental Roles of Associations among the Yakö." *Africa* 31(4): 309-323.

AUTHORITY

According to Leopold Pospisil of Yale, an authority is an individual or group of individuals whose decisions are usually followed by the majority of a group. We can see from this that an authority is a type of political leader, though not necessarily one who leads in the execution of a decision. In every group that has some purpose, there is always a leader, usually an authority as well. Even in a group of boys on the playground (the function of which is to play together), there is one boy whose decisions are usually followed by the rest of the group. Another authority is the classroom teacher, who makes laws and rules as to the kind of behavior allowed in the classroom group. As students know, each classroom teacher is a separate authority whose laws and rules are different from those of other teachers.

It is important to distinguish between formal authority and informal authority. Formal authority is the kind of power that derives from an office and that is strictly defined by law. The limits to the power of the officeholder are spelled out, and even the term of office has a limit; there is a formal assumption and declination of office. Most of us are familiar with formal authority. The president of the United States can order the U.S. military to attack, can launch a nuclear missile, or can pardon anybody in the United States of any crime, but he cannot force a child at the dinner table in a Kansas town to finish his vegetables, which the child's parent, as a legal authority over the child, has the power to do.

An informal authority creates his or her own authority based upon his or her own personal qualities and opportunities. Someone who is charismatic and/or intimidating can create for himself or herself enormous amounts of power. Band headmen and tribal headmen and big men are examples of informal leaders/authorities. These people have titles but no offices. Their positions as headmen or big men often last their entire lives, since, again, it is the qualities of the individual that are important, not a term of office. Further, when new headmen and big men come into power, they do not have the power of their predecessors; the leadership and authority of the new headmen and big men must be created anew by the new leaders/authorities and is always different in character and scope.

One good example of this concerns the succession of headmen for life who were Grand Chiefs of the Micmac Indians of Cape Breton Island, Nova Scotia. From the early twentieth century until 1964, Gabriel Sylliboy held the position. Sylliboy was known for making stringent laws concerning proper behavior. He allowed no drinking to excess, no child neglect, no fighting, and no vandalism. He usually went to visit the offenders and lectured them publicly, humiliating them into complying with his laws. He also lectured each newlywed couple for hours on the proper roles of husband and wife. When he died in 1964, he was replaced by Donald Marshall. Donald was a very quiet and nice man who was well liked. However, he did not pursue any of his predecessor's policies and did not punish people for improper behavior. Two things happened as a result of this. The first is that Micmac behavior in Cape Breton deteriorated. Fighting, vandalism, child neglect, and drinking to excess became far more common. This process went so far that eventually non-Micmac Canadian federal police began to enforce Canadian laws on the reserve, which they had had little reason to do before. The second result was that the Micmac people of Cape Breton lost respect for Donald Marshall and for the position of headman. They came to realize that he could not keep control of the Micmac people for the safety of all, and regarded him as more or less useless to them; he had, in effect, ceased to function as an authority. They came to look to the Royal Canadian Mounted Police, whom they distrust to a great extent, to help them keep conditions safe on the reserve.

One should never confuse the formality of an authority with the power of that authority. The two are functionally not related. Hitler, Stalin, and Mao Zedong are good examples of informal authorities who were able to amass for themselves the power to control the fates of their nations, the power to kill political enemies by the hundreds, thousands, and even millions, and the power to wage wars; to become, in short, dictators with total power. They were charismatic leaders, first of all, intelligent and shrewd in selecting people to help them. They used propaganda to increase popular support and terror to silence their opponents.

The authorities in small societies can also have absolute power over their followers. Pospisil (1971: 62) describes two such authorities, one in New Guinea and one in the Arctic. The Micmac too have had their share of authorities with absolute power. In the seventeenth century, observers described two such men, one in Nova Scotia and another in New Brunswick. The man in New Brunswick would beat his followers if they did not please him, and if they requested something of him, he required a lengthy show of submission before he would condescend to listen to them. The man in Nova Scotia used sorcery to control his followers, even going so far as to wear his death-dealing magic charms around his neck in full view. This would be comparable to the mayor of New York City walking around the city carrying a rocket launcher; it is an arrogant display of naked power. Yet, some authors have described band societies as egalitarian and their leaders as first among equals (Vivelo, 1978: 135)! Rather, the Micmac band looks to the headman for decisive leadership, strong morals, and vigorous punishment of offenders. Both in traditional times and today, the Micmac choose as authorities physically large and strong men who can for this reason stand up to opposition and to those who would try to intimidate them. In the past, if the Micmac failed to change their leader/authority's mind on a divisive issue, then those who disagreed with him simply left his authority.

The traditional authorities of the Navajo Indians of the southwestern United States represent another interesting case study. The Navajo have usually been characterized as having had a very diffuse system of authority, one in which every relatively successful man was considered a headman, with no centralized hierarchy of authority. While this is essentially true, it is also true that each functioning group had an authority. These groups include nuclear families, extended families, local groups, raiding groups, hunting groups, and ceremonial or ritual groups. All earned their authority, and none (with a relatively insignificant exception) had ascribed status that came through the luck of heredity. For example, any man could be a hunt leader if he had demonstrated skill in hunting and if he learned the rituals necessary to lead a hunt. Once he had achieved these goals, he led hunt parties and had absolute authority over how they were to be conducted and over the actions of all members of the party while engaged in a hunt.

A peace chief, or *natani*, was an authority who had the right to speak for a large group of people. He made treaties, spoke before assembled groups on ethical issues, and directed group economic activities, especially those related to horticulture. He also decided legal disputes over all types of matters, especially trespass and land tenure. He was chosen after all the adults in the area had been consulted. Usually, he was chosen by a unanimous vote of all adults. The personal characteristics of charisma, wisdom, speaking ability, and overall level of skills were most important.

Curing rituals were usually held by singers, people who would sing curing music. They had to learn the special chants that were necessary to bring about a cure. During the curing ritual, the singer had absolute authority over the proceedings, which sometimes attracted several hundred people. An especially great singer had political influence beyond the scope of the curing ritual, and most *natanis* were in fact Blessingway Singers.

The raiding party leader was likewise a man of skill, who also had learned the proper ritual magic necessary to conduct a proper raid. He asked for volunteers (four to ten men for a raid, and thirty to two hundred to take revenge for a raid that they themselves had suffered) who would be under the leader's absolute authority.

The Navajo authorities never organized themselves into associations. That is, there were never any groups of *natanis*, or hunting leaders, etc.

See also BIG MAN; HEADMAN; LEADER.

Michels, Robert. (1937) "Authority." In *Encyclopedia of the Social Sciences*, vol. 2.

Pospisil, Leopold. (1974 [1971]) *Anthropology of Law: A Comparative Theory.*

Shepardson, Mary. (1967 [1963]) "The Traditional Authority System of the Navajos." In *Comparative Political Systems*, edited by Ronald Cohen and John Middleton, 143-154.

Strouthes, Daniel P. (1994) *Change in the Real Property Law of a Cape Breton Island Micmac Band.*

Vivelo, Frank Robert. (1978) *Cultural Anthropology: A Basic Introduction.*

AUTOCRACY

Autocracy refers to a situation in which the political power of a society resides in the hands of one person. The term is derived from the Greek *autos* (self) and *kratos* (strength or rule). There are two types of autocratic leaders: the despot and the totalitarian dictator.

The first type, the despot, is a person who does not care what his followers think or believe, so long as they comply with his wishes. Examples of despotic leaders are Ghengis Khan, the Chinese emperors, and some European kings. Despots can also exist in small tribal societies. Watson has found a case of a despot in a small Tairora language society in New Guinea known as Abiera. There, a man known as Matoto came to power as a despot around the turn of the century. Matoto was a strong man, a bully. He came into power as a result of his personal fearlessness and his willingness to fight and to kill others. His fearlessness he proved early in life, when he would go to sleep wherever he was when night fell, oblivious to the dangerous animals or humans who might come across him in

Chinese carry posters of Mao Zedong, the principal leader of the People's Republic of China, in 1950. Chairman Mao, a totalitarian dictator, dominated the policies and politics of his country until his death in 1976.

the forest or in the fields. When he reached adulthood, he became a very dangerous person indeed. He would kill people both inside his society and outside of it, often for no apparent reason. He would also attack people who displeased him, and once killed one of his wives for this reason. He was aided in his fights by the fact that he was larger than other men and, after a while, by his reputation, which caused other people to try to flee rather than fight him. Matoto fought people in a variety of ways, and was not above ambushing or stalking his victims. However, he was said to be an invincible power even in war, despite the fact that it was usually the goal of every warrior to try to kill the enemy's strongman for reasons of personal glory.

Matoto could be seen easily in a battle because of his size and by the fact that he had a distinctive black shield, but he was so dangerous that opposing warriors, out of fear, attempted to avoid him rather than fight him.

Matoto also worked as a mercenary, so well known were his fighting capabilities. Representatives of other villages would visit Matoto and hire him to fight their enemies. In a similar case, Matoto acted simply as a hired killer. A group of men had a grudge against a man who was living in Matoto's village. This man was not originally from Matoto's village, but had married a woman who was, and he lived with her. The group of men went to Matoto to get his permission to kill the man (necessary to avoid a war between the two villages), but wound up hiring Matoto to kill the man instead. This Matoto did without hesitation and, apparently, with no more reason than that he was paid to do so.

Matoto also had sexual intercourse with whatever women he wished. If he desired a woman who was in her house with her husband, Matoto would enter, tell the man to leave, and then have sexual relations with the woman. Matoto's sexual appetite was large, even though he had at least sixteen wives.

Matoto became the leader of his village through intimidation. Simply put, no one would stand up to him. Everybody around him would behave in a manner calculated to escape his attention as much as was possible. That is, they walked slowly, avoided looking at him, and kept their voices low. Visitors to the village would be in particular danger, and Matoto would shout that he would kill the visitor upon seeing him for the first time. A man who visited his sister living in Matoto's village would slip into the village unseen and spend his entire stay in the village behind the walls of his sister's house.

Matoto's leadership was not simply that of a person who bullied everyone else into following his orders, though that was usually how he exercised his power. He also realized the importance of having a united village as a base of support. When a dispute within the Abiera village broke out and caused the murder of one man, Matoto inserted himself between the two armed groups who were firing arrows at each other at the time. Standing in the cross fire, he ordered them to cease their dispute. They did so immediately, since they realized that to continue would have meant facing Matoto as an enemy, which they feared greatly.

Matoto also increased the size of his following by giving political asylum to a group of refugees who had been dispossessed of their land. This group spoke a different language, but later became nothing more than one of the two large kin groups in Abiera society.

Matoto cultivated influence by being a gracious host to those who came from outside of the village because it is politically important to make alliances with such people. Apparently, Matoto did not go far enough in this respect: he was killed in an ambush in an outside village.

The second type of autocratic leader, the totalitarian dictator, is a person who wants to control the minds of his followers as well as their behavior. These people use propaganda, deceit, control of the information that reaches followers, and brainwashing to alter the thinking of other people in the society. Examples of totalitarian dictators are Hitler, Castro, Stalin, Mao Zedong, and Pol Pot. Totalitarian dictators are found only in twentieth-century state societies.

Watson, James B. (1973 [1971]) "Tairora: The Politics of Despotism in a Small Society." In *Politics in New Guinea,* edited by Ronald M. Berndt and Peter Lawrence, 224–275.

primarily by season. Typically, large numbers of smaller bands would congregate in a few places near bodies of water during the summer, thereby making up a few very large bands. At these places, where the fish were plentiful, people socialized, young adults chose mates, and leaders discussed matters of common concern, including disputes. As fall came, the smaller bands reformed, sometimes with different memberships, and they spread out over the land to harvest dispersed food, hunt animals, and find hardwoods for firewood.

The second feature common to bands is informal political leadership and legal authority. Band leaders and authorities, usually one and the same individual, are headmen or big men. Their power and position derives not from any office (there is no such thing in band societies), but from their own personal characteristics, especially charisma. Thus, the qualities of the political leaders and the legal systems that different bands have, even bands who speak the same language and live adjacent to each other, can vary greatly. One band may have a despotic leader who terrorizes his followers into submission, while the next band may have a leader who is followed because he provides food for his followers, and the one next to that has a leader whose most important characteristic is the ability to make just decisions in disputes among his followers. There are also differences in the geographic extent of a leader's power in band societies. Among the Micmac Indians of eastern Canada, for example, each Micmac band was traditionally led by one headman or big man, and no leader had any authority over any band but the one of which he was a member. This was true for all the Micmac except the ones who lived on Cape Breton Island, Nova Scotia, where one headman led all of the bands on the island and had legal authority over all the members of these bands.

The third characteristic of bands is that the leader/authority is, so far as can be determined,

BAND

A band is a type of society and political group that is most commonly found among hunting/fishing/gathering peoples. Bands are usually small societies: as small as a nuclear family or as large as 400 people or so. Bands are almost always legally and politically autonomous, unless some compelling outside influence (such as a war) necessitates bands to work together for a common purpose.

Bands typically have four distinctive features. The first of these is that band membership is usually fluid, in the sense that a person can be a member of one band one year and then live with another band the next year. It also often happens that part of a band's membership will leave the band to start a band of their own. This fluidity occurs for a variety of reasons: to find resources such as food as the seasons change, to join another set of kin living elsewhere, to escape from an undesirable leader/authority, or to avoid revenge.

Among the Algonkian Indians of northeastern North America and the Indians of the subarctic, band size and membership varied almost always male. The simple reason for this is that most bands rely upon hunting for the bulk of their food and clothing, and hunting is a male activity because of the strength and stamina required, as well as the need to hunt even when children are being born and raised. It is the best hunters who attract followers, both male and female, and so become leaders. The best hunters attract male followers because the followers find that the best hunters can help them in their own hunting efforts (locating game and the logistics of hunting). Good hunters have food surpluses, which they can share with their followers, which makes them attractive as leaders to both men and women. Nobody will follow a poor hunter as a leader.

The Micmac Indians provide another reason for why men, particularly strong men, are followed as leaders/authorities. In band societies, there is usually no one to assist a leader or legal authority in enforcing his decisions. There is no separate police force or penal system with the physical power to ensure that decisions are carried out. Further, there is no court bailiff to protect the leader/authority from the physical threats of someone who might seek to intimidate him into changing his decision to benefit the intimidator. For this reason, the Micmac choose physically strong men as their leaders/authorities so as to help ensure that the decisions they make are just ones insofar as they are not influenced by physical intimidation.

The fourth feature of band politics and law is the importance of kinship ties, although it is recognized that kinship ties are also crucially important in other kinds of societies as well. The band headman or big man uses his siblings, children, grandchildren, and spouse as his base of support, since they are his natural political allies. The larger the number of offspring and grandchildren he has, the more powerful he is likely to be. In many cases, one extended family may make up the majority of the band's membership, thus virtually guaranteeing the leadership of that family's head.

The !Kung Bushmen of southwest Africa are a well-known example of a band society. Despite the fact that they live in a hot and arid environment, they are culturally similar in many ways to northern band societies. Their nomadic bands are based upon ties of blood and marriage. The entire population of the !Kung was approximately 1,000 in the early 1950s, and this was divided into thirty-six or thirty-seven autonomous communities. Though autonomous, each band is linked to many others through blood and marriage ties. Each band owns one or more permanent and one or more semipermanent water holes, and the use of these is controlled by the headman so that they are not overused; visitors to the area must ask the permission of the headman before taking water from a water hole.

Each band is also divided into nuclear and extended families, of which the father is leader and authority. The nuclear family becomes extended when there is a relative who comes to live with it, such as a parent of the husband or wife, a sibling of either, or a young man who is providing bride service after marrying a daughter of the family.

!Kung people tend to remain in the bands in which they are born, although people sometimes leave when they marry. The other factor influencing band membership is the resources, particularly water, over which a band has control. If there are not enough resources, people leave to join another band. Bands sometimes split if a man who is a strong leader decides to leave and enough people wish to follow him to begin a new band.

The headman is typically the oldest son of the previous headman, and takes his position as headman upon the death of his father. A headman has prestige and the respect of the people in his band, but only if he makes sure that he does not do things that arouse jealousy, such as

Members of a nomadic !Kung band roam southwest Africa's Kaukau Veld and Kalahari Desert. The !Kung are an example of a band society. A band is a social and political entity that includes members of the nuclear and extended family; such organization is common among hunting, fishing, and gathering groups.

eat better than the others, acquire more material wealth, or fail to be very generous. For this reason, the position of headman is not particularly desirable.

The !Kung headman's principal duties are to control the use of the native food plants and the water, and to direct the movement of band members so as to make the most efficient use of these resources. The headman does not control torts, or private wrongs; these things are handled by the parties to the disputes, and typically involve revenge.

One interesting form of band is the Russian undivided family, which existed in parts of Russia as late as the beginning of the twentieth century. This band consisted entirely of a large, mostly patrilineal, extended family, typically a grandfather and grandmother, father and mother, sons and daughters (natural and adopted), nieces and nephews, and people attached to these through marriage. The Russian undivided family owned all of the family's property in common, and no part of that property could legally be alienated without the express consent of all members of the undivided family.

The individual family was led by the oldest man, who was assisted by the oldest woman in the administration of the affairs of the women and girls. When the old man became incapable of handling his duties, the family elected a replacement. The house elder also represented the interests of the undivided family to the village and district authorities, as well as the tax collector.

The house elder's greatest power lay in his authority over the domestic affairs within the undivided family. He could make decisions between husband and wife, even to the point of ordering a young man to beat his wife. The house elder also assigned the daily agricultural labor of the family members; he determined who would plow, who would thresh grain, etc. If there were too many people in the family to be profitably employed as agricultural laborers, it was the house elder who determined which ones would stay with the family and which ones would have to leave to find some other form of livelihood; those who worked elsewhere, however, were required to share their earnings with the rest of the family. The house elder also signed contracts for the sale of the agricultural produce.

See also AUTHORITY; BIG MAN; HEADMAN.

Kovalevsky, Maxime. (1966 [1891]) "The Modern Russian Family." In *Anthropology and Early Law,* edited by Lawrence Krader, 148–170.

Llewellyn, Karl N., and E. Adamson Hoebel. (1961 [1941]) *The Cheyenne Way.*

Marshall, Lorna. (1967 [1960]) "!Kung Bushman Bands." In *Comparative Political Systems,* edited by Ronald Cohen and John Middleton, 15–43.

Strouthes, Daniel P. (1994) *Change in the Real Property Law of a Cape Breton Island Micmac Band.*

BIG MAN A big man is an informal leader/authority who creates his own position through generosity to others. Usually, the big man has generated the wealth he shares with others through his successful entrepreneurial activities. The big man is found most often in hunting-gathering societies and in pastoral and horticultural societies. Big men differ from headmen in that the former have more economic power over their followers, though both may exercise a wide variety of other types of power. The big man is generous with his wealth, and he uses the actual or implied threat of ending his generosity to induce followers to obey him.

Those who give material wealth away to others not surprisingly become leaders. Those who benefit from this generosity naturally become politically loyal to the big man. The big man is skillful in what he does, otherwise he would not have amassed the wealth that he has; thus, people ask him for advice. Those who depend on the big man for the wealth they need also agree to abide by his legal decisions, or risk losing his generosity. The big man's goal in amassing wealth is to have prestige, political power, and legal authority. Of course, generosity is not the only reason why people follow a big man. A wealthy and generous person who is also personally immoral may not be obeyed no matter how much wealth they give away. Cowardly men also have trouble leading, as do those with low intelligence or poor judgment.

One of the best described examples of the big man is that of the Kapauku Papuans of highland New Guinea, who were studied by Pospisil (1958). The Kapauku big man is called *tonowi* (wealthy man). The *tonowi* is a healthy, middle-aged man who has a great deal of *cowrie* (money in the form of cowrie shells) and credit, twenty or so pigs, a large house, many cultivated fields, and several wives. Wealth is the single most important factor in establishing high prestige and status among the Kapauku. The *tonowi* is middle-aged, because he creates his wealth with his own two hands; young men have not had the time to amass a fortune, and older men can no longer work hard to create sufficient wealth.

However, not all wealthy men can become a *tonowi*. If a wealthy man wishes to become a *tonowi*, he must be very generous with his wealth. He must make cash loans, give pig feasts (without taking part of the pig himself), and support a large household of wives, children, boys from the community, and friends. Further, the *tonowi* himself does not practice conspicuous consumption. He wears the same clothes as others, and eats only a little bit better. The rich Kapauku man who, on the other hand, keeps his wealth for himself is ostracized as immoral and is the target of gossip. Finally, the *tonowi* must be an eloquent speaker in public.

Other qualities that increase the *tonowi*'s hold on his position are experience as a warrior and shamanic expertise. Extraordinary wealth in the hands of a *tonowi* makes him a *maagodo tonowi* (very rich man), and this means that his power and authority are even greater.

The *tonowi*'s political power and legal authority derive primarily from his wealth. Some people obey his decisions because they have borrowed money from him and fear being asked to repay it. They are grateful for the *tonowi*'s generosity and do not wish to lose it. Others obey the *tonowi* because they believe that they themselves may later wish to borrow money from the *tonowi* and do not want to risk losing his future goodwill. A third category of people obedient to the *tonowi* are the boys who live with the *tonowi*. These boys, known as *ani jokaani* (my boys), work in the *tonowi*'s fields and house and fight for him in wars. In return, the *tonowi* gives them food, shelter, education, and a loan to pay the bride-price.

The *tonowi* has authority over his followers only. Of course, most people in a village are indebted to the village's *tonowi* financially or politically. It is also the case that in some villages there is more than one *tonowi* who share power and have followers in common. Within the village, the *tonowi* will decide upon the building of bridges, feast houses, and drainage ditches, and will persuade other men to help him give a pig feast.

Further, a *tonowi* may lend money outside of his village and even outside of his political confederacy, giving him political power over a wide region. These men also influence politics between villages and confederacies by regulating contacts between them.

One *tonowi* led his household, his village, a sublineage, a lineage, and a political confederacy. But because he had authority over his followers only, he could not make binding decisions in cases involving members of different lineages. Rather, he had to try to persuade lineage leaders to accept his decisions.

It should also be noted that big men are not always the only type of leader in a group of people sharing the same language and territory. The Kapauku may have had only big men as leaders, but among the traditional Micmac Indians of eastern Canada, some leaders were big men while others in neighboring bands were headmen who were obeyed for their wisdom, or who ruled their followers by intimidating them with violence. Big men distribute their wealth in different ways in different places; Micmac big men simply gave away their wealth, and never lent it.

Another example of the big man may be found among the Nunamiut Eskimos (Eskimos are sometime also known as Inuit) of Anaktuvuk Pass in the Brooks Range of northern Alaska. An Eskimo big man is called *umialik*, which translates literally as "having an *umiak*." An *umiak* is a large, sturdy, open skin boat, an object of considerable value. Thus, by extension, an *umialik* was a man who had a great deal of wealth, and the Eskimos use the term to apply to any man with a great deal of wealth, whether he actually owns an *umiak* or not. The *umialik* gained his wealth from his great hunting and fishing expertise, as well as his activities in trading meat, pelts, clothing, and luxury goods with other Eskimos and with Indians. But his greatest quality was his capacity for hard work; the typical *umialik* did not hold shamanic supernatural power in too high a regard, since he knew that he could get what he needed through ordinary labor.

Generally speaking, each band had only one dominant *umialik*. The *umialik* had great power with respect to internal band affairs, but never acted as a representative of the band to outside parties. The *umialik*, through his hard work, became an inspiring leader by example to the young men of the band. He was further respected by most or all other members of the band for his hunting abilities. Thus, people listened to him when he spoke of hunting strategies. As a trader, the *umialik* gained power by giving other members of his band very good deals on goods brought from far away. If someone needed material help, food, or clothing, the *umialik* would simply give it. This generosity would increase the good will that the people extended to him. Since the *umialik* always had a surplus of food, people would come to visit and eat with him. If the *umialik* had the personality of a true leader, he would use these opportunities to listen sympathetically and offer advice, which others always wished to hear from someone as successful as the *umialik*. When a serious dispute erupted among the people of a band, the *umialik* used his prestige and notoriety to lead and to mold public opinion on the case. The *umialik* would lead the group of adult men who made and enforced decisions in the formation of those decisions, such as the decision that a serious and recalcitrant thief should be banished from the band. Sometimes, as Gubser reports, the effect of the *umialik*'s efforts to mold opinion in others was so subtle that those whose opinions were being shaped did not always realize what the *umialik* was doing.

However, if an *umialik* led the band in a group hunt of caribou, and it failed, the *umialik* would be held accountable and all of his subsequent opinions and judgments would be held to be bad.

Another type of big man has come into being with the involvement of state societies in the affairs of local indigenous populations. In modern times, government aid to Indian groups in the United States and Canada has created big men out of those local native people designated by the federal governments to distribute this aid.

See also AUTHORITY; CHIEF; LEADER.

Gubser, Nicholas J. (1965) *The Nunamiut Eskimos: Hunters of Caribou.*

Pospisil, Leopold. (1958) *Kapauku Papuans and Their Law.*

———. (1963) *The Kapauku Papuans of West New Guinea.*

———. (1964) "Law and Societal Structure among the Nunamiut Eskimo." In *Explorations in Cultural Anthropology: Essays in Honor of George Peter Murdock,* edited by Ward H. Goodenough, 395–431.

Strouthes, Daniel P. (1994) *Change in the Real Property Law of a Cape Breton Island Micmac Band.*

BLACK MARKET

The term *black market* refers to illegal trade. The term itself is not often used in this country, except to refer to illegal trade in foreign countries, although the illegal trade carried on in this country is nonetheless black market trading. In the United States, most black market activities come in two forms. One is the trading in illegal goods and services, such as prohibited drugs, weapons, and prostitution. Another type of black market trading in the United States is the sale of goods and services that are unreported to the government so as to

Black markets, illegal trade in goods and services, operate beyond the law. Brazilian vendors sell produce on a Rio de Janeiro street in 1989 to avoid governmental bureaucracy and taxes.

avoid the payments of taxes and fees. Some examples of this are the sale of bootleg liquor, untaxed cigarettes, and the practice of working for an employer who does not collect income taxes or social security and medicare taxes, known as "getting paid under the table."

But each society's black market exists for different reasons and operates in different ways, because the trade laws of each society are different as are the needs of its people. For example, in the People's Republic of China, the state until recently had a monopoly on trade so as to prevent capitalism, to which the Chinese Communist government was ideologically opposed. Capitalism is an economic system in which wealth reproduces itself. If the state allowed ordinary Chinese people to engage in trade, they

could use their wealth to buy merchandise in order to resell it. This would be capitalistic enterprise, and was thus forbidden.

However, the People's Republic of China has, until very recently, proven to be inefficient in the production of consumer goods, resulting in a scarcity of many of the things people wanted to own. This scarcity prompted people to use their official positions as workers in factories, farms, stores, warehouses, etc., to acquire control over the distribution of goods and to sell them to other people. The private sale of goods was illegal in China until very recently, although so many people did it that it was rarely punished.

Some of the motivation for engaging in black market activities, which the Chinese call *zhou-houmen* (going in the back door), was to make a profit. But far more important was to use the black market to be able to give or sell goods to friends, relatives, and Communist Party officials, so as to make of them good connections, known as *guanxihu* (special relationships), who will return one's largess with goods, which one later needs oneself. In other words, a worker in a store that sells comforters would save some on the side so that if someone who can help the worker later comes by, the worker would be able to sell him one. In this way, Chinese people would use the black market for many of the things that they wanted, even movie theater tickets or good-quality cigarettes, and so developed a large circle of *guanxihu*.

———

Mosher, Steven W. (1983) *Broken Earth: The Rural Chinese.*

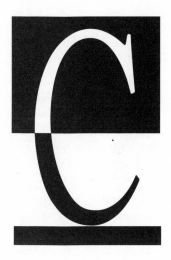

collections of codified canon laws were circulated by priests and others, but many of the laws contained within them were not genuine canon law. As well, as the laws changed over time, older codes began to conflict with the newer. These contradictions were partially smoothed over by Gratian, a Camaldolese monk, who worked the old and new codes together in a single work, known as the *Concordantia Discordantium Canonum.* Despite the fact that this work never received official approval from authorities in Rome, it was widely accepted and used by canonical courts.

Students of Roman Catholic Canon Law were forbidden to study the laws of Rome, which many legal scholars consider to be the most logically consistent in the world. The reason for this was that Roman law was not in accordance with Catholic principles. Roman law, through the institution of *patria potestas,* gave the father of the family great power over his wife and children, while Catholic Canon Law defended the equality of the husband and wife in marriage. The canonical courts also stressed the use of legal measures of dispute resolution as opposed to extralegal measures, such as dueling, which was once popular.

The Roman Catholic Canonical Courts had exclusive jurisdiction over clerics, demonstrating that the personality principle of law was applied. After the year 1279 in Rome, a Roman Catholic cleric who committed a crime and was arrested by secular police had to be turned over to the canonical court. This rule was instituted not by civil Roman authorities, but by the church's Council of Avignon, which provided that the persons in charge of a cleric who did not turn the cleric over would be excommunicated.

The thirteenth century also saw canonical courts grow in their power simply because of the fact that they were deciding so many cases that the secular authorities began to grow jealous of their influence. Some of the French barons in 1225, lead by Peter de Dreux, started a

CANON LAW

Canon law is law made by ecclesiastical courts and may be made by the courts of any church of any religion. Canon law generally deals with matters pertaining to church doctrine, disputes between priests, disputes over rituals and ceremonies, and all other similar affairs pertaining to religious activity.

In the specific case of the Roman Catholic faith, canonical law dealt with disputes on the following civil matters: marriage (adultery, engagements, legitimization of children, distribution of marital property, and separation from bed and board), wills, usury, agreements undertaken on oaths, ecclesiastical goods (benefices, almsgiving, and tithes), as well as vows and sacraments. The canon courts also decided cases involving crimes such as witchcraft, blasphemy, sacrilege, and simony.

In the Catholic Church, canon law was originally derived from the rules (called canons) made by church councils and the decretals (decreed rules) made by popes. These were both codified at an early point in church history. From the fifth century through the eleventh century, movement to have the canonical courts' authority over cases involving wills, usury, and tithes removed from them. In 1245, a second movement to have canonical authority reduced was met by Pope Innocent IV excommunicating the offenders.

Though Roman Catholic Canon Law is today far less powerful in the world outside the church, it did originate a law that still catches the attention of people today, Catholic and non-Catholic alike. This is the law of asylum or sanctuary, *ius asyli*, which provides that any person inside a church building cannot be arrested. At some points in history, right of asylum extended far beyond the church's walls and into the surrounding towns. When the United States military sought Manuel Noriega in Panama, he was protected for several days by church sanctuary.

See also Patria Potestas; PERSONALITY PRINCIPLE OF LAW.

Poulet, Dom Charles. (1950) *A History of the Catholic Church.* Vol. I. Translated by Sidney A. Raemers.

CAPITAL PUNISHMENT

From a cross-cultural perspective, capital punishment is "the appropriate killing of a person who has committed a crime within a political community" (Otterbein 1986). Capital punishment refers, literally, to the punishment of removal of the head and, by extension, to the loss of life by any means. Capital punishment is a near cultural universal, as one survey shows that it is used in 51 of the 53 cultures surveyed. Capital punishment is also generally approved, with people in 89 percent of the 53 cultures expecting it to be used for certain crimes or approving of its use. In only two of the cultures where it occurs do people generally disapprove of its use. Although capital punishment is used or is permitted in nearly all societies, there is considerable variation across cultures in the crimes it is used for, who does the killing, how the criminal is executed, and the purpose people believe it serves. Whether or not capital punishment is an effective deterrent to further crime is unclear, although there is evidence that among the nations of the world, capital punishment does not reduce the frequency of crime.

The offenses most often punished by capital punishment (those so punished in over 50 percent of cultures) are homicide, stealing, sacrilege such as witchcraft, and offenses that threaten the social order, such as rape, adultery, and incest. Traitors are subject to capital punishment in 27 percent of societies while other offenses such as desertion in war, political assassination, arson, and kidnapping are cause for execution in only a few cultures. In most cultures, the crimes punished by execution are those that are most threatening to the society and the well-being of the people, although cultures vary in what is meant by "most threatening" and "well-being." Most executions are carried out in public, but in some cultures they are private or even secret, with the criminal simply disappearing, never to be seen again.

While not much is known about people's motivation for approving of capital punishment or for expecting it to be used, one reason commonly given by people in different societies is to remove an offender so that he can't commit the crime again. Other reasons are for revenge, to show the power of the king, and to wipe out an insult as well as various combinations of these.

Cross-cultural research indicates that the reason a society uses capital punishment is some-

Witchcraft, considered a crime in some societies at some times, led to perhaps 100,000 to 200,000 executions, such as this burning, from the late Middle Ages to the eighteenth century.

what more complex than the reasons given by members of the society. Evidently, different types of societies have different underlying reasons for killing those who commit serious offenses. In small hunter/gatherer societies, capital punishment is used to remove those who commit crimes so serious, or whose behavior is so disruptive to others or the group as a whole, that the survival of the group is threatened. In larger societies, capital punishment is used selectively to punish crimes depending on whether or not kin groups or councils are present and have the authority to punish crimes. Finally, societies with centralized political leadership vested in a chief or king use capital punishment as a social control mechanism to publicly demonstrate and thereby reinforce the power of the chief or king.

See also CRIME; FEUD.

Otterbein, Keith F. (1986) *The Ultimate Coercive Sanction: A Cross-Cultural Study of Capital Punishment.*

| CHARTER MYTH |

The charter myth is a myth that many societies use to explain the existence of, as well as the social, societal, and political structures of their society. The idea of the charter myth was first identified by anthropologist Bronislaw Malinowski.

For example, in the Bunyoro society, in Africa, there is a myth to explain why some of the Bunyoro are born royalty, why some are born cattle herders, and why other Bunyoro are born peasants and servants of royalty, according to which lineages they belong.

The myth is as follows. The first human family on earth (Bunyoro, of course) had three sons who had no names. The parents asked God to name them. God decided to do so after giving the boys a test. He set before them a group of objects and asked the boys to pick which ones they wanted. He also gave each of them a bowl of milk and told them to hold the bowl all night without spilling any milk. The oldest boy chose some food, a ring for carrying loads on one's head, an ax, and a knife. The youngest boy chose an ox's head. The middle boy chose a leather thong. During the night, the oldest boy spilt all of his milk. The youngest boy spilt a small portion of his milk, and the middle boy spilt none of his milk, but gave his younger brother enough of the milk from his bowl to fill it up. Thus, in the morning, only the youngest boy had a full milk bowl.

God saw that the choices the boys had made and the way that they handled their milk demonstrated their natures. The eldest boy chose the kind of goods that were the goods of peasants and royal servants. That he also spilt all of his milk demonstrated his inability to tend cattle. Thus, his descendants are destined to be servants and peasants. The youngest boy's choice of an ox head, as well as his full bowl of milk, determined that he and his descendants are royalty and rulers of all other people. The middle boy's choice of a leather thong, a herder's tool, and his gift of milk to the youngest boy, the royalty, demonstrate that he and his descendants are, by their nature, herders.

The Bunyoro charter myth explains why, according to the will of God, members of some Bunyoro lineages are destined always to be herders, members of other lineages to be peasants and servants, and members of still other lineages to be royalty.

Lienhardt, Godfrey. (1964) *Social Anthropology.*

| CHIEF |

A chief is a formal political leader and authority in a small society, who usually leads and has authority over more than one group. The society governed in this way is known as a chiefdom.

The chief is foremost a formal leader and authority. He or she occupies an office and the officer's rights and duties are defined by law; in some societies they are even written down. The chief's power and authority derive not from his or her own personal qualities but from the office he or she holds. Furthermore, a formal authority has a formal assumption and declination of power in association with the assumption or declination of office.

The institution of the chief is well described for the Cheyenne. According to Cheyenne legend, the institution of chiefship and the number of chiefs within the tribe (forty-four) had their beginnings in the world of the supernatural. The chiefs' offices were created by a young girl who had supernatural abilities and who came to save the Cheyenne people when they were near starvation. She ordered that forty-four chiefs offices be created, that the term of office be ten years, and that five of the old chiefs be kept in office for the next term of office. She further ordered that the chiefs swear an oath to be honest and to take care of the tribe, and, finally, she had them smoke the pipe so that they would never become angry, no matter what anyone said or did to them.

The functions of the Cheyenne chiefs were civil rather than military. The chiefs made the major strategic decisions as to the tribe's general future and destiny. They would decide when and where the tribe was to move. They would decide whether or not to go to war (although the execution of the military raids themselves was left in the hands of the military societies). They would decide on the disposition of murder cases. Other matters of a more mundane sort were left to the military societies.

During the warm months, the forty-four chiefs acted together and in concert as the Council of Forty-Four. When the tribe split up into nomadic bands during the cold months to find food, each band was led individually by one of the forty-four chiefs. The Cheyenne spent their winters living in small bands because the bison, their main source of food, was dispersed; had the whole tribe attempted to live as a single group in the winter, they would have starved.

The chiefs also determined the location and timing of tribal communal hunts. They would send out scouts to look for game, and when it was located, fix the details of the hunt. The Council of Forty-Four then chose the particular military society that would oversee the logistics and maneuvers required by the hunt. The Council of Forty-Four also chose in a like manner the military society that would direct the tribe's moves to other territories.

The chiefs' actions were not only of a secular nature. Many of their responsibilities involved ritual or ceremony. This may be seen even in their preparations for a hunt. The chiefs, before making a decision to hunt, would sometimes call for the services of a spiritual medium. The medium would then contact the appropriate spirits for guidance concerning the proposed hunt. The spirits would then indicate if the hunt should take place and, if so, in what fashion. Failure to heed the directions of the spirits would bring disaster, they believed.

The religious functions of the chiefs were one of its major sources of power, if not the main one. Following a murder within the tribe, the chiefs were more concerned with the supernatural pollution of the sacred center of the tribe, the Sacred Arrows, than with the secular punishment of the murderer. Further, they usually had nothing to do with the creation of new laws by the military societies.

Among the forty-four chiefs were five sanctified priests who acted as the head chiefs. One of these kept and used the forty-four chiefs' medicine bundle (fetish bag) and presided over the council meetings of the chiefs. The medicine in the bundle, called the Sweet Medicine, is a spiritual center of the Cheyenne people, and the spiritual center of the Council of Forty-Four. The chief who carried it had no political power, but instead was considered to be associated with the supernatural center of the world. The remaining priest-chiefs were associated with other spirits and supernatural powers; these included shamanic powers or spirits such as the Spirit Who Rules the Summer. Below these men in formal rank were two Servants, who acted as doormen. Finally, below these in rank were the remaining thirty-seven ordinary chiefs, who had no special or distinguishing rank other than the fact that they were chiefs. On the bottom rank of chiefs was always a non-Cheyenne Indian, usually a Dakota (one of the peoples known collectively as the Sioux). This was probably so that the Cheyenne and the Dakota could always maintain a formal political alliance.

The Council of Forty-Four shared its power with the military societies. The chiefs were older men who were for the most part past their physical prime. They made the great decisions, but it was the mostly younger men of the various military societies who implemented them. Thus, the chiefs could not give orders that the military societies strongly opposed. An example of the political relationship between the chiefs and the military societies can be seen in the efforts of the chiefs to bring the Cheyenne into peaceful relations with the Kiowa and Comanche Indian tribes. The Cheyenne had long been at war with the two tribes, but this was not the major obstacle to peace. The main problem lay in the fact that the young men's favorite activity and most important means of building personal prestige was raiding the enemy for horses and to kill enemy warriors. The interests of the chiefs and of Cheyenne society as a whole lay in peace, since fighting with the enemy cost the Cheyenne the lives of its people. The interests of the young men who made up the military society was to continue raiding to be able to build up personal notoriety. The Cheyenne chiefs resolved the problem by establishing that they favored peace, but then asked one of the military societies, the Dog Soldiers, for its recommendation. The Dog Soldiers noted that the chiefs wanted peace, and then asked the two most militant warriors in its number for their recommendation. The two warriors favored peace, and the rest of the Dog Soldiers voted to agree with them. The Dog Soldiers then reported to the chiefs that they

would agree to peace, and the chiefs thanked them for their recommendation. Then the chiefs concluded the peace. In this way, the Cheyenne were able to secure the compliance of the military societies by allowing them to save face, and this prevented Cheyenne society from splitting over the issue. This solution also demonstrated that the military societies took strong heed of the chiefs' words, even when they were not to their liking.

After the ten-year terms of office for the forty-four chiefs were completed, the council called for a "chief-renewal" ceremony to take place the following spring when the entire tribe was together. At the chief-renewal ceremony, each retiring chief had the privilege of selecting his own successor to his office; it was possible, but considered unseemly, to choose one's own son. Each priest-chief selected his replacement from among the bottom rank of chiefs. If he wished, and was still capable of performing his duties, a retiring priest-chief could take up an office in the bottom rank of chiefs, taking one of the offices being vacated. After the new chiefs took office, they gave their predecessors gifts of an established and unvarying value, just as the previous set of chiefs had given gifts to their own predecessors. The chief-renewal ceremony was in fact a time of general gift-giving generosity, and it was generally considered desirable behavior for the wealthy to give to the poor.

The chiefs were always men, although they listened to what women had to say and took their words into consideration when making decisions. The chiefs were always important men from prominent families, and so were already powerful before becoming chiefs. A chief had to control his temper. He also had to be very generous and give his followers whatever they asked for from his own personal wealth. Finally, Cheyenne chiefs could not lose their office until the chief-renewal, no matter what they did, even if it was to kill another Cheyenne.

Llewellyn, Karl N., and E. Adamson Hoebel. (1961 [1941]) *The Cheyenne Way.*

CITIZENSHIP

Citizenship is the legally recognized membership in a society. Citizenship status carries with it legal rights and duties. For example, citizens of the United States have the right to vote for their leaders upon reaching the age of eighteen, and male citizens of a certain range of ages have the duty to fight to protect the United States during wartime.

In every society, there are also laws regulating who is a citizen and who is not. Among the Kalingas of Luzon, the Philippines, citizenship is determined by residence and by a blood relationship to other members of the society. Each Kalinga society is separate and has its own group of citizens. The Kalinga are largely endogamous, meaning that the Kalinga individual is likely to marry within his/her own society, and so the citizenship requirements of blood ties and residence usually coincide.

On the other hand, blood alone can determine citizenship and can lead to a Kalinga person having dual citizenship. If a man with citizenship in society A marries a woman with citizenship in society B, and they live in society C, then their children will have citizenship in both societies A and B, by virtue of their parents' citizenship.

However, there is yet another dimension to Kalinga citizenship. Kalinga societies are often at or near war with each other. Sometimes, also, someone from one society murders a person from another neighboring society, and then there can be hostilities between the two societies. The Kalinga have developed peace pacts, which they use to end these hostilities and to ensure the safety of the people of a particular society. To be fully a citizen of a particular society is to be covered by one of these pacts, and in fact that is the manner in which the Kalinga state their citizenship. The pact protects the members of the societies making the pact by forcing the pact holder, in order to save the pact, to kill a citizen of his own society if a citizen of his society has killed a citizen of the other society; otherwise, the outcome would be war and many could die.

When a person moves from one society to another, he or she usually wishes to change citizenship to the new society so as to acquire the society's peace pact protection. To become a naturalized citizen, it is necessary to pay a fee to the pact holders. If a man of society A wishes to become a citizen of society B, he pays the member of society B who holds the pact with society A. Half of the payment is kept by this pact holder, and the other half is sent to the member of society A who holds the pact with society B. Both pact holders make public announcements in their own societies concerning the change in citizenship. People who are considered potential troublemakers are not accepted by the pact holder of the society of which they are trying to become a citizen.

If a man, N, a citizen of society A, becomes a naturalized citizen of society B, then his rights, duties, and privileges change. Should N return to society A for a visit, he cannot be the victim of revenge in a feud between his kin and the kin of someone killed by his kin; the peace pact between societies A and B saves N as a citizen of society B. However, if a citizen of society B wants to take revenge against N's family, he can then kill N without endangering the pact, since as a citizen of society B, N has no protection under the pact.

If N moves to society B while remaining a citizen of society A, he has the protection of the pact holder. No one in society B will kill N for

Citizenship, the legally recognized membership in a society, is attained by qualifications such as birth and residence. Upwards of 10,000 non-native-born men and women pledge allegiance to the United States of America at a ceremony in Miami in 1984.

fear that the pact holder will kill the killer in order to save the pact. Further, N can help kill on behalf of his relatives in any society but B, and then escape to society B. If N remained in society A, he could be the target of revenge, but in society B he is protected. If N wishes to kill a person in society C, with which society A has no peace pact, but with which society B does, N can travel with some members of society B to society C in safety, commit murder, and escape to either society A or society B with impunity.

The following is the section of the Civil Code of Japan from 1896 concerning citizenship. As with all nations, the law reflects the importance attached to the question of who may become a citizen. In some cultures, the primary consideration is affording citizenship to those who will be "good" citizens. In others, such as Japan, considerations of marriage, adoption, and racial purity are also important.

Draft of the Law Concerning Nationality

1. A child is a Japanese subject, if at the time of his birth his father is such. The same applies, if the father, having died before the child's birth, was a Japanese subject at the time of his death.

2. If the father before the birth of the child loses his Japanese nationality by divorce or by a dissolution of adoption, the provisions of the preceding article apply with relation back to the beginning of the pregnancy.

The provisions of the foregoing paragraph do not apply, if both parents quit the house, unless the mother returns to the house before the birth of the child.

3. When the father is unknown or has no nationality, the child is a Japanese subject, if the mother is such.

4. If both parents of the child born in Japan are unknown or have no nationality, the child is a Japanese subject.

5. An alien acquires Japanese nationality in the following cases:—
   1. By becoming the wife of a Japanese;
   2. By becoming the husband of a Japanese woman who is the head of a house, at the same time entering her house;
   3. By being acknowledged by his father or mother who is a Japanese subject;
   4. By adoption by a Japanese subject;
   5. By naturalization.

6. The requisites for an alien's acquiring Japanese nationality by acknowledgment are as follows:—
   1. The child must be a minor according to the law of his nationality;
   2. The child must not be the wife of an alien;
   3. The parent who first acknowledges the child must be a Japanese subject;
   4. If both parents acknowledge the child at the same time, the father must be a Japanese subject.

7. With the permission of the Minister of the Home Department an alien may be naturalized on the following conditions:—
   1. He must have had his domicile in Japan for five consecutive years;
   2. He must be at least twenty years old and a person of full capacity by the law of his nationality;
   3. He must be a person of honest behavior;
   4. He must have either property or working ability sufficient for an independent livelihood;
   5. He must have no nationality or must lose his nationality on acquiring Japanese nationality.

8. A wife of an alien can be naturalized only together with her husband.

9. An alien who has at the time his domicile in Japan can be naturalized, even though the conditions specified in Art. 7, No. 1 do not exist, in the following cases:—
   1. If one of his parents is or has been a Japanese subject;
   2. If his wife is or has been a Japanese subject;
   3. If he was born in Japan;
   4. If he has resided in Japan for ten consecutive years.

The persons mentioned in the preceding paragraph under Nos. 1–3 can be naturalized only if they have resided in Japan for three consecutive years; but this does not apply, if a parent of a person mentioned in No. 3 was born in Japan.

10. If a parent of an alien is a Japanese subject and such alien has his domicile at the time in Japan, he may be naturalized, even though the conditions specified in Art. 7, nos. 1, 2 and 4 do not exist.

11. The Minister of the Home Department may with the sanction of the Emperor permit the naturalization of an alien who has done specially meritorious services to Japan, without regard to the provisions to Art. 7.

12. Public notice of a naturalization must be given. A naturalization can be set up against a third person acting in good faith only after such notice.

13. The wife of a person who acquires Japanese nationality acquires it together with her husband, unless she expresses a contrary intention within one month from the time when she had notice of her husband's acquisition of Japanese nationality.

These provisions do not apply, if the law of the wife's nationality provides to the contrary.

14. If the wife of a person who has acquired Japanese nationality did not herself acquire it according to the provisions of the preceding article, she may be naturalized even though the conditions specified in Art. 7 do not exist as to her.

15. A child of a person who acquires Japanese nationality acquires it together with the parent, if the child is a minor according to the law of his nationality.

This provision does not apply, if the law of the child's nationality provides to the contrary.

16. A person naturalized, a person who as being the child of a naturalized person has acquired Japanese nationality, or a person who has become the adopted child of a Japanese or the husband of a Japanese woman who is the head of the house has not the following rights:—

1. The right to become a Minister of State, a Minister of the Imperial Household or Keeper of the Privy Seal;
2. The right to become president, vice-president or a member of the Privy Council;
3. The right to hold the position of a general or admiral;
4. The right to become president of the Supreme court, of the Board of Accounts or of the Administrative Litigation Court;
5. The right to hold the position of Court Councillor;
6. The right to be elected as or to vote for a member of the Imperial Diet.

17. The Minister of the Home Department with the sanction of the Emperor may except from the restrictions of the preceding article a person who has been naturalized under the provision of Art. 11, after five years from the time when he acquired Japanese nationality, or any other person after ten years.

18. A Japanese woman who marries an alien loses thereby her nationality.

19. A person who by marriage or adoption has acquired Japanese nationality loses it on divorce or the dissolution of the adoption only in case he thereby acquires a foreign nationality.

20. A person who voluntarily acquires a foreign nationality loses thereby his Japanese nationality.

21. The wife or child of a person who loses his Japanese nationality, loses the Japanese nationality on acquiring the nationality of such person.

22. The provisions of the preceding article do not apply to the wife or child of a person who loses his Japanese nationality by divorce or the dissolution of adoption, unless the wife in case of the dissolution of adoption of her husband does not procure a divorce, or the child quits the housing following his father.

23. If a child who is a Japanese subject acquires by acknowledgment a foreign nationality, he loses his Japanese nationality; but this does not apply to a person who has become the wife of a Japanese subject, the husband of a Japanese woman being the head of the house, or the adopted child of a Japanese subject.

24. Notwithstanding the provisions of the preceding five articles, a male person of the age of seventeen years or upwards loses his Japanese nationality only if he has already performed his service in the army or navy or is not bound to perform such service.

25. A person who holds a civil or military position can lose his Japanese nationality only on obtaining the permission of his official chief.

A person who has lost Japanese nationality by marriage, but after the dissolution of such marriage has a domicile in Japan may by the permission of the Minister of the Home Department recover Japanese nationality.

26. If a person who has lost Japanese nationality according to the provisions of Arts. 20 or 21 has a domicile in Japan, he may with the permission of the Minister of the Home Department recover Japanese nationality; but this

does not apply to a person mentioned in Art. 16, who has lost the Japanese nationality.

27. The provisions of Arts. 13–15 apply correspondingly to the cases mentioned in the preceding two articles.

28. The time when this law shall take effect shall be determined by Imperial Order.

Barton, Roy F. (1973 [1949]) *The Kalingas: Their Institutions and Custom Law.*

The Civil Code of Japan. (1896)

CIVIL LAW

Civil law deals with legal offenses between private parties. It differs from criminal law in that criminal law deals with legal offenses against the society as a whole. The body of a civil offense (a private wrong) is known as a tort. A good example of the difference between the two is the legal actions that various parties may take after a homicide has been committed. After a homicide, the society may decide that a crime has been committed and try the alleged killer on murder or manslaughter charges. Whether the alleged killer is convicted of a crime or not, the family of the victim may bring legal charges against the alleged killer in civil court. The family can sue the killer to recover monetary awards for the love and affection lost when the victim died, as well as for the services he or she would have performed in the future and whatever monetary earnings the victim would have earned in his or her lifetime. In instances in which someone other than the killer is also responsible for a death, they can be sued as well. An example of this is cases in which a prisoner is killed by another inmate. The prison system, which is responsible for prisoner safety, has been sued by the families of inmates killed in prison for monetary awards.

Justinian I (483–565) ruled the Byzantine Empire from his capital in Constantinople and had Roman statutes compiled into the Codex constitutionum.

Civil law has another meaning as well. It refers to the legal systems that have developed out of the Roman legal system (Justinian Code), mainly the legal systems of continental Europe (such as the French, Austrian, Spanish, etc.) as well as the legal systems of South American nations and of the state of Louisiana in the United States. When civil law is used in this meaning, it is often to contrast it with common law, the legal system that developed in England and is the foundation of the United States, Canadian, New Zealand, and Australian legal systems.

See also COMMON LAW.

CIVILIZATION

The term *civilization*, from the Latin *civis* (citizen), has different meanings for different social scientists. For many, the term is synonymous with the word "state." For others, the term signifies a special complex of cultural traits and social features. Perhaps the best-known definition of civilization is that provided by the archaeologist V. Gordon Childe. He listed a set of attributes that if found together in a society meant that it had undergone an "urban revolution" and is or was a civilization:

1. Urban centers of at least 7,000 people each.
2. A surplus of food produced by peasants, which is used to feed the governmental administrators.
3. Monumental public buildings.
4. A ruling class of priests and military and civilian leaders and officials
5. The use of numerals and writing.
6. The knowledge and use of arithmetic, geometry, and astronomy.
7. Sophisticated artistry.
8. Long-distance trade.
9. An institutionalized political organization that rules by the use of force, which is the "state," according to Childe.

See also STATE.

Childe, V. Gordon. (1950) "The Urban Revolution." *Town Planning Review* 21(1): 3–17.
Service, Elman R. (1975) *Origins of the State and Civilization: The Process of Cultural Evolution.*

CLASS A class is a culturally defined category of people who possess a certain quality or characteristic or set of quali-

ties or characteristics. A class may be based upon any quality or characteristic one wishes to name, including age, sex, height, skin color, last name, or favorite foods. The kind of class social scholars refer to most often is economic class, in which people are classified into categories on the basis of their wealth or their annual financial income. Wealth is considered the most important basis of social position within any society, according to many social scholars, and so the classes to which people belong are assumed to be the greatest factor in social stratification. The classes are conceptualized as running from low to high on a vertical scale, the lower classes being the poorer ones and the higher classes being the wealthier ones. In addition, economic classes are considered to be markers of social class, in that members of a class act in fashions characteristic to their class and exhibit beliefs and attitudes that are also characteristic of that portion of a society whose wealth falls at a certain point on a scale of wealth. Economic classes are found primarily in state societies, since in band and tribal societies wealth and power depends primarily on personal, family, or other group qualifications rather than class associations. Because economic classes are also related to matters of political power, prestige, and access to resources, they are social classes as well as strictly economic classes; they are often referred to as socioeconomic classes.

Classes are considered by many scholars to have some of the properties of a group. They are, for one thing, considered to have relatively stable membership over time. That is, people do not change class affiliation often, since they usually stay with one type of employment over their lifetime, and this type of employment usually pays them an income that is approximately the same relative to other sources of income over time. Class membership is also considered to be largely stable in that children whose parents belong to a certain class also are likely to remain in that class as they grow older. A social and economic system in which it is easy to move from one class to another is said to be open, or it may be said that there is a lot of class mobility in that society.

Caste systems are systems of social class in which there is no class mobility and in which the class is like a group in that it is endogamous (that is, members of the group or caste are required to marry other members of the group or caste). In India, each caste is associated with a certain job or range of jobs in any particular geographic area, so social class frequently determines or strongly affects the economic wealth of the members of the caste. Also, Indian castes traditionally were endogamous.

Those who conceive of classes as grouplike structures usually also accept the grading of them along a vertical range from low to high. Thus, classes are conceived of as vertical layers in a society, in that higher classes are thought of as being above lower classes; this is what is meant by the commonly used phrase "social stratification." However, classes are not groups. Social groups by definition have functions, reasons for being in existence, whereas classes never do.

Another feature of economic classes is that those associated with various classes have, on the whole, different degrees of access to material resources and political power. Those belonging to the lower classes generally have less influence on their society's political situation and political future than do people who are associated with the higher classes. This can be seen in the national politics of the United States, in which candidates need the support of the wealthy before they can afford to mount a campaign that has any chance of success. The candidate who wins an election is expected to remember the interests of those who financed his or her campaign when various legislation affecting those interests appears before the legislature. Sometimes, wealthy candidates for office are able to finance, or largely finance, their own campaigns. Those who are poor have a relatively small chance

to reach elective office unless they work for the interests of at least some wealthy supporters.

The idea of class as a useful concept in the explanation of human societies was first championed by Karl Marx and Friedrich Engels and elaborated on later by Vladimir Lenin. For Marx, Engels, and Lenin, classes were important because the people who were affiliated with each class could be expected to behave in a certain way because their economic interests were the same as other people of the class. Thus, Marx showed how people who ran the industries of nineteenth-century Great Britain and Germany had a common interest in getting cheap labor to work in their factories so that they themselves could become wealthier faster. The industrial ownership class, further, was able to influence laws and legislation so that the factory and mine workers had little or no physical or health protections, which have cost the owners of the factories and mines money.

Marx, Engels, and Lenin wrote to convince people who work for employers and for the lowest wages that they belonged to a class (the working class or, as Marx liked to call it, the proletariat), and that their interests, as a class, were in taking ownership of the factories, fields, mines, and other sources of wealth away from the owners and for themselves. The three men never achieved to their satisfaction an awareness of class, what they called class consciousness, among the workers of the world.

In recent decades, the interests of political anthropologists (as well as sociologists and many political scientists) have largely focused on classes of various types, almost to the exclusion of studies of groups and individuals, which were the traditional units of study of political anthropology. This interest in categories of people by status or some other attribute has branched out from studies of economic categories to categories of people by ethnicity, race, sex, geographic location, and native language as well as other qualities.

Vladimir Ilich Lenin, author of The State and Revolution *(1917) and leader of the Soviet state, in Moscow, 25 May 1919*

The concept of class is useful to explain how certain categories of people are affected by the actions of others. For example, changes in the tax laws that reduce the tax rate for capital gains would benefit people of all classes, but would benefit primarily the wealthy, many of whom make a lot of money through capital investments. Other classes of people, in the United States and elsewhere, including blacks, American Indians, Spanish-speaking peoples, and women, have not always received equal protection under the law and have been the victims of other forms of negative discrimination.

While classes of people thus receive the effects of the actions of others, they do not themselves take action. Only individuals and groups take action. A group may be composed of people who are classed together according to some criterion (wealth, age, race, etc.), but it is a group that exists separately from the class; rarely if ever do all the members of a class work together to do anything. Also, people frequently advocate and work toward political changes that appear to hurt the interests of themselves and of others of their own class, in the belief that they are working to improve society overall. Thus, in the United States we have wealthy industrialists who have supported legislative changes designed to shift wealth from the rich to the poor, and thus reduced their own wealth. Also, in the belief that people should get only what they themselves earn, and all that they themselves earn, there are poor working people who support laissez-faire economic policies, policies that often mean that the poor are poorer than they would be with governmental financial assistance paid by taxes on the wealthy. There are industrial workers who likewise oppose unions, even though their representation by a union would likely mean that they would be paid a higher wage. In other words, people who are affiliated with a class according to whatever criteria may be chosen do not always perceive their interests to be the same of other people of that class. For this reason, classes do not take political action, although a number of people of a certain class may individually or in groups take action.

Lenin, Vladimir I. (1976 [1917]) *The State and Revolution.*

Marx, Karl, and Friedrich Engels. (1968) *Karl Marx and Friedrich Engels: Selected Works in One Volume.*

Tyler, Stephen A. (1973) *India: An Anthropological Perspective.*

Weber, Max. (1947) *The Theory of Social and Economic Organization.*

COLLECTIVE LIABILITY

The idea of collective liability is that an entire group is legally responsible for the actions of any of its members. This idea is all but unknown in our own society, but is common in some parts of the world, and was indeed characteristic of some earlier European societies.

It may seem odd that a group is responsible for the actions of one person. It may even seem unjust. After all, why should I have to pay compensation to the family of a man murdered by my second cousin? Or, even worse, why should I be at risk of losing my own life in retaliation for the death of a person killed by my second cousin?

The idea of collective liability makes a great deal of sense in societies in which one's welfare is insured by one's group. In our society, we depend upon the government or private insurance companies to help us when we cannot take care of ourselves. In many societies, the government cannot do this, and there are no such things as insurance companies. If a plague hits, if one's crops are ruined by insects, or if a drought forces all the game away, one must turn to other members of the group to acquire food, shelter, and clothing. In most such societies, the group to which one turns is a descent group, such as a patrilineage or matrilineage. In other societies, it is often the kindred, the quasi group, that is made up of one's kin on both the father's and mother's side. Naturally, if one depends on these groups and quasi groups for insurance, one wishes to see them prosper, for they cannot help if they themselves fall on hard times. For this reason, a murder of one of the group's members cannot be allowed, because it removes a productive person from the ranks of those who might help you. Thus, it is in the group's or quasi group's interest to seek a payment from the group of the killer to replace the value of the work that would have been done by the murdered person. Among the Anglo-Saxon people, the ancestors of the modern-day English, this compensation payment was known as *wergild* or, literally, "man-payment." The entire group to which the murderer belonged would have to pay the compensation payment, because usually the murderer did not have enough wealth to pay the compensation payment himself. If the murderer's group refused to pay the compensation payment, or if it could not provide an amount acceptable to the murdered man's group, then the murdered man's group would be considered justified in taking revenge by killing a member of the murderer's group. Sometimes, in retaliation for this second killing, members of the murderer's group, especially if they felt the first killing justified, would take revenge for the killing of a member of their own group, and thus a blood feud would start.

The threat of losing a member of one's own group in a retaliation killing was usually enough to prevent most people from killing in the first place. This system worked well in another way. If a man killed another, his own group would have to pay compensation. The members of his group would usually be very unhappy because of this, and would let the murderer know of their unhappiness. Sometimes, the group would be so angry with the murderer that it would banish him from their area or cause him some other punishment as a consequence. In this way then, the method of collective liability worked to keep people from killing one another, especially in the absence of a legal system with authority over a large number of people.

See also CORPORATION.

Gluckman, Max. (1974) *African Traditional Law in Historical Perspective.*

COMMON LAW

Common law refers to the legal system of England, which was brought to many parts of the British Empire and now forms the basis of the legal systems of the United States (and all of the state legal systems with the exception of Louisiana), Canada, New Zealand, Australia, and Hong Kong. It is often contrasted with civil law, which had its origins in Roman law, and which forms the basis of legal systems in continental Europe, South America, and Louisiana.

Common law differs from civil law in that legal authorities in the former system depend more upon previous judicial precedents (as opposed to legislation) than do legal authorities in civil law systems. Of course, many of the precedents set by judges in common law systems do end up being passed as legislation. Thus, the difference between the two is now a matter of degree in this respect.

Of course, the actual laws used by the two systems differ significantly. One of the major differences is that in civil law systems women who divorce are entitled as a matter of basic right to half of the assets of the married couple. On the other hand, common law systems have for centuries been adopting legal principles from civil law systems when they saw them as just. The example of equal division of marital assets is becoming common across the United States, for example. Another example is the old Roman legal principle of dividing the estate of an individual who dies intestate (without a will) per *stirpes,* a practice that common law adopted long ago. When a person dies without a will, his or her estate is divided among his offspring (assuming that there is no living spouse) equally. For example, a man has two sons, one of whom had two sons of his own prior to dying. Thus, an equal division would result in one half of the estate going to the living son, and one half of the estate going to the two grandsons, among whom that half would be equally divided. The estate would not, for example, be divided into thirds.

See also CIVIL LAW.

COMPARATIVE LAW

Comparative law refers to a method of studying law in which legal systems are compared with one another. One may compare large numbers of entire legal systems with each other, one may restrict one's study to one aspect of two legal systems, or one may make a study of any intermediate scope. A single legal system may also be compared with itself at an earlier date, in order to understand the changes the system has undergone. The different types of comparative legal studies differ not primarily with size and scope, but with the goals of the researcher. The practicing attorney or judge, for example, might be primarily interested in learning about foreign legal systems, or even about specific points of law in foreign legal systems, in order to better solve a case at hand; this would be an example of applied comparative law. It is often the case that a foreign legal authority has come across a dispute or legal question that has never before been seen in a domestic court, or the foreign legal authority may have come up with a particularly clever or just answer, or clever or just reason for giving a particular answer, that will serve a

domestic court well, and so may be incorporated into the domestic court's decision.

A good example of the applied use of the comparative method is found in the case of *Greenspan v. Slate*, decided by the Supreme Court of New Jersey in 1953 (*see* Schlesinger, 1980: 2–5). In this case, the teenaged daughter of the defendants injured her leg playing basketball. Her parents believed that the only injury she had was a sprain, and for this reason gave her no medical treatment. A third party saw her condition and took her to a doctor. The doctor took X-rays of her leg and discovered that her leg was fractured. The doctor's professional opinion was that she needed to be treated immediately or risk permanent injury, and so gave her a cast and a pair of crutches on the spot. The doctor then asked the parents for a fee of $45, which they refused to pay. The doctor, Greenspan, sued to recover the fee. The defendant parents relied upon the fact that they had not entered into a contract with the doctor, and thus could not be forced to pay for services they had not requested. The question that the court had to answer is whether or not the parents are legally responsible for taking care of their children in emergency situations. Under the general principles of American law specifically, and common law (law of British origin, including U.S. law) generally, the obligation of parents to care for their children is considered a moral rather than a legal one. However, since there were no good actual legal precedents on this question in U.S. law, the court was able to look to other legal systems for an answer. The court in this case decided to look at the so-called civil legal systems (the legal systems of continental Europe that grew out of Roman law). Under the laws of France, Germany, Italy, Austria, and Switzerland, parents are required by law to support their children until they can support themselves. The court applied this principle to the case at hand in New Jersey and ruled in favor of the doctor to collect the $45 he asked for his fee to treat the girl's leg.

Studies of comparative law are often strongly philosophical in character. This is because when legal systems are compared, their differences show up not merely as different legal principles, but also as the reasons and justifications for the differences in those principles. For example, take the case above. The difference in legal principles revealed was that in the United States, at the time of the decision, the ability of legal parties to make or not to make contracts was superior to the right of children to be supported by their parents. The civil law systems of continental Europe saw the right of children to the support of their parents to be of great importance. The authority in the case determined, in a precedent-setting decision, that the power of people to make contracts was less important than the right of children to receive the support of one's parents. Legal philosophy incorporates a hierarchy of rights that the law protects differentially. In other words, every legal system has made choices as to which rights are more important than others. Thus, virtually all comparative law cases have a philosophical component because, in order for one to understand why a legal system has its own peculiar principles, it is necessary for one to understand the philosophical premises upon which the principles are founded.

A good example of this may be seen in a study that compared product liability awards in the United States and Germany (Stiefel, et. al., 1991), and explained to the reader why not all product liability awards made in U.S. courts are upheld in Germany. Let us say that an American buys a German-made appliance, which because of a manufacturing flaw explodes and injures the buyer. The American goes to court and sues the manufacturer for damages, including pain and suffering, medical expenses, lost wages, and punitive damages. Let us say that the U.S. court decides in favor of the injured

party and awards him $500,000 for pain and suffering, medical expenses, and lost wages. The court also decides to award him another $1 million for punitive damages, so as to give the manufacturer a warning not to continue its shoddy manufacturing practices. If the German manufacturer goes to a German court to protest this award, it is highly likely that the court there would reduce it substantially. In 1991, German courts were allowing at most twice the size of comparable German judgments to be sustained against German corporations by U.S. courts. The highest award for physical injuries in German courts are 350,000 deutsche marks for paraplegia of young people, whereas U.S. courts not infrequently award millions of dollars for any severe injuries that will affect a person for a very long time to come. The reason for the much lower German awards is that the German legal system stringently separates civil law from criminal law. In other words, the private dispute between the company and the injured party is dealt with entirely by civil law, and only the pain and suffering, lost wages, and medical expenses related to the injury are paid by the company to the injured, and these payments are quite low. If the government or public prosecutor, on the other hand, finds that the company has been manufacturing a defective product that has injured or is likely to injure people, they may institute criminal charges against the company, and any fines that the company is forced to pay will go to the government and not to an injured individual. The reason for this approach is that it greatly reduces the number of fraudulent suits against corporations, suits in which people may exaggerate the extent of their injuries, or even make entirely fraudulent injuries, in order to try to enrich themselves by playing on the sympathy of jurors. Further, German courts do not use juries to determine the size of awards to injured parties, but rather specialists trained for just that kind of question. The danger posed by fraudulent claims, especially if they result in large awards, is that companies may resist going into business, developing new and more technologically advanced products, or they may decide to go out of business; all of these results harm a nation's economy and employment rates.

The reason for the American courts' use of high awards for product liability cases is that it is often difficult to fully punish negligent or malicious corporations for selling dangerous products in criminal cases. Therefore, they decided to use civil suits as a means to increase the liability of corporations for producing dangerous products. In short, the philosophical difference between U.S. courts and German courts with respect to product liability awards is that the U.S. courts are primarily interested in punishing companies for producing dangerous products, whereas the German courts are primarily interested in preventing fraud from entering the legal system and possibly causing great harm to the economic system by making it even more difficult for companies to start up or to remain in business.

A second type of comparative law studies is purely philosophical. Some scholars are interested in understanding the philosophical bases of different legal systems as an end in itself. Escarra's comparison of Chinese law with European/Roman legal systems is a good example of studies of this type. All legal systems carry their own reasons for existence. For Western legal systems, which all originated to some degree from the Roman legal system, the law, originally at least, was believed to have divine origins. Laws, that is, especially Natural Law, were given to us by God and are discoverable by a thoughtful mind through philosophical contemplation. In short, Western legal philosophy understood law to be a part of the natural order of things. To a degree, this is still true, although few legal philosophers today are willing to invoke God as a source of law. The idea that law is

a part of the natural order is certainly still alive, as seen in the fact that an adherent of Natural Law philosophy, Clarence Thomas, sits on the United States Supreme Court.

On the other hand, under traditional Chinese philosophy, as Escarra points out, law is nothing more than a necessary evil created by men to control the actions of people who behave poorly. People who are in alignment with the natural world behave well and do not need to be controlled by the law. In fact, when man first appeared on Earth, it was believed, law did not exist. Further, if the emperor is properly virtuous, he brings universal harmony to all of his followers, and so the need for law is removed or at least greatly reduced.

We can also see in comparative studies of the substantive law (the actual legal principles that are used to regulate behavior) of different societies just what people in those societies think is very important and what they use the law to protect. For example, in the United States, as well as in much of Europe, laws are made to encourage the growth of commerce. The U.S. legal system, for example, is effective in enforcing business contracts. It also provides for a lower taxation rate for businesses than for other forms of property. Further, under U. S. law, businesses may deduct many expenses from their taxable income, including business lunches, entertainment, and transportation. U.S. tax law also allows businesses to depreciate business equipment.

By contrast, pre-Communist Chinese law did not protect commerce nearly so well. On the other hand, Chinese law protected something that most Americans do not even consider to be properly within the purview of legal protection, namely filial piety. The law encouraged filial piety in response to the beliefs of the Chinese people, who were tremendously influenced by Confucian philosophy; according to Confucian philosophy, filial piety is one of the requirements for a good society. The law protected filial piety to the point that it made a mourning period for parents mandatory, and in so doing made it a legal offense to engage in certain behaviors, including contracting marriage, during this period. It also made disobedience to a parent or grandparent a legal offense and gave the father the right of life and death over his offspring.

A third type of comparative legal study is the anthropological one. Legal anthropological studies, and anthropological studies in general, are comparative by nature. This is because anthropology is a science, and as such seeks to make generalizations and predictions. Anthropology cannot make accurate generalizations and predictions unless it compares all societies and cultures, and this is no less true of legal anthropology. Could a general statement about law be accurate if it was not tested against all legal systems? Of course, it cannot.

We can see how comparative law helps the legal anthropologist in the following example. The great scholars of international and Natural Law, Hugo Grotius and Samuel von Pufendorf, had asserted that law's ultimate function is to preserve social integrity. This generalization stood for centuries, but conflicted with the modern-day law of a Micmac band on a Nova Scotia reserve, which actively promoted social disunity. Thus, while the generalization made by Grotius and Pufendorf applies to most societies, it is not a universally applicable generalization.

Several excellent examples of the use of comparative law by an anthropologist are to be found in the writings of Pospisil (1974). He was able to develop a theory of law, which has thus far been applicable to all societies against which it has been tested, by using the comparative method and studying a large number of societies. This theory is discussed in the entry on Law. He also invented the theory of legal pluralism/ multiplicity of legal levels by studying a large number of societies, and especially by studying three societies personally and in depth: the Kapauku Papuans, the Nunamiut Eskimo, and the peasants of Tirol. Because the comparative method was used in making this general theory, it has thus far also been applicable to all societies against which it has been tested. Other general theories that Pospisil has formulated and that are cross-culturally valid are theories on the change of legal systems, the change of laws, and justice. The cross-cultural validity of these generalizations is a result of the comparative method being used in their construction.

See also CIVIL LAW; COMMON LAW; LAW; MULTIPLICITY OF LEGAL LEVELS.

Escarra, Jean. (1926) *Chinese Law and Comparative Jurisprudence.*

Pospisil, Leopold. (1974 [1971]) *Anthropology of Law: A Comparative Theory.*

Pufendorf, Samuel von. (1927 [1682]) *De Officio Hominis et Civis Juxta Legem Naturalem Libri Duo.* Translated by Frank Gardener Moore.

Schlesinger, Rudolf B. (1980) *Comparative Law: Cases—Text—Materials.* 4th ed.

Stiefel, Ernst C., Rolf Stürner, and Astrid Stadler. (1991) "The Enforceability of Excessive U.S. Punitive Damage Awards in Germany." *The American Journal of Comparative Law* 39: 779-802.

Strouthes, Daniel P. (1994) *Change in the Real Property Law of a Cape Breton Island Micmac Band.*

Whewell, William. (1853) *Grotius on War and Peace.* Vol. I.

CONDOMINIUM LAW

The term *condominium law* refers to a legal situation in which a society is under the jurisdiction of two or more politically and legally independent societies. Condominium law is less common today than it was in the past.

From 1906 until 1980, the Republic of Vanuatu, a Melanesian archipelago in the Pacific Ocean, was known as the Anglo-French Condominium of the New Hebrides. Under the terms of their agreement, Great Britain and France were strictly equal in their power over the New Hebrides. For example, the two governments each demanded that their own educational system be implemented there, although few schools were actually built and many islanders found themselves far away from schools of any type. Each district was represented by a British officer and a French officer. The condominium law stipulated that both district officers together make a tour of the district three times per year.

With respect to the administration of civil and criminal law, however, the involvement of the British and the French was anything but equal. All behavior was ostensibly regulated according to the provisions of the Native Criminal Code, a legislated code of criminal offenses and sanctions made up by the colonial powers for use by the native people of the New Hebrides. On the other hand, on the island of Aoba (Ambae), the native leaders/authorities, who were big men, controlled minor disputes according to their own native laws and not according to the externally imposed Native Criminal Code. Major disputes, however, were handled differently. In Aoba, the people living on the western side of the island wanted as little to do with the colonial powers as possible, and so did not inform the colonial district officers when legal offenses occurred. They handled all such breaches themselves. On the eastern side of the island, the people disliked the French but tolerated the British. The result was that the French district officer had very little involvement in the lives of the people of Aoba.

The people of east Aoba called upon the British district officer to decide serious criminal offenses. In such cases, the district officer, a British man, was aided by an assessor, a native person whom the district officer had appointed to act as a middleman. The district officer always responded readily to his assessor's requests for help, since this was a good way for the district officer to make sure that his assessor maintained power and authority in the native communities. The two men, the district officer and the assessor, together decided the outcome of the case and the sanction, if any, to be imposed. The assessor, being familiar with the parties involved, as well as native standards of justice, had a great influence on the decisions made.

The question thus is, why did the native big men of east Aoba care to involve a colonial district officer at all in their legal proceedings? Why did they not, like the people of west Aoba, handle their own affairs secretly? The answer was that the colonial government provided a range of powerful legal sanctions that the big men of east Aoba used to punish troublesome people in the area under their control. The big men sponsored the assessors, gave them wealth, prestige, and power, and then used them to bring in the powerful sanctions of colonial Britain to give themselves more control over their own people.

See also BIG MAN.

Rodman, William. (1985) " 'A law unto Themselves': Legal Innovation in Ambae, Vanuatu." *American Ethnologist* 12(4): 603–624.

CONFESSION A confession is a statement made by one accused of wrongdoing in which he or she admits guilt. In the United States, a confession cannot be admitted into a legal proceeding unless it can be proven that the confession was made voluntarily and not under duress, and that the confessor was made fully aware of his or her right not to confess or to say or write anything that could incriminate him or her.

In Japan, the law regarding confessions is quite different. There, most criminal cases are decided by the confession of the person charged in the crime. It is also the case that the police force many people to confess, even if they are innocent. In a 1983 investigation by three bar associations, for example, three people who had been induced to confess to murder were found to be innocent.

The police there often interrogate those who do not freely confess their crimes from early morning until midnight. They are frequently held in special police detention cells, where they are watched twenty four hours a day, and in which the flourescent lights are never turned off. The food served them is of low quality; however, if they confess, they are given a good meal (which they must pay for) as a reward.

Van Wolferen, Karel. (1989) *The Enigma of Japanese Power.*

CONSTITUTION

A constitution may be defined as the fundamental rules and/or legal principles that are used to regulate a society's government. In some societies, constitutions are codes of written rules that are specifically set apart from other written rules as special, as in the United States. In other societies, much of the constitution may be found in written legal principles, although these principles may be dispersed within the overall body of the society's law, as in Great Britain. In yet other societies, the rules and/or legal principles are not written, but are nevertheless well known to those who govern.

The latter situation is of course common in traditional band and tribal societies. Among the Ashanti of West Africa, the constitutional rules that were in place in the Feyiase and post-Feyiase period, when the various divisions of the Ashanti were united into a confederacy, were gathered together by an anthropologist; some of these are described below.

There was a king of all Ashanti, who owned all of the land in Ashanti territory. In addition, each territory within the Ashanti kingdom was ruled by a chief, who took an oath of loyalty to, and could be removed by, the king. The king and the chiefs were political leaders and authorities as well as legal authorities. The king and the chiefs were formal authorities, and their office was known as a stool, just as an English king's office is known as a throne. Each chief was guided by a group of elders known as a *mpanyimfo*. Each territorial division also had its own army in which all adult men served.

The overall organization of the Ashanti kingdom was feudal. As the territorial chiefs were loyal to the king and served at his pleasure, so too were there subordinate chiefs (*birempon*) who were loyal to the territorial chiefs and served at their pleasure. If a lower-ranking chief did not acknowledge loyalty to a territorial chief, he would be forced to do so by armed men under the control of the territorial chief.

Chiefs were sacred while in office (while on the stool), and because of their supernatural powers could not strike an ordinary Ashanti, since it was believed that to do so would cause the ordinary person to become insane. The chief's decisions were considered to be made by the dead ancestors, and thus to be always correct, and for this reason could not be questioned by commoners. However, his every political or legal pronouncement was carefully considered by his advisors before he delivered it, and a chief's failure to say what his advisors had counseled him to say would be grounds for his destoolment. Some chiefs took on the duties of the prosecutor on legal cases, in addition to their usual role as legal authority. This attempt to increase their own power often caused them to become hated by the common people. There is also a group of people, called the *Wirempefo*, who remove the deceased chief's stool, and who may keep it and thus prevent the next chief from taking office if the next chief is not to popular liking.

Each territorial division and subdivision had a special matrilineage that always produced the respective group's chiefs. A chief normally served for life, and when he died, in earlier times, his attendants were killed so that they could serve him in the next world. Before he died, a member of the particular branch of the matrilineage that was to provide the next chief had already been selected by the *mpanyimfo* and groomed for office as the heir apparent to the stool.

The Ashanti government acquired wealth in a variety of ways. One of the most important ways in which it did so was to inherit a portion of each man's valuable personal property upon his death, especially gold, cloth, and slaves. This wealth rose to the higher ranks of government from the common man indirectly and over a long period of time. If, for example, an ordinary man who was subordinate to a member of a *mpanyimfo* or a *birempon* died, the member of the *mpanyimfo* would receive a portion of the man's personal property, but only if he made a contribution to the cost of the man's funeral. When the member of the *mpanyimfo* died, part of his personal property went likewise to the *birempon*, so long as the *birempon* paid a part of the *mpanyimfo*'s funeral costs. The wealth went in the same way from *birempon* to territorial chief, and thence to the king. Thus, the territorial chief, for example, had great potential wealth, but at most points in his life had no assets he could readily expend.

The chiefs and king also gained wealth by trading goods, including kola nuts, livestock, gold, rum, guns, gunpowder, metal rods, and salt. The king and chiefs could not engage in the trading of slaves, as other traders could do; once a chief acquired a slave, it was property that could only be handed down to the next occupant of that stool. Certain of the chief's retinue carried out trading on his behalf; these people included the drummers, horn blowers, hammock carriers, and bathroom attendants. The stools also regulated trade within the borders of their territories, and required traders who passed through their roads to pay a toll.

A third means by which the Ashanti stools gained wealth was through court fines and fees. The chief had the right to keep the fine paid by a man convicted of murder so as to avoid the death penalty. The stools also gained wealth through the profits made by mining gold. They kept two-thirds of the gold that any miner found on his land.

Finally, the stool was entitled to tax people for the chief's funeral expenses, for the chief's enstoolment expenses, for the purpose of conducting a war, and for any other purpose. The stools also collected a portion of all war spoils, and could require the people to give them game and fish.

The revenues that the stool collected were usually spent quickly, and so the wealth of the stool was circulated around within the community. Further, the occupant of the stool, the chief or king, could not become wealthy as a result of his office. If he were destooled, for example, he could keep only one wife, a servant boy, and some gold dust; everything else, even the property and wives he brought with him to the office, would remain with the stool.

Finally, the Ashanti constitution regulates the waging of war. A chief or king may plan to make a military attack upon an enemy over a period of months or even years, during which he plans the attack itself, gathers munitions, and assembles his troops. The troops are adult males subordinate to the chief or king, as well as the chief's or king's slaves, who might number in the hundreds. The chief or king would appoint a captain to help him lead the troops into battle. The captain would then swear an oath before the stool to be brave in battle; however, a person taking this military oath is not subject to a fine for breaking the oath, as he would be if he broke any other kind of oath made before the stool. On the other hand, the Ashanti expected their warriors to be extremely brave in the face of the enemy, and this was especially true with regard to the chiefs and king. The chiefs and king led battle and would never retreat. They would enlist the aid of their ancestral ghosts by standing on their stools, an act designed to enrage the ghosts and make them fight harder. If it looked as if the battle were lost, the king or chief would use gunpowder to blow himself up, or he would kill himself with poison, which he brought with him especially for that purpose. All Ashanti soldiers, in fact, were expected to be brave in war; if one showed cowardice he was usually killed. However, the coward was allowed to pay money in lieu of suffering death, but any man who did so was forced to wear women's waist beads, have his hair dressed as a woman's, and have his eyebrows shaved, and he was unable to seek compensation from a man who seduced his wife into adultery.

If the Ashanti warriors were able to capture an enemy captain, either alive or dead, they tried him, decapitated him, dismembered him, and then sent the head and legs of the enemy to the military leaders of the Ashanti army. If a member of the Ashanti army captured a girl and then had sexual intercourse with her, it would be likely that he would be killed, since captured girls became wives of the chief, and to seduce a wife of the chief was punishable by death.

In contrast, the constitution of the Iroquois Confederacy, also known as the Confederation of the Five Nations, takes a greatly different form, that of the legend of Deganawida and Hiawatha. Deganawida was born to a virgin woman who had been made pregnant by the Creator of the universe. Before he was born, a supernatural being came to his mother's mother and told her that he would be born a male and was to be named Deganawida. After he was born and grew to be a man, he set out on the mission given him by the Creator, to bring his message of peace, known as the Great Peace, to the Iroquois peoples, who at the time were given to internecine warfare with each other. In the pursuit of this goal, he traveled and later met up with Hiawatha, an Onondaga man, who asked Deganawida to prove the truth of his supernatural abilities and mission by surviving a fall off a cliff, which he did. Following this, the two men worked together to bring about peace.

Following a number of exploits involving Deganawida's supernatural powers, Deganawida and Hiawatha gathered together representatives of the five Iroquois nations (Mohawk, Cayuga, Onondaga, Oneida, and Seneca) and told them that they wanted them to come together to form a confederacy. All agreed, with the exception of the Seneca. Deganawida appeased the Seneca by proposing that the Seneca would have the function of military leaders for the entire Five Nations Confederacy, and this caused the Seneca to assent to join. Deganawida then appointed from the representatives of the five nations the members of the first council of the confederacy, and gave them deer antlers to wear on their heads as badges of office. Those chosen selected other members of their own tribes as additional members to complete the full membership of the council.

The five members of the confederacy held positions within the council related to their geographic positions relative to one another. The group farthest to the east, the Mohawk, became the confederacy's Keeper of the Eastern Door. The group farthest to the west, the Seneca, became the Keeper of the Western Door. The group in the middle, the Onondaga, became Keeper of the Sacred Council Fire as well as the

The Ashanti of West Africa were ruled by kings who followed unwritten but widely accepted and understood legal principles, which, by definition, are a form of constitution. This Ashanti chief sits with advisors in 1910.

confederacy's keeper of the wampum, and it was in the central settlement of the Onondaga that the council of the confederacy met. These three groups were called either the "Fathers" or "The Elder Brothers," depending on which particular account of the legend is being told. The other two groups, the Oneida (geographically located between the Mohawk and the Onondaga) along with the Cayuga (located between the Seneca and the Onondaga) were known as either "The Sons" or "The Younger Brothers." When the Tuscarora Indians (another Iroquoian people) moved northward and joined the confederacy approximately 100 years later, they became another "Son" or "Younger Brother."

After giving roles to the five nations, Deganawida assigned a seating plan for the council meetings. The elder brothers sat on one side of the fire and the younger brothers on the other. The Onondaga members of the council were given the responsibility to be the first to address any new business before the council. After giving their opinion on the matter, they passed the problem to the Mohawks. From them, the question was passed to the Senecas. If the Mohawks and the Senecas agreed on a course of action, then the matter was passed across the fire to the Oneida. The Oneida, in turn, passed the matter on to the Cayuga representatives. The Cayuga told their decision to the Oneida, who, if they agreed, told their combined decision to the Mohawk. If the elder brothers' decision agreed with that of the younger brothers, then the Mohawk announced the combined agreement of the four tribes' representatives to the Onondaga. If the Onondaga agreed, then they certified the decision as the final decision of the council. The Onondaga could reject the decision made by the other four tribes, but only if they could point to some great flaw in the decision. If the Onondaga rejected the decision, they stated their reason for the rejection and returned the question to the others. If the disagreement is between the older brothers and the younger

brothers, each side is apprised of the other's position and given another chance to debate it among themselves. If there is no agreement after this, then the Onondaga make a final and binding judgment. If the Mohawks disagree with the Seneca, and the Cayuga disagree with the Oneida, then the separate decisions are given to the Onondaga, who make a final and binding decision on the matter. This procedure is still followed today.

Deganawida chose the original confederacy chiefs. The names of these chiefs became the names of the offices they held. Thus, when the original chiefs died, their replacements took their names and, in so doing, their offices. The names, and thus the offices, belong to the clans of the men who originally held them. Since they are the property of the clans, it is the responsibility of the clan leaders to reassign them when the holders are no longer confederacy chiefs because they have died or were removed from office. The Iroquois are a matrilineal people and for this reason the leadership of the clans is in the hands of the elder female members of the clan. The clan mother, the senior female member of the clan, in conjunction with other female members of the clan, select the next man to take the name associated with a position on the Iroquois Confederacy Council. Thus, while only men can serve on the Iroquois Confederacy Council, only women can select them. If a clan has no appropriate candidates for the name, the name can be lent to another clan for the length of the officeholder's term.

Deganawida made other rules regarding the operation of the confederacy. Only members of the council can speak on matters of their own choosing in council meetings; other parties can only speak if invited to attend by the council and then only to answer the council's questions. The duties of being a member of the council are considerable. Deganawida made attendance of the council members compulsory. If a member failed to attend, and refused one request from the council to attend, the council required that those who appointed him select a replacement. If a council member commits a murder, he is not only removed from the membership of the council but is banished from Iroquois territory altogether. Those members found guilty of rape or theft are also quickly deposed. If a council member who repeatedly acts in a manner that the Iroquois people find to be either contrary to the interests of the welfare of the people or contrary to Deganawida's Laws of Great Peace, he may be removed from office if he continues his poor behavior after the council has given him one warning. Further, a council member who becomes mentally deficient, blind, deaf, dumb, or impotent could not participate, but must defer to a deputy selected by the same clan that selected him. Finally, a council member can only resign voluntarily if the other members of the council accept his resignation.

The Iroquois Confederacy Constitution also provides for three other types of leaders. Two of these are two different types of the War Chief. The first type is a special office, of which there is one in each of the five Iroquois tribes. The men who hold this office are special War Chiefs and do not have seats on the Iroquois Confederacy Council. Their first duty is to lead the warriors in times of war; in an actual military action, the warriors themselves choose one of the five as their supreme commander. Their second function comes into play when the common Iroquois people, particularly the women, are displeased with a council action or decision. In this event, the War Chiefs officially communicate this displeasure to the members of the council, who are then expected to change their behavior. The second kind of War Chief is an Onondaga Confederacy member having the name/office known variously as *Skanatih* or *Skanaawadi* (meaning "across the swamp"). He has the responsibility of notifying the other War Chiefs, just mentioned, of a decision by the Confederacy Council to go to war. This War Chief also has the responsibility of removing the weapons held by a society that the Iroquois have defeated in a war. If a defeated society, and its leader, repeatedly refuses to accede to a peaceful surrender, then the War Chief is bound to kill that leader and initiate warfare once again until the enemy society is ready to accept a peaceful surrender.

The third type of leader included within the Constitution of the Iroquois Confederacy is the Pine Tree Chief. The Pine Tree Chief is a member of the Confederacy Council who has been selected and installed by the members of the council, rather than by the clan heads. Selection as a Pine Tree Chief is done as a mark of honor for someone who is of unusually great ability, wisdom, and honesty. Their positions are not hereditary, and last only so long as the Pine Tree Chief himself is alive. Pine Tree Chiefs may not be deposed, but if they violate the laws of the Great Peace, the other members of the council will cease to listen to them. Pine Tree Chiefs are often men of exceptional personal character and political power, men such as Joseph Brant and Red Jacket. That they are not made into regular members of the council is done so as to limit their already great power; installing them as regular members would place too much power in their hands, the Iroquois feel.

The Constitution of the Iroquois Confederacy also provides that any member society that desires to destroy the Confederacy will be guilty of treason, and if that society fails to heed a warning, will be treated as a military enemy and banished from Iroquois territory. The constitution also includes ways in which other societies may join the Iroquois Confederacy.

As with the Iroquois, a constitution is the basic legal and political document for many nations. Most of these are quite long and detailed and generally cover the issues attended to in the following example of a codified constitution (*The Political Laws of the South African Republic*, 73-86). It is the constitution of the Orange Free

State, a nation that was independent from 1854 to 1900, but is now a province of South Africa. The white people of the region are largely of Dutch descent. Most of the white people of southern Africa are of British descent, and it was the design of Britain to have control over the whole area ever since the British colonized the southern part of Africa. The desire of the British to control the region led them to dominate the people of Dutch descent, in South Africa, who were known as Boers (Dutch for "farmers"). The people of Dutch descent achieved independence in 1854, but lost the South African War in 1900 and came again under British control. In the constitution, notice who is allowed the right to vote.

CONSTITUTION
of the
ORANGE FREE STATE

CHAPTER I.—CITIZENSHIP.
Section I.—How Citizenship is Obtained.

1. Burghers of the Orange Free State are
   (a) White persons born from inhabitants of the State both before and after 23 February, 1854.
   (b) White persons who have obtained burgher-right under the regulations of the Constitution of 1854 or the altered Constitution of 1866.
   (c) White persons who have lived a year in the State and have fixed property registered under their own names to at least the value of £150.
   (d) White persons who have lived three successive years in the State and have made a written promise of allegiance to the State and obedience to the laws, whereupon a certificate of citizenship (burgher ship) shall be granted by the Landrost of the district where they have settled.
   (e) Civil and judicial officials who, before accepting their offices, have taken an oath of allegiance to the State and its laws.

Section II.—How Citizenship is Lost.
Citizenship in the Orange Free State is lost by
   (a) Obtaining citizenship in a foreign country.
   (b) Taking service without consent of the President in foreign military service, or accepting commission under a foreign government.
   (c) Fixing one's residence outside the country with an evident intention of not returning to this State. This intention shall be considered to be expressed when a man settles in a foreign country longer than two years.

CHAPTER II.—BURGHER SERVICE.

2. All burghers as soon as they have reached the full age of 16 years, and all who have obtained burgher-right at a later age, are obliged to have their names inscribed with the Field-cornet, under whom they have their place of residence, and are subject to burgher-service to the full age of 60 years.

CHAPTER III.—QUALIFICATION OF THOSE ENTITLED TO VOTE.

3. All burghers who have reached the age of eighteen years are qualified to exercise the right of voting for the election of Field-commandants and Field-cornets.

4. All burghers of full age are qualified for the election of members of the Volksraad and the President:—
   (a) Who have been born in the State.
   (b) Who have unburdened fixed property under their names to the value of at least £150.
   (c) Who are hirers of fixed property, which has at least a yearly rent of £36.
   (d) Who have at least a fixed yearly income of £200.

(e) Who are owners of movables to a value of at least £300, and have lived at least three years in the State.

CHAPTER IV.—DUTIES AND POWERS OF THE VOLKSRAAD.

5. The highest legislative power rests with the Volksraad.

6. This Council (Raad) shall consist of a member for each Field-cornetcy of the various districts, and of a member for each principal town of a district. This Council is chosen by majority of votes by the enfranchised inhabitants of each ward of each principal town of a district.

7. Every burgher is eligible as a member of the Volksraad, who has never been declared bankrupt or insolvent, his residence being within the State, has reached an age of at least 25, who also possesses fixed property of at least £500 in value.

8. A member of the Raad ceases to be such in any of the following cases:—
   (a) If he neglects to come to the Raad during two successive yearly sessions.
   (b) If he loses one or more of the qualifications as required in Article 7.

9. Members of the Volksraad are chosen for four successive years, and are re-eligible at the end of the period.
   The half shall withdraw after two years, and the first half be regulated by lot.

10. The Volksraad in its yearly meetings chooses a Chairman out of its own members.

11. The Chairman of the Volksraad shall decide in case of any equality of votes.

12. Twelve members shall make a quorum.

13. The Volksraad makes the laws, regulates the government and finances of the country, and shall assemble for that purpose at Bloemfontein once a year (viz., on the first Monday of May).

14. The Chairman shall be able to summon an extraordinary session of the Raad according to the state of affairs.

15. The laws made by the Volksraad shall have force of law two months after the promulgation, and shall be signed by the Chairman or by the President, saving always the right of the Raad to fix a shorter or longer limit of time. The members of the Raad shall, as much as possible, make the laws, which have been passed, known and clear to their own public.

16. In case of insolvency, or if any sentence of imprisonment is passed against the President, the Volksraad shall be able to dismiss him at once.

17. (a) The Volksraad shall have the right to try the President and public officials for treason, bribery and other high crimes.
   (b) The President shall not be condemned without the agreement of three to one of the members present.
   (c) He shall not be condemned without the full Raad being present, or at least without due notice being given, to give all the members opportunity to be present.
   (d) If a quorum is summoned, and is unanimously of opinion that the President is guilty of one of the above-named crimes, they shall have the power to suspend him, and to make provisional arrangements to fulfil the duties of his office. But in that case they shall be obliged to call the whole Raad together to judge him.
   (e) The members of the Volksraad shall take their oath at the commencement of said examination.
   (f) In case the President should come to die, or should resign his post, or be discharged, or become unfit for the discharge of his office, the Volksraad shall be empowered to appoint one or more persons to act in his place till such unfitness cease or another President is chosen.
   (g) The sentence of the Volksraad in such cases shall have no further effect than discharge from their office, and the declaration

of unfitness ever to hold any post under the Government. But the persons so sentenced shall none the less be liable to be judged according to the law.

18. The Volksraad reserves the right to examine the election list of members for the Volksraad itself, and to declare if the members have been duly and legally elected or not.

19. The Volksraad shall have regular minutes of its transactions kept, and from time to time publish the same, such articles excepted as ought in their judgment to be kept back.

20. The agreement or disapproval of the various members on any question put to the vote must, on the request of one-fifth of members present, be inscribed in the minutes.

21. The public shall be admitted to attend the consultations of the Volksraad and to take notice of the transactions, except in special cases, where secrecy is necessary.

22. The Volksraad shall make no laws preventing free assembly of the inhabitants, to memorialize the Government, to obtain assistance in difficulties, or to get an alteration in some law.

23. The furtherance of religion and education is a subject of care for the Volksraad.

24. The Dutch Reformed Church shall be assisted and supported by the Volksraad.

25. The Volksraad shall have the power to pass a burgher or commando law for the protection and safety of this land.

26. After this Constitution shall have been fixedly determined, no alteration may be made in the same without the agreement of three-fifths of the Volksraad, and before such change may be made, a majority of three-fifths of the votes shall be necessary for the same in two successive yearly sessions.

27. The Volksraad shall have the power to inflict taxes or to diminish them, to pay the public debt and to make provision for the general defense and welfare of the State; similarly to take up money on the credit of the State, and also to dispose of Government property.

CHAPTER V.—DUTIES, POWERS, ETC., OF THE PRESIDENT.

28. There shall be a President.

29. The President shall be chosen by the enfranchised burghers; however, the Volksraad shall recommend one or more persons to their choice.

30. The President shall be appointed for five years, and be re-eligible on resignation.

31. The President shall be the head of the Executive Power. The supervision of all public departments and the execution and regulation of all matters connected with the public service shall be entrusted to the President, who shall be responsible to the Volksraad, and whose acts and deeds shall be subject to an appeal before the Volksraad.

32. The President shall as often as possible visit the towns and give the inhabitants of the same and of the district an opportunity to bring forward at the towns matters in which they are interested.

33. The President shall make a report in the yearly assemblage of the Volksraad about the state of the land and the public service, shall assist the same with counsel and advice, and if necessary, lay bills upon the table, without, however, being able to vote upon the same.

34. The President shall also be able to summon an extraordinary meeting of the Volksraad.

35. The President shall have the power to fill up all empty posts in the public offices, which fall vacant between the times of the meeting of the Volksraad, subject to the ratification of that body.

36. The President shall have the right to suspend public officials.

37. The President with a majority of the Executive Council shall exercise the right of mercy in all criminal sentences.

38. The President with the consent of the Volksraad declares war and makes peace.

39. The President shall be able to make conventions, subject to the consent of the Volksraad.

40. The President shall not be able to make any treaty without consent of the Volksraad.

41. The President, or any member of the Executive Council, shall have the right at all times to inspect the state of the finances, as also, the books of the officials.

CHAPTER VI.—EXECUTIVE COUNCIL.

42. There shall be an Executive Council, consisting of the Landrost of the capital, the Secretary of the Government, and three unofficial members, chosen by the Volksraad, to assist the President with advice and assistance.

The President shall be the Chairman, and have a decisive vote.

43. The Executive Council shall hold session on the second Monday of each second month, and at such other times as the President may desire.

44. The Executive Council shall be bound to make a yearly report of its transactions to the Volksraad.

45. A majority of the Executive Council shall have the right to summon an extraordinary meeting of the Volksraad.

46. The President and the Executive Council shall have the power of declaring martial law.

CHAPTER VII.—THE JUDICIAL POWER.

47. The Landrost holds the power of civil commissioner and resident magistrate.

48. The judicial power is exclusively exercised by the courts of law, which are established by the law.

49. Legislation also regulates the administration of criminal justice, as also that in police cases, always understanding, however, that criminal cases brought in the first instance before the Higher Courts are judged by a jury.

CHAPTER VIII.—THE MILITARY SYSTEM.

50. The Field-cornets shall be chosen by and out of the burghers of their wards.

51. A Field-commandant shall be chosen for each district, by and out of the burghers of the same.

52. The assembled Field-commandants and Field-cornets who are united on a commando shall choose from amongst themselves, in case of war, their own Commandant-general, which General must then receive his instructions from the President.

53. The assembled Field-commandants and Field-cornets have the right, during the course of the war, when they have just cause for so doing, to discharge the Commandant-general who had been chosen by them, and to appoint another, they being bound in that case to give notice to the President thereof, who on receipt of such announcement, and on finding the assignment reasons well founded, fixes the day on which a new election shall take place.

54. After the war there exists no longer any Commandant-general as such.

55. The Field-cornets must be resident in their own wards and possess property therein.

56. The Field-commandants must be resident of their own districts, possess fixed property to the amount of £200, and have lived one year in the country.

CHAPTER IX.—MISCELLANEOUS SUBJECTS.

57. The Roman-Dutch law shall be the

principal law of this State, where no other law has been made by the Volksraad.

58. The law is for all alike, always understanding that the judge shall exercise all laws with impartiality and without respect of persons.

59. Every inhabitant owes obedience to the law and the authorities.

60. Right of property is guaranteed.

61. Personal freedom, provisional on remaining within the limitations of the law, is guaranteed.

62. The freedom of press is guaranteed provisionally on remaining within the law.

Morgan, Lewis Henry. (1851) *League of the Ho-De'-No-Sau-Nee, or Iroquois.*

Parker, Arthur Caswell. (1968) *Parker on the Iroquois: Iroquois Uses of Maize and Other Food Plants, the Code of Handsome Lake, the Seneca Prophet, the Constitution of the Five Nations.* Edited by William N. Fenton.

The Political Laws of the South African Republic. (1896) Translated by W. A. Macfadyen.

Rattray, R. S. (1969 [1911]) *Ashanti Law and Constitution.*

Tooker, Elisabeth. (1978) "The League of the Iroquois: Its History, Politics, and Ritual." In *Handbook of North American Indians.* Vol. 15, *Northeast,* edited by Bruce G. Trigger and William Sturtevant, 418–441.

CONTRACT

A contract is a legally recognized promise, the terms of which are protected by the possibility of legal remedy if they are not fulfilled. In order for a contract to be valid, it must be mutually agreed upon by the contracting parties; that is, one person cannot force another person to abide by the terms of a contract if that second person does not wish to enter into the contract. Further, the contracting parties must be legally able to enter into a contract; thus, in most societies, a child is not able to enter into a legally binding contract because he or she is not considered mature enough to be able to distinguish contracts that are to his or her advantage and those that are not.

Traditionally, the Tswana people of South Africa had five main types of contracts. These were (1) contracts pertaining to betrothal, (2) those pertaining to marriage, (3) those pertaining to the alienation of property, (4) those pertaining to permission to use property, and (5) those pertaining to service. Women and children were not allowed to make contracts unless specifically authorized, in the case of women, by their husbands or, in the case of children, by their fathers.

The betrothal contract was preceded by negotiations between the families of the future bride and groom. It was concluded by a payment from the future groom's family to the future bride's family of an animal to slaughter or, instead, items for the future bride, such as cloth or blankets. Either the future bride's family or the future groom's family could break the betrothal contract at any time prior to marriage. If only either the future bride or the future groom wished to break the engagement, then the marriage was still likely to take place, and could be so ordered by the applicable legal authority (chief or headman). If the future groom's family wished to end the betrothal because the future bride had acted badly (failing to take adequate notice of their son when he visited or by keeping company with or becoming pregnant by another man), then the betrothal contract could be broken and the future bride and her family had to return all that had been given them by the future groom's family. If the future bride's family wished to end the betrothal contract because of the future groom's behavior (failing to visit the future bride's family frequently or keeping company with another woman), then the betrothal contract could be broken, but the future bride's family could keep all that the future groom's family had given them. In such a case, the future bride's family could also be awarded by the legal authority a further compensation to be paid by the future groom's family for having wasted the time that the woman had to arrange a good marriage for herself. If a future bride died before marrying, the future groom was entitled to continue his engagement with the dead woman's younger sister. Likewise, if an affianced man died before marrying, his fiancée had the right to marry his younger brother, but her children would be considered the children of the dead man and would inherit from his estate.

A marriage similarly involved a contract between the groom's family and the bride's family. The essential feature of a fully completed marriage was the payment of the bride-price, called *bogadi*. The *bogadi* payment, consisting of a variable number of cattle given by the groom's family to the bride's family, purchased the bride's reproductive powers. Until the *bogadi* was paid, and this could be years after the couple began to cohabit, the couple's children were considered illegitimate and could not be the legal heirs of the father. The *bogadi* was returned to the groom's family if the wife died without having borne children or if the couple divorced on the grounds of the wife's inability to bear children. If the couple divorced after the *bogadi* had been paid and children born, the children remained with the father and his family.

Trading activities also make use of contracts. When a Tswana man needed a manufactured article that he himself could not make, he would have to go to a craftsman and usually would have to place an order for it to be made in the future. If there is a credit transaction, and the buyer does not pay the creditor at the agreed upon time (usu-ally in one year's time), then the creditor reminds the debtor that the payment is due. If he is not paid, he then waits for another period of time before reminding the debtor again. If the debt remains unpaid, then the creditor appeals to the kin of the debtor. If this does no good, then the creditor takes his case to the chief. If the debtor refuses the chief's order to pay the creditor, then the chief will order that the creditor may go to the debtor's house and take whatever is of equal value to the debt; any effort by the debtor to stop the creditor is punished by the chief. The goods that the creditor has seized are not to be used or sold by him, since they are merely security for the payment of the debt. Should a debtor still refuse to pay, or be unable to pay, his debt, his kin are expected to pay the debt. If they refuse or cannot do so, then the debtor will have to perform labor for the creditor to satisfy his debt. Debts are inherited by the heirs to an estate.

If the debt is to be paid at a later date with an article of livestock—for example, a cow—it sometimes happens that the recipient may reject the offered cow as being unsuitable. This would usually lead directly to a lawsuit, with the headman or chief as the legal authority. If the recipient of the cow had not initially specified the condition of the cow that was to be delivered to him, then the legal authority would rule that he must take whatever kind of a cow was offered to him.

Contracts were also used in several types of agreements regarding permission to use property. If someone borrows an item and the item is broken while it is being borrowed, the borrower must inform the owner immediately; otherwise, the borrower will be liable for the repair or replacement of the broken item, even if the damage was accidental. With the exception of wagons and teams of oxen, the Tswana do not expect payment of interest on a loan; wagons and teams are rented out at a rate of two baskets of corn per load.

Cattle owners often lend their cattle to other herdsmen; cattle so borrowed are called *mafisa* cattle. The borrower had to ask the permission of all members of his family before entering into a contract to borrow the cattle, since if the cattle were lost it was possible for the entire family to be held liable for the value of the lost cattle. The one borrowing the cattle benefits because he can use their milk for himself or, if the cattle are oxen, use them for plowing his own fields. The one lending the cattle benefits because his workload is reduced and because, in the event a disease attacks the cattle of his own herd, he may be able to escape total financial ruin by losing only those cattle and not the ones he has lent. The borrower of the *mafisa* cattle must agree as part of the contract to take very good care of them, to keep them separate from his own cattle, and to never slaughter or alienate them or allow them to be seized as payment of a debt. The owner of the cattle also has the right of ownership over any offspring of the cattle, but the owner usually gives the borrower the offspring as a reward if the borrower has taken good care of the cattle. If cattle are lost to theft, death, or straying, this must immediately be communicated to the owner; if a cow or ox dies, the skin must be brought to the owner as proof. Failure to make an immediate report or to bring the skin of a dead animal leaves the borrower liable for the value of the lost animal.

The Tswana also contract for labor. One important kind of contract is between servant and master. Servants are bound by a contract to their masters for life and receive all the necessities of life, the protection of their masters from lawsuits, and the payment of their hut taxes. In exchange, they provide services such as herding, domestic work, and plowing. Servants could not leave the service of their masters without permission and could take no legal action against them even if mistreated by them. Finally, the children of servants were required to serve the family of their parents' masters, also for life.

Another kind of labor contract involves cattle herding. If a man wishes, he may allow his cattle to be herded by another man as if they belonged to this other man. The one taking up the task of herding another's cattle may not sell or slaughter them, but bears no liability for the loss of cattle due to death, straying, or theft. The owner also has ownership of the offspring of his cattle. In this type of contract, the one herding another man's cattle receives no payment for his services.

Cattle owners also sometimes hire another man to work solely as a herdsman of his cattle. The herdsman in this type of contract is liable for the accidental loss of the cattle under his care. The owner pays the herdsman a fee for his services, usually a heifer, and may also supply him with food and blankets.

Tswana manual laborers sometimes sell their labor for such temporary jobs as roofing a hut or clearing a field. Payment and the specifications for the job to be done are decided at the time of the making of the contract. If the work is done and not paid for, the worker can sue the employer. If the work is not completed, the worker has no legal claim to any compensation, even partial compensation.

Work party contracts are also used by the Tswana. If a large job needs to be done quickly, such as clearing a field or weeding it, the owner may ask his friends and kin to help him for a day; the owner pays the workers in beer, milk, tobacco, meat, porridge, and/or salt. If a man's ox dies, he may give the meat away (and quickly, before it spoils) to all who wish to have a portion of it in return for a day's labor at an unspecified later date. If a recipient of the meat repeatedly refuses to work, a legal authority will order him to work or to repay the meat.

Finally, the Tswana make contractual agreements with magicians for their services. The employer will pay a magician for divination, treatment of illnesses, and for good luck magic for their huts, fields, and cattle. The payment for divinations and for the treatment of minor illnesses is small, but for the treatment of major illnesses and for the making of good luck magic, the magician is paid with an ox. The employer only pays the magician for treating an illness if the treatment is successful. If the employer fails to pay for successful medical treatment, the magician can sue him in court. However, people rarely fail to pay magicians for legitimate bills, because of the fear that the magicians will use sorcery against them if they do not pay. Finally, if an employer has paid a magician the substantial payment of an ox, he and his family have the right to the magician's services without further payment at any future time.

The importance of contractual relations among the Tswana may be compared with the importance of contracts among the Naskapi Indians of Labrador, Canada. Among the Naskapi, contracts are of no importance to individuals or the economy as a whole. The first reason is that promises are not protected by the law, and thus there can be no true contracts. The second reason is because everybody does the same kind of work, although there is division of labor by gender. Therefore, nobody typically works for another or trades with another. The exceptions are in the case of older people who cannot any longer do all the things they need to do to live properly, and even these cases are rare. When such promises are made, however, the older people might hire a young unmarried woman to help them and, in the 1940s, would pay her as much as $5 or $10 and the material to make some clothing. If they hire a boy, he is usually expected to help with the trapping, and receives in compensation half of the furs he takes.

In Naskapi society, then, although there are economic promises, they are few and of little importance and hence the provisions of such promises are little protected, and not protected at all under the law. All promises are oral and require no witnesses. There is nothing whatsoever to corroborate the fact that a promise was made. There is no remedy available for a breach of promise, and there is no legal penalty for a breach of promise. The creditor has no right, for instance, to take any property of the debtor if there is a breach, nor can he ask that a legal authority punish the debtor for failing to fulfill the obligations of the promise. In short, the Naskapi have no true contracts as the idea of *contract* is defined. For this reason, it may be supposed that many kinds of commercial activities are not easy to carry out there.

In the former Soviet Union, it was almost impossible for average citizens to make contracts with each other. This was because the Soviet Union wished to stamp out capitalism. So, it was forbidden to make virtually any kind of a commercial agreement with another citizen. The only kinds of contracts allowed were ones in which one let one's own apartment or dacha, or in which one sold agricultural produce grown on one's own plot at the collective farm markets.

Ioffe, Olympiad S., and Peter B. Maggs. (1983) *Soviet Law in Theory and Practice.*

Lips, Julius E. (1947) "Naskapi Law." *Transactions of the American Philosophical Society* 37(4): 378–492.

Schapera, Isaac. (1970 [1938]) *A Handbook of Tswana Law and Custom.*

CORPORATION

The corporation is an artificial person under the law, a legal entity that is recognized by the law as a person. As such, the corporation can be a party to legal action, either as a plaintiff or as a defendant. The corporation is a legal fiction, meaning that it exists only in the eyes of the law.

A corporation may be owned by one person or several persons or, in many parts of the world, it may be unowned, as is the case when groups of people have a corporate identity. A corporations has the capability to exist in perpetuity; that is, it may continue to exist long after any of the people associated with it at any one time are dead.

The main function of a corporation in the modern Western world is to limit individual legal liability. For example, if a man decides to manufacture airplanes, he would probably want to have the airplane company incorporated. If he does so, and one of his airplane designs turns out to be faulty and causes crashes, only the corporation can be sued by those injured by the crashes. The man himself cannot be sued, and his own personal wealth cannot be used to pay damages awarded by a court to the injured. Only the assets of the corporation are legally liable. The obvious benefit to incorporation is that it encourages people to start and to run businesses, because the fear of personal financial ruin is greatly reduced.

In many parts of the world, but particularly in the Middle East and in Africa, lineal societies are found, and it is usually true that the lineages that make up one of these societies are corporate. In some other societies, tribes as a whole can be corporate.

The lineage and tribal corporations typically own the land used by the members of the lineage or tribe. For example, among the Yoruba people of Nigeria, the corporate tribe owns all of the land the Yoruba people use and claim as their own. Under traditional Yoruba law, usufructuary rights to Yoruba land were apportioned to the members of the Yoruba tribe. Since the land was owned by the Yoruba tribal corporation, ownership rights in land could not be alienated. Even a Yoruba king or chief could not alienate any of the real property under Yoruba control; a king or chief was no more an owner of the land as a whole, or of any piece of it, than any other person on the face of the earth; he thus had no right to sell or give away land. An individual's usufructuary rights could not be sold,

and it was required that the holder of such rights bequeath them to his offspring.

The corporate nature of some societies manifests itself in the idea of social substitutability, as Meyer Fortes has called it. In corporate lineal societies, such as the Nuer of the Sudan, Tallensi of Northern Ghana, and the Bedouin of the Middle East, individuals are to a greater degree than in other societies substitutable for each other. There and in similar societies, the social group is conceived of as less of an actual group of living people than as a system of legal and political statuses. When a person holding one of these statuses dies, the society does not face the danger of disintegration, because someone else will inherit that status.

In matters of law and revenge as well, individuals within the corporation are equal and substitutable for each other in corporate societies. If a member of a corporate group commits a murder, and his victim is a member of another group, the relatives of the victim may, if it is appropriate in those societies, seek to kill in revenge. However, it is the corporation as a whole that is responsible for the actions of any one of the members of the corporation. Thus, the people seeking revenge may kill or beat any suitable member (usually an adult male) of the corporation to which the killer belongs; it is not necessary to kill or hurt the killer himself.

This principle of corporate political or legal responsibility for the actions of one member of the corporation can be seen in modern Western business practices as well. If a worker at a factory owned by a corporation makes a bad product, and that product injures someone, then the corporation that owns the factory and employs the worker is legally responsible for causing the injuries, not the worker himself or herself.

Ajisafe, A. K. (1946) *The Laws and Customs of the Yoruba People.*

Fortes, Meyer. (1953) "The Structure of Unilineal Descent Groups." *American Anthropologist* 55: 17–41.

Pollock, Frederick, and Frederic W. Maitland. (1966 [1899]) "Corporation and Person." In *Anthropology and Early Law,* edited by Lawrence Krader, 300–336.

COUP

The term *coup* is short for the French term *coup d'état*, which translates literally as "a blow to the state." A coup is a quick change of government through the actual or threatened use of violence directed specifically at the leadership in power, rather than at the group as a whole. Coups come about when one segment of society seeks to gain from another segment of the society control over the society as a whole; coups do not directly involve forces external to the society, though coup leaders may have ties to external forces and interested parties.

Coups usually take place in societies that already have unstable governments, such as states that recently gained independence from colonial powers. Usually, too, coups are military in origin, since it is the military that usually has the force necessary to bring about a coup and to defeat whatever other forces may wish to defend the leaders whom the coup wishes to replace.

The reasons why coups take place are almost as numerous as the number of coups themselves. There is no one reason for why coups occur. Some coups take place to restore the old ways of doing things in the face of a reform-minded government. Other coups take place because there is insufficient reform of the central government's corruption and inefficiency. Other coups are based in ideological movements, while still further coups come about from a perception that the central government has not been sufficiently nationalistic in its policies.

The coups in Nigeria in the 1960s, which eventually led to civil war and the temporary creation of the separate state of Biafra, resulted from tribalist allegiances and politics. The main dispute centered on the position of the Ibo (also known as Igbo) people of southern Nigeria. The Ibo were, at the time, hard-working, trade-minded people who spread out over the land in Nigeria because their own homelands were densely populated. Wherever they moved, they engaged in commerce and wage labor, and invested their earnings in real property and their children's education. They frequently displayed an arrogant attitude toward others whom they considered backward, lazy, and uneducated, and this aroused resentment in the others, particularly in the Moslem northern part of Nigeria. In 1956, the northern part of Nigeria acquired self-rule, and the largely Hausa population prevented Ibos from holding civil service positions. The Ibos responded by turning their efforts to making money in the private sector.

In January 1966, Ibo army officers staged a successful coup against the central government, killing Prime Minister Balewa and many political leaders in the northern part of the country. The leaders of the coup enjoyed a great deal of popular support, including that of many Hausas. The leaders of the Ibo faction of the army installed General Johnson Aguiyi-Ironsi as the head of the government. Aguiyi-Ironsi established a strong Ibo-dominated central government. This in turn led to anti-Ibo riots in the north, as the northern Hausas believed that the Ibos intended to have total control of the country. Hausas in the north waited until May 1966, and then attacked and killed several thousand Ibos who lived in the north. As the Ibos left to escape to the southern part of Nigeria, their traditional homeland, they were persuaded by the government to remain in the north so as to help build a strong and united Nigeria. But in July of

Kwame Nkrumah, right, the first prime minister of Ghana following independence from Great Britain, visits with Indian Prime Minister Indira Gandhi, left, on 22 February 1966. In his absence, members of the Ghanian army overthrew Nkrumah's government in a coup d'état. Mrs. Gandhi, a Hindu, was assassinated eight years later by two Sikhs who were her guards.

1966, the northerners staged a countercoup, and put into power Army Chief of Staff Yakubu Gowon. Coup leaders killed Aguiyi-Ironsi, and this was followed by a second massacre of Ibos in the northern part of Nigeria. The Ibos continued to stay in the north to help establish a united Nigeria. In September of 1966, there was a third and very large massacre of Ibos in northern Nigeria, and it was this action that convinced the Ibos that a united Nigeria was impossible. Most of those who survived left for eastern Nigeria, thus accomplishing the aims of the northern Nigerians, who wanted a northern Nigeria free of Ibo people.

In 1967, Gowon redrew district lines in Nigeria, creating twelve separate units. The eastern Nigerians rejected this division and seceded from Nigeria, establishing a state known as Biafra. The resulting civil war lasted until 1970, when a defeated Biafra consented to reunify with Nigeria. The civil war cost 1 million Biafran (mostly Ibo) lives through fighting, starvation, and disease.

Gowon attempted to rebuild eastern Nigeria and create a multitribal Nigeria, but his efforts were cut short by another coup in 1975. The man put in charge by that coup was himself the victim of a coup the following year. Democratically elected officials came into power in Nigeria in 1979, but there was another successful military coup in 1983.

The reasons for the successful February 1966 coup against the leader of Ghana, Kwame Nkrumah, were different still from those given above. Ghana became independent from Great Britain in 1957, and Nkrumah became its first prime minister. As time went on, Nkrumah became increasingly intolerant of political opposition, going so far in 1964 as to make the existence of all opposition political parties illegal. He also established increasingly close ties with the U.S.S.R. and other Communist bloc nations. He made extensive use of preventive detention of people who opposed him, fired judges who produced decisions with which he disagreed, and had legal cases retried when the verdicts were not to his liking. Further, he made an error that cost him the support of the military. He asked that two foreign powers, the U.S.S.R. and the former colonial masters, the British, train and equip the army. The army rebelled against these measures and in February 1966, it overthrew Nkrumah. In short, Nkrumah was deposed because he allowed little political freedom and because he was insufficiently nationalistic in his leadership.

Greene, Fred. (1970 [1966]) "Toward Understanding Military Coups." In *African Politics and Society*, edited by Irving Markovitz, 242–247.

Legum, Colin. (1970 [1966]) "The Tragedy in Nigeria" In *African Politics and Society*, edited by Irving Markovitz, 248–251.

Markovitz, Irving. (1970 [1966]) "Ghana without Nkrumah: The Winter of Discontent." In *African Politics and Society*, edited by Irving Markovitz, 252–265.

CRIME

Crime is a legal offense against a society. The society, then, is the subject of legal rights and the object of legal duties to it. It thus differs from an offense against civil law, or tort, in that it involves a public offense rather than a private one. All societies reserve for themselves the right to regulate the behavior of their members so that threats to it do not destroy it. Unregulated behavior can very quickly lead to schisms within a society and to the eventual end of the society.

A very broad range of behaviors are classified as crimes or offenses in cultures around the world. The following is a list of only some behaviors that are considered to be crimes in some cultures, organized into the major categories of crime. There is a great deal of variation among cultures in what is considered a crime and no clear cross-cultural patterning of crimes. Behaviors that are considered crimes in all or most cultures include incest, arson, theft, political assassination, nonpayment of debt, and treason.

Offenses against Life

abortion	evil eye
blood feuds	gossip
cannibalism	insulting
death-hastening behavior	kidnapping

Offenses against the Person

assault	gerontocide
battery	homicide
child abuse and neglect	infanticide
elder abuse	suicide
libel	sorcery
rape	spouse abuse and neglect
slander	witchcraft

Sex and Marital Offenses

bestiality	extramarital sex
bride theft	homosexuality
coercive sex	illegitimacy
desertion	incest

Sex and Marital Offenses, *continued*

miscegenation	prostitution
nonsupport	seduction
premarital sex	sodomy

Property Offenses

arson	malicious mischief
burglary	poaching
cruelty to animals	robbery
diverting water source	stealing
embezzlement	theft
fraud	trespass
livestock rustling	

Nonfulfillment of Obligations

breach of contract	negligence
malpractice	nonpayment of debt

Offenses against the Government

assassination	insubordination
banditry	mutiny
bribery	perjury
conspiracy	piracy
contempt of court	political malfeasance
counterfeiting	sedition
desertion	slavery
electoral fraud	smuggling
espionage	subornation
falsification of	tax evasion
documents	treason
illegal entry	

Religious Offenses

black magic	sale of ceremonial
blasphemy	objects
grave robbing	taboo violations
impiety	theft of
possession of	ceremonial objects
illegal charms	violation of Sabbath
ritual offenses	witchcraft

Social Offenses

breach of etiquette	gambling
disorderly conduct	greed
drug abuse	laziness
drunkenness	loafing

lying	noncooperation
moonshining	quarrelsomeness

In all cultures except those where all people are equals (which are very few in number), different categories of individuals often have different sets of rules governing their behavior. These categories include the wealthy, leaders, warriors, religious practitioners, the young, the aged, and, in many cultures, men and women. The status of some of these categories exempts their members from punishment for offenses that are meted out to others. For example, warriors are often not punished for aggressive behavior within the community, as they are expected to be aggressive. On the other hand, the special status of some other categories places greater burdens on their members. For example, religious practitioners are often expected to follow the laws and norms of behavior more closely than are other people, and they also often have to follow a special set of rules. The major categories and types of punishments include:

Physical Punishments

beating	mutilation
capital punishment	torture
flogging	

Social Punishments

gossip	ridicule
pillory	social isolation

Property Punishments

compensation	destruction of property
confiscation	fines

Deprivation of Rights

banishment	imprisonment
enslavement	military service

Cultures vary in the behaviors that are classified as crimes and how criminals are punished. Among the Micmac Indians of Cape Breton Island, Nova Scotia, crimes include, in addition

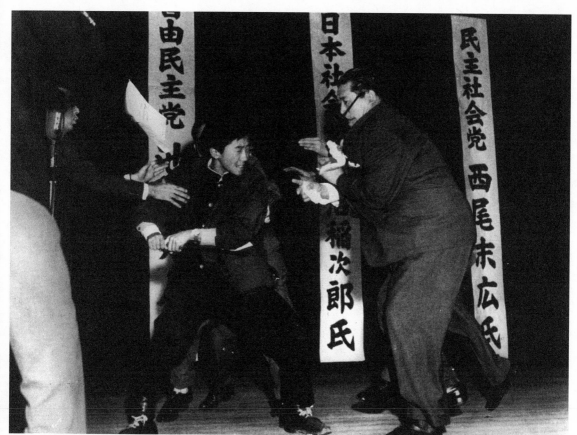

Many societies consider political assassination a crime. A seventeen-year-old student stabbed Japanese socialist leader Inejiro Asanuma to death in 1960; the murderer, Otoya Yamaguchi, hanged himself before he could be brought to trial. Photographer Yasuki Nagao earned a Pulitzer Prize for capturing the crime on film.

to murder and socially disruptive behavior, drinking to excess, child mistreatment, and vandalism. The Micmac were colonized early, and since the early nineteenth century have been nominally under the legal authority of Great Britain and later Canada. However, the federal authorities had little involvement with Micmac affairs until the 1940s. During the era from approximately 1800 until 1940, the Micmac headmen used the Canadian federal legal system as a punishment system. In the case of homicide, for example, the headman would determine the guilt or innocence of the accused murderer. If the accused were judged innocent of the charge, they

would be free of any sanctions, and the federal authorities would never learn of the homicide. People who had committed homicide were judged by the headman not guilty if they killed accidently or if they killed while under the effects of mental illness. If the headman found the killer to be guilty of murder, he or she would be taken to the Canadian federal police (the Royal Canadian Mounted Police), who would then turn him or her over to the court system for trial. The headman would also assist the police in preparing their case against the accused killer. The federal penal system would later mete out the guilty party's sanction.

In many cultures for many crimes there are mitigating circumstances that might influence how serious a specific criminal act will be considered and how harshly the criminal will be punished. Thus, while cultures have a set of laws that define crimes and set punishments for them, these laws often represent the ideal and are not necessarily followed strictly in day-to-day life. Major mitigating circumstances are how much harm the crime caused, the motivation (purposeful or accidental) of the criminal, the relative statuses of the criminal and the victim, whether the criminal is a member of the society or a foreigner, and whether the criminal is insane. For example, if a Kalinga, of Luzon in the Philippines, can prove immediately that he harmed someone by accident, he is immune from pun-

ishment. Or, among the Central Thai, thieves are likely to go uncaught unless they steal from a person wealthy enough to pay the police to investigate the matter.

Probably the most common mitigating circumstance is the status and personal characteristics of the criminal. In nearly all cultures with status distinctions based on either hereditary or earned wealth, power, or education, those with higher status are less likely to be charged with crimes and less likely to be severely punished. In some cultures, rules governing the differential treatment of individuals on the basis of their social status are codified in law, while in others they are simply customary. The Amhara of Ethiopia, for example, have clear rules to assist judges in pronouncing sentence and punishment,

A Muslim in Pakistan convicted of rape receives 100 lashes administered by Islamic officials.

which are expected to decline in severity in the following order (Messing, 1957: 312):

The man who knows the law

The forgetful person (unstable personality)

The "balagär" (rustic peasant)

The poor and ignorant person (illiterates)

The stranger

The ignorant woman

The imbecile or invalid

The Ethiopian from a non-Amharic-speaking province

The child below age twelve

The Amhara judge also considered the personality of the criminal and might adjust the punishment in consideration of whether the individual is known to be lawless, a bully, envious, careless, or proud, among other traits.

Despite the wide variety of types of crime and offenses committed in cultures around the world and the equally broad array of punishments for those crimes, little is known about the causes of crime in general across cultures, although there is fuller knowledge of the causes of some specific crimes such as homicide, suicide, and rape. We do know, however, with some degree of confidence, that personal crime (homicide and assault) is one component of a broader cultural pattern of violence. In cultures where there is much violent crime (committed in all cultures mostly by men), men often also fight in wars, derive personal glory from military successes, are expected to act aggressively, and as children are subjected to harsh disciplinary techniques that might make them mistrustful of and hostile toward other people. And there is also some commonality across cultures as regards theft. Theft is a commonly committed crime in cultures where there are clear wealth differences between individuals and families and where children are raised in ways that stress obedience and self-reliance and, therefore, are left feeling somewhat unloved. In this situation, theft may be an effort to replace the love missing in childhood by acquiring the possessions of others.

See also CAPITAL PUNISHMENT; HOMICIDE.

Allen, Martin G. (1972) "A Cross-Cultural Study of Aggression and Crime." *Journal of Cross-Cultural Psychology* 3: 259–271.

Bacon, Margaret K., Irvin L. Child, and Herbert Barry III. (1963) "A Cross-Cultural Study of the Correlates of Crime." *Journal of Abnormal and Social Psychology* 66: 291–300.

Barton, Roy F. (1973 [1949]) *The Kalingas: Their Institutions and Custom Law.*

Ember, Carol R., and Melvin Ember. (1992) "Warfare, Aggression, and Resource Problems: Cross-Cultural Codes." *Behavior Science Research* 26: 169–226.

Ingersoll, Jasper C. (1969) *The Priest and the Path: An Analysis of the Priest Role in a Central Thai Village.*

Messing, Simon D. (1957) *The Highland-Plateau Amhara of Ethiopia.* Ph.D. dissertation, University of Pennsylvania.

Murdock, George Peter, et al. (1987) *Outline of Cultural Materials.* 5th ed.

Russell, Elbert W. (1972) "Factors of Human Aggression: A Cross-Cultural Factor Analysis of Characteristics Related to Warfare and Crime." *Behavior Science Notes* 7: 275–312.

Seymour-Smith, Charlotte. (1986) *Dictionary of Anthropology.*

Strouthes, Daniel P. (1994) *Change in the Real Property Law of a Cape Breton Island Micmac Band.*

A customary law may be defined as a law that is psychologically internalized by most of the people of a society as a just law. In other words, it is considered fair and morally correct. Customary law is the opposite of authoritarian law, which is not willingly accepted by the majority of people and must be forcibly imposed upon them if it is to have legal effectiveness.

The term *customary law* has another, invidious, meaning as well. In the nineteenth and early twentieth centuries, legal scholars in the Western world, on the basis of inadequate information, speculated that technologically primitive peoples could have nothing so grand, sophisticated, or logical as a legal system. These ethnocentric writers believed that only the technologically advanced societies of Europe and Asia could have something as advanced as a legal system. They believed, and their followers repeated their beliefs, that technologically primitive societies had only custom, rather than law.

Later, a more refined version of this argument, again based upon a paucity of knowledge, was that it was custom that served as law in technologically primitive societies. This gave rise to the term *customary law*. J. H. Driberg, in an article on customary law in East Africa, defined (customary) law as "all of those rules of conduct which regulate the behavior of individuals and communities." In the view of Driberg and others, then, customary law is nothing more than rules of behavior that are generally followed.

This early view of customary law is essentially racist, in that it appears to show that the indigenous peoples of Africa, the Americas, Australia, and elsewhere are simply not as advanced as the people of Europe. This view was the result of assumptions of European superiority and research that was inadequate, in that it did not seek to find out if the non-European peoples had legal authorities, sanctions for misbehavior, and the other features of a legal system.

Once researchers began to genuinely look for legal systems, they of course found them in all societies they investigated. These societies, moreover, had legal systems that were in many respects like those found anywhere else, even Europe. They were not mere collections of custom, but rather dynamic institutions that could, and even did, cause changes in behavior away from the customary.

Still, however, the term *customary law* is used by some writers to refer to the law of technologically less-advanced societies that has not been codified, or written down in abbreviated codes. For others still, *customary law* refers to the indigenous law of a people also under colonial control.

When using it to distinguish the legal systems of smaller, indigenous societies from the legal systems of state societies, the term *customary law* is frequently synonymous with the term *folk law*. The following decision, made by the Tanzanian court system, is interesting because it represents an instance in which the court system of a state society (Tanzania) upheld the legal principles (customary or folk law) used by the smaller, indigenous societies within the borders of Tanzania (*The Law Reports of Tanzania*, 1979: 27–31).

HAMISI ABDALLAH v. SAKILU SUNGI

HIGH COURT, (P.C.) CIV. APP. 88-DDM-76, 19/11/76
CHIPETA, AG. J.

HELD:

(1) Tortious liability exists under customary law to pay compensation for damage to crops caused by tame animals.

(2) Discrepancies in the testimony of various witnesses on material points must be carefully weighed in arriving at the evidence.

(3) A trial Court has the advantage of seeing and hearing witnesses and its findings of facts should not be reversed by the appellate

court unless they were not based on evidence.

Appeal allowed.

CHIPETA, AG. J.—The appellant in this appeal, Hamisi Abdallah, sued the respondent, Sakilu Sungi and one Mghenyi in Ikungi Primary Court, Singida District, for Shs. 220/= being damages for the destruction of the appellant's crops by the respondent's cattle and goats.

The primary court unanimously found for the appellant, but assessed the damage at Shs. 120/=. Dissatisfied with the judgement of the trial Court, the present respondent appealed to the District Court. The District Court allowed the appeal. The learned District Magistrate who heard the appeal in the District Court allowed the appeal on the following grounds:—

(1) that there were discrepancies in the evidence of the appellant and his witnesses regarding dates;

(2) that the appellant did not take legal steps at the first available opportunity;

(3) that there was no evidence that the matter had been referred to elders before whom the respondent and his co-defendant are said to have admitted their liability; and

(4) that on the authority of the case of *Aloice Matanda v. Mamanya Ngapanyi* (1968) H.C.D. 456, the Primary Court had no jurisdiction to entertain the suit because the matter was governed by the Animals (Pounds) Ordinance, Cap. 154 of the Revised Laws, and was therefore outside customary law.

I propose to deal with this appeal on the basis of those four points as they adequately cover the matters in dispute and the questions of law involved.

With regard to the first question, that is, that there were discrepancies in the evidence of the complainant and that of his witnesses, I respectfully agree with the learned District Magistrate that there were discrepancies. However, I respectfully part company with the learned District Magistrate's reasoning that the discrepancies were such as to make the complainant's case suspect.

There is ample authority for the proposition that discrepancies in the testimony of various witnesses on material or broad points must be carefully weighed in arriving at the truth. But trifling discrepancies are to be ignored as they are often a test of truth. Several witnesses testifying to an event witnessed by them are naturally liable to disagree on immaterial points. It is the broad points in the evidence that must be considered in weighing evidence.

In the instant case there is loud and clear evidence that the animals of the respondent trespassed in the appellant's shamba on at least 13 occasions over a period of 20 days. The witnesses are simple peasants. That being so, it would, in my view, be less than just to expect simple peasants to remember all dates of the occurrence of incidents of a similar character over a period of 20 days. To my mind, the discrepancy as to dates was a trifling discrepancy which ought to have been ignored, as it was ignored by the trial Court.

On the second point, that is that the appellant had no reasons for failing to take legal steps at the first available opportunity, I will observe that the learned District Magistrate cannot possibly have pursued the record with care. There is ample evidence that the appellant referred the matter to elders twice over that period. It was only when the respondent and his co-defendant had failed to honor their word to make good the loss that the appellant filed the suit in court. What is so inherently wrong about trying to settle civil disputes out of court and in an amicable manner in the spirit of African tradition?

In regard to the third point, namely, that there was no evidence to show that the matter was referred to elders before whom the respondent and his co-defendant are said to have admitted liability, I must say, with great respect, that that statement flies in the face of overwhelming evidence on that point. With even greater respect, I allow myself the indulgence of feeling that the learned District Magistrate cannot have read the record of the trial Court with the degree of care required of an appellate court. There was low and clear evidence from at least two independent witnesses, one of them being no lesser than a ten cell leader who himself took part as one of the elders in the deliberations on at least two occasions. I can do no better than quote this witness (P.W.2) on this point. He said (and this is a free translation) at pages 12–13, and 14 of the trial Court's record:—

> We warned the defendants not to repeat what they had done. They agreed to pay Shs. 30/= so as to redeem their 6 goats. . . . But they have not paid up to now, and since then their cattle have repeatedly trespassed in the plaintiff's garden. When the elders met again they ordered the defendants to pay the plaintiff Shs. 120/= as damages to his seedlings and damages suffered by him as a result of the damage caused by the defendant's cattle in the plaintiff's entire garden. . . . They admitted the liability to pay Shs. 120/= and were given 30 days to do so at their request.

I therefore fail to see how the learned District Magistrate could have come to the conclusion that there was no evidence on this point.

Before I dispose of the fourth point there is one matter to which I should address my mind. As a first appellate court, the learned Magistrate was entitled to review the evidence and come to his own view based on such evidence. But in doing so an appellate court must always bear in mind that on questions of credibility of witnesses it is not placed in as advantageous a position as a trial Court which had the opportunity of seeing and hearing the witnesses. It is for this reason that it has repeatedly been held that an appellate court should be slow in reversing findings of facts by a trial Court. An appellate court is entitled to reverse findings of facts only where it is clear that those findings of facts were not based on the evidence, or where the inferences are plainly wrong; and a second appellate court will not accept findings of facts by a first ap-

pellate court where such first appellate court misdirected itself on the evidence, as is the case in the instant appeal. The Primary Court fully addressed its mind to the credibility of witnesses, and I see no reason to interfere with its findings.

I will now deal with the last ground of appeal. The learned District Magistrate held that the Primary Court had no jurisdiction to try the suit because it does not come under customary law but is governed by the Animals (Pounds) Ordinance, Cap. 154. He relied on a decision by this Court in the case of *Aloice Matanda v. Mamanya Ngapanyi* (supra).

As I understand the digest of the decision, what the court there held was that a Primary Court has no jurisdiction to hear a suit for costs of keeping a cow that had trespassed on someone's land. That case, in my view, is not an authority for the proposition that a tort arising out of crop destruction by tame animals is not within the purview of "customary law." However, as the matter has been raised I propose to deal with it.

From a couple of decisions by this court, and from my own view, it seems to me that the tort of destruction of crops by tame animals or persons has long been known to customary law. Customary law recognizes this tort and further recognizes payment of damages for the tort to the extent of compensation to the value of the crops destroyed. This court appears to have held that view in the case of *Ali Kindoli v. Tuzihirwe Pendaamani* (1962) Digest of Appeals from Local Courts No. 220 Vol. IX. That view was reaffirmed in the case of *Ruzebe Sweya v. Jacop Kitale* (1968) H.C.D. n. 407.

In Sweya's case the plaintiff claimed that the respondent's cattle had grazed on his shamba, damaging cassava. Citing Ali Kindoli's case (supra) the court held that a Primary Court had jurisdiction in this type of tortious liability because it comes within the phrase "customary law" as used in Section 14 of the Magistrates' Court Act.

I am in complete agreement with these two decisions. There does exist under customary law a tortious liability to pay compensation for damage to crops caused by one's animals.

In the instant case, therefore, the Primary Court had jurisdiction to try the suit within the provisions of Section 14 of the Magistrates' Court Act.

On these grounds, I would allow this appeal. It is accordingly so allowed with costs in this court and the courts below.

Driberg, J. H. (1928) "Primitive Law in East Africa." *Africa* 1: 65.

Hoebel, E. Adamson. (1954) *The Law of Primitive Man.*

The Law Reports of Tanzania. (1979).

Lloyd, Peter C. (1962) *Yoruba Land Law.*

Pospisil, Leopold. (1974 [1971]) *Anthropology of Law: A Comparative Theory.*

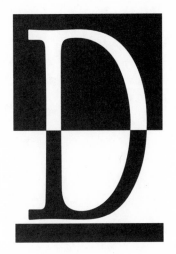

DEMOCRACY

Democracy refers to a political system in which political power rests in the hands of the people of the society. The term itself is derived from the Greek *demos* (the people) and *kratien* (to rule). The democracies with which most people are familiar are various forms of representative democracy that trace their origins to ancient Greece. Greek democracy, really Athenian democracy because it at first was limited to the city-state of Athens, began in the sixth century B.C. Modern democracies such as the United States and other Western nations are characterized by an an elected chief executive with limited or balanced powers, a wide voting franchise, open elections with competing candidates, and the protection of individual civil liberties. Democracy in the modern world is closely linked to economic development; that is, industrialized and postindustrial nations are more likely to have democratic forms of government than are nonindustrialized nations.

Dahl, Robert A. (1971) *Polyarchy.*

Ember, Carol R., Bruce Russett, and Melvin Ember. (1993) "Political Participation and Peace: Cross-Cultural Codes." *Cross-Cultural Research* 27: 97–145.

DESPOTISM

See AUTOCRACY.

DISOWNMENT

Disownment is the legally recognized destruction of all parent-child ties, including all reciprocal rights and duties, by the parent. A parent who disowns a child is legally no longer the child's parent.

Among the Tanala people of Madagascar, it is very important to maintain a good reputation for one's own family. If a family has an adult male member who is poorly behaved, the parents may choose to disown the man so as to maintain their good family name. The Tanala people only do this when the man's behavior is extremely bad, since being disowned is considered a fate worse than death. The Tanala parents will disown their son only if he is a habitual thief or repeatedly engages in incestuous sexual relations. Incest is considered especially bad, since the village's ancestral spirits are believed to cause sickness and crop failure for the whole village when it is committed.

The process of disownment is public. In it, the parents give presents to all the other extended families to compensate the village for the loss of labor that the young man would have provided. The disowned man is then forced to leave the village under threat of death should he return.

Linton, Ralph. (1936) *The Study of Man: An Introduction.*

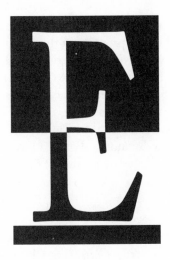

 EQUITY Equity may be defined as law that is especially aimed at achieving just decisions by paying more attention to the spirit of equality in the law than to the letter of the law. Equitable decisions are ones that are concerned more with the merits of the individual case than with the treatment of all similar cases in an identical matter. The term *equity* is a product of the English legal system, although the principles of equity are often practiced in other legal systems under various different names. Equity is an aspect of justice in adjudication.

Systems of equity begin when the usual system of law starts to become very rigid and uncreative, as many legal systems do over time. This rigidity and lack of creativity begin to produce unjust decisions in that the law is unable to take into account all the types of wrongs people suffered. In other words, many types of wrongs simply cannot be remedied by law courts because the law does not address those problems.

The first recorded system of equity was established in ancient Rome. There, the praetor, a special kind of magistrate, had the power to intervene in certain cases being heard by the usual judges and to impose a decision that conflicted with the one that the judge had rendered. The praetor's decision was based entirely upon justice, to the neglect of precedent and statute.

In England, equity in the legal system developed when the common law courts became unable to give just decisions in all cases due to the rigidity caused by following precedent and statute alone. The King of England, therefore, created a special high Court of Chancery at the end of the sixteenth century to give decisions based upon equitable justice rather than upon precedent and statute. Originally, a separate set of rules of equity were set forth that existed in parallel with the common law system. Later, equity became a part of common law, and ordinary judges could use the system of equity in their own courts. The use of equity in the ordinary court system also was a feature of later Roman law. The use of equitable principles is also used in courts in most parts of the United States, and decisions based upon equitable principles rather than statute or precedent are called "decisions at equity." In both Rome and Britain, equity was originally considered to be the conscience of the head of state; in Rome it belonged to the emperor, and in England to the royal monarch.

See also COMMON LAW; JUSTICE.

Maitland, F. W. (1936) *Equity.*

Pospisil, Leopold. (1974 [1971]) *Anthropology of Law: A Comparative Theory.*

EXPROPRIATION The term *expropriation* refers to the government's taking ownership of privately owned property for its own use.

Expropriation cannot legally be prevented by the private owner. In United States law, expropriation is often known as a "taking." The law of expropriation is part of the law of property.

In the United States, the government, whether federal, state, or municipal, may expropriate private property under the doctrine of eminent domain, the right of the sovereign power to use property within its borders for public benefit, and under which the individual property owner has no say in the expropriation. Under United States law, the government cannot expropriate private ownership interests in property unless the expropriation is done to benefit the public, and only if the individual owner is justly compensated for the loss of his interests.

In contrast, the leaders of the Soviet Union carried out expropriations in a much different manner shortly after the Communist revolution in 1917. In November 1917, the leaders of the Soviet Union expropriated the entire banking system that had existed in Russia. First, armed men took control of the State Bank in Petrograd. On 26 November 1917, Lenin ordered that all private banks be taken over by the Soviet Union, and this was done the next day, also by armed forces. Lenin declared all of the banks property of the Soviet Union, and they were combined into the Soviet Union's State Bank. None of the owners of the banks received any compensation for the value of their loss.

Since it was Lenin's purpose that the Soviet leadership control most of the wealth in the nation, he ordered the wholesale expropriation of industrial companies and other business ventures. The problem he faced, then, was what to do about all of the small private investors who held stocks and bonds issued by the expropriated companies. Lenin solved the dilemma simply by declaring that all stocks and bonds were null and void. Further, Lenin ordered that all debts of the former czarist government, whether owed to foreigners or to Russian citizens, were likewise null and void. In this fashion, the So-

viet government expropriated ownership of nearly all of the property in the country.

The wholesale expropriation of industry proved to be disastrous, since the state frequently could not run efficiently the factories they had expropriated. So, in 1921, the Soviet Union reprivatized some industries under the provisions of the New Economic Policy. However, Stalin later expropriated ownership of these businesses once again.

Voslensky, Michael. (1984) *Nomenklatura: The Soviet Ruling Class.* Translated by Eric Mosbacher.

EXTORTION

Extortion is the acquisition of money or other benefit from another person through the use of fear created by illegal threats. Extortion is also known as blackmail.

A form of extortion that is not uncommon in India is the extortion of larger dowries by the groom's family from the bride's family by harassing the recently married bride. In India, Hindu marriage has traditionally included a dowry (in Hindi, known as *daan dehej*), a payment or payments of money and other property by the parents of the bride to the bride and her husband. One function of dowry is to help ensure that the bride's children will be supported, even if her husband dies. Some Indians believe that the use of dowry is endorsed by religious texts such as the *Manusmriti*. The practice of using dowries is very common in the upper economic classes, and thus it is widely considered prestigious to use dowries.

The cost of the dowry is often quite high. In a middle-class area of Delhi, the modal cost of dowries is 50,000 rupees, although dowries

Women in New Delhi in 1980 protest the tradition of dowries, payments by the parents of a bride to the bride and her husband to complete a wedding. Although outlawed by the Indian government in 1961, the tradition continues.

of 200,000 rupees are fairly frequent. This represents a great burden to all but the wealthiest people. Oftentimes, a family will save money for years for a daughter's dowry. Still, it often happens that a father has great difficulty in arranging a marriage for his daughter if he does not have sufficient money for the size of the dowries requested by potential grooms. It is not unknown for girls and young women to commit suicide so as to avoid placing the burden of expensive dowries on their families. Parents, too, consider the cost of dowries. In the past, female infanticide was sometimes practiced. Nowadays, parents use amniocentesis to determine the sex of their unborn children, and many have abortions if the fetus is female. The use of amnio-

centesis and abortion of female fetuses has become a serious problem, to the point that the state of Maharashtra has forbidden the use of amniocentesis for sex determination in all medical facilities but government hospitals.

Extortion takes place after the wedding. The payments of dowry frequently continue after the wedding, though most dowry payments are made no later than a few years after the wedding. In some cases, the husband uses threats of future beatings or verbal abuse on his wife to coerce his wife's family to increase the dowry. Often in such cases, the man's mother also assists her son in harassing her daughter-in-law for more dowry money. Sometimes, the harassment culminates in the wife's suicide. In other cases, the husband becomes enraged by his wife's family's failure to pay more dowry to the point that he kills his wife. The typical method of committing "dowry death," as it is known, is by burning the wife with the kerosene used in cooking appliances. For this reason, dowry deaths are also known as "bride burnings."

In an effort to end dowry and the violence so often associated with it, the Indian government made the payment of dowry illegal in 1961. There have been arrests and convictions under this law, but by and large people in India ignore it and commonly and routinely violate it.

———

Willigen, John van, and V. C. Channa. (1991) "Law, Custom, and Crimes against Women: The Problem of Dowry Death in India." *Human Organization* 50(4): 369–377.

FACTION

A faction is a political group or clique within one or more established, politically active groups or parties; a faction tends to be united for a short period around a single issue or group of related issues. A faction's membership cuts across established political group lines; for example, a faction to support a bill in the U.S. Congress may have members from both the Democratic and Republican parties, but other Democratic and Republican senators and congressmen may form another faction opposed to the bill. Also, as a result of political negotiations, the membership of each faction can change many times before voting on the bill takes place. Both factions cease to exist after the Congress has either finally passed or rejected the bill.

If a society has a tendency to form factions easily, the political process can become unstable and the welfare of the society can suffer. For this reason, people who readily support factions instead of trying to build a consensus of all around a particular issue are sometimes attacked as being self-serving at the public's expense.

One interesting study of factionalism in a town in Burma (now known as Myanmar) was done by Melford Spiro. Spiro found that in the town he studied there were two major political factions that dominated village politics, which were called the *Ayoundaw* group and the *Thamu-hnamu* group. The core of the *Ayoundaw* faction was composed of people who belonged to families that had for a very long time been the traditional elite of the village. These people had recently begun to lose their top economic position, but they had clung to their status as the members of the top social class. The core members of the *Ayoundaw* faction were well educated, schooled in the social graces, and, in general, behaved in the manner of leisure classes the world over. The core members of the *Thamu-hnamu* faction, on the other hand, were people who had only recently become wealthy, usually through the ownership of large parcels of farmlands. They were not well educated and, in general, were concerned primarily with hard work and making money. The core members of the *Ayoundaw* faction resented the success of the core members of the *Thamu-hnamu* faction, which had cost the former their unquestioned top economic status, even though they were still considered socially superior. In turn, the core members of the *Thamu-hnamu* faction resented the *Ayoundaw* faction's efforts to suppress them. Other members of the *Thamu-hnamu* faction included other people who had been hurt by the members of the *Ayoundaw* faction in the redistribution of the nation's land. The *Ayoundaw* faction also included people who were fearful of being hurt by the great economic power wielded by the core members of the *Thamu-hnamu* faction.

Spiro was never able to learn the true origin of these factions, because his informants gave him two different accounts. The first of these is that the factions began shortly after Burmese independence was achieved in 1948. A group of armed guerrilla insurgents occupied the area and were powerful enough to have actual control of the village at night, although the central government had control over the village during the day. The insurgents forced the people of the town to supply them with money and food. The insurgents also installed one of the village men as its representative, and this man (U Pain) collected the payments that the insurgents demanded. According to the *Thamu-hnamu* faction, U Pain kept some of these forced payments for himself and his friends, the people who later became the *Ayoundaw* faction.

The second account of the origin of the factions begins in 1951 when the people of the village organized the Village Development Society to provide low-interest loans for farmers. Each member of the society contributed a payment of one-half bushel of rice to fund the society. After two years of growth, the society had 100 members, a fair amount of money, and a lot of rice in storage. At this point in time, it was discovered that a large amount of money was missing from the society's coffers. U Pain and his friends in the *Ayoundaw* faction were the officers in charge of the society, and members of the *Thamu-hnamu* faction accused them of embezzling the missing money. U Pain made a countercharge that it was in fact the *Thamu-hnamu* faction that had stolen the money and was merely accusing the *Ayoundaw* faction with the offense to camouflage its own complicity. Later, another *Ayoundaw* member became treasurer of the society. Still later, the society folded and offered each member of the society five bushels of rice in the liquidation of its assets. The treasurer discovered that there was insufficient rice to give each member five bushels, so he took what he needed from the private granary of a *Thamu-hnamu* member and claimed that the rice actually belonged to the society.

Another factional conflict took place over the imposition of the federal Land Nationalization Act, the intent of which was to take some land from wealthy landowners and distribute it to the landless poor. The committee set up to administer the land redistribution was made up entirely of members of the *Ayoundaw* and was also entirely self-regulating. The wealthy landowners attempted to bribe the committee so as to avoid losing portions of the land they owned. On the other hand, the members of the committee extorted bribes from landowners, threatening that they would expropriate lands to which the landowners were legally entitled under the Land Nationalization Act. The committee also failed to give lands to the eligible poor unless they also paid bribes. Finally, one of the most serious charges was that land expropriated under the act was never delivered to the poor, but rather kept by committee members, given to their friends and relatives, or transferred to peasants in return for even greater bribes.

The factionalism manifested itself in yet different ways. There was an election for the office of headman of the village. The office had traditionally belonged to the elite, now the core of the *Ayoundaw*. However, the growing economic power of the *Thamu-hnamu* made their candidate a strong contender. The *Thamu-hnamu* candidate in point of fact lost, but had he won, his faction, with both its wealth and its control of the headman's office, would have permanently ended the influence of the members of the old elite, the *Ayoundaw*.

One important quality of the factionalism in this Burmese village is its absence of physical confrontation. There were no public arguments, let alone fights, as a result of the factionalism. The members of the two factions displayed their antipathy toward each other by withdrawing their cooperation from activities associated with the other. The withdrawal of cooperation by the *Thamu-hnamu* was even more pronounced after it lost the election for headman.

After the election, the headman, as one of his duties, organized the village's observation of Wazou, a Buddhist holy day. Some members of *Thamu-hnamu* refused to attend the event, because it was organized by the *Ayoundaw* headman.

On the grounds that an *Ayoundaw* member had failed to participate in a mandatory work party crew to maintain the village's chapel, all members of the *Thamu-hnamu* refused to join the work party. They also refused to use the chapel.

The factionalism spread to performances of the village orchestra during public celebrations. The orchestra, being under the control of the ruling *Ayoundaw*, refused the entry of a drummer belonging to the *Thamu-hnamu* faction. *Ayoundaw* members accused the *Thamu-hnamu* of sending the drummer to subvert the other orchestra members to support the *Thamu-hnamu*. The members of the *Thamu-hnamu* became angry at this charge, and as a result declared that they would found their own orchestra. The village elders, all appointed by the headman, became concerned that this could mean the end of their village and so proposed that certain musical instruments would be played by members of one faction and other instruments by members of the other faction. The *Thamu-hnamu* agreed to this, but later the only *Thamu-hnamu* member of the orchestra, the drummer, resigned.

The village as a whole was also expected to provide money for the building of a pagoda at a nearby Buddhist pilgrimage center, and the headman of the village was expected to collect this money. The members of the *Thamu-hnamu*, in opposing the *Ayoundaw* headman, refused to contribute, and since they had the majority of the village's wealth, the village was unable to meet its obligation that year.

The existence of two factions caused internal political difficulties, but their disputes did not lead to any differences in social solidarity with respect to the outside world. For example, when a member of the *Thamu-hnamu* faction faced federal governmental opposition, all members of the village rallied together behind him, in large part to maintain a good name for the village as well as to assist the fellow villager.

Another feature of factions in this Burmese village is that factions are themselves prone to splintering and internal dissension, and there is little solidarity within a faction's membership beyond the issue that formed the factions in the first place. An interesting example of this is that of U Lum Byei, the village's wealthiest man and the *Thamu-hnamu* faction's candidate for village headman. His affinal kinsman Kou Swe was also a fellow faction member and a great supporter of his in the election. Yet, when Kou Swe fell ill and could not fulfill a contract to deliver bamboo to a Malay businessman by the promised date, U Lum Byei did not help his kinsman and fellow faction member transport his bamboo; rather, he offered to sell his own bamboo to the businessman in place of the bamboo of Kou Swe, so as to keep the profit for himself.

The membership of factional groups is tied very closely to the particular interests of the individuals involved in making up the factions. In other words, a faction that develops over one issue may contain two people who had been in opposing factions over another issue. For example, take the case of the village's wealthiest woman, Do Ci. She brought legal charges against Kou Khin Maung for allegedly molesting her granddaughter. The dispute became a political as well as a legal one, and Kou Khin Maung received the support not only of the *Ayoundaw* headman, but also of the two most powerful supporters of the former *Thamu-hnamu* candidate for headman. On the other hand, the former *Thamu-hnamu* candidate for headman lent his political support to Do Ci against Kou Khin Maung.

The last characteristic of factionalism in this Burmese village was that factionalism was well camouflaged behind a public display of friendliness between the members of opposing factions. When the members of one faction make allegations of wrongdoing against the members of the other faction, they do it privately and through third parties. Written allegations filed with formal authorities bore no signatures. Those involved in a plot to remove the

Ayoundaw headman from office also invited him to coffee, as they would any friend, just hours before they attempted to carry out their plan. This pattern of behavior meant that conflicts rarely were resolved, and that resentments built up over time, leading eventually to a schism within the entire village. Much is said privately, but almost none of what is spoken about ever comes to pass.

In contrast, in band societies, factionalism is the chief means by which two or more bands are created out of one former band. In such cases, factionalism may be viewed as a positive event. When a band grows to be too large for the local resources to support all of its members, it makes sense for the band to divide into two or more groups and for the groups to move away from each other and form separate bands. The two new bands will thus not deplete the resources around them. A second reason why factionalism benefits band societies (as well as other types of societies) is that it allows people who have disputes to move away from each other. In this way, the likelihood and severity of conflict between the disputants are both reduced without the need for legal remedies.

But single bands can also form out of two or more separate bands, in which case the original populations often coexist as separate factions within the band. Such was the case of the Nunamiut Eskimo of Anaktuvuk Pass in the Brooks Range region of Alaska. There, the two factions, known as the Tulugak Lake people and the Killik River people for their earlier homes, largely kept separate from each other in many respects. They were mutually distrustful and often gossiped about each other, sometimes making accusations about a member of the other faction's use of sorcery. The two factions also tended toward endogamy, although there was some intermarriage. Also, the two factions carried out their economic activities separately and in greatly different fashions. The Killik River faction sold their furs, manufactured goods, and bounty money (earned by killing wolves) to a white trader who came through the area. The Tulugak Lake people, on the other hand, spent much of their time in the bush working, and chartered their own plane to send the products they made, their furs, and their bounty money to other traders where they could get a better deal. This meant that the Tulugak Lake people enjoyed a higher standard of living, and this, in turn, meant that the Killik River people were often jealous of the Tulugak Lake people.

Despite the existence of these factions, the Nunamiut band was stronger with the two factions living together than it would have been had the two factions lived as separate bands. When difficult times demanded it, differences between the two factions disappeared, and all of the members of the band worked together as a single team to conquer the troubles of the moment.

This is not to say that Eskimo bands did not split into two or more bands on occasion. Band fission occurred when the band's population exceeded 150 people for a period of time, thus making it difficult to find enough food nearby for all. When a band split up, it usually did so along factional lines.

See also FISSIONING.

French, David. (1948) *Factionalism in Isleta Pueblo.*

Gubser, Nicholas J. (1965) *The Nunamiut Eskimos: Hunters of Caribou.*

Spiro, Melford. (1968) "Factionalism and Politics in Village Burma." In *Local-Level Politics,* edited by Marc Swartz, 401-421.

FAMILY LAW

Family law is law that applies to the membership and functioning of the family. Specifically, family law includes laws pertaining to parent-child relationships, sibling-sibling relationships, husband-wife relationships, marriage, divorce, and adoption; in more recent times in some nations, the legal regulation of surrogate parenthood, abortion, as well as disputes over postdivorce child custody and the rights of natural parents who do not have legally recognized parenthood have become important. Additional laws may be involved if the society normally has extended families living together, since grandparent-grandchild relationships and relationships between an individual and his or her parent's sibling may also be legally relevant and regulated.

A critical part of family law in any culture is the question of maintenance. Maintenance is the material or financial support that one person is legally required to pay to another person who is incapable of supporting himself or herself. In the United States, the only people who have a legal right to maintenance are spouses, divorced spouses who receive maintenance in addition to alimony payments (sometimes maintenance is included in the alimony payment), and minor children.

In pre-Communist China, however, where the family was the most important unit of society, maintenance was required by law for a great number of kin. Following are the statutory rules concerning maintenance in the Chinese Republic (*The Civil Code of the Republic of China*, 1931: 39–41):

Chapter V
Maintenance

Article 1114.—The following relatives are under a mutual obligation to maintain one another:—

1. Lineal relatives by blood;
2. Spouse and the parents of the other spouse living in the same household;
3. Brothers and sisters;
4. The head and the members of a house.

Article 1115.—In case there are several persons bound to furnish maintenance, the order in which they are to perform such obligation is as follows:—

1. Lineal descendants;
2. Lineal ascendants;
3. Head of the house;
4. Brothers and sisters;
5. Members of the house;
6. Daughter-in-law and son-in-law;
7. Parents of either spouse.

Among lineal ascendants or lineal descendants, the person nearest in degree of relationship comes first.

If there are several persons of the same degree of relationship bound to furnish maintenance, such obligation shall be borne by them according to their respective means.

Article 1116.—In case there are several persons entitled to maintenance, and the means of the person bound to provide it is not sufficient to maintain all of them, the person to receive maintenance shall be determined in the following order:—

1. Lineal ascendants;
2. Lineal descendants;
3. Members of the house;
4. Brothers and sisters;
5. Head of the house;
6. Parents of either spouse;
7. Daughter-in-law and son-in-law.

Among lineal ascendants or lineal descendants, the person nearest in degree of relationship comes first.

Where there are several persons of the same degree of relationship entitled to maintenance, each shall receive maintenance according to his needs.

Article 1117.—Persons entitled to maintenance are limited to those only who have no means of maintenance and have no ability to earn a living.

The aforesaid limitation in respect of inability to earn a living does not apply to the case of lineal ascendants by blood.

Article 1118.—A person who can no longer support his own living if he assumes the obligation of furnishing maintenance to another, shall be exempted from such an obligation.

Article 1119.—The extent of maintenance shall be determined according to the needs of the person entitled to maintenance, and the means and social status of the person bound to furnish it.

Article 1120.—The manner in which maintenance is furnished shall be determined by mutual agreement between the parties, or if they cannot agree, by the family council.

Article 1121.—Either party may demand an alteration in the extent and the manner of furnishing maintenance on the ground that circumstances have changed.

See also ADOPTION; MARRIAGE; *PATRIA POTESTAS;* RIGHTS, CHILDREN'S.

The Civil Code of the Republic of China. (1931) Book IV, Family. Translated by Ching-lin Hsia, James Chow, Liu Chieh, and Yukon Chang.

Rwezaura, Barthazar Aloys. (1985) *Traditional Family Law and Change in Tanzania: A Study of the Kuria Social System.*

FEUD

A feud is defined as prolonged, unauthorized violence between two subgroups of a larger group or between two groups who reside in the same political community (Pospisil 1971: 10). It differs from war in that war is authorized, or approved by the authorities, and takes place between independent groups or societies. Feuding groups are usually large kinship groups such as fraternal interest groups (groups of brothers who live in the same community), lineages, clans, or extended families.

Some anthropologists have claimed that the feud is a form of primitive law, since the threat of revenge forces people to abstain from committing homicide. Bronislaw Malinowski, a famous anthropologist, wrote (1964: 261) "fighting, collective and organized, is a juridical mechanism for the adjustment of differences between constituent groups of the same larger cultural unit." Robert Spencer (1959: 161) said that after a North Alaskan Eskimo was killed, "his own kin became embroiled and the legal mechanism of the feud was put into action." These statements are misleading. The feud continues, on and on, because there is no authority who can stop it, and authority is one of the necessary attributes of law. Feud, because it can continue so long, can be very destructive to society, sometimes killing off whole families, bands, or even tribes. That is why law always tries to prevent killings, revenge killings, and feuds, even though the parties to the feud may remain angry with each other. Feud cannot be law, further, because feuds do not lead to final settlements or peace (except when the other party is exterminated), as does law. Feud is the opposite of law.

One of the most commonly described types of feud is the blood feud, in which two groups, usually kin-based groups such as kindreds, or descent-based groups such as lineages, avenge the murder of a member of their own group by killing one of the members of the killer's group. If simple revenge is taken, and the dispute is put to rest, then it is a case of revenge and not of feud. Feud occurs when the process of taking revenge goes back and forth, and it is often the case that the original killing, or other offense, is forgotten. Feuds can last generations.

A recent study of feuding in 186 societies indicates six levels of feuding in cultures around the world, noted below with the percentages of societies that practice that form of feuding:

feuding is considered morally imperative	22.0 percent
feuding is considered the most appropriate response	8.9 percent
feuding occurs only in certain circumstances	10.7 percent
feuding is considered a last resort	11.9 percent
feuding occurs but is punished	37.5 percent
kin groups are not recognized as an avenging unit, so feuding does not occur	8.9 percent

As these percentages show, feuding is permitted in 53.5 percent of societies. These figures apply to the situation in the early 1900s. Since World War I, feuding has diminished or disappeared in many societies where it was previously common, evidently because these societies were incorporated into modern nations where the local, regional, or national police and legal systems were the primary mechanisms for settling serious disputes and they eventually replaced feuding. Feuding was especially common, and vestiges remain, in societies near the Mediterranean Sea, such as among Sicilians, Calabrians, Albanians, Serbs, Montenegrins, and Libyan Bedouins.

In societies with feuding, the offenses that require blood revenge are the murder of a kinsman by a member of another kinship group or an affront to the honor of a kinswoman by a male member of another kinship group. An affront to the honor of a kinswoman is the more frequent precipitator of violence, and is a major cause of feuding in societies in the Mediterranean region because of the status of women in these societies and the economic arrangements between families whose children marry one another. In many of these societies, when a woman marries she moves to the community of her husband's family. In addition, she often brings

with her a substantial dowry and recognizes that her children will belong to her husband's kin group, not the group to which she was born. Thus, a woman and her family give up much at marriage. In turn, the husband's family makes little material contribution to the marriage, except to give its name and honor, which the wife gains upon marriage. Thus, it is important that kin groups maintain their good name and honor, and any slight to that honor must be erased through revenge. And, since it is girls and young women who will marry out, slights to their honor, and especially their sexual purity, must be revenged. Since it is a family matter, it is often the brothers (fraternal interest groups) of the unmarried sisters who initiate the feuding.

The Sarakatsani, a Greek-speaking pastoral people of northern Greece, display the major features of this type of feuding. Family honor is a vital matter to the Sarakatsani and comes into play when a male member of the family is physically or verbally attacked by an outsider, when a kinswoman is the victim of sexual assault or insult, or when a kinswoman is guilty of sexual misconduct. The notion of honor is much concerned with the concepts of manliness and sexual shame and serves as the basis for the social value of the family as judged by outsiders.

In accord with their conception of honor, the Sarakatsani seek revenge for two types of attacks on their honor—killing of a man and sexual assault of a woman. The killing of a man requires revenge by killing the murderer or driving him permanently away, with the former preferable. To kill the murderer means "to take out the blood" of their murdered kinsman, as the Sarakatsani believe that by taking the blood of their kinsman, the murderer took strength from the family. The sexual behavior of daughters, sisters, and wives is of central concern, as the sexual behavior of women is controlled by the family. If a woman commits adultery, she and her lover are killed by her husband to restore honor to the family. If a daughter loses her virginity before marriage, she and her lover are killed by her father or brothers. If a woman is raped or sexually dishonored, such as by having a betrothal broken, only the man is killed.

All of this might suggest that the Sarakatsani are in a constant state of feuding, with a real possibility that the men may kill each other off completely. This does not happen, because insults that require blood revenge do not occur too often, the guilty man can flee and stay away permanently, the Greek police often intervene and arrest the guilty man, or the offended family might choose not to seek blood revenge because the cost of the revenge (the likely death of one of their own men) seems too high.

The Micmac Indians of eastern Canada have an ingenious nonlegal means to stop feuds before they start. If a man kills another, or commits some other offense to a family or patrilineage, he is safe from the threat of revenge so long as he remains outside of the victim's family territory. The victim's family would appear to all to be dishonorable if they attacked the killer in the killer's own family territory or anywhere outside of their own family territory. If the killer enters the family territory of his victim, he may be severely beaten if he is caught there, and the community will treat the revenge as just. Thus, the usual behavior of the killer is simply to avoid the family territory of his victim for as long as he lives, and thus the social peace is preserved. At the same time, the family of the victim gains some satisfaction in that everyone in the community is constantly reminded of the killing, because the killer is always avoiding part of the community in his travels, and thus the killer is ostracized by other members of the community as long as he lives. Further, the killer is disgraced by being obliged to avoid a part of the community for the rest of his life; in other words, he behaves as a coward, and his loss of face is permanent.

See also HOMICIDE; WAR.

Campbell, J. K. (1964) *Honour, Family, and Patronage: A Study of Institutions and Moral Values in a Greek Mountain Community.*

Caudill, Harry M. (1963) *Night Comes to the Cumberlands.*

Ericksen, Karen Paige, and Heather Horton. (1992) "'Blood Feuds': Cross-Cultural Variations in Kin Group Vengeance." *Behavior Science Research* 26: 57–86.

Malinowski, Bronislaw. (1964) "An Anthropological Analysis of War." In *War: Studies from Psychology, Sociology, Anthropology,* edited by Leon Bramson and George W. Goethals, 245–268.

Otterbein, Keith F., and Charlotte S. Otterbein. (1965) "An Eye for an Eye, a Tooth for a Tooth: A Cross-Cultural Study of Feuding." *American Anthropologist* 67: 1470–1482.

Pospisil, Leopold. (1974 [1971]) *Anthropology of Law: A Comparative Theory.*

Spencer, Robert F. (1959) *The North Alaskan Eskimo.* Smithsonian Institution Bureau of American Ethnology Bulletin 171.

Strouthes, Daniel P. (1994) *Change in the Real Property Law of a Cape Breton Island Micmac Band.*

FISSIONING

Fissioning is the splitting of a community. Fissioning occurs when the groups that form a community separate completely to form new communities or when one group moves away and forms a new community or joins another community. The opposite of fissioning is fusion, which is the formation of a community through the joining together of two or more previously independent groups or the expansion of a community through the arrival of a formerly separate group.

Fissioning occurs in a number of cultures for a variety of reasons, including better economic opportunities elsewhere, population expansion that makes the group too large to survive on local resources, and disputes or the threat of disputes that disrupt social cohesion within the community. In non-Western cultures, the groups that form a community (village or band) are kinship groups such as lineages or families and are often linked to one another politically, socially, and economically. Thus, fissioning is not just moving away, but might also involve severing ties between groups and establishing ties with new groups. However, fissioning does not always result in the severing of all ties and, in fact, in some cultures it can be a mechanism that creates cultural cohesion and greater cooperation between groups. For example, Tiv compounds in Nigeria often fission after the death of the compound head, especially when there are disputes about succession or the cause of death, or when some families are dissatisfied with the new head. Sometimes, all the families will separate and settle elsewhere, although more often only one family leaves. The families continue to farm together, or as the Tiv say, they are "sitting separately" but use "one field."

Among the San of Botswana, families continually leave a band to join new ones. While unresolved disputes are sometimes the reason for leaving, more often it is simply a desire to live elsewhere or because food is more plentiful elsewhere. This continual movement of families creates ties among different San bands that help unite them together as a single culture.

As a form of conflict resolution, fissioning is quite common around the world, with at least some fissioning taking place after disputes in 78 percent of a sample of sixty-four cultures. It is usually the group that is unhappy with the outcome of the dispute that moves away. In general, fissioning occurs only in response to serious or ongoing disputes or disputes that threaten the survival of the community. The Mbuti of central Africa have both internal and external fissioning. In the internal form, families who are not wanted are isolated within the camp, as the other groups build their huts apart from the undesirable group. External fissioning generally occurs when disputes disrupt the cooperation needed in hunting and the community then splits into two separate groups or one group leaves and joins another band. Among the Yanomamö of Brazil it is a combination of group size and violent disputes or the likelihood of continual violence that leads to fissioning. The Yanomamö live in circular villages with men and women encouraged to marry others from the same village, and with new groups added through fusion. Large villages are preferred and important because some Yanomamö groups are in a continual state of war with other groups, and the larger the village the less likely it is that it will be attacked and the more successful it will be in attacks on other villages. However, when the village grows to between 100 and 150 residents, disputes and especially fights and club duels over women and extramarital affairs become so common that the internal order of the village is threatened and weakens the effectiveness of the men of the village as a military force. When the threat of internal disorder or actual disorder reaches this point, the village fissions. Sometimes, the village will separate in half and each group will establish separate gardens near one another so that they can support each other in raids on and by other villages. At other times, when the disruption is too great, one small faction will leave and establish a new village or join another existing village.

See also FACTION.

Bohannan, Paul J. (1957b) *Tiv Farm and Settlement.*

Chagnon, Napoleon A. (1968) *Yanomamö: The Fierce People.*

Ross, Marc H. (1983) "Political Decision-Making and Conflict: Additional Cross-Cultural Codes." *Ethnology* 22: 169–192.

Tanaka, Jiro. (1980) *The San Hinter-Gatherers of the Kalahari.* Translated by David W. Hughes.

Turnbull, Colin M. (1965) *Wayward Servants: The Two Worlds of the African Pygmies.*

have not been examined, verified, and branded, shall be punished as if it were an illegal manufacture with 40 blows.

The Chinese Government. (1887) *A Chapter of the Chinese Penal Code.*

The Law Codification Commission. (1919) *The Criminal Code of the Republic of China (Second Revised Draft).*

FRAUD

Fraud is the practice of deceiving another party so as to cause him or her a loss and is prohibited by law. One type of fraud involves the use of incorrect weights and measures in trade so as to cheat the other party in a business transaction. Another type of fraud is counterfeiting. Fraud is recognized and prohibited by most legal systems. Following are statutes from the Qing Dynasty and the Chinese Republic regarding fraud. Note how the Chinese Republic used incarceration as a common sanction, whereas the government previous to it, the Qing Dynasty, preferred to use beatings.

Chinese Republic

Article 204. Whoever counterfeits or fraudulently alters any current coin, paper money, or bank-note with the intent that the same may be put into circulation as standard currency, shall be punished with imprisonment for life, or with imprisonment for a period of not less than five years, or with both imprisonment for life and a fine of not more then three thousand yuan, or with both imprisonment for a period of not less than five years and a fine of not more than three thousand yuan.

Qing Dynasty

Anyone using weights, measures, or scales on the market, which, though being accurate,

FUNCTIONS OF LAW

Since law itself is culturally relative, it should not be surprising to find that ideas on its function also differ from group to group and even individual to individual. According to the anthropologist E. A. Hoebel (1954: 275), the law has four functions:

1. To maintain orderly relations between members of society so that social integration may be maintained.

2. To select an authority who will choose properly how to apply force to the end of maintaining order.

3. To adjudicate actual trouble cases.

4. To change relations between members of society as social and cultural conditions change, this adaptability makes law better able to accomplish its other functions.

Across cultures, these basic functions are manifested in a variety of ways. Among the Barotse of Zambia, in Africa, the purpose of law as conceived of by the legal authorities in that society is to allow the parties to a dispute to continue to live together, and to be able to carry out their mutual social obligations to each other. In doing this, the court aims to employ the use of ethical principles in determining the law in each case. The legal authorities do not assess the law only on the basis of abstract principles and precedents, but actively try to make the outcome just.

For theorists of Natural Law, the ultimate function of law is to preserve society, and this is done by preserving peaceful relations among the people. The law thus seeks to prevent societal fragmentation, so as to keep the society whole. The reason for this is to help the society survive. If a society does not have a sufficient number of people who can coordinate their efforts to defend a society, then it follows that another society with the ability to cohere and to raise an army can defeat the society that does not have that ability. Similarly, a society with the ability to cohere and to coordinate its population enough to raise an army or militia can more readily defeat internal threats to the survival of the society, such as terrorist groups or secessionists.

See also NATURAL LAW.

Gluckman, Max. (1965a) *The Ideas in Barotse Jurisprudence.*

Grotius, Hugo. (1925 [1625]) *De Jure Belli ac Pacis Libri Tres.* Translated by Francis W. Kelsey.

Hoebel, E. Adamson. (1954) *The Law of Primitive Man.*

Pufendorf, Samuel von. (1927 [1682]) *De Officio Hominis et Civis Juxta Legem Naturalem Libri Duo.* Translated by Frank Gardner Moore.

Seidler, Michael. (1990) *Samuel Pufendorf's On the Natural State of Men.* Translated and annotated by Michael Seidler.

Whewell, William. (1853) *Grotius on War and Peace.* Vol. I.

FUNDAMENTAL LEGAL CONCEPTIONS

In 1923, Wesley Newcomb Hohfeld proposed four legal conceptions that have become widely accepted as basic to an understanding of all legal relationships. His conceptions were in the form of pairs of jural opposites (also called jural correlatives). All jural relations fall into sets of pairs; one party cannot be characterized by one-half of a pair without some other party being characterized by the other half. They are as follows:

1. **Demand right versus duty.** This may be more easily understood simply as right versus duty. Legally speaking, this is a relationship of behavior that must be followed. A legal right is the legal expectation that someone else will behave toward me in a certain way. A duty is the expectation that I must behave in a certain way to another person or else I will be punished by the law. A worker who works for an employer has a right to be paid for his work, and the employer has a duty to pay him, for example. A man who enters a store and gives the storeowner the price of a sweater has a right to have the sweater, and the storeowner has a duty to give it to the purchaser. An owner of a shirt has the right to wear it as he wishes, and everyone else has the duty to allow him to do so. An owner of a car has the right to alienate it (to sell or to give it to whomever he chooses), and the buyer has the duty to pay whatever price the owner agrees to.

2. **Privilege right versus no-demand-right.** This may be more easily understood as privilege (or no duty) versus no right. Legally speaking, this is a legal relationship in which a person may behave in a certain way if he or she wishes to do so, and someone else has no right to stop him or her. A factory worker, for example, has the privilege of taking a workday off for illness, and the

employer has no right to fire him, refuse to pay him, or treat him differently. An army general has the privilege of eating in the officer's mess, while a private has no right to eat there. The president of the United States has the privilege of granting pardons for criminal convictions, but a convicted criminal has no right to demand a pardon.

3. **Power versus liability.** Power means that party A can initiate a right with respect to party B. Party B has liability, meaning that he or she is possibly subject to a duty imposed upon him or her by someone else. For example, the United States government has the power to draft men for military service, and men in the United States have a liability to serve in the military when drafted.

4. **Immunity versus no power.** This may be better understood as immunity versus disability. If A is an immune party, then A is immune to any liability imposed by B, another party. Party B has no ability to create a liability in party A. For example, a university may have an immunity against the payment of property taxes, whereas a city or state has a disability to tax it. The president of the United States has, as a diplomat, immunity from the criminal laws of another country, and the police force and courts of another country have a disability to arrest him or to try him for a crime.

The value of Hohfeld's jural correlatives is that they may be used to help analyze, and to clarify in our own minds, the often complex and multifaceted legal relationships between the various parties in all types of legal cases.

————

Hohfeld, W. N. (1923) *Fundamental Legal Conceptions as Applied in Judicial Reasoning and Other Essays*. Edited by Walter Wheeler Cook.

sense of morality as well. Morality develops within people over time, as does its force in guiding behavior. Of course, some few people never develop a strong sense of morality, but it is true that older people are more strongly guided by their society's mores than are younger people.

We can see this very clearly in two examples. During the Nazi regime in Germany, those running the death camps that were used to kill Jews, Gypsies, Slavic peoples, and others whom the Germans found offensive, discovered that older Germans, generally speaking, could not bring themselves to operate the machinery that killed people. They may have disliked or even hated those who were to be killed, but they could not bring themselves to take their lives in cold blood. The job of killing people in gas chambers and by other means was given to young people, few of whom had the moral scruples of the older people.

In a second example, Pol Pot of the Khmer Rouge (Communist Cambodians) enlisted young adults and children (some of whom were quite young) to carry out his orders to execute political opponents of the Khmer Rouge who had been taken prisoner. He found young people more willing to give themselves wholeheartedly to killing for no other reason than that they were ordered to do so.

The Micmac Indians of eastern Canada traditionally chose gerontocracies to lead them. They valued the wisdom of older men. This pattern changed in the 1950s and 1960s when the Micmac realized that they needed to be able to communicate clearly with the federal government in Ottawa. Since clear communication with the government required a good knowledge of English, and since only younger people had this knowledge, the Micmac have in recent decades been choosing younger people to lead them. The Micmac experience is typical of that of many indigenous peoples around the world in recent times. In many of these societies, traditional leadership practices that have

GERONTOCRACY The term *gerontocracy* refers to a type of government in which the majority of political power rests in the hands of old people; the word is derived from the Greek words *gerontos* (old man) and *kratos* (rule). The United States, for example, is to a considerable degree a gerontocracy. Gerontocracies have the advantage that they are led by people with a great deal of experience, people who are less likely to make rash or impulsive decisions or to make decisions without gathering all the necessary facts.

Gerontocracies are common throughout the world, both in technologically advanced societies and in technologically primitive societies. People know that when their leaders have a lot of experience in life, they are less likely to lead their followers in ways that might hurt them. An older leader, for example, is less likely to lead his or her people to war, since he or she has probably seen war in his or her lifetime and would be loathe to repeat it, knowing the kind of death and misery it can bring.

Societies often choose older leaders because they usually have a more strongly developed given authority to older and more experienced members of the community have given way to structures that favor younger leaders who are believed to be better able to deal with the complexities of the modern world and to manage relations with outside economic and political interests.

Strouthes, Daniel P. (1994) *Change in the Real Property Law of a Cape Breton Island Micmac Band.*

GUARDIAN

A guardian is someone who is legally responsible for the care of a person who cannot care for himself or herself and, if applicable, for his or her estate as well. The individual who is cared for in such a manner is known as a ward of the guardian. People protected by guardians may be children or people mentally unfit to take care of their own affairs. Under U.S. law, a ward must live where directed by the guardian, and he or she can be prevented by the guardian from entering into contracts. The conduct of a guardian is subject to the direction of the courts.

Among the Yoruba people of Nigeria, guardianship is not altogether different. The guardian of an orphan child is the ward's nearest male relative on the mother's side, and is selected by the head of the extended family. The head of the extended family also supervises the guardian's performance of his duties. The guardian's duties are to take care of the orphan ward's needs. The financial needs of the orphan are met from the income from the orphan's property, and whatever is left over from providing for the orphan's needs goes to the guardian in payment for his effort in working the orphan's fields and taking care of the orphan. The guardian also lives in the orphan's house until the need for a guardian has passed.

The Yoruba guardianship relationship ceases once the orphan either reaches puberty or marries. If the orphan wishes to become independent of his or her guardian after puberty but before he or she is sufficiently mature to look after his or her own property, his or her relatives will forbid the end of the relationship. Wards end the guardianship relationship simply by claiming possession of their property. Boys claim their property by the time they reach adulthood. Girls and women claim their property by the time they marry; since all Yoruba women marry, there is always an end to the guardianship relationship.

The guardianship of the mentally ill among the Yoruba is handled differently. Guardians of mentally ill persons are responsible for any damages their wards do. Normally, the guardians of the mentally ill are doctors, and the parents of the wards pay the doctors for their care. Sometimes, however, the ill person is a ward of his or her own parents. Dangerous mentally ill persons are made the wards of the keeper of prisons, and again, it is the ward's parents who pay for his or her requirements. The mentally ill person's property is managed and worked by his or her own parents, and the profits produced are the property of the parents. Should a mentally ill person recover sanity, he or she regains possession of his or her property, but not of the crops on the land or any profits made by his or her parents while the illness was manifest.

Ajisafe, A. K. (1946) *The Laws and Customs of the Yoruba People.*

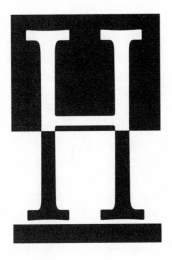

to their decisions, or at least avoid the intimidation of others in making their decisions. In the Micmac Indian society of Nova Scotia, a society with headmen as rulers, it is believed by many that a woman would not have the ability to resist a man who wanted to physically intimidate her.

In some societies, headmen retain their titles for life. This means that men who are well past their physical prime continue to lead and to make decisions. Sometimes these men have made their followers respect them to such an extent that they continue to be followed. Such men may even be more endearing to their followers because they have gained wisdom as they grew older. However, in some cases, once the headman has declined physically, and especially if some accident or disease has impaired his physical or mental powers, he may be a headman in title alone. Other members of his band may continue to address him as a headman, but will refuse to obey his decisions or follow his leadership. They may, in fact, follow another man, one whom they privately address as headman.

No matter which society they are found in, headmen usually, if at all possible, have many children. The number of children a headman can have can be especially large in polygynous societies. A large number of children does two things for the headman. First, it demonstrates that he has the wealth or the hunting and fishing ability to feed a large number of people. This is very impressive to potential followers. Second, and more importantly, a large number of children means that he has a large number of loyal followers who will continue to be loyal to him in years to come. The sons, especially, will help him implement his decisions when they grow older. As well, the daughters can potentially bring their husbands and their own children into the band their father heads.

In some societies, the title of headman traditionally is passed from father to son, usually to the oldest son. The son is typically prepared

HEADMAN

A headman is an informal leader and authority of a band society. As an informal leader and authority, his rights and duties do not arise from occupation of a formal office and are thus limited by his personal abilities and qualities and by the willingness of his followers to follow him and his decisions. Some headmen are thus relatively weak leaders and authorities, while others, even those speaking the same language but living in another band, may be ruthless dictators. Headmen, as the name implies, are men. Women, it appears, are never headmen for two reasons. Headmen live in hunting/fishing/gathering societies, in which the most vital ability is the ability to hunt and to fish. If a band's members fail in their hunting and fishing tasks, which are male tasks, then the band will likely starve to death. Therefore, a good hunter or fisherman will attract followers who are eager to share in his success, or at least to acquire whatever knowledge and skills he has. Such men often become headmen. Headmen are also usually strong men in the prime of their lives. Headmen can thus coerce others into adhering for the position he is to assume while still young. His father tells him about the proper ways to lead the group and about legal cases he has had to decide and the reasons for his decisions. Further lessons are given in the kinds of behavior appropriate for the headman to engage in. But, of course, sometimes a headman's first son will not be physically, intellectually, or temperamentally suitable for the job of headman. In such cases, a younger son, the headman's brother, or the headman's nephew will be chosen as the next headman. Sometimes, the first son is chosen even if he is not a good person for the job of headman. In such instances, he may retain the title of headman but lose his authority and leadership because no one will follow him or abide by his decisions. Again, the headman has no office, and people follow him not because of his title but because of his personal abilities and other qualities. Often, a poor leader will cause many or most of the members of the band to leave the area to form a new band. There are also cases known in which headmen in hereditary systems have told their sons to refuse to accept the title, because the job of the headman is so difficult and time consuming, and because in some cases people become angry with the headman.

One especially well described example of a headman is the headman of the Naskapi Indians of Labrador, Canada. The following example is of the Naskapi headman as he was during the first half of this century. The Naskapi headman traditionally was the first-born son of the previous headman. If without a son, the headman's brother became headman. If neither a son nor a brother was available, the next headman was elected. The headman holds his position for life. If there was to be an election for the next headman, there would be a period of months between the death of the former headman and the election of a new man. During this period, people would think about and discuss their choices for

headman. Once the majority had decided in favor of one man, a respected member of the band would speak on behalf of the chosen man before the group, which was assembled for the summer. If there was no opposition, the man was thereafter the headman. There were only rarely men who opposed the popular choice on their own behalf, and it was considered bad form to do so.

A Naskapi headman must be first of all a good hunter. When he gets too old to hunt well, he loses influence, but not his title. The headman must also show skill in negotiating with the Hudson's Bay Company (to which the Naskapi sell their furs) and with other Naskapi. All headmen are also married, and many have large numbers of children.

The Naskapi headman indicated his position by wearing a feather headdress and, later, a special coat that was given to him by the Hudson's Bay Company. Of course, everyone knew whom he was even without the paraphernalia, and the headman wore his special costume only during the summer meetings and then only to request that people congregate to discuss some important public matter.

The primary duties of the headman were to represent his band to people from the outside world and to maintain peace within his band. The headman had his authority limited by three important factors. The first was that during most of the year the band was split into small hunting groups who lived in a very dispersed fashion, meaning that most people could not contact the headman for assistance even if they wanted to do so. Second, the Naskapi consider it unbecoming to rely on another person for help, especially the headman. It is much more creditable, they believe, to handle problems on one's own. Third, there was a predisposition to solve one's disputes on one's own. This is because the people had to rely upon one another in the harsh environment, and so they were very quick to smooth over most social problems.

Hamilton, W. D. (1984) *The Julian Tribe.*

Lips, Julius E. (1947) "Naskapi Law." *Transactions of the American Philosophical Society* 37(4): 378–492.

Strouthes, Daniel P. (1994) *Change in the Real Property Law of a Cape Breton Island Micmac Band.*

HOMICIDE

Homicide is the killing of a human being by another human being. Murder is the criminal killing of a human being; criminal acts are legal offenses against a society. But killing a human being can involve more than just criminal repercussions. There may be a taboo against killing a human being; if so, the killer may expect to receive supernatural punishment for the killing. Killing a human being can also be a civil offense, and the family of the murdered person may have a legal claim against the murderer for killing one of their number, for loss of services and income, among other things.

While Western conceptions of homicide usually assume that some direct physical action such as shooting, stabbing, poisoning, hitting with vehicle, etc., must occur for a homicide to take place, in many cultures homicide may also take place through witchcraft or sorcery. That is, an individual calls upon supernatural forces to kill another individual, usually through making them ill or by causing them to have an accident. In cultures where people use witchcraft or sorcery to harm others, it does not matter whether or not witchcraft or sorcery genuinely causes a person to die or whether it only explains a death that resulted from another cause such as illness or a serious injury. What does matter and what qualifies witchcraft and sorcery as forms of homicide in some cultures is that the people

believe they can kill another individual or be killed by these means. For example, the Kapauku of New Guinea use witchcraft and sorcery to kill enemies, who are usually people from other communities, but sometimes also from one's own village. In one case, a Kapauku groom died shortly after his wedding and the death was attributed to the actions of a jealous sorcerer. The sorcerer was judged guilty by the village leader and executed by the victim's older brother.

In most cultures the norms that govern social behavior and the legal system delineate different types of homicide. The three criteria used most often to differentiate among types of homicide are intent, premeditation, and the closeness of the relationship between the murderer and the victim. Intent means that the killer wanted the victim to die. Premeditation means that the killer thought about killing the victim before acting and planned the homicide. Closeness means whether the killer and the victim were blood relatives, relatives by marriage, neighbors, members of the same community, members of the same society, or members of different societies.

Western legal systems differentiate on the basis of intent and premeditation (as in legal concepts such as manslaughter, murder, homicide, etc.) and also differentiate on the basis of relationship, as indicated by the use of specific words for certain types of homicide such as infanticide, matricide and patricide, and gerontocide. Western legal systems also differentiate on the basis of the status and role of the victim in the community. For example, assassination refers to murder of a public official for political purposes, while the punishment for killing a police officer is often more severe than the punishment for killing a civilian, indicating that killing a police officer is a more serious form of homicide.

In most non-Western cultures, similar sets of rules distinguish among types of homicide, although these rules may not always be codified into a set of written laws. These rules are important not only because they differentiate among types of homicide and indicate which are acceptable and which are criminal, but also because they determine the severity of punishment meted out to the killer. For example, the Ifugao of the Philippines recognize four types of homicide and have different levels of punishment for each (Barton 1969, [1919]: 78):

(a) The taking of life when there is an entire absence of both intent and carelessness. As for example . . . when a party of hunters have a wild boar at bay. The boar . . . charges the most advanced of the hunters, and in retreating backwards, the latter jabs one of his companions with the shod point of his spear handle. There is no penalty for such a taking of life.

(b) The taking of life when there is clearly an absence of intent, but a degree of carelessness. For example, a number of men are throwing spears at a mark. A child runs in the way, and is killed. The penalty is a fine varying from one-third to two-thirds the amount of the full fine for homicide according to the degree of carelessness.

(c) Intentional taking of the life of another, under the impression that he is an enemy when in reality he is a co-villager or a companion. In case the killer can make the family of the slain understand the circumstances, only a fine is assessed. This fine is called *labod*. If the killer be unrelated to the slain, the full amount of the *labod* is demanded: if related, the amount is usually lessened.

Example: Dumauwat of Baay was irrigating his fields at night. Some of his companions told him that there were some head-hunters from an enemy village near. In the darkness, Dumauwat encountered another man, Likyayu, the betrothed of his daughter. He asked him who was there. On account of the noise of water falling from the rice fields, Likyayu did not hear the inquiry, and said nothing. Dumauwat speared him. Likyayu

cried out. Dumauwat recognized his voice, and carried him home. He furnished animals for sacrifice to secure Likyayu's recovery. Likyayu recovered. Had he died, Dumauwat would have been called on for the full amount of the fine; but had Likyayu been firmly engaged to Dumauwat's daughter, that is, had the *bango* ceremony been performed, the full amount of the *labod* fine would not have been demanded, since the relationship would have been an extenuating circumstance.

(d) The taking of life by persons in a brawl or by an intoxicated or insane person. In case the slain died before his slayer could agree to provide animals for sacrifice, the latter would probably be killed by the kin of the slain if he were of a foreign district. He might be killed if a non-related co-villager. He would be fined the *labod* if a kinsman. He would probably go scot free if a brother or uncle.

The Ifugao also differentiate attempted murder from actual murder, with punishment again inversely related to the closeness of the relationship of the murderer and the intended victim.

In many cultures, whether or not the killer and victim are kin or are members of the same political community is a major consideration in determining whether a homicide is considered a crime. For example, the Kapauku consider the premeditated murder of a member of one's own kin group or political confederacy a crime and execute the killer. However, killing a member of another confederacy is not considered a crime and the killer is not punished, although it might lead to a war between the confederacies. Because the killing of a close relative is an especially serious offense in many cultures, those who kill their children or parents or any close kin in kin-based cultures are often thought to be insane, which sometimes though not always excuses their behavior and forestalls punishment. For example, among the Ona a woman who kills her infant is considered insane and the behavior excused. Among the Dogon, "the murderer is an unfortunate person, the object of pity as much as of repulsion, who could only act as he did at a moment when an unknown force dominated him" (Paulme 1940: 113). However, a Dogon murderer does not escape punishment and is banished from the community, often for life, with his wife allowed to remarry and his property divided among his relatives. The murderer is considered to be dead.

Criminologists and others who study homicide often distinguish among different general types of homicide, some of which are listed below:

assassination
the killing of a political leader or other important public figure for a political purpose

capital punishment
the killing of a criminal that is approved of by the political community

familicide
the killing of an entire nuclear family by a member of the family, usually the husband/father who then kills himself

feuding (blood revenge)
after a homicide, the killing of the murderer or a member of his kin group by the kin of the victim

filicide
the killing of a son or daughter by a parent

fratricide
the killing of a brother by a brother

gerontocide
the killing of the aged

infanticide
the killing of an infant, usually by a parent, a relative, or with the parents' approval

mass murder
the killing of a number of individuals at the same time in the same place usually by one individual

matricide
the killing of a mother by her child

parricide
the killing of a parent by his or her child

serial killing
the killing of a number of individuals over a period of time by one individual

spousal homicide
the killing of an individual by a spouse

suicide
killing oneself

terrorism
the killing of civilians by a political group for a political purpose

The supernatural sanctions against murder are in many societies the strongest of all supernatural sanctions. Among the Cheyenne Indians of the Great Plains, the killing of a Cheyenne by another Cheyenne would cause the sacred arrows of the tribe to become polluted. The sacred arrows are the supernatural center of the tribe, and when they have been polluted bad luck of a supernatural origin could be expected for all the tribe. Two kinds of misfortune were particularly expected and feared: game would disappear from the area, leading to starvation, and the Cheyenne would lose in their battles with their enemies, costing the Cheyenne the lives of many of its people. The Cheyenne could end the supernatural stain on the arrows through a renewal ceremony, but the murderer remained polluted for the rest of his or her life and could not attend any arrow renewal ceremony or come in contact with any other Cheyenne individual's eating or smoking utensil without polluting it.

In many societies, it is legal, and even expected, that the kin of the murdered victim will receive compensation for the death from the killer or from the kin of the killer. In many societies, it is likewise legal and expected that the kin of the murdered person can kill the murderer in revenge.

Homicide is not always criminal or even illegal. During times of war, it may even be a criminal offense for a soldier not to kill members of the enemy forces. The person who carries out the sentence of one who has been given the death penalty is certainly considered no criminal. Also, there are in all societies of which I am aware circumstances under which a person might kill another with no legal repercussions, including killing in self-defense (or, as it is often termed in Western law, justifiable homicide).

Under traditional Cheyenne Indian law, homicide was not considered illegal if it occurred under one of the following four circumstances:

1. To defend against incestuous rape.
2. To rid society of a repeated murderer.
3. When necessary for the military police to carry out an important function.
4. When accidental.

Killing was considered less of an offense if it occurred under conditions of drunkenness, provocation, or an apparent need for self-protection.

Among the Nuer of the Sudan, in Africa, homicide was traditionally always treated as a civil offense. This was due in large part to the absence of a centralized political and legal apparatus; in short, there was no authority who could punish a man who killed another.

Homicide among the Nuer carried with it a genuine threat of prolonged blood feud. The kin of the slain had a duty to avenge the death of their kinsman, and the threat of retaliation was the usual means of preventing future homicides. Moreover, the kinsmen of the slain man could take his revenge upon any of the kin of the killer, and not only upon the killer himself. This made it doubly difficult to kill, since a potential killer would have to deal with his own angry kinsmen (who would be potential victims of retaliation) if he decided to take a life. Normally, however, the killer and his kinsmen try to arrange a peaceful end to the whole affair by paying the kin of the slain person compensation for the death.

After a man killed another, he would normally try to get to the house of the Leopard-Skin Chief, a man who acts as a mediator in such matters. As soon as the killing has taken place, a feud between the kin of the slain and the kin of the killer exists, but once inside the Leopard-Skin Chief's house, the killer cannot be harmed by the kin of the man he killed. Sometimes, the killer's entire family will also live in the house for protection. The killer must observe a taboo of not eating or drinking until some of his blood has been let by the Leopard-Skin Chief. Then a bull calf is slaughtered in a ritual.

The Leopard-Skin Chief will then attempt to negotiate a settlement for the homicide by appealing to the kin of the slain man. Usually, the kin of the slain are willing to accept a settlement, since they gain financially by it and would gain nothing if they simply killed in retaliation. The negotiations are a fairly drawn-out affair and require the sacrifice of several cattle. The total cost of compensation for most types of killing is forty head of cattle. These include the payment to the Leopard-Skin Chief for his efforts and payments to some of the kin of the deceased, especially his father and mother, as well as maternal and paternal uncles. However, the majority of the payment goes to the deceased man's heir for the purpose of paying the bride-price of the deceased man. The deceased man's wife will then bear children who are biologically those of another man, but who are legally the offspring of the deceased. The Nuer consider it very important that the lineage be continued, and this is the reason for this practice. The compensation is paid by the killer and his kin.

The two sets of kin are expected to observe taboos against eating and drinking together and intermarrying, and this taboo can last for generations, even if the civil offense has been peacefully settled. The supernatural sanction for violating the taboo is a bout of painful diarrhea.

Under Nuer law, a death caused by another person is a homicide no matter what the circumstances. However, Nuer law recognizes degrees of homicide, and they are reflected in the rates of compensation paid. The degree of intention is a key factor, for example. The Nuer believe that the weapon with which a man kills another indicates the degree of intention, and they figure compensation on that basis. If a man is killed accidentally, then the one responsible for the circumstances surrounding the death is held accountable, but is usually made to pay only a token compensation. An example would be if a man died because of a fall while working for another man; the employer would pay a compensation of grass and rope.

The honesty of the killer also comes into play in degree of culpability. If the killer denies that he committed a homicide, then he has committed a second offense and will be forced to pay a greater compensation.

If a man causes another a wound that kills him within a period of approximately one year, then the one who inflicted the wound must pay full compensation. If the wound causes death after several years or more, the compensation to be paid is reduced.

The killing of a woman is compensated at the same rate as for men, but it is her family (if she is unmarried) or her husband (if she is married) who receives the compensation. If a married woman commits homicide, it is her husband who must pay compensation, and not her or her family. A woman could not be killed in the pursuit of revenge for a killing or in a blood feud.

Witches, ghouls, and werewolves could be killed without having to pay compensation. Killing a person who had the evil eye was compensated at the rate of only six cattle.

An unmarried woman who died in childbirth was considered the victim of homicide by the man who impregnated her, and he had to fully compensate the death.

See also CAPITAL PUNISHMENT; FEUD.

Barton, Roy F. (1969 [1919]) *Ifugao Law.*

Howell, P. P. (1970 [1954]) *A Manual of Nuer Law: Being an Account of Customary Law, Its Evolution and Development in the Courts Established by the Sudan Government.*

Llewellyn, Karl N., and E. Adamson Hoebel. (1961 [1941]) *The Cheyenne Way.*

Palmer, Stuart. (1965) "Murder and Suicide in Forty Non-Literate Societies." *The Journal of Criminal Law, Criminology, and Police Science* 56: 320–324.

Paulme, Denise. (1940) *Social Organization of the Dogon.* Translated by Frieda Schutze.

Pospisil, Leopold. (1958) *Kapauku Papuans and Their Law.*

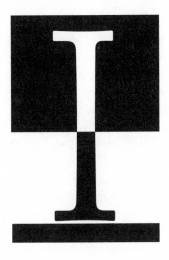

the man's property was given away as a stylized means of showing the family's grief at having lost someone so important and dear to them, and to purify the family of the supernatural pollution caused by the death. It sometimes happened that the man's widow, brothers, and father gave away their own belongings as well, as part of their mourning.

A man could also give his property by means of a will, though the will was oral and not written as in modern U.S. legal practice. Most of the men who did this were old or ill and foresaw the nearness of their deaths. All of the wills made gave the man's property to family members. It was typical that these wills gave most of a man's horses to his daughters, since it was felt that the sons had the ability to get their own horses by raiding. The man's oldest son usually executed the will unless the widow decided upon another male as executor.

The property of an unmarried man who died was handled in a like manner by his parents. He was buried in his finest clothing, and his horse was killed and placed on his grave. His parents gave away the rest of his property to people who were not related to him. If he died in a battle as a result of injuries caused by the enemy, the disposition of his property was somewhat different, however. A portion of his property was kept by his parents and then given to another man, usually the deceased's best friend, as an obligation for him to take an enemy's scalp and thereby to please the deceased man's father.

Among the Naskapi Indians of Labrador, the most valuable and important property a person has to leave to an heir is the right to hunt in a hunting territory, because this is the main source of wealth and food in Naskapi society. In cases of intestamentary succession, the oldest son inherits his father's hunting rights as well as all of the apparatus his father had used in hunting and trapping. If the oldest son is too young to hunt and trap, the deceased man's property goes to his widow until the son is old enough to make

INHERITANCE

Inheritance is tranferance of rights in real or personal property to one's heirs according to the laws of testamentary and intestamentary succession. In other words, the laws of inheritance deal with the disposition of the property of a deceased person. Inheritance may occur by either intestamentary succession (descent) if there is no will, or by testamentary succession (devise) if there is a will and if its provisions deviate from the laws of intestamentary succession. The law also sometimes places limits and conditions upon both the form and the content of a will.

Among the Cheyenne Indians of the Great Plains, the traditional laws for intestamentary succession were that all of a man's property that was not buried with him was to go to his widow. If she wished to behave in an ideal Cheyenne widow's fashion, she would then give the rest of her husband's property to people who were not related to him. Buried with the man were a set of his best clothing, his weapons, pipe, and other personal belongings, and his best horse, which was killed and placed over his grave. The rest of use of them. However, if the oldest son was born elsewhere and a younger son was born on the father's hunting territory, the one born on the hunting territory inherits it from the father.

If the deceased dies without any sons, all of his property goes to his widow. When she dies, the property that was once her husband's is inherited by her oldest daughter and her oldest daughter's husband. If the couple had no children, the property goes to the widow's brothers after she dies. If she has no brothers, the property goes to the husband's brothers. Next in line to inherit are the husband's nephews and then his sisters. If a family line completely dies out, the hunting territory goes to the band, which then redistributes the land to other band members.

A Naskapi man may use a will to give some of his personal property to whomever he wishes after he dies. This will is oral and is communicated to the wife, oldest son, or daughter. The only guarantee that the deceased has that the provisions of the will are to be enforced is that of supernatural sanction. Bad luck is said to come to a whole family if it neglects the instructions of a will.

Among the Micmac Indians of Nova Scotia, the laws regarding intestate inheritance are quite similar to those of the Naskapi. However, among the Micmac both men and women may own real property, although it is usually men who do so. If either spouse should die before the other, the remaining spouse becomes the sole owner of the real and personal property of the deceased. When the remaining spouse dies, all of the property of both parents normally goes to the oldest child regardless of sex. It is believed that the oldest, whether a man or a woman, has the best ability to take care of the needs of the younger offspring. Of course, the remaining parent has the right to do with the property whatever he or she wants while alive, but it is considered proper for the property to pass on to the oldest offspring.

The sequence of heirs in Micmac law conflicts with that of the federal Canadian Indian law, as expressed in the statutes of the Canadian Indian Act. According to that act, real property that is lawfully possessed is part of the possessor's estate and is to be divided between the remaining spouse and the offspring. This means that the widow or widower may be without a house in which to live. This legal sequence of heirs reflects modern Canadian and U.S. law, which is designed to protect the interests of the offspring before the interests of anyone else. The result has all too often been, among the Micmac as well as other Canadian Indians, that a father or a mother has been evicted from the house in which he or she lived by his or her own children. For this reason, the Indian Act was amended to allow the Minister of Indian Affairs and Northern Development to grant permission for the widow to occupy the house in which she and her husband lived at the time of his death. There is no similar protection for men. Among the Micmac, most people do not have lawful possession of the land upon which they reside, so this provision of the Indian Act does not apply to them. Those who occupy the land simply follow traditional Micmac law on this point and allow the remaining spouse to "own" the house (the Micmac conceive of this interest as ownership, no matter what the federal Indian Act says), the land, and all personal property of the deceased spouse.

If there is no spouse and no offspring, the Micmac may rely upon wills to leave their property to a niece, nephew, or an offspring of a niece or nephew. Wills can also be used to invalidate the normal sequence of heirs in intestate succession. Wills are usually oral and are communicated to other family members. It is up to those family members, however, to observe the provisions of the will, and this is not always done; sometimes, there is even a fight over the property, with victory going to the strongest or the most cunning. It is frequently the case that the remaining spouse will use a will to leave his or her house and land to a grandson or granddaughter, because their own children are fully grown and established with their own families and houses by the time they die and have less need of material assistance than do grandchildren.

As the situation involving the Micmac suggests, inheritance law is quite complicated and decisions are influenced by a mix of sociocultural considerations. The following is a legal decision from 1924 in India on the subject of inheritance as it may be affected by adoption according to Hindu law (*The Indian Law Reports, Bombay Series*, 1925: 520-526).

APPELLATE CIVIL.

Before Sir Norman Macleod, Kt., Chief Justice, and Mr. Justice Crump MANIKBAI kom VISHNUDAS GUJJAR and another (Original Plaintiffs), Appellants v. GOKULDAS RAMDAS KARADGI and others (Original Defendants), Respondents.

Hindu Law—Adoption—Rights of daughter of adopted son on adoption.

The adoption of a married Hindu, the sole owner of ancestral property acquired by survivorship on the death of his father, does not deprive his daughter of her right to inheritance to that property.

The rights of a daughter on the adoption of her father considered.

This was an appeal against the decision of N. K. Bapat, First Class Subordinate Judge of Bijapur, in Suit No. 327 of 1920.

Suit to recover possession.

The suit property belonged to one Narsidas, who died in 1883, leaving him surviving his son Ramdas. Ramdas has a wife (plaintiff No. 2) and a daughter (plaintiff No.

1). On October 26, 1908, Ramdas was adopted by Dhondubai, the widow of a near relative.

In 1920, the plaintiffs sued as heirs to Ramdas to recover possession of the property from the defendants. They alleged that even after his adoption Ramdas was in possession of the property in his natural family but that defendants Nos. 1 to 5, who were children of the sisters of Ramdas, dispossessed him in 1910 and 1914.

The defendants by their written statement contended that the suit property was given in gift to the father of defendants Nos. 1 to 3 by Ramdas in 1898 and that they had become owners of it by adverse possession: that neither Ramdas nor plaintiffs Nos. 1 and 2 were the heirs to Narsidas's property but defendants were the heirs: that it was so held in previous litigation between the same parties and hence the present claim of the plaintiffs was barred as *res judicata*.

The trial Judge held *inter alia* that the defendants were the Heirs of Narsidas after the adoption of Ramdas: that Ramdas had made a gift of the suit property to defendant No. 3's father: that defendants Nos. 1 to 4 were not in adverse possession for over twelve years before suit. The suit was dismissed.

H. C. Coyajee, with *A. G. Desai*, for the appellants.

Nilkanth Atmaram, for the respondents.

MACLEOD, C. J.:— The plaintiffs sued to recover possession of the plaint property after a declaration that plaintiff No. 1 was the owner or, in the alternative, if plaintiff No. 1 was not an heir, that plaintiff No. 2 should be declared the owner.

It was alleged that the property originally belonged to two brothers, Narsidas and Shankerdas, but it has been found by the Court below, and that finding has not been disputed in this Court, that the brothers were not in union, and so the following pedigree will be sufficient for the purposes of his appeal. . . .

The property was held jointly by Narsidas and his son Ramdas. Narsidas died in 1883. Ramdas was adopted in 1908 by one Bhagwandas, a first cousin of Narsidas. At the time of his adoption Ramdas had a wife, plaintiff No. 2, and a daughter, plaintiff No. 1.

The plaintiffs claim that they were entitled to the property originally owned jointly by Narsidas and Ramdas, as against the defendants who are the grand-children of Narsidas by his daughters, Radhabai and Ratnabai.

It was decided in *Kalgavda Tavanappa v. Somappa Tamangarda* that when a married Hindu having a son is given in adoption, the son does not like his father lose the *gotra* and right of inheritance in the family of his birth, and does not acquire the *gotra* and right of succession to the property of the family into which his father is adopted. It was also held that when a married Hindu is given in adoption his wife passes with him into the adopted family because according to the Shastras husband and wife form one body. The 2nd plaintiff, therefore, can in no case succeed. But the rights of a daughter in the event of her father being adopted have, as far as we can ascertain, not being considered either in the texts or reported cases, neither have they been discussed by any of the writers on Hindu law. It is not surprising that the texts are silent on the question as in olden times the adoption of a married man having children would be repugnant to orthodox Hindu customs.

The trial Judge has taken it for granted that the main issue was "Who was the heir of Narsidas after the adoption of Ramdas?", and it cannot be disputed that the defendants were never heirs to Narsidas than plaintiff No. 1.

Para. 12 of the judgment says: "After Ramdas left the family by adoption Ekambribai was the heir of Narsidas to whom the property belonged and she lived in the house till her death which took place on September 12, 1912"; and para. 75 says: "the property in dispute belonged to Narsidas. Defendants Nos. 1, 2, 3, 4, and 6 are sons of

the daughters of Narsidas and are his heirs preferable to plaintiff No. 1 or plaintiff No. 2". He had some justification for so holding, as in *Ramchandra v. Manubai*, Ramdas attempted to execute a decree obtained by his father. The case came up to the High Court when it was held that Ramdas by his adoption lost all rights in his father's estate which thereafter went to the heirs of Narsidas. The judgment-debtor was the only party to the proceedings, and rights of the present plaintiff No. 1 as daughter of Ramdas were never taken into consideration. It would have been sufficient for the Court to decide that Ramdas was incompetent to execute the decree without going on to say in whom the right to execute lay. In any event plaintiff No. 1 is entitled to raise the point in the present suit, the question is not *res judicata*, and the dictum of the High Court being obiter must at the best be treated with the respect usually attached to such dicta.

The trial Judge says: "By his adoption Ramdas lost all rights of inheritance in his natural family as completely as if he was never born in it. Inheritance must be traced from the previous male holders".

It is true that his right to the property of his adoptive family accrued as if he had been born in it, and it is equally true that he lost all rights to the property of his natural family. But I think the Judge is led into a fallacy by using the words "rights of inheritance" without regard to the varying circumstances which may exist in different cases. If Narsidas had been alive in 1908 Ramdas would have lost all rights to the family property which he had as coparcener, and all rights to succeed to any self-acquired property of Narsidas. The adoption would have put an end to those rights in the same way as if he had died, but it is quite unnecessary to add a further fiction "as if he had never been born in the family".

It is unfortunate that when we get within the realm of fiction the ordinary rules of logic no longer apply. If the adopted son is to be considered as having been born in his adoptive family, the ordinary result should follow that he takes the whole of his family then in existence into the adoptive family, but as I have pointed out above he does not take his sons with him, and presumably his unmarried daughters are left behind as well. There can be no difficulty with regard to the rights of the son in his father's property. If father and son are joint the son on his father's adoption succeeds by survivorship. If there are other co-parceners the result is the same. If there is a daughter unmarried she is entitled to mainte-nance and marriage expenses. The difficulty arises when the adopted son is the sole owner of ancestral property as Ramdas was. If he is to be treated as having civilly died in the natu-ral family when he was adopted, the property should go to his heirs, as he was the last male-holder, and not to the heirs of his father. If in 1908 he had died a natural death, undoubt-edly plaintiff No. 1 would have been his heir-ess, and if he is to be treated as dead by a fiction, there can be no possible reason for de-parting from the ordinary rule of devolution of property under the Hindu law. One result of tracing descent from the next generation above would be, that if Narsidas and his brother, Shankardas, had been joint, as the plaintiff contended, since Shankardas survived Narsidas the property would go to his heirs and not to the heirs of Narsidas, with the re-sult that Ramdas would have become entitled to the property as son of Bhagwandas, his adoptive father, first cousin of Shankardas, in preference to his brother's son's daughter or his brother's daughter's sons. The fallacy in the passage of the judgment under review lies in the failure to recognize that Ramdas had no right of inheritance to the property of Narsidas to lose. He had already acquired it by survivorship. In *Dattatraya Sakharam v. Govind Sambhaji,* it was held on the authority of the text of Manu, Adhyaya 1, Verse No. 142, that a Hindu, the sole owner of ancestral property, lost his right to the suit property on adoption, but in the case of property acquired by partition it was held in *Mahableslavar*

Narayan v. Sabramanya Shieram, that the suit property was not the estate of the natural fa-ther within the meaning of the above men-tioned text, and therefore the son was divested of it on adoption. Consequently the question who would succeed to it if he were divested did not arise. But I expressed the opinion that then the heir of the defendant at the time of his adoption would have had to be ascertained as if he were dead.

In *Dattatraya Sakharam v. Govind Sambhaji,* also the question was not decided as the mother of the adopted son was the heir of her son and also of the father.

Though there is an objection to referring to an adopted son as civilly dead in his natural family (cf. *Sri Rajah Venkata Narasimha Appa Row v. Sri Rajah Rangayya Appa Row*), I can-not see myself that there is any reason in this case for holding that the property should go to the heirs of Narsidas and not to the heirs of Ramdas.

In my opinion, therefore, plaintiff No. 1 is entitled to succeed to her father's property. There will be a decree for possession and an inquiry as to mesne profits from date to suit with costs throughout.

CRUMP, J.:— I agree.

Appeal allowed.
R. R.

The Indian Law Reports, Bombay Series. (1925) Vol. XLIX. Edited by K. McI. Kemp.

Lips, Julius E. (1947) "Naskapi Law." *Transactions of the American Philosophical Society* 37(4): 378–492.

Llewellyn, Karl N., and E. Adamson Hoebel. (1961 [1941]) *The Cheyenne Way.*

Strouthes, Daniel P. (1994) *Change in the Real Property Law of a Cape Breton Island Micmac Band.*

INTERNATIONAL LAW

International law may be defined as the law that is used to decide disputes between nations, or disputes between individuals of different nations where jurisdiction by the principle of territoriality cannot readily be relied upon. Since no nation will always agree to relinquish its own powers of sovereignty to an external authority by being bound by its decisions, international law is not always law. In other words, each party to the conflict must agree to abide by the decision of a court of international law for law to exist. No court of international law has the ability to force a disputing nation to accept its decisions, especially in the matter of sanctions.

The United Nations (U.N.) is one of the modern sources of international law. It has in recent years been attempting to acquire the ability to force some nations to accept its judgments whether they wish to or not. For example, after Iraq took control of Kuwait in 1990, the U.N. first requested that member nations cease trading with Iraq, and later asked them to participate in an attack on Iraq. Thus, while Iraq was forced to accept a decision that it did not agree to accept (that it withdraw from Kuwait), the U.N. was only able to enforce its decision with the voluntary help of member nations. Of course, these other nations, especially the United States, would most likely have driven Iraqi military forces from Kuwait whether the U.N. had asked them to do so or not. Thus, the U.N.'s ability to enforce its decisions rests upon the political will of a few powerful nations.

The U.N. does not have this kind of power in most decisions and has been generally ineffective in resolving international disputes. The United States, for example, does not ask the U.N. to make decisions when it has a trading dispute with Japan or a dispute over fishing rights with Canada.

The Charter of the United Nations calls for the development and eventual codification of international law, and the U.N. has commissions to pursue that goal.

Another modern source of international law is the International Court of Justice (sometimes informally known as the World Court), a part of the United Nations located at The Hague in the Netherlands. It has fifteen members who are elected by the General Assembly and the Security Council for definite terms. Judgments made by this court may be appealed to the United Nations Security Council.

One example of early international law, and a theoretical and historical basis for modern international law as we know it today, is Roman law's *ius gentium,* or general law. The Romans developed a law called *ius quiritium,* which applied to *quirites,* or Roman citizens. It applied to disputes between two Romans no matter where in the Roman Empire they were. If two non-Roman parties to a dispute originated in the same place within the Roman Empire, for example Judea, Judean law was applied by the Roman courts. But if the two parties came from different parts of the Roman Empire, say Judea and Gaul, *ius gentium* was applied. This was a body of law that the Romans developed to apply to different peoples in the various territories Rome had conquered. *Ius gentium* was made up of laws taken from various parts of the Roman Empire, although the majority of its laws were Roman laws from which specifically Roman features had been removed.

Other theoretical foundations for modern international law are as follows: (1) abstract reasoning, including Natural Law, (2) judicial precedents from earlier cases and from the decisions of courts within various nations, and (3) custom.

When legal scholars today speak of international law, they speak about a social movement that began in Europe in the seventeenth century and that depended initially on the fact that Roman law formed a common basis of law in all of the European nations. In the seventeenth century, Hugo Grotius, a Dutchman, had been alarmed by the destructiveness of the Thirty Years War. He wished to reduce both the causes and the destructiveness of war, and to do so he wrote a book called *De Jure Belli ac Pacis* (*The Law of War and Peace*). He relied upon Natural Law as a philosophical basis for his work. The principles of Natural Law and of Roman law were similar, and so many of his ideas were fairly readily understood by Europeans. These same principles were the basis for the laws of the North and South American legal systems. Grotius was the first to discover that all Natural Law falls into one of two categories: either it is public law (the law dealing with matters of government) or it is private law (law dealing with the private affairs of individuals).

A later major voice in the movement towards international law was Sir Henry Maine, who in his book *International Law* also sought a way to make war less destructive. These movements later bore fruit in the various Conventions of Geneva and Lausanne and many others, the Treaties of Westphalia and many other international treaties, the Permanent Court of International Justice (later reconstituted as the International Court of Justice under the control of the United Nations), the League of Nations, and the United Nations. The actual basis for nearly all international law in the modern world of nation-states are the agreements that nations make with each other. The sovereign powers of the nations have acknowledged that they will be bound by these agreements and, in effect, have had to relinquish some of their power as sovereign states to comply with these agreements.

A critical portion of international law concerns jurisdiction. International courts are sometimes asked to decide which nation has jurisdiction over a specific territory. These kinds of questions are usually answered on the basis of which nation has sovereignty, and laws have been established to answer such questions. The interests of nation-states always take precedence over the interests of indigenous tribal or band societies in determining jurisdiction.

A second question of jurisdiction has to do with cases in which the territorial principle of jurisdiction is unclear or conflicting, and this usually happens in cases that involve travel on ships. Take, for example, the case of *Regina v. Anderson* (Great Britain, Court of Criminal Appeal, 1868). In this case, an American man stood accused of murdering another man while on a British ship, which was at the time in French waters. Arguments could be made on behalf of jurisdiction in American courts (because the accused was American), on the basis of the nationality principle of law, in which the state wishes to have jurisdiction over its own citizens and any other people who have special ties to the state. An argument could also be made for British jurisdiction, since the offense occurred on a British ship, by the territorial principle of law. However, the territorial principle could also be invoked by the French, since the offense occurred in French waters. The British Court of Criminal Appeal noted that the French courts certainly could have tried the case, but by the provisions of the treaties of Ortolan, the French do not claim jurisdiction over foreign vessels in French waters unless requested to do so by the master of the ship or if the case involves a disturbance of the peace at a port. It is generally regarded in cases of this type that a ship is a "floating island" and is part of the nation in which the ship is registered. Further, one of the chief principles bearing on the selection of jurisdiction in legal cases of international involvement is comity. The term *comity* refers not to a legal principle but rather to a principle of courteous behavior, in which one court that could claim jurisdiction allows another court, which could also claim jurisdiction, to try the case if it has claimed jurisdiction first. In the case above, the British claimed jurisdiction first, and the French courts did not try to take jurisdiction by virtue of comity.

Hugo Grotius (1583–1645), Dutch jurist and author of De Jure Belli ac Pacis (The Law of War and Peace)

One of the most important parts of international law concerns extradition. Because nations wish that those who break their own laws be held accountable to their courts, they agree with other nations to surrender an alleged criminal to the jurisdiction where the crime took place. The basis for extradition is treaty, usually a bilateral agreement between two nations for one to extradite to the other wanted alleged criminals. Originally, the treaties specified the crimes for which one could be extradited, but this method did not work very well since some important crimes were often accidentally omitted; therefore, the usual way is to specify extradition for crimes that carry possible sentences of, for example, two years or more. In modern times, nations will extradite alleged criminals only if they are to be tried on the charges for which they are extradited (and not some other new charges), only if the alleged offense is a crime in both nations, and only if sanctions are relatively congruent. This allows the extraditing nation to make sure that the individual extradited is tried more or less in concert with its own laws and morals. For example, Canada, which has no death penalty, will not extradite U.S. citizens to the United States if they are to face the possibility of the death penalty once in a U.S. court. Nations also sometimes give preference to their own citizens; Germany, Italy, and France, for example, will not extradite their own citizens to a foreign country. As a further protection for the rights of the accused, modern nations will not extradite an individual if they determine that there is insufficient evidence to take the case to trial.

Following is an actual treaty of extradition between the United States and Norway (*Treaties and Other International Agreements of the United States of America.* (n.d.) Vol. 10, 445–449).

NORWAY
EXTRADITION

Treaty signed at Washington June 7, 1893

Ratified by Norway July 10, 1893
Senate advice and consent to ratification November 1, 1893
Ratified by the President of the United States November 3, 1893
Ratifications exchanged at Washington November 8, 1893
Proclaimed by the President of the United States November 9, 1893
Entered into force December 8, 1893
Amended by treaty of December 10, 1904
Supplemented by treaty of February 1, 1938.

28 Stat. 1187; Treaty Series 262

The United States of America and His Majesty the King of Sweden and Norway, being desirous to confirm their friendly relations and to promote the cause of justice, have resolved to conclude a new treaty for the extradition of fugitives from justice between the United States of America and the Kingdom of Norway, and have appointed for that purpose the following Plenipotentiaries:

The President of the United States of America, W. Q. Gersham, Secretary of State of the United States, and
His Majesty the King of Sweden and Norway, J. A. W. Grip, His Majesty's Envoy Extraordinary and Minister Plenipotentiary to the United States,

who, after having communicated to each other their respective full powers, found in good and due form, have agreed upon and concluded the following articles:

Article I
The Government of the United States and the Government of Norway mutually agree to deliver up persons who, having been charged with or convicted of any of the crimes and offenses specified in the following article, committed within the jurisdiction of one of the contracting parties, shall seek an asylum or be found within the territories of the other: Provided,

that this shall only be done upon such evidence of criminality as, according to the laws of the place where the fugitive or person so charged shall be found, would justify his or her apprehension and commitment for trial if the crime or offense had been there committed.

Article II

Extradition shall be granted for the following crimes and offenses:

1. Murder, comprehending assassination, parricide, infanticide, and poisoning; attempt to commit murder; manslaughter, when voluntary.

2. Arson.

3. Robbery, defined to be the act of feloniously and forcibly taking from the person of another money or goods, by violence or putting him in fear; burglary.

4. Forgery, or the utterance of forged papers; the forgery or falsification of official acts of government, of public authorities, or of courts of justice, or the utterance of the thing forged or falsified.

5. The counterfeiting, falsifying or altering of money, whether coin or paper, or of instruments of debt created by national, state, provincial, or municipal governments, or of coupons thereof, or of bank notes, or the utterance or circulation of the same; or the counterfeiting, falsifying or altering of seals of state.

6. Embezzlement by public officers; embezzlement by persons hired or salaried, to the detriment of their employers; larceny.

7. Fraud or breach of trust by a bailee, banker, agent, factor, trustee, or other person acting in a fiduciary capacity, or director or member or officer of any company, when such act is made criminal by the laws of both countries and the amount of money or the value of the property misappropriated is not less than $200 or Kroner 740.

8. Perjury, subornation of perjury.

9. Rape; abduction; kidnapping.

10. Willful and unlawful destruction or obstruction of railroads which endangers human life.

11. Crimes committed at sea:

(a) Piracy, by statute or by the law of nations.

(b) Revolt, or conspiracy to revolt, by two and more persons on board a ship on the high seas against the authority of the master.

(c) Wrongful sinking or destroying a vessel at sea, or attempting to do so.

(d) Assaults on board a ship on the high seas with intent to do grievous bodily harm.

12. Crimes and offenses against the laws of both countries for the suppression of slavery and slave-trading.

Extradition is also to take place for participation in any of the crimes and offenses mentioned in this Treaty, provided such participation may be punished, in the United States as a felony, and in Norway by imprisonment at hard labor.

Article III

Requisitions for the surrender of fugitives from justice shall be made by the diplomatic agents of the contracting parties, or in the absence of these from the country or its seat of government, may be made by the superior consular officers.

If the person whose extradition is requested shall have been convicted of a crime or offense, a duly authenticated copy of the sentence of the court in which he was convicted, or if the fugitive is merely charged with a crime, a duly authenticated copy of the warrant of arrest in the country where the crime has been committed, and of the deposition or other evidence upon which such warrant was issued, shall be produced.

The extradition of fugitives under the provisions of this treaty shall be carried out in the United States and in Norway, respectively, in conformity with the laws regulating extradition for the time being in force in the state on which the demand for surrender is made.

Article IV

Where the arrest and detention of a fugitive are desired on telegraphic or other information in advance of the presentation of formal proofs, the proper course in the United States shall be to apply to a judge or other magistrate authorized to issue warrants of arrest in extradition cases and present a complaint on oath, as provided by the statutes of the United States.

When, under the provision of this article, the arrest and detention of a fugitive are desired in the Kingdom of Norway, the proper course shall be to apply to the Foreign Office, which will immediately cause the necessary steps to be taken in order to secure the provisional arrest or detention of the fugitive.

The provisional detention of a fugitive shall cease and the prisoner be released if a formal requisition for his surrender, accompanied by the necessary evidence of his criminality, has not been produced under the stipulations of this Treaty, within two months from the date of his provisional arrest or detention.

Article V

Neither of the contracting parties shall be bound to deliver up its own citizens or subjects under the stipulations of this Treaty.

Article VI

A fugitive criminal shall not be surrendered if the offense in respect of which his surrender is demanded be of a political character, or if he proves that the requisition for his surrender has, in fact, been made with a view to try to punish him for an offense of a political character.

No person surrendered by either of the high contracting parties to the other shall be triable or tried, or be punished, for any political crime or offense, or for any act connected therewith, committed previously to his extradition.

If any question shall arise as to whether a case comes within the provisions of this article, the decision of the authorities of the government on which the demand for surrender is made, or which may have granted the extradition, shall be final.

Article VII

Extradition shall not be granted, in pursuance of the provisions of this Treaty, if legal proceedings or the enforcement of the penalty for the act committed by the person claimed has become barred by limitation, according to the laws of the country to which the requisition is addressed.

Article VIII

No person surrendered by either of the high contracting parties to the other shall, without his consent, freely granted and publicly declared by him, be triable or tried or be punished for any crime or offense committed prior to his extradition, other than that for which he was delivered up, until he shall have had an opportunity of returning to the country from which he was surrendered.

Article IX

All articles seized which are in the possession of the person to be surrendered at the time of his apprehension, whether being the proceeds of the crime or offense charged, or being materially as evidence in making proof of the crime or offense, shall, so far as practicable and in conformity with the laws of the respective countries, be given up when the extradition takes place. Nevertheless, the rights of third parties with regard to such articles shall be duly respected.

Article X

If the individual claimed by one of the high contracting parties, in pursuance of the present Treaty, shall also be claimed by one or several other powers on account of crimes or offenses committed within their respective jurisdictions, his extradition shall be granted to the state whose demand is first received: Provided, that the government from which extradition is sought is not bound by treaty to give preference otherwise.

Article XI

The expenses incurred in the arrest, detention, examination, and delivery of fugitives under this Treaty shall be borne by the state in whose name the extradition is sought: Provided, that the demanding government shall not be compelled to bear any expense for the services of such public officers of the government from which extradition is sought as receive a fixed salary: And, provided, that the charge for the services of such public officers as receive only fees or perquisites shall not exceed their customary fees for the acts or services performed by them had such acts or services been performed in ordinary criminal proceedings under the laws of the country of which they are officers.

Article XII

The present Treaty shall take effect on the thirtieth day after the date of the exchange of ratifications, and shall not operate retroactively. On the day on which it takes effect the Convention of March 21,1860, shall, as between the governments of the United States and of Norway, cease to be in force except as to crimes therein enumerated and committed prior to that date.

The ratifications of the present Treaty shall be exchanged at Washington as soon as possible, and it shall remain in force for a period of six months after either of the contracting governments shall have given notice of a purpose to terminate it.

In witness whereof, the respective Plenipotentiaries have signed the above articles, both in the English and the Norwegian languages, and have hereunto affixed their seals.

Done in duplicate, at the city of Washington this seventh day of June, one thousand eight hundred and ninety-three.

Walter Q. Gersham   [Seal]
J. A. W. Grip   [Seal]

Another field of international law deals with domestic courts that are called upon to make decisions concerning companies that do business in more than one nation. The laws regulating business activities differ from nation to nation, and one branch of a business in one nation may be forced by law to do things that are forbidden by law in another nation. For example, German bank secrecy laws prohibit the disclosure of some types of bank documents. But in the case of *U.S. v. First National City Bank* (U.S. Second Circuit Court of Appeals, 1968), the court subpoenaed documents in the possession of the German branch of the First National City Bank. The bank protested that it could not release the documents, because to do so would result in their prosecution by German authorities. The U.S. court said that the bank must comply, because whatever liabilities the bank suffered were insufficient to excuse its not releasing the document. The courts have generally said that, in this and similar cases, local law always precedes the law of other nations.

In reading studies of international law, one will almost always see authors referring to the tradition of Western law as the only source of international law. Many will claim that international law did not exist before a point in time shortly after the turn of the twentieth century, when Western philosophical and social movements came together, prompted by the carnage of World War I, to begin to build institutions to dispense international law. Others have said that international law only came about after the development of modern nation-states, and could not have preceded them. This is not true. International law has been observed in several tribal and band societies, though there probably have been more societies in which international law existed but for which we have no evidence. We find international law in band and tribal societies where we find efforts to improve relations between adjoining societies.

The Choctaw Indians of what is now the Mississippi region, for example, concluded a treaty with a group of Cherokee Indians to the effect that if a Choctaw murdered a Cherokee, or vice versa, only the offender could be killed in revenge, and that any other person, even a member of the family of the killer, could not be harmed in revenge. The Choctaw also made a similar treaty with the nearby Chickasaw Indians. After much of the population of the Choctaws and of other Indian peoples of the Southeast were forced to move to Oklahoma, the Choctaws, along with other relocated peoples, the Cherokees, Chickasaws, Creeks, and Seminoles, made a code of international law in 1859 to govern their relations. This code provided for extradition of accused criminals, for the trying of criminal acts (including the harboring of escaped slaves) according to the principle of territoriality, for the changing of tribal citizenship, and for intertribal cooperation in reducing the sale of alcoholic beverages.

Other societies also came together to regulate their intergroup relations through the use of international law. The five Iroquois tribes of what is now New York State (the Mohawk, Seneca, Cayuga, Oneida, and Onondaga) united in the Iroquois Confederacy, well before European contact, in an effort to end their hostilities with each other. This confederacy was similar in structure, function, and purpose to the much-later League of Nations and United Nations. This confederacy also served to coordinate international military activities, just as the present-day United Nations does in fighting its common enemies. In fact, a group of Indians further to the northeast, the Penobscot, the Passamaquoddy, the Maliseet, and the Micmac, who were long-time enemies of the Iroquois, also came together among themselves in the Wabanaki Confederacy in order to coordinate their military resistance to the Iroquois and to the English; in the process, they developed international law amongst themselves.

Perhaps the best described case of international law in a tribal society is that of the Kapauku Papuans of New Guinea. The Kapauku live in villages that are frequently united under a powerful big man into confederacies. In the 1950s, when their society and legal system were studied, it was the case that when members of the same Kapauku confederacy had disputes, most were handled legally or in accordance with established legal principles. However, when disputes involved two people of different confederacies, the law came into play in only a minority of disputes. In fact, disputes between members of different confederacies sometimes became the basis for war between the confederacies. Other disputes were settled peacefully without the involvement of authorities. In cases involving legal decisions in disputes between private parties of different confederacies, the cases were usually decided by an authority who was a member of the confederacy to whom the offender belongs. It was up to the authorities of the same confederacy to which the offender belonged to punish the offender, or to require him to pay compensation, in order to maintain good or peaceful relations with the confederacy to which the victims belonged. The authority did so to avoid warfare against the entire membership of the village or even confederacy. The entire village was considered by the victim of an offense liable for the damages or thefts caused by any member of the village. Thus, a group, usually including the victim, would come to the village of the offender to press the case of the victim, or to take revenge or whatever compensation they felt was just from anyone in the village, and by force if opposed. This is seen in the following case, which occurred in 1955 in the village of Botu (and which is taken from Pospisil, 1958: 223–224).

A man of the village, named Ij Bun, made his living primarily by theft and fraudulent transactions involving the buying and selling of swine, rather than by horticulture, which was the normal way of making an honorable living. One time, Ij Bun, who belonged to the Ijaaj-Pigome Confederacy, was travelling in the Tigi region, where there was another confederacy. There, he met Ba Amo, who, on Ij Bun's promise of three large pigs, loaned Ij Bun a considerable sum of money (pigs, being the major source of wealth in the Kapauku world, were worth a good deal of money). Some months later, people from the Tigi region came to collect the pigs, and found out that not only did Ij Bun have no pigs, but had also spent the money he had received from Ba Amo, and thus could not return it. The people from Tigi threatened to forcibly take what was justly due them from the other members of the village. The people of Botu pleaded with them not to do that, but to take their revenge upon Ij Bun, who was away and who, when summoned, refused to return. Some men of the Ijaaj-Pigome Confederacy called for Ij Bun's death. Then a large party of armed men from the Tigi region returned two weeks later, and confronted Ij Bun, who had returned to Botu. After his promise to pay his creditor, as guaranteed by the village headman and Ij Bun's relatives, the armed men left.

Then Ij Bun's trial began. The authorities included three village headmen, a lineage headman, and the headman of the entire Ijaaj-Pigome Confederacy. At the trial, which took several days to complete and which involved much public denunciation of Ij Bun and public speeches by members of the village, the authorities finally decided on leniency with respect to Ij Bun. He was not killed, but merely reprimanded. In addition, the authorities collected from Ij Bun's kin the amount of the debt so as to pay off his creditor. They reprimanded him by warning him that he would come to a bad end if he did not change his ways, and that he had narrowly escaped such a fate this time.

See also CONSTITUTION.

Bishop, William W., Jr. (1971) *International Law: Cases and Materials.*

Debo, Angie. (1961 [1934]) *The Rise and Fall of the Choctaw Republic.*

Kratochwil, Friedrich. (1985) "The Role of Domestic Courts as Agencies of the International Legal Order." In *International Law: A Contemporary Perspective,* edited by Richard Falk, Friedrich Kratochwil, and Saul Mendlovitz, 236–263.

Maine, Henry Sumner. (1978 [1888]) *International Law: A Series of Lectures Delivered before the University of Cambridge 1887.*

Pospisil, Leopold. (1958) *Kapauku Papuans and Their Law.*

Swift, Richard. (1969) *International Law: Current and Classic.*

Treaties and Other International Agreements of the United States of America, 1776-1949. (n.d.) Vol. 10, Nepal-Peru. Compiled under the direction of Charles I. Bevans, LL.B.

The term *jurisdiction* refers to the authority to decide a legal case. It is derived from the Latin *juris dictio* (the judge's speaking). Jurisdictional issues are questions as to which legal authority is to decide any particular case. This issue is of central importance in discussions of the subjects of the territorial principle of law, the personality principle of law, and international law. Jurisdictional issues come up in U.S. courts and in the very similar Canadian courts more frequently than one might suspect. In Canada, the wills of Canadian Indians have been probated by provincial courts, even though the federal Indian Act gives jurisdiction over the probate of Indian wills to the federal Department of Indian Affairs and Northern Development. We might also take as a hypothetical case one in which a Native American who is a corporal in the army murders another Native American who is a captain in the army while both are on the Navajo reservation in Arizona. Because they were in Arizona, an argument could be made for the trial to be held in an Arizona state court. Because they were Indians on

a reservation, an argument could be made that the trial should be held in a federal court because the reserve is federal land and Indians are administered by the federal government and not by the states. Because they were both active military personnel at the time of the murder, an argument could also be made that a military court should hear and decide the case.

Jurisdictional issues in the Tibetan legal system were equally complex. There were nine factors that could influence the selection of jurisdiction in a particular case.

The first of these factors was the territoriality principle. Normally, a case was handled within the territorial unit in which the offense occurred. However, if the parties to the case wanted their legal hearing to be conducted in another court, the local courts of the territory could not prevent them from doing so. Further, if the local courts wished, they could refuse to hear and decide a case that occurred within the territory they represented.

The type of offense committed was also a factor in Tibetan jurisdictional issues. The territorial principle, as noted above, could be neglected if the parties to the dispute so chose. However, this option did not exist for cases involving serious crimes such as murder, rioting, or large-scale robbery; it was compulsary for local courts to hear and decide such cases.

Consent was a third factor in deciding jurisdiction. It was required in all but a few types of cases that both parties involved in the dispute and the court itself agree that the case be handled by the chosen court. If any of the three (either party or the court) did not agree to the choice of court, the legal hearing would be held elsewhere. This factor was operative unless the case concerned the serious crimes noted above or a government official commanded that he himself would decide the case in his court.

A fourth factor was the power of the government to refer some cases to particular courts. It was the Cabinet and the Highest Ecclesiastical

Office that referred most of these cases, and it was these governmental bodies that decided the appropriate court for any particular case. For example, the Cabinet was known sometimes to refer relatively small property cases or civil suits to the High Court of Tibet.

It was also possible for those who had worked for a particular court, or who had relatives who worked for a particular court, to have their legal hearings at these courts. Of course, the likelihood that the court would decide in favor of someone related to or on friendly grounds with the legal authorities was considered, and the opponent in the case always had the right to refuse his or her consent to the use of that court. However, the opponent might allow the court to be used, especially if he or she had a strong case, because the party with relatives or friends in the court would be more likely to accept that court's verdict.

Jurisdiction also depended on the factor of the social rank of the individuals involved. Those of very high rank were not brought before ordinary courts. The father of the Thirteenth Dalai Lama once beat a man in the city of Lhasa, and he could not even be arrested by ordinary police; his case was dealt with by a specially assembled group of governmental officials. The Dalai Lama himself was a legal authority for at least some disputes among royalty. Some of the disputes involving the highly ranked were treated in political rather than legal forums, including the National Assembly and the Cabinet. On the other hand, disputes among the lowest social ranks, including blacksmiths, beggars, butchers, and executioners, were almost never tried in the courts. Such people often settled their disputes by means of self-redress. They were further unlikely to be taken to court by a plaintiff, since they rarely had any money that could be taken from them in a legal settlement.

Foreigners frequently had court systems of their own in Tibet. Cases involving Nepalese in Lhasa were handled by the the Office for Nepalese, while those in the rural hinterlands were handled by the local district courts. Legal disputes involving all other foreigners were decided by the Office for Foreigners, located in Lhasa.

Tibetan monks also had their own courts, which dealt with cases involving disputes between monks that occurred within the monastery. Disputes that occurred outside the monastery, involving either two monks or a monk and someone who was not a monk, were usually resolved by secular courts.

Finally, military men also had their own courts that decided disputes between military personnel. If a member of the military was a defendant in a case involving someone who was not in the military, the case was also decided by the military court system. On the other hand, if the military man was the plaintiff or victim of a crime, the case was decided by the ordinary Tibetan courts.

See also INTERNATIONAL LAW; PERSONALITY PRINCIPLE OF LAW; SELF-REDRESS; TERRITORIAL PRINCIPLE OF LAW.

Barton, Roy F. (1973 [1949]) *The Kalingas: Their Institutions and Custom Law.*

French, Rebecca. (1990) *The Golden Yoke: A Legal Ethnography of Tibet Pre-1959.*

JURISPRUDENCE

Jurisprudence may be defined in two ways. One commonly used meaning for the term is as a synonym for *law*. Legal scholars, on the other hand, use the term to refer to the science of law. As a science, *jurisprudence* refers specifically to the lawyer's study of legal precepts and technique in light of information supplied by disciplines other than law. Much of what is called jurisprudence in modern U.S. legal journals is not this, but rather simple discussions of recent trends in legal decision making.

The noted legal scholar Roscoe Pound proposed four categories of jurisprudence, as follows.

1. **Analytical.** Analytical jurisprudence involves the study of legal precepts to understand how they form logical and consistent patterns. One of the most important tasks of analytical jurisprudence is to prevent laws from becoming contradictory with each other and with principles of justice, something that is not done very well in U.S. law. For example, people who commit manslaughter may receive prison sentences of only a few years, but in one case a man who pinched two women was sentenced to ten years in prison. In this example, we see an obvious conflict between the law and principles of justice; principles of justice are supposed to be built into sentencing laws in the United States. Another subject studied by scholars of analytic jurisprudence is theories of justice, such as Natural Law.

2. **Historical.** Scholars of historical jurisprudence study the history of jurisprudence itself, as well as the history of particular legal systems. They want to answer questions like "How did we arrive at the legal system we have?"

3. **Philosophical.** Philosophical jurisprudence involves the application of philosophical reasoning to the problems of justice in the law.

4. **Sociological.** Scholars of sociological jurisprudence study a range of related subjects. Some study human behavior and how it conforms to the law or how it differs from the law. Others are interested in how human behavior influences the law. Still others study the relationship between law and society in order to make scientific generalizations about the law, such as whether laws have the intended effect on behavior. Legal anthropologists are most interested in this last category of sociological jurisprudence.

The following decision (*The All Pakistan Legal Decisions*, 1993 45: 44–53) shows how legal authorities in an Islamic country solved a potentially difficult legal dilemma. They had to decide whether the statutes made by the Pakistani legislature were in conflict with the rules set down in the Qur'an (Koran). In predominantly Islamic countries, governments attempt to implement rules in the Qur'an in the nation's actual legal system. Thus, ideally, all legal statutes made by the legislatures should agree with the rules laid down in the Qur'an, and if they do not they are frequently cast aside by the legal authorities.

PLD 1993 Federal Shariat Court 44

Before Tanzihur Rahman, C. J., Fida Muhammad Khan *and Abaid Ullah Khan, JJ*

SOHAIL HAMEED—Petitioner
versus
FEDERATION OF PAKISTAN—
Respondent

Sariat Petition No. 4-K of 1992, decided on 12th November, 1992.

(a) Islamic Jurisprudence—
—Crime and punishment—Person who commits a crime, he alone would be liable to punishment for the commission of the crime and no other person would be liable in his place. [p. 46]A
Al-Qur'an: 165:6; 79:38; 2:286; 16:126 and 6:164 ref.

(b) Islamic Jurisprudence—
—Crime and punishment—Intention—Mere

intention not coupled with any preparation or attempt to translate the intention into action is not liable for any punishment—Even after having an intention to commit a crime followed by preparation to commit same, if a crime is not committed for some reason the mere intention or preparation is not liable to punishment specified for the crime itself, unless the preparation by itself is a crime. [p. 47]B

(c) Islamic Jurisprudence—
—Crime and punishment—Intention—If a person performs a bad deed with good intention, the badness of that action will remain there. [p. 47]C

(d) Islamic Jurisprudence—
—Crime and punishment—Qisas—If a group of persons kill a person, then the entire group involved in the murder would be put to death in Qisas. [p. 49]D

(e) Islamic Jurisprudence—
—Crime and punishment—Common intention—If several persons commit an act of aggression against a single person in furtherance of common intention, all of them would be liable to punishment. [p. 50]E

(f) Penal Code (XLV of 1860)—
—S. 34—Scope and implication of S.34, P.P.C. [pp. 51, 52]F & G
    Inam Bux v. The State (PLD 1983 SC 35); Sultan v. Emperor (AIR 1931 Lah. 749) and Ibra Akanda v. Emperor (AIR 1944 Cal. 339(358): 45 Cr. LJ 771 ref.)

(g) Penal Code (XLV of 1860)—
—S.34—Constitution of Pakistan (1973), Art. 203-D—Repugnancy to Injunctions of Islam—Provision of S.34, P.P.C. does not offend any Injunction of Islam.
    An individual involved in a criminal act may not be sufficiently motivated to execute his criminal design but aided, abetted and encouraged by the presence and participation of others may provide him the sufficient tools to complete the offence. The culpability of all the accused in such cases is co-extensive and embraces the principal actor and his accessories to the act. All the participants with common intention deserve like treatment to be meted out to them in law.
    Section 34, P.P.C. does not offend any Injunction of Islam, laid down in the Holy Qur'an and Sunnah of the Holy Prophet (p.b.u.h.). [p.53]H

Petitioner in person.
Iftikhar Hussain Ch., Standing Counsel for Respondent.

Date of hearing: 7th October, 1992.

JUDGMENT

TANZIL-UR-RAHMAN, C. J.—1. This Sariat Petition challenges section 34 of the Pakistan Penal Code on the ground of its being repugnant to the Injunctions of Islam as laid down in the Holy Qur'an and Sunnah of the Holy Prophet (p.b.u.h.). The said section is reproduced as under:—

> "S.34. When a criminal act is done by several persons, in furtherance of the common intention of all, each of such persons is liable for that act in the same manner as if it were done by him alone."

According to section 34, when a criminal act is done by several persons in furtherance of the common intention of all, each of such persons is liable for that act in the same manner as if it were done by him alone.

2. The contention of the petitioner is that in Islam there is no punishment for intention. Reliance has been placed on the following verse:

> "No bearer of the burden can bear the burden of others." (Al-Qur'an, 165:6).

It, however, seems relevant to also quote the following verses of the Holy Qur'an:—

"Every soul will be held in pledge for its deeds." (Al-Qur'an, 79:38).

"In his favor shall be whatever good he does, and against him whatever evil he does." (Al-Qur'an, 2:286).

"If you have to respond to an attack (in argument) respond only to the extent of the attack leveled against you." (Al-Qur'an, 16:126).

"And whatever (wrong) any human being commits rest upon himself alone." (Al-Qur'an, 6:164).

3. According to the above verses of the Holy Qur'an the basic principle of Islamic criminal justice seems to be that the person who commits a crime, he alone would be liable to punishment for the commission of the crime and no other person would be liable in his place.

4. As regards the contention of the petitioner that there is no punishment for the mere intention, the following Hadith seems to be relevant and are thus quoted below:—
(i) "It is reported from the Holy Prophet (p.b.u.h.) To have said that—

"Allah Almighty has exempted their followers from any penalty for what is in their hearts unless it is translated into action."

(ii) "It is also reported from the Holy Prophet (p.b.u.h.) To have said that—

"The person who intends to do any virtuous act but does not perform it, a reward shall be written in his account and the person who intends to commit a crime but for some reason, does not act upon it in such circumstance, nothing shall be recorded against him."

5. Abu Zahra, a renounced renowned jurist of Egypt in his Al-Jarima wal Uquba fil Shari'ah Al-Islamia page 350 writes that—

"Mere intention is not subject to punishment unless it is done practically."

6. On account of his principle mere intention not coupled with any preparation or attempt to translate the intention into action is not liable for any punishment. Thus even after having an intention to commit a crime followed by preparation to commit it, if a crime is not committed for some reason the mere intention or preparation is not liable to punishment specified for the crime itself, unless the preparation by itself is a crime.

7. The petitioner also submitted that the actions (liable to reward) go into intentions. This phrase is, in fact, a part of a long Hadith of the Holy Prophet (p.b.u.h.) narrated from him by Hazrat Umar. This Hadith is narrated by Imam Bukhari in his Sahih as first Hadith under Kitab al-Wahi and is also mentioned in Al-Mishkat as the first Hadith under Kitab al-Imam. After the above part of the Hadith the Holy Prophet (p.b.u.h.) Said, i.e., a human being will get (in result) what he intends for.

It was then stated by the Holy Prophet in the said Hadith that:

"i.e., who migrates with the intention to seek pleasure of Allah and His Apostle, his migration from Makka to Madina will be for the sake of Allah and His Apostle and who migrates (from Makka to Madina) for worldly gain and marrying with certain woman, his migration will be relatable to that intention with which he migrated."

Therefore, it can be inferred that if one performs a bad deed with good intention, the badness of that action will remain there, e.g., if a person steals another's property with the intention that he will help the poor with that stolen property, the mere intention will not render the theft as lawful. The theft will remain theft and he will be liable to punishment in accordance with law. No matter the intention of committing theft may be good.

8. In so far as the question of doing an act jointly in furtherance of common intention and its liability on each of them is concerned, it seems pertinent to refer to an incident that occurred during the days of Umar, the second Caliph. It is narrated in Al-Musannaf Abi Shaibah, Vol. IX, page 347 that—

"The husband of a woman of the city San'a disappeared by leaving her step-son in the house. In his absence, the woman had illicit relations with a person and said to her friend that this child will nickname them by disclosing their relation and asked him to kill the child. When he refused to do so she discontinued her illicit relation with him. Ultimately, the woman, her friend, her servant and another person jointly agreed to kill the child. After killing, they cut his body into pieces and then threw it into a well. When the incident came to the knowledge of the people the Governor of Yemen arrested the persons concerned. He and other culprits make confession before him. The Governor of Yemen brought the matter into the notice of Hazrat Umar. In reply, Hazrat Umar ordered him to kill all of them and said "By God, if all the inhabitants of San'a participated in committing this crime, I would have killed all of them."

9. The same incident has been stated in Al-Mufiqat by Imam Shatibi. It reads as under:—

"Hazrat Umar executed five or seven persons in retaliation of a single person, whom they had killed treacherously. Because Hazrat deemed it expedient for the protection and security of human lives. If several persons are not killed in retaliation of a single person, then the crime of human massacre will not be completely eradicated by the law of retribution. Here wisdom may hesitate, because it does not seem to be a protection of human lives to kill several persons in retaliation of a single person. It was an Ijtihad of Hazrat Umar to have said, 'If all inhabitants of San'a participated jointly in committing this crime, I would have killed all of them.' The object of his declaration was the protection of human lives and to deter others from committing the crime. However, Hazrat Umar was not sure about the correctness of his decision until he asked Hazrat Ali that 'if you apprehended several persons in committing a crime of theft, would you order amputation of their hands?' Hazrat Ali said, yes! 'The same principle would be applied here.' Then, Hazrat Umar ordered to kill all of them." (Al-Mufiqat fi Asul al-Shari'ah, Labi Ishaque Al-Shatibi, Vol. III, page 11 Dar al-Ma'rafat, Beirut, Lebanon).

10. There is another incident that Hazrat Ali had also ordered the execution of three persons in retaliation of killing a single person. It is thus so stated in as under:—

Likewise, Hazrat Ali also executed, many persons in retaliation of one person (This precedent is followed by the majority of Jurists and Companions of the Holy Prophet).

11. Imam Malik, in Mu'atta has also been quoted as saying that if a person catches hold of a person and another kills him and then it is found that he had caught hold of him for being killed, then both would be put to death. (Mu'atta: Imam Malik, Vol. II, p. 873 Kitabl Aqul-Babul-Qisas fil-Qatl).

12. Maulana Salmat Ali in his translation of Kitabul Ikhtiyar known as Islami Faujdari Qanun has also stated on the authority of Al-Kafi that if a group of persons kills a person, then the entire group involved in the murder would be put to death in Qisas. (Article 560, p. 194).

13. In Fiqh terminology, two words Tawafuq and Tamalu' are very common to denote such a situation. There is, however, a big difference between the Hanafis and the rest of the Jurists in determining the meaning of Tamalu'. According to Jamhoor Tamalu' is like Tawafuq to commit a crime jointly without having prior agreement or conspiracy, that is to say they just agree on the spot to commit a crime jointly without prior planning and agreement. While according to Malikis Jurists, Tamalu' meant to commit a crime jointly by several persons in furtherance of common intention and prior agreement. According to them each member of the group shall be liable to punishment specified for the commission of the crime regardless of their direct participation in the crime. Each of them would be considered as it was done individually.

14. In other words, according to Malikis, mere presence at the spot of occurrence of crime with an intention of such commission is sufficient to make a person liable to punishment for such crime irrespective of the nature of his participation and assistance. According to Hanafis, however, all participants shall be punished with a punishment of Qisas in the case of murder and the person, who after agreement, merely assists at the place of occurrence he will, however, be awarded Ta'zir punishment which may go to the extent of death punishment but only as Ta'zir, not as Qisas.

15. According to Shafi'is and Hambalis, all will be liable to the same punishment provided they all intended to commit the said crime and participate in the commission of the crime, even if other person or persons engage themselves in some minor act like beating with a stick, etc. However, the preferred opinion of the Jumhoor of the Fuqaha (multitude majority overwhelming of the Jurists) is that if several persons participated in killing a single person, all of them shall be liable to death punishment. Their opinion is, in fact, based on the decision of Hazrat Umar who had executed seven persons, in retaliation of killing a single person and is reported to have said that if all inhabitants of San'a had participated in committing the said crime, I would have killed all of them, as referred to above.

16. It is reported that there seems to be consensus of opinion among the Companions of the Holy Prophet (p.b.u.h.) That if several persons commit an act of aggression against a single person in furtherance of common intention, all of them would be liable to punishment. It is, however, stated in Al-Muhalla by Imam Ibn Hazam Zahiri that the Companions of the Holy Prophet (p.b.u.h.) Cannot be said to be unanimous as Ma'az bib Jabal, a prominent Companion of the Holy Prophet (p.b.u.h.) Is reported to have not agreed on the issue of joint liability with Hazrat Umar and Hazrat Ali. This is so stated in Abu Zahra's book, page 402 (ibid).

17. However, the jurists are of the opinion that if the concept of joint liability is ignored, then "Mischief in the land" will spread on earth. The criminals will conspire to commit a crime jointly for the purpose of availing acquittal of some of the participants. Therefore, it is also in the interest of keeping peace and harmony in the society, if the acts committed with common intention be made punishable for all and each of them for committing such crime.

18. It appears that this Court in exercise of its suo motu jurisdiction under Article 203-D(1) of the Constitution, had issued public notice dated 30-8-1987 in S.S.M. No. 41-A of 1987 to examine some of the provisions of the Pakistan Penal Code, 1860, including section 34, and had invited the opinions of lawyers, jurists and ulema etc. A public notice appeared in the National Dailies of Pakistan, both Urdu and English and the Court started examination of the said section 34 along with certain other provisions of the Pakistan Penal

Code from 17th to 21st January, 1988 at Islamabad and the matter was heard on different dates at Karachi, Lahore and Quetta during 1989 and 1990, but there appears to be no judgment written or pronounced in the said S.S.M. No. 41-A of 1987, with the result that section 34, P.P.C., now under consideration also remained undecided.

19. It may, however, be mentioned that in response to the earlier publication of the public notice in the Dailies of Pakistan, a number of Scholars submitted their comments on the different provisions of law in a general form. However, Professor Fazle Hadi Qasmi of Peshawar, made his comments on certain sections of the Pakistan Penal Code as asked for. About section 34 his comments are reproduced as below:

20. Section 34, as reproduced (supra), only enacts a rule of co-extensive culpability when offence is committed with common intention by more than one accused. Meeting of more than one mind in doing an act (intended as agreed) to an offence can be said to result in having common intention in doing it. That creates co-extensive criminal liability under this section. The principle which is embodied in section 34, is participation in some act with the common intention of committing a crime. If one such participation among more than one person is established section 34 is attracted. The Hon'ble Supreme Court of Pakistan in Inam Bux v. The State (PLD 1983 SC 35) has thus held that:

"Section 34 of the Penal Code, 1860 is intended to meet a case in which it may be difficult to distinguish between the acts of individual members of a party who act in furtherance of the common intention of all. It does not create a distinct offence but merely enunciates a principle of joint liability for acts done in furtherance of common intention animating the accused leading to the doing of a criminal act in furtherance of such intention. Common intention usually consists of some or all of the following acts; common motive, pre-planned preparation and concert pursuant of such plan, common intention, however may develop even at the spur of the moment or during the commission of the offence.

The principle enunciated is that if two or more persons intentionally do a thing jointly the position is just the same as if each of them had done it individually by himself."

21. To understand and appreciate the implications of section 34 it seems necessary to also refer to sections 35, 37 and 38, P.P.C. Section 34 deals with the doing of separate acts, similar or diverse, by several persons; if all are done in furtherance of a common intention, each person is liable for the result of them all as if he had done them himself. Section 35 in effect provides for a case where several persons join in an act which is not per se criminal, but is criminal only if it is done with a criminal knowledge or intention; in such a case each of those persons who joins in the act with that particular knowledge or intention will be liable for the whole act as if it were done by him alone with that knowledge or intention, and those who join in the act but have no such knowledge or intention will not be liable at all. Section 37, in effect, provides for a case where several persons cooperate in the commission of an offence by doing separate acts in different times or places, which acts, by reason of intervening intervals of time, may not be regarded as one act or which may not be necessarily committed with a common intention. Section 38 provides that if several persons are engaged or concerned in the commission of a criminal act, having been set in motion by different intentions, they may be guilty of different offences by means of that act. This section, which is the converse of section 34, provides for different punishments for different offences where several persons are co-accused in the commission of a criminal act, whether such persons are actuated by the one

intention or the other. The basic principle which runs through all these sections is that an entire act is to be attributed to a person who may have performed only a fractional part of it. Sections 35, 37 and 38 begin by accepting this proposition as axiomatic, and each of them then goes on to lay down a rule by which the criminal liability of the doer of a fractional part (who is to be taken as the doer of the entire act), is to be adjudged in different situations of mens rea. The axiom itself is laid down in section 34 is which emphasis is on the act. What has to be carefully noted is that in section 35 and in section 37 and in section 38 this axiom that the doer of the factional act is the doer of the entire act is taken up as the basis of a further rule. Without the axiom these sections would not work, for it is the foundation on which they all stand. Reference may be made to Sultan v. Emperor (AIR 1931 Lah. 749 (750) and Ibra Akanda v. Emperor (AIR 1944 Cal. 339 (358): 45 Cr. LJ 771).

22. Mr. Iftikhar Hussain Chaudhary, learned counsel for the Federal Government, submitted that the principle of collective responsibility is well-established in history. The Holy Qur'an mentions extinction of the tribes of 'Ad and Thamud. These people had abandoned the worship of true god and lapsed into incorrigible idolatry. To 'Ad, Hazrat Hud was sent but they did not believe him and the tribe was obliterated from the face of the earth by a hot and suffocating wind that blew for seven nights and eight days without intermission and was accompanied by a terrible earthquake. The idolatrous tribe of Thamud was bestowed with the presence of Hazrat Salih but the unbelievers persisted in the incorrigible impiety and a violent storm overtook them and they were found prostrate on their breasts in their abodes. Thus, groups, tribes, people or nations were given punishment for their collective wrongdoings and males, females and children were treated alike.

23. The above instances, as quoted by the learned Standing Counsel for the Federation,

seem to be out of context as they relate to the law of creation/extinction whereas we are at the moment concerned with the legislation as to the law of crime and punishment.

24. It may thus be stated that an individual involved in a criminal act may be sufficiently motivated to execute his criminal design but aided, abetted and encouraged by the presence and participation of others may provide him the sufficient tools to complete the offence. The culpability of all the accused in such cases is co-extensive and embraces the principal actor and his accessories to the act. All the participants with common intention deserve like treatment to be meted out to them in law.

25. We are, therefore, of the considered view that the above section 34, P.P.C. does not offend any Injunction of Islam, laid down in the Holy Qur'an and Sunnah of the Holy Prophet (p.b.u.h.).

26. The petition is, therefore, dismissed as being without merit.

Petition dismissed.

The All Pakistan Legal Decisions. (1993) Vol. 45. Edited by Malik Muhammad Saeed.

Austin, John. (1954) The Province of Jurisprudence Determined and the Uses of the Study of Jurisprudence.

Pospisil, Leopold. (1974 [1971]) Anthropology of Law: A Comparative Theory.

JUSTICE

The subject of justice is a very complex one. Justice may play a role in virtually all aspects of the law. In many societies,

Justice, represented as a blindfolded woman holding a sword and scales on which to weigh truth, rests on a throne in an eighteenth-century engraving.

the concepts of law and justice are virtually indistinguishable from one another, and it is believed in those societies that the purpose of the law is to provide justice.

However, it is not true that the law is always just, or even that law always provides justice. In Nazi Germany, for example, Adolf Hitler committed many injustices in killing people in his concentration camps, but these injustices were strictly legal at the time in Germany.

While it is probably true that all societies have concepts of justice, ideas about what specifically constitutes justice vary from society to society. Among the Koreans, justice is often conceived of as being synonymous with virtue. In Western legal traditions, equality, or equity (in France, *égalité*), is often thought to be the goal of justice. Among the Kapauku Papuans of New Guinea, justice is known as *uta-uta*, or "half-

half," showing that they conceive of justice as a balance between the parties.

Most questions of justice focus on the justice of the law. However, there is another category of justice known as justice of the facts. In order for a legal authority to render a decision, he or she must discover and investigate the facts of the dispute. Justice of the facts concerns the quality of the information that the legal authority uses to decide a case. What is important in a legal action is what the legal authority assumes happened, and not what actually happened. It is usually the job of the legal authority to objectively seek the truth with regard to the facts of the case, and so the authority must consider the possibility that witnesses lie and that both parties to a case have committed offenses. The legal authority must determine credibility, and will sometimes use the standard of the *reasonable man* in determining this.

Among the Kapauku of Papua, New Guinea (Pospisil, 1971: 237), the legal authority has an advantage over legal authorities in Western courts in that he has the opportunity to hear the parties to a case argue violently over it, and in so doing may hear more of the truth than he would hear in a calm courtroom in the West.

The legal authorities of the Micmac Indians of eastern Canada are lucky in that they usually never have to worry about justice of the facts. All of the true facts of the case are presented to them in short order by the parties to the case. The plaintiff will tell the headman or Indian act chief (legal authority) truthfully what the alleged wrongdoer has done, but will omit whatever offensive acts he or she has himself or herself committed. Then the headman or chief will go to the alleged wrongdoer. The alleged wrongdoer will admit the truthful allegations made by the plaintiff, and will then accuse the plaintiff of the commission of offensive acts, which the plaintiff had neglected to mention. In short, the usual legal strategy of the alleged wrongdoer is to claim that the plaintiff is without "clean hands" (has himself or herself done wrong things in relation to the case, and should not therefore have just cause to complain). The alleged wrongdoer will also argue the interpretation of the facts, and the application of the appropriate law or rule to the facts, but will rarely deny true facts.

The second branch of justice is the justice of law. This may be further broken down into justice of adjudication and justice in principles of the law. Justice in adjudication may either be formal, involving uniformity in application of legal principle and equal sanction for equal crimes, or it may be on a case basis, with the merits and demerits of each case weighed separately. For example, the Micmac Indians are firm believers in formal justice in adjudication. They believe that all similar offenses should be treated in exactly the same way. Their insistence on uniformity is largely a result of the not uncommon practice of legal authorities making decisions on the basis of political self-interest and in the interest of benefitting kin and friends with light sanctions; corruption of the legal system is all too common in a community in which all people know each other and/or are related through kinship to each other.

When deciding principles of law, it is important to treat crimes of relative equality in much the same manner, to decide which crimes are more reprehensible than others, and, in democratic systems, to ensure that certain classes of people do not receive preferential treatment. Accordingly, among the Ifugao people of the Philippines, fines are adjusted on the basis of wealth. The poor pay one amount for a particular offense, those of the middle class pay a higher amount, and the wealthy pay the greatest fine.

Natural Law, equity, and the standards of the reasonable man, discussed in their own entries, are all doctrines applied to the question of justice in adjudication.

Many legal scholars, on the other hand, have been interested in justice in principles of the law. That is, they want to know whether the principles behind the legal decisions themselves are just.

How is it that one assesses the justice of legal principles? One has to look at questions of substantive justice, the goal of which is to provide a scale of values in order to make such assessments. One such scale of values was provided by the doctrine of Natural Law.

The other part of substantive justice is procedural justice. This involves the way in which large philosophical doctrines, such as Natural Law, are converted into actual laws to be used in the regulation of human society. Ideas on this subject are, like those pertaining to substantive justice, largely philosophical, and are treated in the entry on Legal Anthropology.

See also EQUITY; LEGAL ANTHROPOLOGY; NATURAL LAW; REASONABLE MAN.

Barton, Roy F. (1969 [1919]) *Ifugao Law.*

Bohannan, Paul J. (1957a) *Justice and Judgement among the Tiv.*

Gluckman, Max. (1967 [1955]) *The Judicial Process among the Barotse of Northern Rhodesia.*

Pospisil, Leopold. (1974 [1971]) *Anthropology of Law: A Comparative Theory.*

Strouthes, Daniel P. (1994) *Change in the Real Property Law of a Cape Breton Island Micmac Band.*

of the society's people and its lands. These characteristics, along with the characteristic of divine rule, are all that kingdoms around the world seem to have in common. Differences in succession, power, duties, responsibilities, and a host of other factors distinguish one society's royalty from that of another.

For instance, Yoruba kings (only males can be monarchs) are in an alternating fashion elected from one of two segments of the royal lineage. In comparison, the British and Japanese monarchs descend according to primogeniture, while the Tibetan monarch, the Dalai Lama, is by ordinary kinship reckoning unrelated to his predecessor. Some monarchs can abdicate the throne, such as those in Great Britain, but Yoruba kings can only leave office in death (on the other hand, those who elected the Yoruba king could require him to commit suicide by drinking poison).

The supernatural qualities ascribed to monarchs vary along with differences in the official religions to which the monarchs belong. The British monarch is the head of the Church of England, but not a god, whereas the Japanese emperor and Polynesian kings and queens are themselves deities. Neither the Japanese emperor nor the Polynesian monarch may be touched by a commoner.

The reason that the Polynesian monarch may not be touched by a commoner illustrates the differences and similarities in the divine power held by monarchs. The Polynesian monarch was believed to possess more of a supernatural power called *mana* than anyone else. *Mana* is a formless supernatural power that may be likened to an electrical charge, in that it can be transferred by contact. A person with very little *mana* can be killed by touching someone with a great deal of *mana*, and someone with a great deal of *mana* could lose it by touching supernaturally polluted objects. *Mana* is universal, the Polynesians believe, and present to some degree in all objects. A fish hook that has caught

KINGSHIP Kingship may be defined as a type of political leadership in which the leader of a society rules with divine right or divine power. In many kingdoms, the king or queen is believed to have descended from a god, or to himself or herself actually be a god. Kingdoms differ from theocracies in that the latter are governed by religious practitioners, such as priests, rather than by the objects of veneration themselves.

Kingship was found in many places throughout the world in traditional times, including Europe, India, Polynesia and other parts of Oceania, China, Cambodia, Japan, West and East Africa, Mexico (the Aztec), and Peru (the Inca). Where monarchies remain in the modern world, they have lost most of their power. Yoruba kings, for example, are under the power of the Nigerian government, and the monarchs of Great Britain, Japan, and the Netherlands are subordinate to national parliaments.

Kingdoms are generally regarded as state societies. Furthermore, in most if not all cases, the monarch is regarded as the personification a lot of fish has more *mana* than one that has not; the same is true for a spear that has killed many men. An army that wins a battle has more *mana* than the losing army. The king, of course, has more *mana* than anyone, and therefore cannot be touched without killing the person who touches him. In fact, the king was believed to have so much *mana* that he had to be carried everywhere so that the ground would not become contaminated and later kill any commoner who walked on the same spot.

People inherited *mana* through both their father's and their mother's lines. Thus, a child had more *mana* than either of his parents, and it is for this reason that the king of Tahiti abdicated his throne in favor of his son. When different types of *mana* came into contact, they discharged each other, much like electrical forces of opposite polarities. Thus, the best way to accumulate *mana* in one's family is for siblings, who have the same kind of *mana*, to marry each other, and this was actually done by the royal families of Polynesia in the past.

The practice of children marrying each other was also practiced by some Egyptian royal families, and for the same reason: to conserve and

The royal family of Japan rules by divine right and follows the tradition of primogeniture—the firstborn son becomes the ruler upon the death of his father. Emperor Hirohito, shown mounted on his favorite horse in 1936, succeeded his father Emperor Yoshihito in 1926 and was succeeded by his son Akihito in 1989.

increase the royal essence in the royal line of descent. We see, then, that although the divinity or supernatural power held by royalty differs in kind from one society to another, there is a common belief among all that this supernatural power can be quantified, in the sense that it can be determined that one person has or does not have it, or that one person has more than does another. British royal family members must marry others who have "blue blood," as they say, or give up any claim they have to occupy the throne.

The fact that the royal essence, however it is expressed, runs through a line of descent (in most cases) means not only that royal incest was practiced at times and in places, but that the monarch's own siblings had large amounts of it as well, and thus represented possible rivals to the throne. It was not unknown, therefore, for European kings and princes to kill the members of their immediate families whom they regarded as threats to their own rule, present or future.

Among the Zulu of South Africa, the king as a matter of course killed all of his brothers to prevent their assassinating him in order to take the throne.

Beattie, John. (1960) *Bunyoro: An African Kingdom.*

Gluckman, Max. (1940) "The Kingdom of the Zulu of South Africa." In *African Political Systems,* edited by Meyer Fortes and E. E. Evans Pritchard, 25–55.

Hocart, A. M. (1927) *Kingship.*

Lloyd, Peter C. (1967) "The Traditional Political System of the Yoruba." In *Comparative Political Systems,* edited by Ronald Cohen and John Middleton, 269–292.

Oberg, K. (1940) "The Kingdom of the Ankole in Uganda." In *Comparative Political Systems,* edited by Ronald Cohen and John Middleton, 121–162.

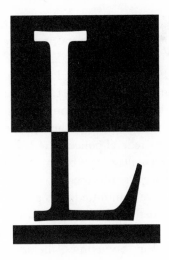

ship between the two parties to the dispute, called *obligatio*. It states the rights of one party and the duties of the other with respect to each other. For example, if a man steals the wallet of another man, the legal authority might say in his decision that, before the theft, the first man had the duty to not take the wallet and that the second man had the right to keep it. The authority would also say, once the theft occurred, that the second man had the right to have the wallet restored to him and that the first man had the duty to return it. There is, thus, a two-directional relationship between the parties to a dispute, and the authority states what that relationship is, how the initial relationship became unbalanced by the offense, or delict, and how the relationship may be repaired.

3. The third criterion is that law must be regularly applied or, in other words, that the authority must apply the law in the same way in all similar cases. This criterion may be called the intention of universal application. A legal authority must, for example, use the same law whether the disputants before him are his personal friends or not. If the authority gives preferential treatment to his friends, he is dealing not in law but in politics, and we may say that his decisions are politically corrupted. This does not mean that all individuals are treated the same way by authorities. For example, juveniles in our society are treated by the courts very differently than adults. Among the Inca of Peru, there were two separate legal codes, one for commoners and one for nobles. Commoners faced different sanctions than nobles when found guilty of a crime. The commoners faced physical sanctions (beatings, death, forced labor), while the nobles faced primarily psychological ones (public ridicule, loss of office).

4. The fourth and last criterion for law is sanction, or detriment. Legal authorities must have the ability to impose sanctions or their decisions will carry no weight. Sanctions may be either negative, in which case rewards or

LAW

The definition of law that has proven to be the most useful, as well as one that can be used in all societies, is the one developed by anthropologist Leopold Pospisil: law is "principles abstracted from decisions" (Pospisil 1978: 30). For example, a Micmac Indian headman, when told that a man had killed another while both were out hunting, decided that the homicide was not murder and that the killer had no legal liability because the killing was an accidental shooting. We may abstract from this decision the legal principle, or law, as follows: the individual who kills another through an accident is not guilty of an offense.

Law further has four criteria that must be met for a legal principle to be truly a law.

1. The first criterion is that the legal decision that contains the law must be made by a legal authority. Only someone who is authorized to make legal decisions can make a legal decision. Decisions made by someone else are not legal decisions and have no bearing.

2. The second criterion is that the decision contains a statement of the proper legal relation-

favors that would have been granted had the law not been violated are withdrawn, or positive, in which case some painful physical or psychological experience is inflicted. When we think of legal sanctions, we usually think of the physical sanction of imprisonment. Many societies, however, almost never use physical or other coercive sanctions. The traditional Micmac of Cape Breton Island, Nova Scotia, for example, almost never used physical sanction. Most often, they used psychological sanctions. Often, the legal authority would lecture the offender in public, thereby humiliating and embarrassing him. During an annual religious festival near one of the reserves, people who acted improperly were placed on a small island near the festival. The island was almost bare of vegetation; therefore, the offenders could be seen by everyone at the festival. Though the offenders could easily swim away and escape, most did not as a matter of honor; instead, they simply sat out this period of intense public humiliation.

Among the Kapauku Papuans of highland New Guinea, on the other hand, economic sanction was usually preferred. A killer could sometimes pay blood money to avoid losing his own life. If an individual refused to pay what he owed in a contract, his personal property was sometimes seized or destroyed. If a legal authority loaned money to a poor man, the authority would sometimes ask for the loan to be repaid early if the man was insubordinate to him.

Pospisil, Leopold. (1974 [1971]) *Anthropology of Law: A Comparative Theory.*

———. (1978) *The Ethnology of Law.*

Strouthes, Daniel P. (1994) *Change in the Real Property Law of a Cape Breton Island Micmac Band.*

LAW ENFORCEMENT Law enforcement consists of giving force to the laws made by the legal (and sometimes moral) authorities. In the United States, two different kinds of professions enforce the law. The first is the police, whether they are municipal, state, or federal police. The police stop the commission of illegal acts by arresting and bringing to the legal authorities those whom are believed to have committed such acts. If the legal authorities determine that the accused individual has committed an illegal act, they may prescribe some sanction. Sometimes, the sanction must be administered by a person or persons, and these persons constitute the second kind of law enforcement personnel, known as penal officers. Since the penal officers carry out the imposition of the sanction, which is part of the law, they too are law enforcement officers. In the United States, we see that law enforcement officers and legal authorities are separate. This helps to keep any group from having too much power. Imagine if a police officer had the power to determine an alleged offender's guilt, impose a sanction, and then execute the sanction. Such a person would have a great deal of power in a society and would be able to force a lot of people to do whatever he or she wanted, even illegal or unjust things.

However, in many technologically primitive societies, the police, legal authority, and penal officer are all found in one and the same person. A good example of this is the military societies of the Cheyenne Indians of the North American Great Plains. The military societies were given the responsibility, among others, of making sure that the tribe's large communal bison hunts went well. Cheyenne bison hunts were large so that many bison could be killed at once. Each time the bison herd was hunted, it would run away from the hunters. This meant that individual members of the tribe could not go about hunting the bison by themselves, because this would cause the herds of bison to become frightened and to move far from the Cheyenne tribe, making it difficult or impossible for the tribe to hunt the bison and endangering the survival of the whole tribe.

At one point in time, the Shield Soldiers, a military society, had ordered that no one was to hunt the bison. A Cheyenne man named Man Lying On His Back With His Legs Flexed heard this and told the Shield Soldiers that because his family was hungry, he was going to go out and kill some small game. The Shield Soldiers approved this. However, when Man Lying On His Back With His Legs Flexed went hunting, he came across by accident a herd of bison and could not restrain himself from killing one. Someone reported this to the Shield Soldiers, and they went to pay a visit to the offender. They decided his guilt on the spot and immediately began to impose the sanction of destroying his tipi. Man Lying On His Back With His Legs Flexed did not say a thing; he knew that he was guilty and that he would suffer the sanction.

Of course, concentrating all this power in the hands of one group could easily lead to abuses, and it did sometimes happen. Last Bull, one of the chiefs of the Fox Soldiers, another Cheyenne military society, became too harsh in his punishments when he acted as a policeman, often beating people too severely. However, the military societies are legal authorities when it comes to the conduct of their own members, too. As a result, the Fox Soldiers decided to remove Last Bull from office.

The Naskapi Indians, a hunting and gathering people of Labrador, Canada, use considerably different methods in enforcing their laws. For the Naskapi, the prime means of law enforcement is public opinion. The strength of public opinion is much stronger in a society like the Naskapi than in our own because of the homogeneity of the society. Everyone is of the same class and has the same interests, problems, and concerns; once public opinion begins to turn against an individual or group, it involves virtually all of the band's population.

In one case, a couple spent so much time together that the rest of the band considered them legally married, despite the fact that no minister had formally married them.

In a second instance, a man repeatedly hunted outside of his band's territory, in the territories of other bands. This caused political trouble for the members of his band, and so by unanimous public opinion he was banished from the band and the band's territory. Unable to be admitted to any other band, he and his family starved to death; no family can long survive on its own in the forests of northern Canada.

Ostracism is used to enforce moral as well as jural law. We have, for example, the case of Camatuet, a Naskapi man who married his own sister. Incest is not a criminal offense in Naskapi law, and the headman took no notice of the matter. However, the rest of the community was outraged, and treated Camatuet as an outcast, making him very anguished. His treatment made him so miserable that he left the band.

Public opinion, finally, compels people to render assistance to others in need, even if those people are despised personal enemies. If an individual or family is in the forest in the winter and starving, he puts up signals to that effect where they are likely to be seen. If someone passing by does not help, he will likely face the same fate if he is ever in trouble.

There are, however, three weaknesses in public opinion as a means of law enforcement in Naskapi society. The first is that public opinion comes into play only after an offense has been committed. It cannot stop the commission of a crime, though it can act as a deterrent to those who think of it before deciding to commit an offense. The second weakness is that public opinion only functions in the warmer months when the entire summer band is collected. In the winter, when small bands split up to live and to hunt in the forest, it has little effect because few people can know of an offense. Finally, public opinion is not usually aroused unless an offense affects the welfare of the entire band. Offenses that affect only a nuclear or extended family are not likely to bring the wrath of public opinion unless they are truly serious.

Another agent of law enforcement among the Naskapi is the headman and council, the latter of which is composed of the oldest and most respected men. The headman and council met in the summer, when the entire band was collected in one place, to decide legal cases. In most instances, the guilt of the accused was already an established fact, which is not unusual for small societies in which everyone knows everyone else's business. The council was also responsible for carrying out the sanction after the hearing concluded.

Law enforcement is also provided in Naskapi society by the shaman, who deals primarily with cases of hunting law, especially that of hunting territories. The shaman also functions primarily during the winter months when the band is dispersed and the headman and council are not in session. Winter is also the time that hunting territories are utilized and their borders infringed upon. If one man discovers that another man has been hunting on his territory, he will usually ask the second man to refrain from doing so. If the one breaking the law continues to do so, the territory owner may ask the shaman for his help. The shaman will then try to discover the facts of the alleged offense on his own. If he finds that the allegation is true, he will warn the trespasser to cease trespassing by informing him that he had had a dream in which the trespasser was identified to him as a trespasser and then cautioning him that continued trespassing will cause him injury or other damage. Failure to heed the second warning will bring the shaman to the trespasser in the form of a very large supernatural bird of a wholly unnatural shape who will give the trespasser one more warning. Failure to heed that warning will bring a bear or a wolverine that will destroy the trespasser's traps. At this point, the trespasser's hunting magic, which the Naskapi believe is essential for the ability to hunt, and thus to survive, will be destroyed. The shaman thus enforces secular law by using the supernatural world to punish those who break it.

Lips, Julius E. (1947) "Naskapi Law." *Transactions of the American Philosophical Society* 37(4): 378–492.

Llewellyn, Karl N., and E. Adamson Hoebel. (1961 [1941]) *The Cheyenne Way.*

LEADER

According to Leopold Pospisil of Yale, a leader is an individual who makes a decision and leads in the execution of the decision; thus, one who is followed. A leader may also have authority.

Among the peoples of the Trobriand Islands, in Melanesia in the Pacific Ocean, village leadership is acquired in a very special and precise manner. First, to become a village leader, a man must become a subclan leader. However, he cannot lead just any subclan in order to achieve this status; the subclan must be of elite status. Such subclans are known as *guyau* subclans, and these are considered by the Trobrianders as elite because their members are believed to hold special powers, often supernatural ones, that make the male members especially powerful and dangerous. In one region, for example, members of the Tabalu subclan are believed to have magical control over weather and economic wealth, and thus were thought responsible for the prosperity of the entire island, making them the leading subclan in that area. In another area, the Toliwaga subclan was thought to control supernatural military powers and the men were thought to be great fighters; therefore, the Toli-waga subclan was the most powerful in that district. Thus, the leadership of these subclans, and other *guyau* subclans, was a matter of great importance to all people of a village and, sometimes, larger areas. Those who became leaders of the commoner subclans earned the notice only of the members of those subclans.

To become a leader of a subclan, especially one of the *guyau* subclans, takes determination and perseverance, and many men simply do not have the qualities of persistence and ambition required. To become a village leader, one must be the legitimate successor to the previous leader, who held his position until death. It is the process of becoming a legitimate successor that takes drive and determination because of the amount of work entailed. The young man who sets his sights on becoming a leader of a subclan begins by giving gifts to and working for older members of the subclan who are either older brothers, mother's brothers, or mother's mother's brothers; this activity is known as fulfilling the *pokala* responsibility. Typically, the gifts range from fish to firewood, and the help given includes that of helping the older person with his gardening work and with his commitments to garden for others. While all young men must provide these services, the one who wishes to be noticed and selected to be a successor to the existing subclan leader must work far harder; as a subclan leader, he will be expected to assume a great many responsibilities involving physical labor, and one who does not work hard would be unsuitable. Not only does the hardworking young man achieve notoriety, he also has the right to ask those whom he has been assisting for land or coconut palms of his own.

In addition to demonstrating an ability to work hard, a man who wished to become a village leader needed to have a large number of the village people as his kin, since kin are likely to support one of their own as the village leader.

The best way for a man to do this was to marry a number of women, especially women who are related to the right people. The more wives a man had, the better were his chances of being selected as the successor to the existing village leader. Of course, for the young man this is not merely as simple as marrying several women. These women, and their children, must be supported materially. This means more work for the ambitious leader-to-be. Not only must he grow more food in his own gardens, he must also be diligent in his *pokala* activities so he can acquire more land on which to grow this food.

But having wives brings not only an obligation to feed them and their children. In addition, men also must bear *urigubu* responsibilities. These typically involve gifts to close relations. In other words, a man who marries must give gifts, typically of garden produce, to some members of his wife's consanguineal family. So, to marry many wives in the pursuit of the position of village leader becomes a great burden.

Finally, it often happens that the existing village leader is old and feeble for some years before his death. Often, the man who is chosen by the old leader to bear the burden of his *pokala* responsibilities is the man who will become the next village leader. While the man who takes on the task of helping the old leader must feel assured of becoming the next leader himself, he can be, for years at a time, a slave to his own *pokala* and *urigubu* responsibilities, as well as the responsibilities of the elderly leader.

Frequently, the ambitious man may be just one of several men who seek to become village leader. In their competitive efforts, the men must work very hard to show themselves to be superior to each other. Often, however, men attempt to eliminate the others from competition through the use of sorcery and poison.

The village leader plays several roles in the village. He is the spokesman for the village and the chairman of village council meetings, where the adult men of the village discuss and decide village matters. He has the right to make the final statement of village council decisions and to lead the execution of these decisions, and he has the responsibility to lead public opinion in support of the council's decisions. It is in this last role that the village leader is perhaps most powerful, for it is difficult for the individual to ignore public opinion. Should an individual disregard public opinion, the other members of his or her subclan usually will shame the dissenter and even banish him or her from the village. Shame sometimes leads a dissenter to commit suicide.

A tool at the disposal of the village leader is sorcery, and in his hands it is an acceptable sanction. However, he does not overuse sorcery, since to do so would call into question his abilities as a leader.

A third device by which the subclan or village leader can enforce compliance with his decisions is to withhold from dissident individuals land that they request through *pokala*. The village leaders and the subclan leaders all have control of lands that are owned by either the village or the subclan, respectively, but not by individuals. Those who do not defer to the leader's wishes typically are unable to receive allotments of this land.

The village leader, by having a great measure of personal power and control, sometimes uses it to enrich himself. If he enriches himself at the expense of other members of his village, he cannot expect to have his position indefinitely, however. But if he enriches himself and his village at the expense of outsiders, he may very well be lauded by other members of his village.

Finally, it often happens that several villages are united under the leadership of a village cluster leader. This position is analogous to that of the subclan leader and the village leader. A cluster leader must first be a village leader, and then become the recognized successor to the existing cluster leader. In order to gain power in other villages, however, the person who aims to become a cluster leader marries women from other villages in the cluster; if these women come from subclans that are at odds with his own, he often has to threaten them with war before they will allow him to marry one of their women. Just as importantly, a man who wants to be a village cluster leader gives festivals that allow him the opportunity to display his wealth and generosity. The man who is successful in these power-gathering activities can sometimes extend the reach of his influence into village after village, creating for himself a truly great amount of power that sometimes becomes dictatorial in nature. The Trobriand Islander leader is an informal leader whose potential power is limited ultimately only by his own characteristics and abilities.

See also BIG MAN; CHIEF.

Powell, H. A. (1967 [1960]) "Competitive Leadership in Trobriand Political Organization." In *Comparative Political Systems,* edited by Ronald Cohen and John Middleton, 155–192.

LEASE

A lease is a kind of contract in which the owner of a property gives up to another party possession of the property in return for a consideration (usually known as rent). The lessee has exclusive right of possession against all other parties in the world.

In the following case, the owner of a piece of property in Rhodesia (now Zimbabwe) that he had leased attempted to end the lease and eject the tenant because he could no longer supply water to the tenant, as the lease had required (*The Rhodesian Law Reports, 1968,* 1968(1): 192–194).

TUCKER v. BUCHAN

Appellate Division, Salisbury
Quénet, J. P. and Macdonald, J. A.

September 27th; October 11th, 1968

Landlord and tenant–lease–statutory tenant–supplied with water by landlord–landlord unable to continue supply–whether sufficient grounds for ejectment under s. 34 (1) (f) of Rent Regulations 317 of 1949.

Under a lease between the parties, the landlord (respondent) agreed to supply the tenant (appellant) with water for domestic use. Because of a rapid depletion of his water supply the landlord could not continue to supply water to appellant without jeopardizing his own future supply. The landlord gave the tenant (who was a statutory tenant) notice to quit and subsequently brought an action for ejectment. The claim was upheld on the ground that the shortage of water was a sufficient reason under s. 34 (1) (f) of the Rent Regulations for ejectment. The tenant appealed against this decision and claimed that the proper course for the landlord was to cut off the tenant's water supply and leave him to obtain his own water.

Held, dismissing the appeal, that the landlord's inability through no fault of his own to continue to fulfill his contractual obligation to supply water without serious risk to his own requirements justified his termination of the tenancy and the magistrate was entitled to "deem" that the acute shortage of water was an "additional ground" within the meaning of s. 34 (1) (f) of the Regulations. The cutting off of respondent's water was not an appropriate or legal remedy and failing an agreement resolving the difficulty, the landlord acted correctly in giving notice to quit and claiming ejectment.

N. J. McNally for the appellant, referred to: *Akoon v. Thoolasmiah,* 1963 (4) S.A. 498 (N).

J. C. Andersen, for respondent, referred to: *Herbstein and van Winsen,* CIVIL PROCEDURE IN SUPREME COURTS, p. 572.

MACDONALD, J. A.: The respondent instituted an action in the Magistrate's Court for the ejectment of the appellant from a cottage situated in the grounds of the residential property owned and occupied by the respondent. The appellant, a statutory tenant, [footnote: A statutory tenant is one who is a tenant as described by the relevant statutes.] had been given notice to quit.

The respondent based his claim for ejectment on the provisions of s. 34 (1) (f) of the Rent Regulations, Government Notice 317 of 1949, as amended. The relevant portion of s. 34 reads as follows:

"... no order for the recovery of possession of any dwelling or for the ejection of a lessee therefrom, which is based on the fact of the lease having expired either by the effluxion of time or in the consequence of notice duly given, shall be made by any court so long as the lessee continues duly to pay in respect of the dwelling ... the agreed rent, and performs the other conditions of the lease, except on the additional ground—

(f) in the case of a dwelling only, on other such ground which, regard being had to all the circumstances, is deemed sufficient by such court."

The ground relied on by the respondent was his alleged inability to continue to supply the appellant with water for domestic purposes in accordance with the agreement of the lease. This inability arose from the rapid depletion of the underground water which was the respondent's only source of supply.

The magistrate was satisfied on the evidence led that the respondent could not continue to supply the appellant with water from this underground source without jeopardizing his own future supply and he accordingly "deemed" this acute shortage of water to be "a sufficient additional ground" within the meaning of s. 34 (1) (f) and made an order for the appellant's ejectment.

The magistrate's finding that the respondent "was faced with a very serious water shortage and before the beginning of the next rainy season might have to transport water for household use" is not challenged and this appeal was noted on the following ground:

"The learned magistrate erred in holding that the shortage of water (his findings on which are not disputed) constituted a ground for ejectment within the meaning of Section 34 (1) (f) of the Rent Regulations, 1949, as amended."

In amplification of this ground of appeal, Mr. *McNally* submitted that "inability on the part of the lessor to carry out one term of his contract with the lessee cannot entitle him to withdraw from his other obligations. The lessor's remedy was to cut off the water supply and leave the lessee to seek whatever remedy he could. The lessee had made it clear that he would have remained on, and made alternative arrangements about water."

The defence raised before the magistrate was that there was in fact no shortage of water as alleged by the respondent. In the course of his evidence, but not in his plea, the appellant, without resiling from his defence on the merits, suggested that if in fact there was a shortage as alleged he would be prepared to arrange for the delivery of water to his cottage from an outside source.

The respondent's inability through no fault of his own to continue to fulfill his contractual obligation to supply water to the appellant without serious risk to his own requirements justified his decision to terminate the tenancy and the magistrate was entitled to "deem" that the acute shortage of water was an "additional ground" within the meaning of s. 34 (1) (f). I agree with Mr. *Andersen's* submission that the remedy suggested by Mr. *McNally*—to cut off the water supply to the cottage—was not an appropriate or a legal remedy and in the absence of an agreement between the parties resolving the problem which had arisen without fault on the respondent's part, the respondent acted correctly in giving notice to quit and instituting action for ejectment.

Mr. *McNally* has submitted, however, that justification for an ejectment order fell away when the appellant intimated in evidence that he would be prepared to make his own arrangements for the supply of water.

I am satisfied that this belated suggestion by the appellant could not, in the circumstances in which it was made, constitute a defence to the claim for ejectment. At most, it might found a plea for a stay of execution but since the case for the appellant has never, even at this late stage, been placed upon this restricted basis, I do not propose to consider whether under s. 40 (3) of the Rent Regulations a stay of ejectment order for an indefinite period could properly be ordered. Even if the magistrate had been prepared to grant the indulgence of an indefinite stay of execution, he would still have been obliged to make this ejectment order claimed and award the costs of the action to the respondent.

Accordingly, in my judgment, the appeal must be dismissed with costs.

QUENET, J. P. concurred.

The Rhodesian Law Reports, 1968. (1968) Part 1.

Though the history of legal anthropology as a discipline dates back perhaps only as far as the publication of Llewellyn and Hoebel's *The Cheyenne Way* in 1941, most of the issues central to legal anthropology, particularly justice, comparative law, the evolution of legal systems, and even the definition of law itself, have been of interest to legal scholars, philosophers, historians, and other thinkers for centuries. Thus, legal anthropology provides a very broad cross-cultural perspective to the study and understanding of law in the human experience.

The history of legal thought in the West essentially begins with the theory of Natural Law. The doctrine of Natural Law is based upon the idea that law exists independently of man and thus does not change from one region to another, nor does it change over time. Natural Law, because of its immutable character, may be discovered only by philosophical contemplation, and the basic ideas behind it were developed by such ancient Greek philosophers as Aristotle and Plato. The theory of Natural Law held prime importance until the nineteenth century, and its emphasis on timelessness kept most legal scholars from considering the question of legal change.

Though Natural Law held center stage until quite recently, it had been attacked for some time as a means for understanding law as it actually existed in different societies. The first person to make a significant attack on the idea of Natural Law was Charles-Louis de Secondat, Baron de La Brède et de La Montesquieu, who lived from 1689 to 1755. Montesquieu advanced the proposition that law was a phenomenon, not a preconceived philosophical notion. In other words, law exists separately from the human mind and can be studied as such. This revolutionary thought, in fact, launched the whole field that we know as social science, including the subdisciplines of sociology and anthropology.

Montesquieu conceived of law as a part of an individual culture. Thus, each legal system was a part of a single culture and was adapted to fit in with the other parts of the culture. Montesquieu thought of each particular culture as a whole. When the overall government of the culture is bad, he said, even the best laws are bad, and when the overall government is good, even the worst laws are good. In other words, law does not exist by itself, but only as part of a government and a culture as a whole. Law is in this sense relative, and Montesquieu thought that law could not be brought from one society to another (unless the two societies were culturally almost identical) because the law would not fit the recipient society's culture and needs. Law, he believed, could only be just if it was made to fit in with the needs of a particular society at a particular time; law cannot be judged either bad or good unless the society and time for which it was designed is known.

Montesquieu also distinguished jural laws from scientific laws. The first, which are laws dealing with disputes, are completely relative in place and time. The second, which are generalizations made on the basis of empirical evidence, are absolute and timeless. The former, Montesquieu said, derive from social nature, and the latter from human nature.

Montesquieu attempted to make some scientific laws concerning systems of jural laws. He claimed that jural laws are congruent with the kinds of government in a society at a particular time. Montesquieu, for example, noted that harsh laws went together with despotic leaderships. In societies with republican governments, social equality under the law is sought, since the lawmakers were forced to live under the same laws that they made for everyone else.

Montesquieu also noted that the legislator, the one who makes the rules that guide the legal authorities in the making of laws, can only make legislation out of the ideas present in his own culture and not from some philosophical absolute applicable to all people, as supposed by the Natural Law theorists. For Montesquieu, it is the legislator who takes the central place in the formation of every society's legal system. Another social thinker of renown, Emile Durkheim, writing at the end of the nineteenth century, was a social determinist who believed that invisible social forces within a society ultimately produce legislation and laws, and that the legislator is simply the tool by which the social forces are translated into legislation. Durkheim attacked

Montesquieu for allowing the legislator too much importance in determining the laws of the society.

Montesquieu also distinguished, from a scientific point of view, legislative, executive, and judicial functions, distinctions that are crucial to the scientific understanding of law in any society. He also noted that law is but one of several types of social control. He considered all of the following types of social control: governmental principles, laws, religion, mores, and manners. Whether one accepts these as stated or not, one must say that for an eighteenth-century scholar, this is a good accounting. However, Montesquieu was unquestionably correct in stating that all of the various means of social control influence each other, and that if one changes, so too do all of the rest. Here Montesquieu was far ahead of his peers in showing the interconnectedness of cultural traits and complexes with each other. He also found that in different societies the different means of social control have different importances. In some, religion was predominant, in others laws, and in yet others mores; when one declined in importance, one or more of the others had to increase in power to maintain social control and social integrity.

Montesquieu's intellectual contributions, unfortunately, were not recognized by his contemporaries, and, in fact, it was not until the nineteenth and twentieth centuries that he received the acclaim he was due. One who did see the value of Montesquieu's work early on was the German scholar Friedrich Karl von Savigny, who lived from 1779 to 1861.

Savigny rejected the validity of Natural Law and sought to find a pattern linking each society's legal system to its overall society and culture. Savigny claimed that law, along with other aspects of a society's culture, developed out of the historical evolution of the society's *Volksgeist* (national spirit), which was entirely unique to the particular society. Savigny's idea of the *Volksgeist*

is that it is essentially mystical. Laws emanate mystically from the *Volksgeist*, and it is the job of the legislator to watch for their appearance and then to employ them without altering them. Savigny limited his thinking about legal change to specific concrete societies rather than theorizing about legal change in general. For example, he looked at the German legal system. The German legal system was made up primarily of old Roman laws, which had largely displaced the previous Germanic law. Savigny's emphasis on *Volksgeist* led him to conclude that Roman law, because it was adopted over the previous Germanic law, proved that Roman law was superior to Germanic law for the national spirit of the German people.

For Savigny, law and the society in which the legal system existed grew and matured together, and then, using an organic analogy, died together when the nation lost its nationality. A young nation begins with legal ideas that are not clearly formulated or stated, he said. For this reason, it is useless to try to codify the laws. A nation in its middle age reaches the full flower of its legal development. The jural system acquires a great deal of skill, and there is considerable thought given to the law by specialists dedicated to the operation of the legal system. It is at this point that law may be profitably codified, though the only real reason to codify law, in Savigny's opinion, is to preserve it for history. When a society reaches the final stage, that of decline and the destruction of national identity, the legal system becomes divorced from the needs of the people and is controlled by a very few people. Savigny's theories suffered from a lack of information about legal systems outside of Europe, and from an overly great reliance on the socially deterministic idea that nations must pass through three stages that are the same for all peoples and that, no matter how aware of the process a people might be, they are powerless to alter the course of those changes. Finally, Savigny's idea of *Volksgeist* was to be revived in altered form in the ideology of the Nazis in the twentieth century, for whom it became a justification for a great many atrocities.

Following somewhat in the footsteps of Savigny was the great British jurist Sir Henry Maine, who lived from 1822 to 1888. Maine was also a law professor at Cambridge University and a professor of jurisprudence at Oxford. Maine advanced the study of law by rejecting the idea that each nation has a mystical *Volksgeist* that guides the development of its legal system. Maine stressed instead the study of empirical phenomena to understand how legal systems changed over time. His overall approach was heavily influenced by the theoretical interest of the time, Darwinian biological evolution. Consequently, he phrased his explanation of the change of legal systems as evolutionary. He did say that forces of evolution acted similarly on legal systems everywhere, but argued against a unilineal model of evolution in which all legal systems went through the same uniform progression of stages in exactly the same way.

For Maine the law developed along a string of a single set of stages, although many societies' legal systems went through them slightly differently. On the whole, however, similarities among legal systems in their evolution are far more numerous than differences between them due to the fact that human nature is the same everywhere, he said.

The first stage in Maine's legal evolution is known as the "archaic society," which we today would call the extended family. In societies at this level, Maine believed, the family was run by the eldest male, who made decisions, but the decisions had no basis in a clear principle that he would use again in similar circumstances.

Maine's second evolutionary stage, called the tribal state, also had no law. This state was similar to the archaic society in that it was dominated by the eldest male. The tribal state, Maine believed, was nothing more than a group of archaic societies that were grouped together under the fictional idea of a common male ancestor. As the tribal state continued to evolve to the next stage, the importance of territory to social groups increased.

The next stage Maine called the territorial society. In this society, the unifying principle of a common kinship became less important as the size of the group increased. Instead, the social bonds created by the sharing of a common territory became important. Towards the end of this stage, law began to take shape. This was accomplished by the emergence of aristocracies—elites who replaced the old family leaders. These elites were priests and lawyers and claimed special knowledge of the law. Because the rest of society distrusted the elites, they were forced to write the law down in a codified system so that it could be seen by all and applied to all equally.

The following stage of legal evolution came about due to the very nature of the legal codes themselves. Since the codes were written, it now took special effort to change them, as opposed to the previous situation in which laws would change as people failed to remember them accurately from one point in time to another. The result of the codification of law was that at this point two types of societies began to develop, one progressive and wanting always to change its legal system, and one stationary, always wanting to preserve its legal system as it was. The progressives used three methods to achieve their goal of changing the legal system. The first was the use of legal fiction. Here, Maine gives the term *legal fiction* a special meaning that it does not have elsewhere. For Maine, a legal fiction was a situation in which the codified law had not changed, but the law itself had, and those dealing with the law maintained a fiction that the law had not, in fact, changed by pointing to the codification to show that it was unchanged. This promoted acceptance of legal change in the population at large by making people believe falsely that no change had occurred. Legal change also occurred through the use of equity, which by overriding normal legal systems allows for new principles to be introduced into the law, as was done in ancient Rome. The third and most powerful way in which Maine saw legal change as occurring at this stage was through legislation, which allowed those in power the right and ability to change the law according to their wishes.

Overall, Maine asserted that, although different societies' legal systems evolved at different rates, the overall direction of evolution was away from law centered around the family (for example, *patria potestas*) to law focused on the individual. At the same time, as part of this overall development, the law's central concern went from that of status (especially ascribed status) to contract. As the society became more and more egalitarian, status became less important as a regulatory mechanism and the law shifted to the use of contract as a mechanism of social control. People who live in societies in the later stages of legal evolution are regulated by the law more by the type of contracts into which they enter than by their status.

Another advance in legal evolution was the development of criminal law. Wrongs were, in earlier stages, only torts, or private wrongs between the two parties to the case. As legal systems developed, they made wrongs a matter of interest to the whole society. That is, they made many types of wrongs offenses against the group, or crimes.

The flaws in Maine's work are many. First, he had no information on technologically primitive societies. Thus, he was left to speculate on them and their legal systems. Subsequent studies of technologically primitive peoples has shown that the patrilineal family bond is not universal and that many technologically primitive peoples are territorially bound. There are many other faults in this theory; in fact, most of what he said about the development of legal systems has turned out to be incorrect. Maine's contribution lies not in the specific details of his theory but rather in his example of trying to use empirical data to make general conclusions.

Another evolutionist who attracted a good deal of attention in the field of legal studies was Herbert Spencer. Spencer, a former railway engineer, was known for an evolutionist approach that was completely unempirical in either its methods or its goals. Rather, Spencer relied entirely upon rational speculation. For this reason his theory of legal evolution should not be given much weight at all today. He believed that the direction of legal evolution is towards the eventual dissolution of the legal system in favor of a purely ethical system of regulating human behavior.

A third evolutionist who gained notoriety is E. A. Hoebel, a legal anthropologist. According to his theory of legal evolution, the earliest stages of legal development may be seen in band and tribal societies. In such societies, he says, homicide and adultery are the sources of dispute, and these are treated by the legal authorities as private disputes rather than as crimes. At this stage of development, he says, criminal law as a whole is weak. Further, offenses against persons are the largest part of law, and law dealing with property offenses is poorly developed because there is little property to be the source of trouble. The next higher stage of law, Hoebel says, is found in horticultural (or gardening) societies, where the law has to take into account disputes over land.

Yet another evolutionist and his collaborator gained a great deal of attention and indeed became two of the nineteenth and twentieth centuries' most influential social thinkers. These are Karl Marx and Friedrich Engels, whose ideas are discussed in the entry on Marxism.

Emile Durkheim, the father of sociology, also had his own unique ideas concerning the evolution of law. For him, the question was not primarily one of law, but rather of social solidarity, the forces that help keep societies together. In technologically primitive societies, the social fabric is maintained by mechanical solidarity. That is, people are kept together by the similarity of their beliefs, attitudes, desires, behaviors, and values. In other words, societies are culturally homogeneous. Law comes into the picture when somebody disturbs the status quo, and the rest of the members of the society punish the offender. In such cases, the collective action against the offender helps bind the other members of the society together. Law in technologically primitive societies, according to Durkheim, is entirely penal, and its only goal is to punish. From there, societies and legal systems progress into the kind of societies and legal systems we have in technologically advanced societies, where legal sanctions are restitutive in nature (restitutive sanctions attempt to restore the original relationship between the two parties; if someone steals, restitutive sanctions would demand that he return to his victim what was stolen and apologize for the theft). In his generalizations, Durkheim has since been proven wrong by a multitude of studies of the peoples in technologically primitive societies. Also, his division of legal systems and societies is unwarranted; there are many similarities between societies, and differences do not always obtain on the basis of whether they are technologically advanced or not. As far as the matter of legal sanctions go, we can see that in technologically advanced societies, we often use punitive sanctions and do not rely always on restitutive sanctions. Also, in many technologically primitive societies, restitutive sanctions are preferred. Durkheim's beliefs were wholly speculative in nature.

Legal scholars have also long been interested in the subject of legal justice, especially the subdiscipline of procedural justice, which is concerned with how ideas of justice are implemented in actual laws. An early thinker on the subject was Jeremy Bentham, who lived from 1748 to 1832. Bentham's primary interest was in procedural justice. Bentham believed that the best laws

were those that produced the greatest utility. But his use of the term *utility* is different from the usual use of the word. By *utility*, Bentham referred to the amount of pleasure produced in relation to the amount of pain produced by something else. For Bentham, a just law was one that resulted in the greatest amount of pleasure and the least amount of pain. The problem with this theory is that what is *pleasurable* and what is *painful* differs from society to society, and thus Bentham's theory cannot be applied equally everywhere. Further, the idea that all people everywhere are primarily interested in pleasure for themselves as individuals is untrue, since there are many people who undergo painful experiences or who deny themselves pleasures in order to advance the interests of others or to benefit themselves or society in general.

A later figure in the field of procedural justice, one who is ultimately responsible for the interest of legal anthropologists in the subject of cultural values in law, is Josef Kohler. For Kohler, a just law must reflect the values held by the people to whom the law applies.

Roscoe Pound, an American who lived from 1870 to 1964, expanded upon Kohler's idea. Instead of looking at the values held by the people as a model for just law, Pound said, just law must rest upon the values the people say they want reflected in their law. In other words, if the majority of the people actually believe in something that is perhaps good for them individually, but bad for the group as such, then they should want the law to reflect the best interests of the group. For example, if people in the United States each want to drive their own cars at 100 miles per hour on the highways so that they can get where they want to go more quickly, they also realize that if everyone drove at 100 miles per hour, many more people would be killed. Therefore, they support speed limits that are much lower.

Another theory of justice was developed by the legal anthropologist Leopold Pospisil. He discovered while working with the Kapauku

Papuans of New Guinea that people often did not agree with the laws their authorities used in making legal decisions. These laws, Pospisil decided, were not psychologically internalized. That is, the people did not consider them proper Kapauku laws, but rather as foreign to their culture and thus immoral. However, Pospisil noted that as time went on, the values of these laws often became accepted, or psychologically internalized, and so became regarded as moral and just after a period of time. Likewise, laws that had previously been regarded by the people as just and moral were no longer considered so, and they were either discarded or imposed against the will of the people by the legal authorities. The degree of psychological internalization, therefore, provides a useful measure of the justness of any particular law. Further, this standard can be used as a measure of legal change as well, showing how new laws come into use and later are repealed.

Pospisil is known for two additional contributions to the field of legal anthropology. One of these is the theory of the multiplicity of legal levels, or legal pluralism, discussed in its own entry. The other is his cross-culturally applicable theory of law, discussed separately in the entry on Law.

Another major figure in twentieth century legal anthropology is Max Gluckman, who is well known for his fieldwork in Africa and his theoretical contributions. He is probably best known for finding the legal standard of behavior known as "the reasonable man" among the Lozi people. Gluckman hypothesized that this standard exists in every society in the world. Gluckman's other major theoretical contribution is to elucidate how law is a process that takes place over time.

Oliver Wendell Holmes, the well-known jurist and member of the United States Supreme Court, was also a theoretical scholar of some repute. His major contribution was to point legal scholars, including legal anthropologists, in the direction of closer attention to law as it really is and away from the logical examination of abstract rules. Law should be studied, he said, in concert with the study of other phenomena of the same society. The approach that Holmes pioneered is known as the American School of Legal Realism, which is discussed in the entry on Legal Realism.

A follower of Holmes's legal realism, Karl Llewellyn, actually put the idea of legal realism to use in his study, with E. Adamson Hoebel, of the legal system of the Cheyenne Indians, *The Cheyenne Way*, which properly began the field of legal anthropology. The book makes use of case studies that tell the reader in concrete detail about the Cheyenne legal system.

The anthropologist and Africanist Paul Bohannan has done famous work on the laws of the Tiv of Nigeria. Bohannan is best known for calling attention to the theoretical distinction between folk (native or indigenous) systems of classification and theoretical (cross-cultural) ones. Bohannan essentially repudiates the use of theoretical systems to describe alien folk legal systems as ethnocentric.

See also JUSTICE; LAW; LEGAL REALISM; MARXISM; MULTIPLICITY OF LEGAL LEVELS; NATURAL LAW; *PATRIA POTESTAS*; REASONABLE MAN; TERRITORIAL PRINCIPLE OF LAW.

Bentham, Jeremy. (1876 [1780]) *Introduction to the Principles of Morals and Legislation.*

Bohannan, Paul J. (1957a) *Justice and Judgement among the Tiv.*

Durkheim, Emile. (1933 [1893]) *The Division of Labor in Society.*

———. (1953) *Montesquieu et Rousseau.*

French, Rebecca. (1990) *The Golden Yoke: A Legal Ethnography of Tibet Pre-1959.*

Gluckman, Max. (1955) *Custom and Conflict in Africa.*

———. (1965a) *The Ideas in Barotse Jurisprudence.*

———. (1965b) *Politics, Law and Ritual in Tribal Society.*

———. (1967) "The Judicial Process among the Barotse." In *Law and Warfare*, edited by Paul J. Bohannan, 59–92.

———. (1974) *African Traditional Law in Historical Perspective.*

Gluckman, Max, ed. (1969) *Ideas and Procedures in African Customary Law.*

Hoebel, E. Adamson. (1954) *The Law of Primitive Man.*

Llewellyn, Karl N., and E. Adamson Hoebel. (1961 [1941]) *The Cheyenne Way.*

Maine, Henry Sumner. (1963 [1861]) *Ancient Law.*

Malinowski, Bronislaw. (1959 [1932]) *Crime and Custom in Savage Society.*

Montesquieu, C. L. J. de Secondat, Baron de la Brède et de. (1750) *De l'esprit des lois.* Vols. I, II.

Moore, Sally Falk. (1978) *Law as Process.*

Nader, Laura. (1964) "An Analysis of Zapotec Law Cases." *Ethnology* 3(4): 404–419.

Nader, Laura, and Duane Metzger. (1963) "Conflict Resolution in Two Mexican Communities." *American Anthropologist* 65(3) part 2: 584–592.

Offner, Jerome A. (1983) *Law and Politics in Aztec Texcoco.*

Pospisil, Leopold. (1974 [1971]) *Anthropology of Law: A Comparative Theory.*

Pound, Roscoe. (1942) *Social Control through Law.*

———. (1965) *An Introduction to the Philosophy of Law.*

Savigny, Friedrich Karl von. (1831) *On the Vocation of Our Age for Legislation and Jurisprudence.* Translated by Abraham Hayward.

Spencer, Herbert. (1893) *The Principles of Ethics.* Vol. II.

———. (1899) *The Principles of Sociology.* Vol. II.

Stone, Julius. (1950) *The Province and Function of Law.*

Stark, W. (1960) *Montesquieu: Pioneer of the Sociology of Knowledge.*

Starr, June. (1978) *Dispute and Settlement in Rural Turkey: An Ethnography of Law.*

LEGAL DECISION

According to Leopold Pospisil of Yale, legal decision is a statement by a legal authority (headman, judge, chief, father, mother, etc.) by which a dispute is settled, by which a party or parties is advised before legally relevant behavior takes place (declaratory decision), or by which approval is given to a previous solution of a dispute made by the parties before the dispute was brought to the attention of an authority (such as approval of self-redress).

Legal decisions in the same type of cases change as the legal authority himself or herself changes. The authority's behavior is dynamic, changing over time, and decisions he or she would have made at one time would not be the same later on. Another characteristic of legal decisions is that they are common to all functioning groups. Groups that have a function, or purpose, always have a leader who makes the decisions necessary to the group's functions. If this were not the case, the group would have no reason to be, and would likely cease to exist.

A declaratory decision is one in which a legal authority rules on what the legal consequences of a future act might be. For example, if a third-grade boy wants to hit one of his classmates in class, he might ask the teacher, "What would happen if I hit Billy?" The teacher would reply with a declaratory decision, which might be "Then I would have to tell your mother that you behaved badly in school today." This consequence might cause the boy to refrain from hitting Billy.

Sometimes a legal decision gives approval to an act that already solved a dispute. If a man shoots and kills an intruder in his house, there might be a court hearing, where the judge might exonerate the man who did the shooting of all legal charges.

_____

Pospisil, Leopold. (1974 [1971]) *Anthropology of Law: A Comparative Theory.*

LEGAL FICTION

A legal fiction is an assumption of something as factual under the law that is not actually true. Legal fictions in the legal systems of the United States include adoption (the law treats an adopted child as if he or she were the parents' natural child, and treats the natural parents as if they were never the adopted child's parents), corporation (an artificial person under the law, a corporation has no existence whatsoever outside of the law), and statutory rape (in which a person below a certain age who has sexual intercourse with a person above a certain age is deemed under the law as having given no consent to sexual intercourse, whether or not consent was given).

See also ADOPTION; CORPORATION; LEGALISM.

LEGAL REALISM

Legal realism is the idea that for a true understanding of the laws in effect in a society, one must study actual legal decisions rather than rules or statutes made by legislatures. The expression of this idea was first made strongly in the United States by Oliver Wendell Holmes, who is credited in doing so with starting the American School of Legal Realism. Prior to Holmes's argument, legal scholars were accustomed to studying the statutes for an understanding of how the law works. The influence of the American School of Legal Realism dramatically changed the way in which law schools teach law. In fact, law schools today pay almost exclusive attention to legal decisions (which are called "case law" by U.S. lawyers) in their lessons, and little or no attention to rules (which are called "statute law").

See also LEGAL ANTHROPOLOGY.

_____

Pospisil, Leopold. (1974 [1971]) *Anthropology of Law: A Comparative Theory.*

LEGAL RIGHT

A legal right may be defined as the legal expectation that someone else will behave toward the holder of the right in a certain way. A legal right is one-half of a jural relationship between the holder of a right and another party, who may be one person or all persons. A right only exists when another party has a duty to the holder of the right. *Duty* is defined as the expectation that one will behave toward the holder of a right in a certain way or be punished by law. A citizen of the United States, for example, has the right of freedom of speech when in the United States. Everyone else has a duty not to infringe upon that right. This is discussed further in the entry on Fundamental Legal Conceptions.

In Western legal systems, legal rights have long been divided into rights *in personam* and rights *in rem*. The Latin term *in personam* may be translated as "into or against the person." The term *in rem* signifies that the rights are against the *res* or thing, rather than against the person. Most rights are rights *in personam*.

Rights *in rem* are exercised against property, with the object of disposing of property without reference to the title of ownership of claimants to the property. An example of a legal action *in rem* would be for foreclosure of a lien upon a house. The holder of a lien (such as a bank) will go to court to acquire title of ownership to the house if the owner of the house has not kept up with his or her mortgage payments. The original owner would not need to appear in court, since he or she is not a party to the action.

This dichotomy between rights *in rem* and rights *in personam* is a false one that only Western legal systems use. Legal relationships can actually exist only between living people. The example of foreclosure on a lien is a legal action between the bank and the mortgage holder, in which the bank seeks to take away the rights of ownership from the owner. Only persons may be party to legal actions, in reality. If rights resided *in res,* or in a thing, then someone could legally give ownership of a house to a tree. This is impossible in any legal system, since ownership consists of jural relationships between people only.

See also FUNDAMENTAL LEGAL CONCEPTIONS.

American jurist Oliver Wendell Holmes (1809–1894)

LEGALISM

Leopold Pospisil has defined legalism as "an extreme emphasis upon abstract rules, which are regarded as the objective revelation of the legislator's will, as the exclusive manifestation and source of law. The individual rules themselves are seen as the exclusive and concrete answers to particular disputes."

Legalists believe that all undesirable behavior may be controlled through rules that are specific to every possible situation. It is the rules themselves that are the foundation of law rather than, as in many societies, various principles of justice that guide the legal authority. The law under a legalist system considers a party to a case not as a person, but as a role-player as described by the rule. To the legalist, the legal authority should have no creativity, but should merely find the facts of a case and match them to the applicable rule.

Some legalistic ideas:

1. Law is *a priori*.
2. Law is the final answer to every problem.
3. Law is autonomous.
4. Law can only be changed by another rule explicitly changing the original rule.

Nineteenth-century author Victor Hugo attacked French legalism in his novel Les Misérables, *published in 1862. A contemporary artist, Honoré Daumier, represents a courtroom scene of the period.*

Court procedure under a legalist system also differs from that practiced, for example, in the United States (which, though somewhat legalistic, is not extremely so). Evidence that does not apply to a rule is inadmissable. In Victor Hugo's great novel *Les Misérables*, which was an attack on French legalism, the question that faced the protagonist in court was "Did he steal?," and the court could not consider the facts that he stole only a loaf of bread and that he did so in order to feed his starving children. Questions of justice in any particular case are unimportant; what is important is the rule.

Since human behavior and human social relations are so complex, no set of rules (which in legalistic societies are usually written down together in a code) can take all offenses into account, but legalists believe that it is necessary to try to describe in their statutes all of the possible variations of a particular offense, so that the statute can control the prohibited behavior with little action by the legal authority except to match the actions of the accused with a particular statutory rule. For example, rather than simply making a statute against the fraudulent alteration of elections in Canada, legalism there prompted the legislature to pass the following legislation covering every imaginable means of altering the election process (*Prefix to Statutes, 1960*: 54–55):

Section 29. Everyone who

(a) forges, counterfeits, fraudulently alters, defaces or fraudulently destroys a ballot paper or the initials of the deputy returning officer signed thereon;

(b) without authority supplies a ballot paper to any person;

(c) not being a person entitled under this Act to be in possession of official ballot paper or of any kind of ballot paper, has any such official ballot paper or any ballot paper in his possession;

(d) fraudulently puts or causes to be put into a ballot box a paper other than the ballot paper which is authorized by this Act;

(e) fraudulently takes a ballot paper out of the polling station;

(f) without due authority destroys, takes, opens or otherwise interferes with a ballot box or book or packet of ballot papers then in use for the purposes of the election;

(g) being a deputy returning officer fraudulently puts, otherwise than as authorized by this Act, his initials on the back of any paper purporting to be or capable of being used as a ballot paper at an election;

(h) with fraudulent intent, prints any ballot paper or what purports to be or is capable of being used as a ballot paper at an election;

(i) being authorized by the returning officer to print the ballot papers for an election, prints without authority more ballot papers than he is authorized to print;

(j) being a deputy returning officer, places upon any ballot paper, except as authorized by this Act, any writing, number or mark with intent that the elector to whom such ballot paper is to be, or has been, given may be identified thereby;

(k) manufactures, constructs, imports into Canada, has in possession, supplies to any election officer, or uses for the purposes of an election, or causes to be manufactured, constructed, imported into Canada, supplied to any election officer, or used for the purposes of any election, any ballot box containing or including any compartment, appliance, device or mechanism by which a ballot paper could be secretly placed or stored therein, or having been deposited during polling, may be secretly diverted, misplaced, affected or manipulated; or

(l) attempts to commit any offence specified in this section;

is disqualified from voting at any election for a term of seven years thereafter and guilty of an indictable offence and liable, if he is a returning officer, election clerk, deputy returning officer, poll clerk or other officer engaged in the election, to imprisonment, without the alternative of a fine, for a term not exceeding five years and not less than one year, with or without hard labour, and if he is any other person to imprisonment for a term not exceeding three years and not less than one year, with or without hard labour.

The repetitive nature of the statutes of legalists are a product of the legalists' belief in the central importance of the statutes rather than of allowing legal authorities to make up their own minds as to what constitutes a transgression of the law. But it is still possible for someone to offend the spirit of the law while not breaking an actual statute. What do the legalists do then?

Section 281.2 of the *Canadian Criminal Code* of 1987 prohibits public incitement of hatred by communication of statements in which communication takes place by "telephone, broadcasting or other audible or visible means." But one can imagine a situation in which incitement of hatred occurs through communication in Braille! What does the legalistic legal system do in such a case? The judge would apply *analogia legis* (analogy of rule), which would make the rule applicable in this situation because case and rule are similar.

Legalists typically like to extend the application of the rules as far as possible, even to the point of resorting to legal fictions. There is, for example, the fiction of corporation, in which a business is literally given the legal status of a person. Here, the legalists have simply extended the rules regarding persons to businesses, rather than draw up a whole new set of rules to apply to businesses. There is also the legal fiction of no evidence. In U.S. statutes, there is a rule that evidence cannot be legally collected in certain manners. The U.S. courts have extended that rule so far that they treat evidence collected in an illegal manner as if it did not exist by making it inadmissible in court. In European courts, by contrast, illegally collected evidence is admissible, although the person who collected it illegally could face criminal prosecution. Another legal fiction in U.S. law is statutory rape in cases in which the underage individual gave consent to sex. The legalists simply extended the rules on rape to apply to those who have sex with underage persons rather than draft a new rule to prohibit sex with underage persons (as was done in Canada).

Legalists sometimes will find the rule that they want to apply and then apply it even if the facts do not fit the case. A good example of this was the case in which Dr. Mudd was found guilty of being an accessory to murder because he set the broken leg of John Wilkes Booth after he killed Abraham Lincoln. Dr. Mudd could not have been an accessory to murder because the murder had occurred long before Dr. Mudd and John Wilkes Booth met. Legalists typically care little for the extenuating circumstances involved in a case.

In some respects, legalism does promote justice, since it requires that all like cases be treated uniformly. The United States has a somewhat legalistic legal system. Thus, a judge in western New York State treats a drug dealer much the same way as does a judge in Long Island, New York.

However, extreme legalism can also create many injustices. It is often the case in legalistic societies that there are stiff penalties for minor wrongs and light penalties for major wrongs. Drug dealers convicted of selling small amounts of drugs now face mandatory sentences in the United States, and the crowding in prisons means that violent felons are being released early so that drug dealers can be incarcerated.

In the former Soviet Union during Stalin's reign, harsh sentences were thought to be effective ways to curb undesirable behavior. So, rather than rewrite all of the statutes, legal authorities would use the principle of analogy and determine that a civil infraction was actually a criminal one because of some resemblance to the criminal offense, and so give a much harsher sanction. Likewise, minor crimes were held to be like major crimes on the principle of analogy, and the sanctions that the offenders would bear would be those of the major crime and not the minor one they had actually committed.

A famous case in the United States involved a sheriff who arrested a mailman for murder. The sheriff was then himself arrested for delaying the mail, because the mailman was on his delivery rounds at the time that he was arrested. The sheriff's conviction was upheld by all courts until it reached the Supreme Court, which overturned the sheriff's conviction as unreasonable.

Another amusing case of injustice being created by following the legal rules too closely occurred in the 1960s and involved a Micmac Indian woman who was in the state of Maine to participate in the potato harvest. She and her husband were parked in the woods in October, which is moose mating season. At this time of year, male moose are easily irritated and will attack things that they dislike for no clear reason. A male moose, which can weigh more than one ton, saw the car and attacked it, threatening to tip it over. The Micmac woman left the car, opened the trunk, and picked up the bumper jack. With this, she beat the moose on the head and killed it. She was arrested for killing a moose out of season and jailed (though she was released later).

Yet another problem with making laws rigid is that, when society changes, the laws do not reflect social reality, which is why we have so many so-called dead laws on the books. Dead laws are actually dead statutes or statutes that are no longer being applied by the courts.

Legalistic societies tend to have harsher punishments than societies that are not legalistic. Legalism is generally the result of judges and lawyers who want more power in society. The storming of the Bastille during the French Revolution was a revolt against legalism; the Bastille held not only prisoners, but also the offices of judges and lawyers. Ever since then, the French have continued to fight legalism by prohibiting lawyers from becoming members of the French parliament (though special permission may be granted in some individual cases).

One significant example of legalism is that of China during the Ch'in Dynasty (221–206 B.C.). To understand the impact of the movement toward legalism at that time, it is necessary to have some knowledge of China's previous legal system and Chinese society generally.

Confucian philosophy was an important set of guiding principles in Chinese life prior to the Ch'in Dynasty. One of the important principles advanced by Confucius was to push the concept of *li* into prominence in daily life. *Li* may be defined as custom based on ethical principles, principles that were formerly the nobleman's code of behavior. At the time, these principles were considered binding above all legal precedent and were far more important than statutes. *Li* was taught paternalistically and by example. Leaders were expected to follow the principles of *li* very scrupulously.

According to Confucian philosophical tenets, law punishes wrongs but does not make for better people. In fact, Confucius argued, law only encourages people to avoid punishment rather than to develop a sense of shame. What is needed, Confucius said, is for peoples' hearts to improve, and this was to be done through *li*.

Li is modified by *I*, or "justice." It was permissible under *li*, for example, for a man to return a sterile wife to her family, but *I* demanded in one notable case that, since she had no home to return to, she must remain with her husband.

The Chinese called rules (or statutes) *fa*. Their purpose was to aid inexperienced judges. In the Confucian era, *li* was always paramount and *fa* was not followed closely. The Ch'in legalists, however, disregarded *li* entirely and made *fa* the legal standard. Whereas *li* was expressed in short, vague general principles, *fa* was far more applicable to actual legal disputes. The Ch'in legalists promoted legalism so as to increase the power of the state and to unite China, which at the time was a collection of states that often fought each other. A central authority would, of course, need a strong legal code, since it could not exist if judges in different parts of China applied the law differently, basing their decisions on the vague principles of *li*. The legalists ended the variations in what was considered a crime and what was considered an appropriate sanction. The following are central ideas of Chinese legalism:

1. Human ethics may be changed at the stroke of a pen, by writing a new rule.

2. Obedience cannot be learned by example. A good mother, they said, may have a spoiled child.

3. Man is basically evil.

4. Good law is law that strengthens the state and the power of authority.

5. Law originates from authority, not from justice.

6. Law can provide all answers to social problems.

7. The function of law is to stop wrongs, and not to encourage goodness.

8. Criminal offenses are an attack upon the state, and therefore should be severely punished.

9. There is no difference between the good man who commits no crimes and the bad man who is too afraid of punishment to commit a crime.

The radical legal change that occurred under the Ch'in was too much for the Chinese people, and there was a counterrevolution that ended the dynasty. Later, *fa* and *li* were paired together in the legal system, combining moral education with uniform sanctions.

Legalism is prominent in the societies of Europe, the Middle East, China (now and during the Ch'in Dynasty), as well as in the Inca and Aztec societies at the times of their cultural climaxes. The United States and Canada are significantly legalistic and growing more so. Outside of these areas, legal dependence on rules has not been especially important. Legalism develops in times of social turmoil and heterogeneity, under circumstances in which there is a desire to create central authority, and when legal practitioners have an influence in the writing of legislation.

See also CORPORATION; JUSTICE; LEGAL FICTION.

Ioffe, Olympiad S., and Peter B. Maggs. (1983) *Soviet Law in Theory and Practice.*

Offner, Jerome A. (1983) *Law and Politics in Aztec Texcoco.*

Pocket Criminal Code and Miscellaneous Statutes. (1987).

Pospisil, Leopold. (1974 [1971]) *Anthropology of Law: A Comparative Theory.*

Prefix to Statutes, 1960. (1960).

LEGITIMACY IN LAW

Legal legitimacy refers to the legal rights and duties that exist between a man and his legally recognized child. Legitimacy is established by the legal recognition of filiation. In all societies of which I am aware, the legitimate child has a right to be cared for and supported by his or her legal father, and the man has a right to custody of his legal son or daughter. The illegitimate child typically has no right to be financially supported by his or her natural father, nor to inherit any or all of his or her father's estate when he dies, unless the father specifically instructs that part of his estate go to the illegitimate offspring. And in most societies, legitimate offspring are unavoidable heirs; that is, they may inherit from their father's estate unless the father has specifically disinherited them in a will.

The idea of legitimacy is universal among human societies. Its purpose is to provide for the material support of the society's children. Normally, legitimacy is determined by marriage. The children born to a married couple are considered legitimate. Marriage is used to establish paternity and legitimacy. A child's maternity is, of course, easily known, but in the days before modern blood tests paternity was often difficult or impossible to establish beyond a reasonable doubt. Thus, marriage was used to determine legal paternity. Even if a married woman's child was not the natural child of her husband, the law considered the child the legitimate offspring of the woman and her husband. In contemporary industrialized countries, sophisticated genetic testing can prove that a child is not the natural child of his or her mother's husband. Most of the world's people, however, do not have access to this type of testing and rely on marriage to determine legitimacy and paternity.

Every society has its own laws regarding the rights and duties entailed by legitimacy. One of the best-described systems in the non-Western world is that of the Shona of Zimbabwe. Children are legitimate if born to a married or betrothed couple. If a married or betrothed woman has a child by a man other than her husband, the natural father may gain full rights in the child by payment of compensation to the mother's husband, and only if the mother's husband agrees to the compensation. This, however, is the exception, and in most cases the natural father has no rights in his children and all rights belong to the mother's husband.

While it is common in many societies for some men to wish to have no legal ties to their children, because such ties entail costly responsibilities for the raising of the children, the Shona are patrilineal and so wish to have their children as part of their own lineages to build up the lineage's size and wealth. For this reason, in the case of a woman who is neither married nor affianced but who bears a child, the child remains as a member of her own patrilineage and the natural father has no right to claim him or her as his own nor to include him or her as a member of his patrilineage. In normal Shona marriages, the groom must pay to his fiancé's father a bride-price consisting of cattle and sometimes cash. This payment is intended to compensate the family for the loss of the woman's labor and for their interest in the children she will bear. If the payment is not made or the marriage is dissolved for some other reason, the ex-husband loses all of his rights in his children. These rights go to the mother's family.

Children have legal rights with respect to their fathers on the basis of their legitimacy. Children of married parents can expect to be fed, clothed, sheltered, and healed at the expense of their father. Further, the fathers are obligated to find their sons wives and to supply the cattle for the bride-price. Moreover, fathers are legally liable for whatever damage their children do to others or to the property of others. When their fathers die, the male children can expect a share of their father's estate and a share of the cattle given him by the husbands of their sisters. Finally, sons can rise in the patrilineal genealogical hierarchy to their father's position.

Male children born as a result of adulterous affairs who have been legitimated by their natural father's payment of compensation and who live with their natural fathers are legally legitimate. However, such a child faces difficulties after his father's death in gaining his father's position in the patrilineal hierarchy and in getting a portion of his father's cattle because of political pressure from his father's wives and their children. This is because he was not raised by these women in one of their houses, but lived with the family as something of an outsider, and he cannot count on the political support of any of the women or his half-siblings.

Children of a woman's adulterous affair who are raised by the woman's husband are legally legitimate children of their mother's husband. Male children face the problem that although they have all the legal rights of their mother's other male children, they are not of the same blood as their father's patrilineage, but rather of the blood of their natural father. In this respect, then, they are not considered part of the patrilineage. They are admitted to their mother's husband's position in the patrilineage, but their words are given no weight by the other members of the patrilineage.

Children who are not legitimate at all face the greatest obstacles. They are socially stigmatized and addressed by derogatory names. Girls rarely find themselves growing up illegitimate. When girls mature and marry, their fathers receive cattle in compensation, and for this reason, men are likely to wish to be their legitimate fathers. Boys, on the other hand, face a different future. They are raised by their maternal grandparents, who give them food, clothing, shelter, and the cattle they need to marry. But they can never be a member of any lineage, a very significant handicap.

It sometimes happens that a son becomes incorrigible and costs his father a great deal of wealth settling claims for damages he has caused. In some such cases, the father may publicly disavow his son as his own in an attempt to escape any further liabilities for the damages his son may cause. This will usually be followed by his forbidding the son from living with him. These actions do not, however, mean that the father is no longer legally responsible for his son. It only means that he is protesting the son's actions and his responsibility for paying for the son's actions. The father may later recoup some of his losses by refusing to find his son a wife and pay the bride-price, and by denying him a share in his estate when he dies.

Among the Ifugao people of the Philippines, a natural father must give his illegitimate child a rice field if he has one that he is not using. The father's kin also support the illegitimate child in all legal and nonlegal disputes as if he or she were legitimate. However, the illegitimate child, as is the case virtually everywhere, has no right to inherit from his natural father or his mother's husband.

Among the Kuria people of Tanzania, offspring are an asset because sons and unmarried daughters represent a source of labor and, in the parents' old age, material security. The offspring of married women are the legally recognized children of her husband. For his right to the children, a man pays a bride-price to his wife's patrilineal family. If he does not pay the bride-price, normally in cattle, the children that he and his wife produce belong to the wife's family. The husband also has full rights in his wife's children even if the natural father of the children is a man other than himself; the only important factor, again, is whether or not he has paid the appropriate bride-price. If a couple divorces, the woman may take some or all of her children to become part of the family of her second husband, and those children become his. This feature of the law is for the emotional and material benefit of the women; they could thus avoid being separated from their children, and they also had the opportunity to bring a son with them if the second marriage produced no sons (as sons were their means of material security in old age). However, she may do this only with the permis-

sion of her first husband, or with the permission of his heirs if he is dead; further, the children do not become the children of their stepfather until the stepfather pays his wife's first husband one head of cattle for each child. The first husband could later cancel the agreement to turn over his children to his ex-wife's new husband by returning the cattle. The children who are themselves involved may also cancel the arrangement so as to once again become heirs of their natural father; however, they must return the cattle paid on their behalf to their stepfather for such an arrangement to be valid.

Barton, Roy F. (1969 [1919]) *Ifugao Law.*

Holleman, J. F. (1952) *Shona Customary Law.*

Rwezaura, Barthazar Aloys. (1985) *Traditional Family Law and Change in Tanzania: A Study of the Kuria Social System.*

LEGITIMACY IN POLITICS

Legitimate political rule may be defined as political rule that is valid in terms of adherence to the positive ideals of established political tradition. Legitimacy, then, basically refers to the acceptability of a leader or a type of leader to the people led. A specific type of leader may be illegitimate in a particular society; for example, a monarch cannot be legitimate in the United States.

A leader's legitimacy typically varies in his or her adherence to the ideals of a political tradition and by the degree to which the ideals are actually accepted by the people. Another way in which legitimacy varied was described by Max Weber. He noted that some leaders are legitimate because of their personal qualities, and that others are legitimate for reasons not directly related to their personal qualities. The leaders legitimated on the basis of their personal qualities Weber called "charismatic" and noted that they tended to be religious or military leaders. Weber called the other type of legitimacy "nonindividual legitimacy," and it is of two kinds. The first he called "traditional legitimacy," and this was legitimacy ascribed to a leader on the basis of mores and jural norms. An English monarch is an example of a leader with "traditional legitimacy." The other kind he called "rational legitimacy," and this was legitimacy achieved through a position in a bureaucracy or other governmental structure. In other words, a bureaucrat has political legitimacy by virtue of his or her position alone.

An interesting example of those qualities that legitimize or act against legitimacy in a leader was provided by Paul Friedrich's 1968 study of a Tarascan Indian cacique in Mexico. The term *cacique* can refer to a number of different positions, from headman to labor boss to a head of state. In Friedrich's study, the cacique was a political leader of a type known as an agrarian cacique, whose name was Pedro Caso. Pedro held power through his use of violence against political enemies and his efforts in promoting the agrarian land ownership reforms that were part of the outcome of the Mexican Revolution, usually by expropriating the lands of landlords and farmers. Agrarian caciques typically work to prevent the abuse of people within their villages by usurious moneylenders.

Pedro had several legitimizing factors in his favor as a leader. Although he claimed the title of cacique for himself, he was part of a politically powerful family that had provided caciques in the past. And though the people of the town were not always happy with the existence of caciques, since they tended to acquire power through violence, they were usually resigned to the caciques' presence.

Pedro was also legitimized by his abilities. He brought some genuine improvements to the lives of the poorer people of the town. He brought about a good deal of land ownership reform, generally following the guidelines of the Agrarian Code, and in this manner provided land for the poor. One way he acquired land for the poor was to have the poor work a plot of land belonging to a wealthy landowner for two years, a time period that gives the person working it ownership according to Article 165 of the Agrarian Code; Pedro was able to do this by forcibly preventing the original owners from working that land for the two-year period.

He brought electricity, water, and a highway to the town. He was a skilled speaker who could also help settle personal disputes and call upon a large network of contacts, including official government bureaucrats, to help people with their efforts to achieve their own goals. Pedro, further, accepted the traditional values of a united and peaceful pueblo. He did not use his wealth and position to create a social gulf between himself and the peasants of the village. His clothes and house were ordinary, and he described himself as an Indian peasant. All of these factors were also legitimizing.

Another type of factor contributing to Pedro's legitimacy were his connections with national politicians. This made him seem more important and thus more valuable to the local peasants. Pedro represents himself to the national leaders as an authentic voice of Indian peasants, thus making himself valuable, and legitimate, to the national leaders.

Pedro also established his legitimacy by attempting to create an ideological and historical link with Emiliano Zapata, the legendary leader of the revolutionary forces of the Mexican Revolution.

On the other hand, there were factors working against the full legitimacy of Pedro as a leader. One of these is the fact that the position of cacique is not an elected one. It is a position that is more or less created by one who seeks to become a cacique. Further, Pedro could never have won an election in the town. Ideologically, he was very far to the left, much too extreme in his beliefs to enjoy popular support. His leftist ideology also made him hostile to the leadership of the church in town, and this further eroded his legitimacy. Pedro opposed the church not only on socialist ideological grounds, but also as a means of reducing the political influence of the priests. Pedro and other agrarian caciques opposed the use of Catholic rituals such as weddings, baptisms, and wakes, and publicly and verbally attacked those who participated in them. To some degree this strategy worked, and some couples eloped as a result; but for many, it was a reason to dislike Pedro. Further, Pedro could not gain democratic support because of his commitment to violence as a means of securing political power. The people of the village may respect the use of violence, but they do not like it. Pedro also had problems with respect to legitimate leadership in that he was not a charismatic individual. People simply did not find him a likeable person. In short, although there were delegitimizing factors in Pedro's leadership, there were enough legitimizing ones that he could effect political leadership and bring about political change.

Friedrich, Paul. (1968) "The Legitimacy of a Cacique." In *Local-Level Politics*, edited by Marc Swartz, 243–269.

Weber, Max. (1958) *From Max Weber*, edited and translated by H. H. Gerth and C. Wright Mills.

LICENSE A license is a right granted by one party to another to do something that would not be legally permissable without the license; licenses may normally be revoked at any time by the grantor of the license. In United States law, a person with a license to use real property does not by virtue of the license have an interest (a right that can be alienated) in the property.

When governments of state societies grant licenses, they usually do so for two distinct reasons—to regulate behavior and to acquire money. One of the most common types of regulatory licenses is a license to dispense alcoholic beverages, the object of which is to control alcohol consumption. Following is a set of statutory sections regulating the selling of alcoholic beverages in railway stations in the Northern Territories of Austrailia from 1939 until 1960. Its main purpose is to restrict the sale of liquor at railway stations to train travelers only, and so to keep the railway stations from becoming pubs or bars for all people in the area (*The Ordinances of the Northern Territory of Australia*, 1961: 1031–1032).

97. Subject to the provisions of the Ordinance, there may be granted to any lessee of premises at any railway station in the Territory which have been leased by the Commonwealth Railways Commissioner for refreshment-rooms a licence to be called a railway licence, in accordance with Form 7 of the Second Schedule.

98. A licence under the last preceding section shall authorize the holder thereof to sell and dispose of liquor in any quantity, at the refreshment-rooms mentioned in the licence to *bona fide* travellers within the meaning of section one hundred and fifty-nine of this Ordinance and to persons other than *bona fide* travellers upon such days and during such hours as are authorized by the licence, any law regulating to the sale of such liquors to the contrary notwithstanding.

99. A railway licence shall not authorize the sale of any liquor to persons other than *bona fide* travellers as defined by section one hundred and fifty-nine of this Ordinance ex-

cept at times to be specified in the licence, and each of those times shall commence not more than half an hourt before the time fixed for the arrival of any passenger train at the station at which the refreshment-rooms are situated and shall continue for not more than half an hour after its departure from that station.

100. A railway licence shall not continue in force or be granted or issued for a longer period than twelve calendar months from the day of its issue.

As previously mentioned, the governments of state societies issue some licenses primarily to increase income. Most of the licenses of this type are applied to profit-making and pleasure activities, behaviors behind which there is a strong motivation and for which people will pay money to engage in. Following is a statute providing for the licensing of boats, whether used for pleasure or profit, from Norfolk Island, a part of Australia some 900 miles northeast of Sydney, in 1934 (*Territory of Norfolk Island Consolidated Laws*, 1934: 156–157).

1. This Ordinance may be cited as the *Licensing of Boats Ordinance 1934*.

2. In this Ordinance, unless the contrary intention appears—

"boat" means any whaleboat or other vessel, whether propelled by oars, wind, steam or other power, and includes a lighter;

"boatman" means the owner, master or person in charge of any boat;

"overseas ship" means any ship employed in trading or going any place in Norfolk Island and places beyond Norfolk Island.

3.—(1) The Administrator may, upon application in writing being made to him, and subject to such conditions as he determines or as are prescribed, grant to the applicant a boat licence or a boatman's licence, as the case may be.

(2) A boat licence shall not be issued under this section to a company unless the company is registered in Norfolk Island according to law.

(3) A boat licence issued under this section shall be in respect of one boat only and the fee for a boat licence shall be One pound.

Provided that no fee shall be payable for a boat licence where the boat is already licensed in pursuance of section five B of the *Customs Ordinance* 1913-1934.

(4) The fee for a boatman's licence shall be Two shillings and sixpence.

4. Any person who uses any boat that is not licensed under this Ordinance or under section five B of the *Customs Ordinance* 1913-1934 for the conveyance of persons or luggage to or from any overseas ship shall be guilty of an offence.

Penalty: Ten pounds.

5. Any boatman who engages in the conveyance of persons or luggage to or from any overseas ship unless he is the holder of a boatman's licence under this Ordinance shall be guilty of an offence.

Penalty: Five pounds.

The Ordinances of the Northern Territory of Australia, in Force on 1st January 1961. (1961) Vol. II.

Territory of Norfolk Island, Consolidated Laws, Being the Norfolk Island Act 1913; the Laws Proclaimed by Proclamation Dated 23rd December, 1913, Which Repealed All Laws Heretofore in Force in Norfolk Island; and Ordinances Made under the Norfolk Island Act 1913, and Rules, Regulations, By-Laws, Proclamations and Notifications Made or Issued under Such Ordinances as in Force on 31st December, 1934. (1934).

LITIGATION Litigation refers to the actual hearing and judgment of a dispute by a legal authority. All legal systems, therefore, use litigation, although the forms it takes in various societies can differ quite remarkably. In some, the dress of the people involved is important (as in Great Britain, where the judge and lawyers must wear special wigs). In the United States, everyone in the courtroom must stand up when the judge enters in order to show respect for his or her office and authority. But in other legal systems, such as that of the Micmac Indians of eastern Canada, there is not even a courtroom, let alone proper courtroom dress or behavior. And there, the two parties to the dispute rarely even meet the legal authority at the same time.

There are a great many issues regarding litigation, which is part of the law of procedure. One of the most vexing is litigation that has no merit, that is, frivolous litigation. Sometimes various parties initiate frivolous lawsuits against an enemy simply to cause the enemy discomfort or expense. Other times, in legal systems in which the process of legal decisionmaking is slow, such as that of the United States, a party can initiate a lawsuit against another party simply to get it to accede to another request it would not otherwise grant. For example, a large company with a great deal of money may want to buy a patent from a small company, which does not wish to sell it. The large company could initiate a frivolous lawsuit against the small company on some unrelated matter, hoping that the expense, time, and effort that the lawsuit would cost the small company, even if the small company won the suit years later, would be more damaging than to sell the patent. This practice of using a lawsuit to gain an advantage in another matter is known as a shakedown suit.

In some societies, the initiation of a frivolous lawsuit may result in sanctions against the one who brings the lawsuit. The same is true for those who repeatedly sue an adversary hoping that one of the suits will cause the adversary some loss or misery.

In feudal times in Japan, parties that brought frivolous lawsuits to the High Court, or repeat-

edly brought a suit that had already been turned down in any court, stood to receive a punishment. Following are some of the rules in feudal Japan on this matter (Hall, 1906: 695–697):

4.—OF SUITS WHICH ARE BROUGHT A SECOND TIME AFTER HAVING BEEN REJECTED AND OF SUITS BROUGHT BEFORE A WRONG TRIBUNAL.

When a suit has been instituted and, when examined in common form, has been found to be unsustainable, it is to be returned to the plaintiff with an endorsement to the effect of its invalidity. If it is again instituted, the plaint is to be returned to the suitor with an order that he is to receive a public reprimand. If the plaint be again preferred to the court the suitor is to be fined. (1720)

If, after bringing a suit in the Magistrate's court and after being fined for persisting in bringing it after its repeated rejection, a suitor abruptly drops his plaint into the Plaint-box and applies to the Council of State (*Goroju*) or the Junior Senators (*Waka-doshiyori*), he must be summoned to appear before the Magistrate, and his plaint shall be again considered, and if it still be found lacking in validity, he shall be again punished by a fine. (1720)

If the parents, children, brothers or other relatives of an obstinate suitor who has been subjected to public reprimand (e.g. handcuffs, fine, house seclusion [note: In *oshikome* the culprit was confined to a room in his won house, was barred up in it, his food passed through a hole and the *nanishi* and his *goningumi* had to keep him under constant surveillance.]) petition for his pardon over and over again, they are not to be subjected to public reprimand for their persistence. (1720)

In general, whenever a plaint is brought before a wrong court the suitor must be directed to bring it before the proper court; should he nevertheless, bring it a second time before the same court, there must be a conference between the two Magistracies, and if they find that the suit is one that cannot be enter-

Traditionally, British judges and barristers wear wigs in court. Two members of court greet each other outside of Westminster Abbey, London, in October 1937 on the occasion of the beginning of the September-to-December court term, called the Michalmas sitting.

tained the suitor must be informed that his petition is inadmissible; and the proper court whose jurisdiction he sought to avoid is to inflict on him a suitable public reprimand. (1722)

If a suit which had once been rejected as inadmissible in a Magistrate's court is again brought before the judge's colleague in the same Magistracy, the suitor, if the manager of a temple, shall be sentenced to close confinement in a single cell, or, if a rustic or a townsman, shall be sentenced to wear handcuffs. [note: The length of the punishments is left to the discretion of the tribunal.] (Customary)

If, without being brought before one of the three Magistrates, a suit is brought direct before the High Court (*Hyojosho*), the suitor must be instructed to bring it before the proper magistrate, by whom it shall be enquired into, and when he has reached his decision, it shall be discussed by the three magistrates and the judgment pronounced by the full bench. (Customary)

If a suit is brought by relatives or connections in the name of a party and no valid reason is given why he should not sue in person, they must be directed to let the party sue in person and their petition is not to be entertained. (Customary)

5.—OF THOSE WHO REPEATEDLY PUT THEIR PLAINT INTO THE PETITION-BOX IN FRONT OF THE HIGH COURT.

If a person puts an inadmissible petition into the Plaint-box in front of the High Court he shall be handcuffed and put in charge of a security [generally the keeper of his provincial hostel in Yedo]; and if his security (the landlord of the hostel at which his provincials put up) petitions a second time for his forgiveness, he shall be directed to caution the offender that if the offence be repeated he will be subjected to a public rebuke (*togame*), and the offender himself must sign a bond pledging himself not to repeat the offence under the said penalty. Thereupon he may be at once released from the handcuffs, whatever might be the number of days for which he was sentenced to wear them.

If the improper petitioner be an ecclesiastic (Buddhist) he shall be given in charge to his head monastery or to the Noticiary (*furegashira*) of his sect: if he be a free lance (literally a waveman [*ronin*], *i.e.* a *samurai* no longer in the service of a feudal lord), he shall be secured by the landowner or the householder of the place where he is stopping; and when they petition for his forgiveness they shall be directed to caution him in the same terms as in the former case, and when his bond not to repeat the offence has been given in, he shall be released. (1741)

Appendix: same year.—A person who, for persistently petitioning through the Plaint-box, has been handcuffed and who after being forgiven again puts his plaint into the box is to be expelled from Yedo, whether he be a resident in the city or in the suburbs.

Any person who, for bringing an inadmissible plaint before the High Court direct (not through the Plaint-box), has been put under bail or been handcuffed, and yet will not cease from urging his suit, is to be dealt with in the same way as above (*i.e.* expulsion from Yedo). (Customary)

Hall, John Carey. (1906) *Japanese Feudal Law: The Institutes of Judicature: Being a Translation of "Go Seibei Shikimoku"; The Magisterial Code of the Hojo Power-Holders* (A.D. 1232).

MARRIAGE Marriage is the legally recognized union of a man and a woman for the purpose of producing legitimate children. Among societies, laws on marriage differ considerably, from what is necessary to create a genuine marriage and how a marriage is dissolved to the kinds of behavior in which married people may engage with respect to each other and each other's families. The Laws regarding marriage are part of the larger field known as family law.

In many societies, the couple who is to marry must become formally betrothed before they can be married. Betrothal is a formal contract to marry in the future. In some societies, betrothal is made by the parents of the male and female who are to marry; in some cases, when the people betrothed are but small children.

In some societies, marriage is at least as much of a union between families as between a man and a woman. Traditionally, among the Cheyenne Indians of the Great Plains, the family of the bride would decide whom a young woman was to marry, oftentimes regardless of her wishes. They had the authority to make a contract to marry by accepting horses sent by the groom's family.

Also among the Cheyenne, the decision as to whom a young woman would marry was left to her brothers, and if she had none, to her father. If a man promised his sister to a particular man, and his sister ran away to elope with another man, then the sister was disowned by her family and the brother was disgraced. It sometimes happened that the brother committed suicide, so great was his disgrace.

Such arranged marriages were common among the Micmac Indians of eastern Canada until the 1970s. Parents of children of marriageable age would decide whom their children were to marry. The prime consideration was that their children marry a mate who was not lazy. Many of the prospective brides and grooms disliked this system intensely, but had no choice but to accept it. They had no choice because, unless their circumstances were very unusual, the young people depended upon their parents for food and shelter for a few more years at least. The system only began to change in the 1960s, when young adults began to go in significant numbers to the state of Maine in August to harvest the blueberry crop. From there, they found that they could easily go to Boston, where they could readily find a job and a place to live. There, they were beyond the control of their parents. They could use their source of livelihood in Boston to force their parents into dropping their insistence on a choice of mate.

The laws regarding marriage among the pre-Soviet Russians are also of interest. Marriage was considered a religious affair as well as a legal one; no marriage was legally binding unless it was performed by church authorities. Marriage was also indissoluble; divorce was impossible. In Russia, marriage also gave men a great deal of power over their wives. Men could abuse and beat their wives so long as they did nothing to endanger life or limb, and if they did they were punished with a prison term. Otherwise, the legal authorities would do nothing to help an abused spouse.

Among the Yoruba people of Nigeria, marriage is very much different. In that society, a bride-price is traditionally paid to complete a marriage, and the payment assures that any children born of the union are considered the husband's legitimate offspring. However, a man has the right to give his daughter or niece in marriage to a friend or benefactor without requiring a bride-price. The Yoruba practice polygyny.

Yoruba law does not recognize divorce. If a woman decides that she would prefer to be with a man other than her husband, she may separate from her husband and live with the man whom she prefers. The second man must pay to the husband the bride-price that the husband originally paid, though none of this money goes to the woman's family. The woman is still considered married to her husband, and her children are still regarded as his.

The Yoruba traditionally took the matters of adultery and of the seduction of betrothed women and girls very seriously. If a man seduced a woman or girl who was betrothed to another man, then he must pay whatever bride-price was asked, and pay to the man originally affianced to the female whatever expenses he had paid in the courting of the female; after this was done, the seducer and the girl or woman were married. If a man seduced a married woman and then walked near the house of the husband, the husband had the right to seriously wound the seducer with impunity. It was also legally appropriate for the seducer and the husband to fight over the wife. If one of the combatants became scared to fight, he relinquished his claim on the woman, and the two men became lifelong friends. If the two fought, and one man was killed, then the survivor could claim the woman

as his. If both men died as a result of their duel, then the woman was punished with the death penalty as a murderer for having caused the deaths.

Among the Kuria people of Tanzania, the law regarding husbands and wives provides that a woman who divorces her husband to marry again may return to her first husband if her second marriage produces no sons. This is because sons support their parents in old age, and such support is crucial if the parents are to survive when they get old.

Kuria law does prohibit adultery, but generally no legal cases concerning adultery are brought to the attention of legal authorities unless it is a case of a woman who commits adultery in a flagrant manner. In other words, husbands do not mind that their wives have affairs with other men so long as they do not do so in a way that embarrasses the husband publicly.

Under Muslim law (Islamic law), one may divorce one's spouse by repeating the words of repudiation or divorce, known as the *Talak*, three times.

Ajisafe, A. K. (1946) *The Laws and Customs of the Yoruba People.*

Kovalevsky, Maxime. (1966 [1891]) "The Modern Russian Family." In *Anthropology and Early Law,* edited by Lawrence Krader, 148–170.

Llewellyn, Karl N., and E. Adamson Hoebel. (1961 [1941]) *The Cheyenne Way.*

Rwezaura, Barthazar Aloys. (1985) *Traditional Family Law and Change in Tanzania: A Study of the Kuria Social System.*

Strouthes, Daniel P. (1994) *Change in the Real Property Law of a Cape Breton Island Micmac Band.*

MARXISM

Karl Marx had two main objectives in his writings. The first was to help bring about a Communist revolution. He made this call most clearly and expressly in 1848 in *The Communist Manifesto,* which he cowrote with Friedrich Engels, and called for, above all else, the abolition of private property, the dictatorship of the working class, and particularly the control of the means of production by the working class and the abolition of capital.

The second, which is of interest to us because of its bearing on the cross-cultural study of society, was to provide a scientific analysis of human economic, political, and social evolution. Marx developed a novel form of scientific analysis that used historical, political, economic, and anthropological data, and analyzed them to demonstrate their intimate connections to each other, particularly with respect to nineteenth-century Europe.

Scientific analyses provide generalizations and predictions. Marx, along with his collaborator, Friedrich Engels, made specific social generalizations and predictions. As a general principle of social evolution, Marx and Engels advanced what they called "the materialist conception of history," saying that the true analysis of social evolution should concentrate on the production of the goods that support human life and the exchange of those goods, which they called "the basis of all social structure" (Marx and Engels, 1968: 417). With regard to the actual progression of social evolution, they said that after a long period of social and technological development, mankind reached a stage in which civilization was formed, at which time socioeconomic classes and the state came into being. At first, the state is feudal, and the aristocracy, or upper classes, is dominant. Later, as technology advances with the invention of productive machinery, capitalism develops, and the capitalist middle class (or bourgeoisie) becomes dominant.

Marx and Engels also made the prediction that as society further developed, the working class (or proletariat) would become dominant, communism would destroy capitalism, and the state would "wither away."

Marx and Engels devoted much of their efforts to understanding capitalism and evaluating its moral implications. Capitalism has been defined in several ways, but to Marx and Engels, it is "living labour serving accumulated labour as a means for maintaining and multiplying the exchange value of the latter" (Marx and Engels, 1968: 82). In this definition, Marx refers to capital as accumulated labor, though capital is usually defined as collected accumulated wealth. The capitalist reproduces his capital by hiring workers, whom he pays with his capital, and who create for him additional capital.

Marx and Engels, and later Lenin, were clearly opposed in their writings to the moral implications of capitalism. Their principal objection to it is that it denies the wage laborer the full measure of the value of his labor, but gives part of it instead to the owner of the capital. Thus, the capitalist's capital grows, but the wage laborer may have no benefit from his relationship with the capitalist (the owner of the capital and the employer) other than to acquire enough material goods to survive. Finally, as Marx and Engels discovered and described, capitalism cannot exist without the wage laborer.

Several other features of classical capitalism (capitalism as it was practiced in nineteenth-century Europe, before the advent of significant social welfare legislation) drew fire from Marx and Engels. First, they attacked the great disparities in wealth between the wealthy classes and the working class. Second, they decried the wretched living conditions that faced many of those belonging to the working class; this was a special interest of Engels, who described it in some detail. Third, they described the competition among workers for employment; when there

Karl Marx (1818–1883)

are more workers than available jobs, as is usually the case in capitalist societies, employers can keep wages low and still be able to acquire workers, since workers will work at low wages to avoid starvation. Fourth, Marx and Engels criticized the automation of industry, which serves to reduce the skills required of workers and to reduce the number of workers needed, both of which they claimed lead to reduced wages.

Marx and Engels were primarily interested in technological and economic data in their analyses. Marx called his style of analysis "materialist." He paid especial attention to which people or groups of people in a society had control of the majority of the society's material wealth and, even more importantly, who had control of the ability to produce that material wealth, which he called "the means of production." Marx's theory of materialism argued that relations between different components of society are material in nature and not primarily religious, kinship-related, geographic, political, or legal. For example, in *The Communist Manifesto,* Marx and Engels went so far as to say "The bourgeois [man] sees in his wife a mere instrument of production."

In making their argument in favor of a Communist revolution, Marx and Engels faced many problems, the chief being the then commonly accepted idea that the social and economic systems in place in Europe had been there all along and were timeless and immutable save for minor technological advances. How, the problem seemed to be, could Marx and Engels convince people that a new social-economic system—communism—could come about if they believed that no other social-economic system other than capitalism had ever existed.

Marx and Engels began attempting, as much as possible, to be scientific in their analysis and rely upon empirical evidence. They opposed their approach to the religious, which depends upon faith. This made them two of the world's earliest social scientists. They gathered primarily historical data, intending to prove that other forms of social-economic systems had, in fact, existed in Europe, and that therefore still other forms (particularly communism) could exist in the future. Marx was interested in the data collected by the national governments of Europe at the time, especially British data. He assembled data on production, technology, wages, and wealth accumulation in his book *Das Kapital.* He also undertook studies of medieval history and wrote about feudal society.

Marx and Engels also made use of philosophy to support their arguments in favor of historical materialism/political economy as a means of analysis, as well as to support their arguments that social-economic systems change, as do all natural phenomena. They used a special form of philosophical inquiry known as dialectics, which originated with Plato and the Platonists. Dialectics is concerned primarily with distinguishing truth from error. In the nineteenth century, a major thinker in the field of dialectics was the German philosopher Georg Wilhelm Friedrich Hegel. For Hegel, truth was to be found in the mind and in ideas, not in the objective world. The dialectics of Marx and Engels was a reaction against Hegelian dialectics, and they named their theory dialectical materialism. Dialectical materialism holds that the only truth is the material truth, and that matter is always changing. Matter, in fact, says Marx, is the source of all change; change cannot occur without matter, and matter cannot exist without change. Change occurs through a struggle of opposites. Marx called these opposites contradictions. Any particular socioeconomic system, such as capitalism, produces its own contradictions that inevitably cause it to fail and to be replaced by a more advanced system. For capitalism, Marx said, one major contradiction lies in its need for growth. As technology improves due to a desire among capitalists for greater productivity and thus greater profits, competition among producers actually results in a lowering of profits and a reduction in the number of capitalists, as the smaller capitalists' enterprises are swallowed up by those of the larger capitalists. The contradiction that Marx saw as most damaging to capitalism was the ever-increasing development of technology; here again, Marx's materialistic emphasis can be seen. As technology improves, and the smaller capitalists lose out to the greater productive power of the large capitalists, wealth becomes concentrated in fewer and fewer hands, and the working class grows larger and larger. The increase in technology allows members of the ever-larger and ever-poorer working class to communicate with each other, to unite and cooperate in a revolt against the few remaining large capitalists and thus bring about a Communist revolution. The process that Marx believed would bring about the end of capitalism was the same general process by which capitalism brought about the end of feudalism. Engels (Marx and Engels 1968: 625) gave the following example of the latter:

> At a certain stage the new productive forces set in motion by the bourgeoisie—in the first place the division of labor and the combination of many detail laborers [Teilarbeiter] in one general manufactory—and the conditions and requirements of exchange, developed through these productive forces, became incompatible with the existing order of production handed down by history and sanctified by law, that is to say, incompatible with the privileges of the guild and the numerous other personal and local privileges (which were only so many fetters to the unprivileged estates) of the feudal order of society. The productive forces represented by the bourgeoisie rebelled against the order of production represented by the feudal landlords and the guildmasters. The result is known: the feudal fetters were smashed, gradually in England, at one blow in France. In Germany the process is not yet finished. But just as, at a definite stage of its development, manufacture

came into conflict with the feudal order of production, so now large-scale industry has already come into conflict with the bourgeois order of production established in its place.

We see also in the quote above one of the hallmarks of Marx's and Engels's theory, that social evolution proceeds in stages, just as does biological evolution, as shown by Darwin, and the history of ideas, as shown by Hegel. In all cases, more complex and advanced stages replace the simpler and less-advanced stages that preceded them. Evolution, whether biological, intellectual, or social, is thus seen by Marx and Engels as both revolutionary in its character and unstoppable.

However, the philosophical theories of Marx and Engels have a logical inconsistency. Marx and Engels said that everything is always in a state of change and that there is a struggle of opposites. Marx and Engels apparently did not mean that these processes continue to operate once human society entered the stage of development of communism. At that time, there would be no more struggle of opposites and no more changes. They did not say why the laws of nature as they described them would suddenly cease to operate when communism came about, though it is obvious that they believed that communism is the most perfect state for humanity.

The third major source Marx and Engels used to assist their arguments came from another branch of the social sciences, anthropology. Marx and Engels had wanted to be able to show that all societies go through a series of stages of development, ending up with capitalism and then, of course, communism. But they had no data for societies before the period at which the Greeks and Romans began writing down their history. They turned to the writings of a man whom many consider to be America's first anthropologist, Lewis Henry Morgan. In his book *Ancient Society*, Morgan had attempted to trace the development of mankind's society from its earliest beginnings to modern European civilization (note that Morgan believed in a single line of social evolution, and that European society represented the most advanced society). Morgan noticed from the accounts of various societies written by missionaries and explorers that people in these societies were at different levels of technological development and had different systems of classifying kin by the terms of address they used. Morgan believed that these levels of technology represented levels of social evolution. He argued that technology always advanced from the simple to the more complex, and that thus peoples with simple technologies were less advanced than peoples with more complex technologies. Each society passed through a single line of stages of technology, he argued, graduating from one level to the next most complex; this kind of theory is known as a unilineal theory of social evolution. Morgan described three stages of savagery (lower, middle, and upper), which are followed by three stages of barbarism (lower, middle, and upper), which are in turn followed by civilization (which begins with the invention of an alphabet). For example, the middle stage of savagery begins with the invention of fishing and fire, and the upper stage of savagery begins with the invention of archery. Morgan claimed that by studying other societies with less-advanced levels of technology, we can see in them the same stages of social evolution that Europeans must have passed through before reaching the stage of civilization. Morgan tried to tie levels of technology to the evolution of social organization by using data on kinship terminological systems. Engels used the data and analysis that Morgan supplied to trace the social evolution of all peoples and to show how the European civilizations of his time were the product of long periods of social evolution. This he did in a work called *The Origin of the Family, Private Property*

and the State in Light of the Researches of Lewis H. Morgan (Marx and Engels 1968: 468–593). The conclusion that one should draw from the fact that European civilization was the product of a long period of social evolution, Engels argued, is that further social evolution will occur, and that it will be in the direction of communism.

Marx's and Engels's analyses and predictions may be criticized on several grounds. With regard to their analyses of non-Western peoples, the two men may be criticized for using data insufficient for their purposes. At the time, little data was available on non-Western societies, and much of what was available was simply incorrect due to poor collection methods. This same problem hampered the work of other early social scientists, including Montesquieu, Morgan, and Durkheim. Thus, for Marx and Engels to make generalizations and predictions about humankind in general, as they purported to do, was impossible since they were essentially limited to data from Europe. For Marx and Engels to predict human social behavior on the basis of European social behavior alone is comparable to the biologist who would try to explain the behavior of all mammals using as his source of data only rats; it cannot be done.

Another critique that may be offered is that Marx became emotionally attached to the subject matter of his analysis. Scientific analysis must be pursued dispassionately, for if a scientist is not dispassionate in his or her work, the scientist's generalizations cannot be trusted, and the results will show what the scientist wishes them to show rather than the truth. That Marx and Engels passionately wished for a Communist revolution is made clear in *The Communist Manifesto*. It also cannot be doubted that this emotional attachment to their cause was one of the main factors for their prediction of inevitable Communist revolutions in industrialized societies and the "withering away" of the state, predictions that have not come true.

Marx and Engels may also be criticized in two respects with regard to their theory of unilineal evolution. The first is the theory itself. Societies change, it is true, but not in orderly and predictable fashions, and certainly not in the stages Morgan outlined. Various peoples may have used at the same time technology specified as characteristic of several different stages, and may have technology of a more advanced stage but not the technology associated with a lower stage. Take, for example, the Micmac Indians of Nova Scotia, who at contact with white people had domesticated dogs (a characteristic of the middle stage of barbarism), but knew nothing of pottery (a characteristic of the lower stage of barbarism). To which stage of social evolution would we assign them? This was a serious flaw in the theories of Marx, Engels, and other unilineal evolutionists. The consequences of this flaw may be seen in most of Soviet anthropology, which was dedicated to categorizing groups of people by stage of development. Soviet anthropologists, who were expected to be consistent in their work with the principles Marx and Engels laid down, spent much of their time trying to justify the classifications of peoples into stages they had made. Western anthropologists long ago cast aside theories of unilineal social evolution and their stages of development as useless.

The second aspect of the theory that has been proven invalid is its reliance on measures of technology as the decisive characteristic for judging social progress or level of advancement. This itself is a characteristic of Western ethnocentrism. Because many of us in the West like to think of ourselves as more advanced than the people in the rest of the world, we judge all peoples on the basis of what we do the best, namely create new technologies. For example, we can say that the United States has the most advanced technology. But can we say that the United States is the most advanced nation when it has not been able to produce philosophy as great as did the ancient Greeks or the nineteenth-century Germans? Our legal system is far less logically elaborated than that of the ancient Romans. We do not even have as effective a nonlegal means of controlling damaging behavior as the Micmac Indians of Canada. In other words, technological advancement is but one way to measure social progress, and we cannot say that any one society's social progress is greater than another's if we only measure one criterion, as did Marx and Engels.

Kolakowski, Leszek. (1978) *Main Currents of Marxism: Its Rise, Growth, and Dissolution.* Vol. 1.

Lenin, Vladimir I. (1976 [1917]) *The State and Revolution.*

Marx, Karl. (1906 [1883, 1885, 1894]) *Capital: A Critique of Political Economy,* edited by Friedrich Engels. Translated by Samuel Moore and Edward Aveling.

Marx, Karl, and Friedrich Engels. (1968) *Karl Marx and Friedrich Engels: Selected Works in One Volume.*

Morgan, Lewis Henry. (1963 [1877]) *Ancient Society.*

MILITARY SOCIETIES

Military societies were voluntary associations of men among many of the Indian societies of the North American Great Plains. Men of all ages could join simply by volunteering to do so. The military societies coordinated hunting and raiding parties, made decisions on less-important day-to-day matters, and acted as the tribe's law enforcement apparatus. They were also social clubs for the men.

One of the best-described systems of military societies is that of the Cheyenne Indians. The Cheyenne had six military societies: the Fox Soldiers, the Dog Men, the Northern Crazy Dogs, the Elk Soldiers, the Bowstring Soldiers, and the Shield Soldiers. Some of these societies were known among the Cheyenne by other names as well.

With the exception of the Dog Soldiers, the members of each military society were spread among numerous winter bands (the Cheyenne congregated as a single group in the warm months and spread out into forty-four bands during the winter months to hunt the smaller bison herds). The Dog Soldiers, members formed a band of their own and lived in that band only. They were led by military chiefs rather than by a civil chief, as in other bands. In addition, some military societies were limited to bands of a particular geographic range. For example, the Northern Crazy Dogs only lived among northern Cheyenne bands, whereas the Bowstring Soldiers only had members among southern Cheyenne bands.

Each military society had two "headmen" and two "servants" or doormen. These four men were also war chiefs of the Cheyenne tribe. The headmen were the ones who made the decisions for the military society unless they were deadlocked on a particular matter, and then the two servants would make the decision.

Military society chiefs held office for life, although the chances of being killed in battle were rather high. In such a circumstance, the office was filled by a member of the society who had been elected by all members of the society. Further, if a war chief decided that he had become too old for the job, he could bestow his office on a younger man of his own choosing. Finally, a military society chief could be removed from office if he broke the laws pertaining to his duties. Take, for example, the case of Buffalo Chief, a chief of the Dog Men society. A Cheyenne man had gone hunting bison during a time in which the Cheyenne had prohibited bison hunting. Buffalo Chief was supervising the punishment, which was to destroy the offender's tipi, when the offender decided to fight back by hitting one of the people destroying his tipi. Buffalo Chief saw this and wrongly shot and killed the offender. When the offender's wife then ran to him with a knife, he wrongly shot and killed her too. Buffalo Chief not only lost his office for the murders, but was exiled from the Cheyenne tribe. Another military society chief, Last Bull, was removed from office for dealing too harshly with offenders while carrying out his police duties.

Military society members could become civil chiefs as well, though they had to relinquish their military society memberships to do so. This kept the military societies from gaining undue influence over the most important decisions affecting the tribe as a whole, since it was the duty of the civil chiefs to make decisions that would affect the strategic future of the entire Cheyenne people.

One of the principal duties of the military societies was to make and enforce the law with regard to certain types of behaviors. They made sure that no one spoiled the large tribal bison hunts by scaring away the bison by hunting them before the rest of the tribe was ready. They would whip or destroy the tipi of one who hunted without permission. They also policed warfare activities. In one case, men who failed to kill an enemy warrior were whipped severely. They also punished a young woman who had aborted her fetus by banishing her until the tribe's sacred arrows had been renewed; in Cheyenne society, all Cheyenne have the right to life, even the unborn.

Llewellyn, Karl N., and E. Adamson Hoebel. (1961 [1941]) *The Cheyenne Way.*

MISPRISION

Misprision is the illegal act of failing to report to the proper authorities knowledge that one has concerning the commission of a crime. In the United States, as well as in many other societies, misprision is not recognized as a legal offense. This is changing, however, in some parts of the United States, where doctors and teachers who see evidence of child abuse may face criminal liability if they fail to report it to the proper authorities.

The use of misprision is common in Communist countries, where it is one tool among many that governments use to control the behavior of people. The negative side to misprision as a legal offense is that it degrades morally acceptable behavior by forcing friends and family members to report each other for the commission of crimes.

Following are two statutes from the formerly Communist Hungarian government regarding misprision with respect to civil and military desertion (Ministry of Justice of the Hungarian People's Republic, 1978: 133, 189):

Section 219

(1) A person who obtains credible information:
  (a) of preparation for the perpetration of an offence defined in Section 217, pars. (2) through (4) [dealing with leaving the country without permission], or the offence defined in Section 218,
  (b) of a soldier making preparations for deserting abroad [Section 343, par. (3)],
  (c) of an offence as defined in the clauses above, committed yet still undetected, and fails to report this to the authorities as soon as possible, commits a misdemeanour and shall be punished with deprivation of liberty up to one year, or with reformatory and educative labour, or with a fine.

(2) The kin of the perpetrator is not punishable for misprision.

Section 344

A person who obtains credible information of preparations made by a person to desert to a foreign country, or of such offence committed but not yet discovered, and fails to report it to the authorities as soon as he can do so, commits a felony and shall be punished with deprivation of liberty up to three years. The kin of the perpetrator is not punishable for misprision.

Ministry of Justice of the Hungarian People's Republic. (1978) *The Statutes of the Hungarian People's Republic, Act IV of 1978 on Criminal Code.*

MONARCHY

Monarchy is a form of government in which only one person rules; the term is derived from the Greek words *monos* (alone) and *archein* (to be first, to rule). The existence of a monarchy does not mean that only one person has power (such a government would be an autocracy), but rather that one person ostensibly makes the decisions. For example, the British government is a monarchy, although the ruler, the king or queen, has little genuine power. On the other hand, those who do have the true power of the government, the legislators who sit in Parliament, do everything in the name of the monarch. Likewise, the court system operates in the name of the king or queen; the judges speak on behalf of the king or queen and the criminal prosecutors (known as crown prosecutors) act as legal representatives of the king or queen, who is the one ostensibly offended by criminal acts rather than the society as a whole.

The term *monarch* is most often associated with a monarch of a particular type, a king or queen, who is royalty. Thus, the term *monarch* is often used synonymously with a royal ruler, a king or a queen. However, the term can also be applied accurately to autocratic leaders such as Adolf Hitler, Joseph Stalin, Mao Zedong, and Fidel Castro. All autocrats are monarchs, but not all monarchs are autocrats.

MULTIPLICITY OF LEGAL LEVELS The theory of a multiplicity of legal levels, also known as the theory of legal pluralism, was developed by anthropologist Leopold Pospisil. The theory, briefly stated, is that society is composed of various functioning groups and subgroups at various "levels" of society, from small, less inclusive groups (such as families and schools) at the bottom levels to large and more inclusive groups (such as the state of Nebraska or the United States of America) at the top levels. Each of these groups has its own legal system, usually subordinate to the legal systems of the group or groups at the next higher level, until one reaches the top level of the nation and its supreme legal system.

The theory depends upon the idea that a society has a societal structure, meaning that it is composed of groups and subgroups that have a system of mutual interrelationships. In other words, these groups are ultimately connected to one another, each through its connections to yet other groups and its partially shared memberships with other groups. For example, if one is a student at a state university in New York State, he or she is a member of the group of people who are members of the State University of New York. The State University of New York group is tied to the New York State government, another group, which is tied to the United States government, which is in turn tied to many of the other groups in the United States, and so on.

Haile Selassie, emperor of Ethiopia, ruled as a monarch from 1930 to 1974.

Groups typically have functions. That is, they are composed of people brought together to get something done. The function of the third-shift group of workers at an auto parts plant might be to make spark plugs or fuel pumps. The function of a classroom at a high school in Kentucky is to teach young adults knowledge. The function of a nuclear family is to socialize and to provide for the physical needs of children and prepare them for membership in the larger society.

All groups that have functions also have leaders and authorities. This must be so because otherwise nothing would ever get done by the groups, and they would cease to be functioning groups. For example, take the example of the group that operates a factory. Decisions, requiring an authority, must be made about the product the factory produces, about who the workers are and who selects them, about when and how much workers are to be paid, about procuring the materials the factory uses, and many other things. Also, there must be an authority who settles disagreements among the members of the group. If two workers disagree about how something is to be made, a decision has to be made as to which method will be used. Behind these decisions are principles, the laws that guide behavior in the factory. In the nuclear family, as well, decisions have to be made, and someone or some subgroup (usually the parents) have to lead the implementation of the decisions made. The "rules" laid down by parents for their children are some of the laws of that family.

An important feature of groups themselves is that they have absolute membership. Either one is a member of a group or one is not. This feature can be seen in combination with that of leadership and authority. The leaders of a group and the authorities of a group have the right to lead and to make decisions only with respect to members of that group. A father and mother can make decisions concerning their own children, but not the children of the family down the street. A plant manager's decisions affect the people who work in his or her factory, not another factory across town.

Finally, we can see all of these patterns in terms of a larger pattern of legal levels. At the lower legal levels, we have the family, the factory, the school, etc. All of these groups have their own legal systems and their own laws. But these groups are also parts of larger groups. All of them may be part of the group known as the membership of the city of Chicago, for example. The members of the city of Chicago in turn are members of a larger group, the state of Illinois. Finally, the members of the state of Illinois are members of the larger group known as the United States of America. Each of these more or less inclusive groups have their own legal systems and laws that apply to all members. These

levels of inclusiveness are thus also legal levels, for the legal decisions made at one level affect all of the levels below it.

In contemporary U.S. society, there are numerous legal levels. There are also numerous low legal level groups to which an American citizen may belong, including family, church, school, employment group, social club, etc. Between the family legal level and the top legal level of the federal government, there are at least two legal levels, the municipal level and the state legal level. In some places, there is the community legal level, which may regulate such things as building codes and the admission of children. In some places also, the county or parish, an intermediate level between municipal and state levels, is of some importance.

In technologically primitive societies, the number of groups to which one belongs is usually much fewer, although the number of legal levels may not differ greatly. The woodlands Cree of northeastern Canada, for example, traditionally had the following groups of which an individual was a member: the nuclear family, the extended family, the winter band, and the summer band. Each one of these represents a separate legal level.

However, some legal systems can exist in a society in conflict with the legal system that is authorized by the society's central government. For example, the legal system that the mafia uses to control the behavior of its members is often in conflict with the laws of the United States. Under mafia law, for instance, it is legal for one "made" (or full) member to kill another "made" member under orders from the appropriate mafia authorities; such a killing is of course illegal under U.S. law. Thus, one way in which an unofficial legal system can exist within a society is for that organization to create its own laws.

Another way for unofficial law to come about is for a local legal system to continue to exist even after a national legal system is extended to cover the small society that gave birth to the local system. A good example of this is the legal systems of some North American Indian peoples, which continue to exist and function despite the imposition of the U.S. and Canadian federal legal systems. In such cases, the indigenous legal systems fulfill social and cultural needs that the large national systems were not designed to fulfill.

Another example of a traditional legal system continuing to function despite the imposition of a new national legal system can be found in India. There, the traditional village *panchayat*s (not to be confused with the *Nyaya Panchayat*s [or "justice panchayats"] developed by the federal government in recent times) still work to resolve disputes among members of the village in some rural areas. Though they do not enjoy the recognition of the federal government, they are known to and are tolerated by federal officials, including court officials. The *panchayat* continues because in many parts of India, use of the official courts has not yet become common. It also continues primarily in single-caste villages. In earlier times, the *panchayat*s of mixed-caste villages were controlled by the higher castes, who used their social position to intimidate the lower castes, especially the *Harijan*s (also known as the low-caste people, the people without caste, or the untouchables). When India gained its independence, the government called for social equality and the end of the caste system; it also set aside jobs for *Harijan*s. As a result, the relationships between members of different castes became contentious, and those in the lower castes became much less likely to submit to the insults and degradations of the upper castes; thus, where upper castes controlled the *panchayat*, people frequently turned to the Indian court system rather than the *panchayat*. However, in many rural single-caste villages (as well as in some rural mixed-caste villages), the *panchayat* continues.

Where the village is predominantly *Harijan*, and people of upper castes later come to live there, the *panchayat*, composed of *Harijan*s, will often refuse to become involved in a dispute between a *Harijan* and an upper-caste person, especially if the upper-caste person aggressively asserts his position using violence, as was common in earlier times. Simply put, the *Harijan panchayat* in such a situation would fear for its members' own safety if it intervened. In some other cases, though, the *panchayat* will pursue political means and either make a display of force itself on behalf of a wronged *Harijan* or supplicate itself before upper-caste antagonists and plead for mercy on behalf of a *Harijan* man whom the upper-caste men have been beating. Overall, however, the *Harijan panchayat* is largely ineffective in dealing with aggressive upper-caste people, and for this reason some *Harijan* villages have forbidden members of other castes from settling in their midst.

The *panchayat* is composed of older, married men, and employs primarily psychological rather than physical sanctions; most often, the offender is expected to confess his wrongs and then is lectured and cautioned to mend his ways. Thus, the function of the *panchayat* is primarily restitutive rather than punitive. That is, its intent is to restore social relations as they existed prior to the commission of the offense rather than to punish the offender; this is especially important in small villages, in which all members know and interact with each other on a daily basis. This is another reason why the *panchayat* has been replaced by Indian courts in urban centers. In the cities, there is less need for restitution, because the people involved will frequently have little need to work together cooperatively in the future; thus, in the Indian court system, punishment of the offender is more likely and more severe. Though the *panchayat* is still alive today, its numbers and relative influence are on the wane.

A second important source of unofficial law within a larger society is discontent among various subgroups of the larger society with regard to the way in which the legal system of the larger society handles disputes. If the larger society cannot control disputes effectively, small sub-groups within the larger society will often attempt to control these disputes themselves. Such was the case in rural west-central Tanzania in the 1980s. Tanzania as a whole saw a great increase in criminal activity during the 1970s, and the Tanzanian government proved unable to control it. The Nyamwezi and Sukuma peoples of west-central Tanzania responded by inventing their own legal system to control crime, a legal system whose laws were based upon their own traditional values and social organization. This system, which they brought to life in the 1980s, is operated by groups of people known as *Sungusungu;* each *Sungusungu* group normally includes all of the people of the village that the group administers. The group is led by a chief (*ntemi*), a chief's assistant (*ntwale*), a secretary (*katibu*), and a chief commander (*kamanda mkuu*). A major role of the *Sungusungu* groups is to retrieve stolen cattle and to punish the thieves. The activities of a village's *Sungusungu* are essentially secret, both to avoid attacks by the thieves, who are willing to die in the commission of thefts, and to avoid the notice of the Tanzanian authorities who would punish them for the killing of the thieves. The *Sungusungu* also provides food of those who chase the thieves, since the pursuit is likely to be long and arduous.

Two other sources of trouble that the *Sungusungu* deals with are adultery by wives and witchcraft. In the case of witchcraft, the witch is discovered and fined. In the case of adultery by wives, the main concern of the *Sungusungu* is to prevent the men involved from fighting. The *Sungusungu* deals with this by tracking down the deserting wife and returning her to her husband, as well as fining the man for whom she left her husband. In the case of adultery, the bulk of the fines go to the husband; in all other types of cases, all of the fines imposed go to the

Sungusungu. The Sukuma and Nyamwezi people prefer the *Sungusungu* to the Tanzanian courts for disputes over adulterous wives because the Tanzanian courts were said to be unjustly unpredictable in their decisions. The *Sungusungu* also returns girls who elope to their parents.

The *Sungusungu* further tries cases of ordinary disputes between members of the village. After a complaint has been made to one of the officers of the *Sungusungu,* the alleged offender is summoned before the *Sungusungu* committee. After making formulaic greetings, the alleged offender is persuaded to confess his or her wrongs. Then, the accused offers to pay a fine. His or her first offer is always too small for the gravity of the offense, but he or she gradually increases the offer until one at last meets with the standard used by the *Sungusungu* committee, which then applauds to show its approval of the appropriate offer. This method has the advantage that the guilty cannot readily complain to the federal authorities, since he or she has participated in the determination of his or her own guilt and its punishment.

The individual who refuses to admit guilt, or who admits guilt but does not pay a fine, is usually ostracized. A further inducement to admit guilt and to pay fines is the ostracism of the guilty party's entire household as well. Ostracism in these societies means that the members of the household may expect no assistance from the other members of the village. The entire membership of the village works together to ensure that the ostracism is complete; those who do not ostracize the guilty may themselves receive punishment. Members of the village also assist the *Sungusungu* by reporting serious disputes to the officers of the *Sungusungu;* failure to do so is noted and is taken into account when the person involved is brought before the *Sungusungu* on a charge of improper behavior. People who do not take part in any *Sungusungu*-ordered activities, such as searching for a lost child, are fined.

See also LEGAL ANTHROPOLOGY; MISPRISION.

Bukurura, Sufian Hemed. (1994) "The Maintenance of Order in Rural Tanzania: The Case of the Sungusungu." *Journal of Legal Pluralism and Unofficial Law* 34: 1–29.

Pospisil, Leopold. (1974 [1971]) *Anthropology of Law: A Comparative Theory.*

Vincentnathan, S. George. (1992) "The Social Construction of Order and Disorder in Two South Indian Communities." *Journal of Legal Pluralism and Unofficial Law* 32: 65–102.

N

Charles-Louis de Secondat, Baron de La Brède et de Montesquieu (1689–1755)

Natural Law may be defined as law that agrees with human nature and that therefore is essential for social peace and happiness; a knowledge of Natural Law is derived by pure reason. Natural Law is thought of as a group of principles belonging to the world of natural objects that, if fully implemented by man, would cause the world to exist in a state of universal harmony. Theorists of Natural Law believe that human nature is the same everywhere, and that Natural Law is the same for everyone. They also believe that Natural Law is *a priori*, independent of culture, time, and space, natural to mankind and common to all men. Natural Law may be thought of as a moral philosophy; actual laws, of course, can never completely conform to Natural Law, though Natural Law is often used in the formulation of actual laws and rules. Natural Law is an invention of the philosophical traditions of European culture, and its basic tenets had their origin in ancient Greece.

Since Natural Law is a matter of morality and philosophy, and since each culture has its own ideas about morality and moral philosophy, it should come as no surprise that there can be no one Natural Law. Each culture has different ideas about what is moral behavior and what is not. Therefore, the idea that there is one set of morally correct laws (Natural Law) for all of humankind is absurd. In terms of morality, human nature is not everywhere the same, an idea first broached by the French social thinker Montesquieu, who lived from 1689 to 1755.

A good example of this is can be had by comparing the treatment of patricide in our society and in pre-Communist China. By the moral standards of our society, the killing of a man by his son is considered as reprehensible as the killing of a man by his father. In some cases, the killing of a man by his son is considered less reprehensible than the reverse; for example, in cases in which the father has been abusing his son,

179

courts have often been lenient. In pre-Communist China, on the other hand, the killing of a man by his son was considered one of the most reprehensible of acts, no matter what the circumstances. Even if the father abused his son, patricide was harshly punished and there were no grounds for leniency. On the other hand, there were many justifiable reasons for a man to kill his son with impunity. The Chinese, of course, considered their laws in this regard perfectly "natural," and the fact that people in United States society do not is the reason that there is no such thing as a truly natural law.

See also JUSTICE; LEGAL ANTHROPOLOGY

Gierke, Otto von. (1957 [1934]) *Natural Law and the Theory of Society: 1500 to 1800.*

Grotius, Hugo. (1925 [1625]) *De Jure Belli ac Pacis Libri Tres.* Translated by Francis W. Kelsey.

Montesquieu, C. L. J. de Secondat, Baron de la Brède et de. (1750) *De l'esprit des lois.* Vols. I, II.

Pospisil, Leopold. (1974 [1971]) *Anthropology of Law: A Comparative Theory.*

Pufendorf, Samuel von. (1927 [1682]) *De Officio Hominus et Civis Juxta Legem Naturalem Libri Duo.* Translated by Frank Gardner Moore.

Seidler, Michael. (1990) *Samuel Pufendorf's On the Natural State of Men.* Translated and annotated by Michael Seidler.

Whewell, William. (1853) *Grotius on War and Peace.* Vol. I.

ordeals and oaths are used to settle disputes. Unlike ordeals, which are not distributed around the world, oaths are used by cultures in all regions.

Oaths are most commonly used to settle disputes in which members of the community cannot easily decide which party is telling the truth. For example, among the Wolof and Tiv of West Africa, a person's willingness to take an oath is interpreted as a sign that he is telling the truth while resistance is a sign that he is not telling the truth. The dispute is then likely to be resolved in favor of the oath-taker. The Crow Indians of the Great Plains of the United States used oaths when there were disputes over counting coup. In that society, male warriors placed great positive value on counting coup, or touching the body of an enemy. The one who touched the enemy first enjoyed much greater prestige than anyone who counted coup on that body afterwards. Thus, it sometimes happened that more than one person claimed to be the first man to count coup on any particular enemy. In this event, the two warriors would each put a knife in his mouth, point the knife in the direction of the sun, and say a formula that asked the sun to witness the oath and called for the death of the warrior who lied. The first of the two men to suffer a significant injury was believed by the rest of the group to be the imposter, and the accolades would go to the other man. In the society of the Ostyak, in Siberia, the oath-taker swears the truth of his statements by saying, over a bear's nose, "may a bear eat me if I tell a lie." If the oath-taker is later killed by a bear or in an accident, this is believed to be proof that he had not told the truth.

Oaths are effective only when people are generally truthful and when they believe that the supernatural will harm them if they lie under oath. It is, of course, the belief that they will be punished for lying that causes them to be truthful. Thus, it is not surprising that societies that rely on oaths are ones in which children are

OATH An oath is a solemn attestation to the truth of statements uttered. It is often used in legal proceedings to help the legal authority discover the true facts of a case. It is common for oath-takers to call for supernatural sanctions to befall them if they tell falsehoods. In cultures where people believe strongly in the power of the supernatural to influence the lives of the living, oaths can be an important way of encouraging compliance and settling disputes. Oaths are used for a variety of purposes and in a variety of contexts. In the United States, they are used to encourage witnesses to tell the truth in judicial proceedings, to encourage compliance and allegiance among members of restricted membership organizations such as fraternal organizations and the military, and to hold public officials to high standards of conduct. Elsewhere, oaths are often used in non-Western cultures to settle disputes and to maintain social order.

A cross-cultural survey of oaths used to ascertain the truth in 150 cultures shows that oaths are used in 37 percent of cultures. In 19 percent oaths alone are used, while in 18 percent both

Lt. Col. Oliver North, United States Marine Corps, raises his right hand and swears an oath to tell the truth before the House and Senate Iran-Contra Committee of the U.S. Congress. Such oaths to elicit the truth are used in 37 percent of 150 cultures surveyed.

reared to be responsible, an emphasis that likely produces adults who are truthful. Additionally, people in societies with oaths generally believe strongly in a high God and they share the belief that those who lie while under oath will be punished. For example, the Crow Indians believed that those who lied would be cursed and that they or their children would be punished. As with ordeals, it seems that oaths occur mainly in societies where the political leadership is weak and the group is fragmented into a number of different subgroups, usually kinship groups such as lineages or clans. In these cultures, oaths allow the weak leadership to maintain control by appealing to a higher authority in judicial decision making.

Oaths are also used commonly across cultures by the state as a means of ensuring loyalty among citizens. For example, in most nations today, naturalized citizens are required to take an oath of allegiance to their new nation. Similarly, oaths are commonly required for individuals joining various government or private organizations, as with the following oath required of individuals who join the Sudanese State Security Bureau:

I _____ being apppointed an active member in the State Security Bureau (_____) swear by Almighty God (or solemnly affirm) that my sincerity and loyalty shall be to the Democratic Republic of the Sudan and to the May Socialist Revolution. I shall perform my duty devotedly and sincerely for the protection of the Revolution and securing its achievements, exert my utmost effort to continuously combat reactionaries, imperialism and Zionism and their intelligence agencies, whether within or outside the Republic, obey my superiors, maintain the safety of myself and not lose whatever I obtain of information whatever their source may be and not disclose any secret I carry or know during my work in the Bureau or after I terminate my work save where the name is required by maintenance of the safety or security of the State and abide by this Oath even if it leads to the sacrifice of my life, my God bear witness of what I say.

Signature

Certificate

I _____ post _____
certify that Sayed/ _____
has taken the above Oath before me in the presence of Sayed/ _____
post _____ .

Signature

Signature of Witness

As with oaths used to ascertain the truth, these loyalty oaths also use appeals to a higher, usually supernatural, authority, as well as requiring the presence of a higher human authority, in the Sudanese case a Muslim official.

See also ORDEAL; PROCEDUREAL LAW

Laws of the Sudan. Vol. II, 1978–1979–1980–1981.

Lowie, Robert H. (1961 [1920]) *Primitive Society.*

Roberts, John M. (1967) "Oaths, Autonomic Ordeals, and Power." In *Cross-Cultural Approaches,* edited by Clelland S. Ford, 169–195.

OLIGARCHY

Oligarchy refers to a government that is ruled by a few people; the term is derived from the Greek words *oligos* (few) and *archein* (to rule). Most modern state societies, including the United States, are in fact oligarchies, since they are ruled by a small number of people relative to the overall population.

ORDEAL

An ordeal is a painful or dangerous test, thought to be controlled by a supernatural being, that is used to determine guilt, innocence, or the veracity of testimony. The underlying operating principle is that the tests are controlled by supernatural beings who will intervene to protect the innocent from failure and harm and allow the guilty to be discovered and, often, injured. Failure to pass the test thus proves guilt. There are a variety of types of ordeals, including those in which the outcome is based on chance or the knowledge or skill of the participants and those used as part of initiation rites or to prepare men for combat. Ordeals are also used to settle disputes and maintain social order; this is a category of ordeals called autonomic ordeals. In autonomic ordeals, the outcome is determined by the involuntary reactions of the participants to painful or dangerous stimuli. The reactions are usually physiological because the ordeals often involve burning, scalding, bleeding, or drowning.

Autonomic ordeals were common in medieval Europe and often involved fire and heat, water, and direct appeals to God. For example, an individual was judged guilty if his hand was burned after insertion in boiling water or by carrying a red-hot piece of iron. In water ordeals, the guilty were thought to float and the innocent to sink. These tests were not, of course, especially reliable. Direct appeals to God were more contests than ordeals, with the innocent party the one who could stand longest in front of a cross with his hands upraised. Ordeals faded from use in Europe when they were replaced by more rational procedures such as due-process litigation and the use of empirical evidence.

A cross-cultural survey of ordeals in 150 cultures in more recent times indicates that autonomic ordeals are used in 26 percent of cultures. Ordeals are not distributed uniformly around the world. Rather, two-thirds of societies with ordeals are in sub-Saharan Africa, and no native North or South American culture is known to have ever used ordeals. Ordeals are usually the method of final resort, called for by those in power only when other methods of resolving a dispute or discovering the facts have proved fruitless.

One society that used ordeals in the past is the Ifugao of the Philippines. The Ifugao used ordeals in criminal cases when the accused repeatedly professed innocence, in disputes over ownership of property in which the facts of the case were difficult to determine, and in disputes over boundaries between adjacent agricultural fields.

Both the accuser and the accused could challenge the other to an ordeal. If the one challenged refused the ordeal, then the challenger was declared the victor in the dispute. If the challenged individual underwent the ordeal and emerged uninjured, he was declared the victor in the dispute and had the right to collect from his challenger a fine for false accusation. If two people accused each other of committing a wrong to another, both had to undergo the ordeal. If both were injured by it, then both had to share the payment of damages to the injured party. If only one person was injured, he had to pay all of the damages to the injured party, as well as a fine for falsely accusing the other accuser.

One of the more popular ordeals was the hot water ordeal. A pot of water more than one foot deep was brought to a boil, and a pebble was placed in it. The party undergoing the ordeal had to reach in and retrieve the pebble and then replace it without being burned, but he had to do these things slowly. If the pebble was taken and replaced too quickly, it was indicative of guilt; it was as if the person undergoing the ordeal had been burned. The hot water ordeal could not be used in adultery cases. This is because it was believed that the gods of fertility look kindly upon all sexual intercourse, and thus will not allow a party guilty of adultery to be burned by the hot water ordeal.

In cases in which two people accuse each other of wrongdoing, the Ifugao used the hot bolo ordeal. Each accuser placed one hand beside the hand of the other accuser. The *monkalun*, or referee, then took a very hot bolo (large knife much like a machete) and put it on their hands together. The guilty one was the one whose hand was more seriously burned. It was believed that the gods of war and justice would cause the knife to bend away from the innocent person's hand, but would cause it to adhere to the guilty person's hand.

When the dispute was over rice field boundaries, the Ifugao used the wrestling ordeal. The outcome of the wrestling match between the disputants was believed to be determined by the disputants' own ancestral spirits, and the winner was declared to be the one in the right. To get a fair outcome, however, the spirits had to be placated by prayers made by priests and sacrifices of chickens and pigs.

The Kalingas, also of Luzon in the Philippines, used ordeals as well, although procedures differed. The Kalingas did use the hot water ordeal. But they also used a supernatural test that was not dangerous or painful, and this was the rice-chewing test. This test demanded that all those who could possibly be involved in committing an offense chew a handful of dry, uncooked rice. The person who chewed rice for a while without being able to make it wet with saliva was judged guilty of the offense.

The Rundi of Zaire are a society that traditionally made heavy use of ordeals in judicial proceedings. The preferred ordeal was one in which the accused was forced to inhale a poisonous powder mixed with water and tobacco. The mixture caused some to have seizures and hallucinations, proving their guilt. Those who confess immediately are administered an antidote that reverses the effects of the poison. Other ordeals included ingesting materials that will cause sickness, such as cow dung or certain plants, immersing a hand in boiling water, sitting a person in a basket into which others thrust spears, as well as more benign methods that do not subject the accused to harm.

The severity of an ordeal often reflected the severity of the wrong being investigated. Thus, not all were as harsh as those that have been described. For example, the Dogon of Mali determined if a boy stole sorrel by tickling along the spine of his back with a stick of straw. If he cannot control his laughter, he is considered guilty. These ordeals are now a custom of the past among the Rundi and Dogon and in Africa in general. They were banned first by the European colonial powers who instituted their own legal systems, and which have now been replaced by the legal systems of the African nations.

Little is known about why some cultures use ordeals and others don't, although it is clear that they fall into disuse when an effective legal system becomes the primary means of settling disputes in a society. In Africa and medieval Europe it seems, though, that ordeals occured mainly in societies where the political leadership was weak, the group was fragmented into a number of different subgroups such as kinship groups, and there was a strong belief in the supernatural. In this context, ordeals allowed the weak leadership to maintain control by appealing to a higher authority in judicial decision making.

See also OATH; PROCEDURAL LAW.

Barton, Roy F. (1969 [1919]) *Ifugao Law.*

———. (1973 [1949]) *The Kalingas: Their Institutions and Custom Law.*

Griaule, Marcel. (1938) *Dogon Games.* Translated by Michael A. Marcus.

Pagès, G. (1933) *A Hamitic Kingdom in the Center of Africa: In Ruanda on the Shores of Lake Kiva (Belgian Congo).* Translated by Bernard Scholl.

Roberts, John M. (1967) "Oaths, Autonomic Ordeals, and Power." In *Cross-Cultural Approaches,* edited by Clelland S. Ford, 169–195.

Teksbury, William J. (1967) "The Ordeal as a Vehicle for Divine Intervention in Medieval Europe." In *Law and Warfare: Studies in the Anthropology of Conflict,* edited by Paul Bohannan, 267–270.

OWNERSHIP

Ownership is "a bundle of rights belonging to the holder, including possession, alienation, testamentary disposition, and *ususfructus* (usufructuary rights), unless yielded to a nonowner; also, when the nonowner's possession of these rights is extinguished, these rights automatically revert to the owner without any legal action" (Pospisil 1971).

The English word *ownership* was first used, according to available records, in 1583, and at the time it meant "to hold" or "to belong to." The owner of real property, as we use the term today, refers to a person or person who holds a freehold estate, also known as an estate in fee simple. The owner must have all of a particular set of rights in order to own his or her real property. At the time that the word *ownership* came into being, however, the holder of all the rights that we now call a freehold estate was known as a tenant of the king, the latter of whom held the basic rights in all British lands. Ownership rights ultimately depend upon the power of the government, which guarantees them; for example, after a war individuals in the losing society may find that their rights to own land and businesses have been lost.

The above definition of ownership applies to a society in which those rights are important, such as the modern nation-states. In many smaller and less technologically advanced societies, not all of these rights can even be said to exist, simply because they are not important.

For example, among the Micmac Indians of Nova Scotia, Canada, until the twentieth century or so, the right to alienate (to sell or to give away rights in) land or the right to be able to leave real property to an heir in a will (the right of testamentary disposition) were not important simply because there was a much greater supply of land than was needed. The ability to do these things only becomes important when land is scarce.

Until sometime in this century, the situation was not too different among the Yoruba of Nigeria. There, rights in land were divided between the individual possessor and the community as a whole. The possessor traditionally had the right to clear the land of jungle, to plant crops and trees on it, and to keep the produce of the crops and trees. The other members of the community, however, had the right to go upon the land and to take from it wood, stone, and water. Wood, stone, and water were at the time not commercially valuable, and therefore not something that the possessor of the land wished to control for himself. When something becomes valuable, the law of rights in that thing arises, and these rights are added to other ideas of ownership in that society.

———————

Lloyd, Peter C. (1962) *Yoruba Land Law.*

Pospisil, Leopold. (1974 [1971]) *Anthropology of Law: A comparative Theory.*

Strouthes, Daniel P. (1994) *Change in the Real Property Law of a Cape Breton Island Micmac Band.*

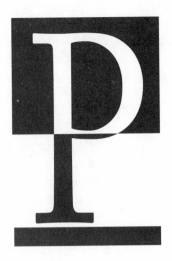

The term *pacification* is used to describe the processes used by colonial nations to render colonized indigenous peoples unlikely to attack colonists and to assure that they are politically and legally controlled. The processes involved have differed from place to place, time to time, and colonial power to colonial power, but in all cases pacification has involved the extension of the jurisdiction of the colonial power's legal system over the indigenous peoples of the colonies.

The term is used somewhat inconsistently by social scientists and government officials, and is most accurate only in reference to those situations where the explicit government policy is to "pacify" indigenous cultures rather than to conquer or destroy them. Thus, the term is used primarily in reference to one aspect of native-colonial relations in Melanesia and South America, and less used in reference to native-colonial relations in North America or Africa. In North America, the native peoples were in some cases conquered and displaced to reservations. In Africa, some were encouraged initially to raid for slaves, were then colonized or exploited as a labor force, and eventually achieved political independence.

One form of warfare to be controlled through pacification is indigenous peoples reacting in a warlike fashion to the encroaching dominant culture. For this reason, pacification always proceeds intensive efforts to develop the resources in the native peoples' territories. A second type of warfare to be controlled by pacification is warfare between indigenous peoples. When the culture or cultures to be pacified are known to be, or are strongly suspected of being, warlike (which is often the situation), the wars that are meant to be prevented are those between the culture and other native peoples, which do not directly threaten the colonists but are an impediment to their controlling the region and governing the native peoples.

Two major arenas for pacification have been South America (especially Brazil) and Oceania (Polynesia, New Guinea and the associated islands of Melanesia in the South Pacific). Comparison of pacification efforts in these two regions illustrates the major objectives, causes, techniques, and outcomes of pacification around the world.

Pacification in Brazil

Although localized efforts by traders, missionaries, land agents, and government officers had occurred previously, full-scale pacification began in Brazil in the early 1990s under the direction of the Indian Protection Service (SPI) for the express purpose of protecting Indian cultures from traders, land developers, and others. The SPI strategy was to make contact with hostile tribes and convince them to end hostilities directed at outsiders and to trust the government to protect them and their interests. Beginning in the early 1900s, teams of unarmed SPI agents would approach an Indian village, leave gifts such as beads, mirrors, and steel machetes at the entrance and then wait weeks or months for the Indians to accept the gifts. After again waiting some period of time, the agents would enter the village with an interpreter and convince the Indians to cease hostilities and to trust the government agents to protect their interests. The agents were pacifists and patient and operated under the dictum: "Die if it be necessary, but never kill" (Davis 1977: 4). This approach to pacification is referred to as "classic pacification."

Such classic pacification was successful and over sixty tribes were pacified, sixty-seven Indian posts were established in the region, and no Indians and only a few agents were killed. However, the long-term effects of this pacification effort were devastating to the Indians. Between 1900 and 1957, more than eighty tribes were destroyed by disease, and others fled to the interior or were placed on small, resource-poor reservations (called "parks"). The traditional territories of the pacified groups are now coffee or rubber plantations or the sites of towns, farms, factories, or mineral extraction operations. In addition, many of the surviving groups exist on the margins of Brazilian society and have lost their native languages, beliefs, and customs.

Beginning about 1950, pacification efforts became overtly linked to Brazilian development and economic policy, with protection of Indians no longer a major consideration. Economic development of the Amazon Basin was the driving force, with an emphasis on building roads, mining, farming, establishment of towns and industries, and settlement by non-Indians. Indian policy stressed pacification followed by relocation on small reservations isolated from areas of development. When existing reservations were in the way of development, they were further reduced in size or divided by roads. As with the more humanely motivated pacification of the early 1900s, the Indian tribes were devastated. For example, the highway program that began in 1970 has resulted in the disappearance, relocation, fleeing, or deculturation of all 29 tribes

living in the vicinity of the proposed roads. The official policy today is a combination of placement on reservations and integration into mainstream society

Pacification in Oceania

A not atypical case of pacification may be seen in the history of the Tiwi people of Melville and Bathurst Islands in northern Australia. The Tiwi are an Australian Aborigine people. For much of the recorded history of contact between the Tiwi and non-Aborigines, the Tiwi greeted peoples from other lands with outright hostility and killed many of those who came to Tiwi territory. The colonial powers' first contacts with the Tiwi came in the seventeenth and eighteenth centuries, when Dutch sailors visited them. Relations between the two peoples at the time were good. Then, Portuguese people in Timor began raiding Melville Island for slaves, and the Tiwi became hostile to all outsiders. This slave raiding ended approximately around 1800.

The next outsiders to visit the Tiwi were Indonesians, who wanted to collect sea slugs (trepang) in order to sell them to the Chinese. The Indonesians were usually killed by the Tiwi wherever they were found.

The British established Fort Dundas on Melville Island in 1824, but its inhabitants came under Tiwi attack. The commander of the fort tried to capture a Tiwi man in order to teach the Tiwi man enough English so that he could be returned to the Tiwi people with the message that the British would start shooting back if the Tiwi did not cease their attacks. The only Tiwi man successfully captured escaped before learning any English. The British later abandoned the fort.

From then until 1900, the Tiwi's main contact with colonists was when ships wrecked on their islands, from which the Tiwi took cloth and iron.

The colonists then tried to buy the goodwill of the Tiwi by giving them trade goods. Iron they liked, because it could be made into axes and knives. Matchlock and flintlock guns, on the other hand, held no special value. The Tiwi watched colonists use firearms against them and developed a strategy to counter them. The Tiwi waited until the gun was fired, ducked to escape being hit by the bullet, and then attacked the gunman with a spear to kill him. The Tiwi had no use for either rice or flour, and they killed the water buffaloes that were given to them to prevent them from muddying up the best water holes. A later group of colonists came to the islands looking for mother-of-pearl shell and firewood and were met by Tiwi canoeists. The colonists fed the Tiwi and gave them iron and other goods.

Complete pacification and true political control of the Tiwi began when Joe Cooper, an Australian buffalo hunter, came to the Tiwi territory with a number of Aborigines from the mainland as his helpers. He also brought quite a few modern rifles, and the Tiwi could not withstand a battle against men armed with these. Cooper also captured two Tiwi women so that they could teach his helpers the Tiwi language, which they did. It was Cooper, then, who established a safe place for other people of European ancestry to come. Cooper was soon joined by an Alsatian priest doing missionary work. Cooper tried to dissuade the missionary from coming by telling him that the Tiwi were armed with guns. The missionary came anyway, and Cooper himself left five years later.

The Tiwi did not accept the missionary as a man of importance because he had no wives, and all big men, as any Tiwi person knew, had many wives. When the missionary was joined by a group of nuns, the Tiwi changed their minds and accorded him the status of a big man!

The missionary had a clever plan to convert the Tiwi and, especially, to end their practice of polygyny. He would purchase, for iron, tobacco, or other trade goods, a baby girl when she was born. The girl would be raised as a Catholic in the convent until she was eighteen or so. At that time, she was allowed to choose a young man as her husband, and the missionary allowed the wedding only after the young man promised that he would marry only one wife. Thus, the Tiwi became monogamous Christians.

Davis, Shelton H. (1977) *Victims of the Miracle: Development and the Indians of Brazil.*

Hart, C. W. M., and Arnold R. Pilling. (1960) *The Tiwi of North Australia.*

Rodman, Margaret, and Matthew Cooper, eds. (1983) *The Pacification of Melanesia.*

PATRIA POTESTAS The Latin term *patria potestas* refers to a very unusual legal institution of the ancient Romans. Among the ancient Romans, for a time at least, the father of a nuclear family had unquestioned authority over the behavior of his offspring, including the authority to punish them or even to take their lives. The father had *jus vitae necisque,* the power of life and death over his offspring as well as the power to inflict corporal punishment in any fashion and to any degree, the power to alter the lives of his offspring in any way he chose, the power to select a wife for his son and to give his daughter in marriage, the power to divorce his offspring from their spouses, the power to give his offspring to be adopted by other parents, and the power to sell his offspring. The father also had the right to acquire ownership of much of his son's property; only property of the category *peculium* was exempt from parental rights. All property an offspring inherited from his or her mother was under the absolute control of the father until the emperor Constantine the Great limited the father's rights so that they lasted only as long as he lived (in other words, he could not allow other people to use the son's property after he, the father, was dead). As the Roman Empire spread, so did the *patria potestas* feature of Roman law, although children born before their own region had been conquered by Rome were not affected by this legal institution.

Patria potestas gave fathers not only rights over their children but duties to them as well. A father bore full responsibility for any legal offenses his offspring committed. This particular feature of the law reduced the number of offenses by young people, since their fathers tended to try to control the behavior of their offspring very rigidly so as to avoid any penalties for themselves. This in effect reduced the number of cases coming before the courts. The offspring, of course, feared their fathers and so were less likely to commit offenses. They also feared the father's power to give them to aggrieved parties in full restitution of any offense they had committed.

A third feature of the institution of the *patria potestas* was that the father and the offspring could not sue each other in court.

Patria potestas was dismembered piece by piece until it ceased to exist. There have been a number of theories as to why it disappeared, but probably the best has to do with simple logistical difficulties. As the Roman Empire grew, sons in the military were posted farther and farther away. It simply became too difficult for a father to be transported to the site of a son's offense.

Maine, Henry Sumner. (1970 [1861]) *Ancient Law.*

Nisbet, Robert. (1973) "Kinship and Political Power in First Century Rome." In *The Social Organization of Law,* edited by Donald Black and Maureen Mileski, 262–277.

PATRON-CLIENT RELATIONSHIPS

Patron-client relations are special political relationships in which a politically or economically powerful individual (the patron) provides protection, material benefits, or other desirable resources available to someone in his or her position to someone who is far less powerful politically or economically (the client) in return for labor or political loyalty, depending on the situation. In other words, a patron-client relationship is like other types of contract relationships, in which each party contracts to supply the other with what he or she wants, except in this case one of the two parties has far more economic or political power than the other. As a rule, clients are dependent upon their patrons, but patrons, while dependent upon their clients in general, are far less dependent upon any particular client and have many potential clients from whom to choose. Thus, the patron usually benefits far more from a patron-client relationship than does the client.

Most of the patron-client systems in the world today are found in the Third World. This is because, in many parts of the Third World, a single wealthy landowner may control much of a region's economic power and may use it to buy political and legal power. The average commoner who lives in the area might have to go to the wealthy landowner if he wants a job. He thus becomes a client, and the landowner a patron. In return for giving his client a job, the patron may require that the client vote for the patron's choice of candidates in the next election, or render him some other service. The patron may also have a great deal of influence with the local bureaucracy, and with this influence be able to assist his client with his legal affairs.

One interesting example of Third World patronage takes place in parts of Mexico. There, parents will attempt to acquire as their child's godfather (in an institution known as *compadrazgo* or coparenthood) a wealthy man, with the intent of later using the relationship to ask the godfather for a loan. In return, the godchild's parents will be expected to help the godfather by giving labor or other help when asked to do so.

An even more powerful system of patronage is found among the Mandari people of the southern Sudan in Africa. Mandari landowners accept poor people from their own tribe and from neighboring tribes (such as the Dinka) as their clients. The patron provides the client with food and shelter, which the client cannot get otherwise because he or she has no living kin or because the client's kin no longer wish to have any association with him or her. Also, children are sometimes sold into clienthood by their parents. The Mandari patron defends his clients in court, pays their fines, and assists them in bringing legal actions in court. Finally, the patron allows his client some land for a house and garden, and grazes his cattle with his own. In return, a male client works in his patron's fields and repairs his buildings, and he serves as a personal servant and guard to the patron. Female clients cook. The clients of chiefs are also supposed to spy for them.

What makes the Mandari patron-client relationship unusual is the client's legal status. Once an individual becomes a client, he or she remains a client until death. The children of a client man, no matter his wife's status, also have client status. Furthermore, while a client has ordinary legal rights against other people, he or she does not have ordinary legal rights against his or her patron. The patron is under no legal obligation to treat the client well and may beat the client with virtual impunity. If the client tries to escape, the patron is well within his legal rights to catch and to kill the client.

Though more common in the Third World, patron-client relations are not uncommon in North America. In the United States, for example, it is well known that many of the ambassadors whom the president of the United States sends to serve in foreign countries are people who have contributed heavily to the president's election campaign. It is also well known that individuals and organizations who contribute to the election funds of U.S. senators and congressmen expect that those senators and congressmen will vote in favor of legislation that benefits the contributors and against legislation that injures their interests.

Patronage is also found in American Indian societies. It is the key element of the modern political system of the Micmac Indians of Nova Scotia, Canada. The Micmac began electing their governing officials according to the rules set forth in the Canadian Indian Act in the years around 1960. Since that time, the governing officials of several bands in Nova Scotia have limited their activities primarily to handing out federal monies to other members of their bands. The elected Micmac officials give away new houses, supplies for house repair, jobs, and loans. The primary requirement that the band member must have met in order to receive these benefits is to have voted for the official to whom the request for help is made. If a band member votes for the loser in an election, he or she may receive no more assistance than federal laws require that he or she be given. As one woman band member said after an election, "a lot of people are going to get nothing." In other words, the patron (the elected official) helps his or her clients with financial benefits, but in return requires political loyalty in the form of votes at elections.

Albuquerque, C., and D. Werner. (1985) "Political Patronage in Santa Catarina." *Current Anthropology* 26(1): 117–120.

Amsbury, Clifton. (1979) "Patron-Client Structure in Modern World Organization." In *Political Anthropology: The State of the Art,* edited by S. Lee Seaton and Henri J. M. Claessen, 79–107.

Boissevain, Jeremy. (1966) "Patronage in Sicily." *Man,* n.s. 1:18–33.

Buxton, Jean Carlile. (1967 [1957]) "'Clientship' among the Mandari of the Southern Sudan." In *Comparative Political Systems,* edited by Ronald Cohen and John Middleton, 229–245.

Gellner, Ernest, and John Waterbury, eds. (1977) *Patrons and Clients in Mediterranean Societies.*

Kottak, Conrad. (1983) *Assault on Paradise.*

Strouthes, Daniel P. (1994) *Change in the Real Property Law of a Cape Breton Island Micmac Band.*

PERSONAL PROPERTY

Personal property is property that is moveable. It is contrasted with real property, which consists of land and things that are permanently attached to the land, such as most types of buildings. An item of personal property is also known as a chattel. The term *personal property* is often abbreviated as "personalty."

Among the Cheyenne Indians of the Great Plains, all property was personal and was individually owned. Even horses taken in a raid involving a number of Cheyenne were immediately assigned to individual owners. This was done most often on an equal basis among those who took part in the actual raid and excluded members of the raiding party who were scouts or cooks.

Llewellyn, Karl N., and E. Adamson Hoebel. (1961 [1941]) *The Cheyenne Way.*

PERSONALITY PRINCIPLE OF LAW

Law applied by the personality principle is applied according to the status of the party rather than the place where the delict occurred, as would be the case under the territorial principle of law. Normally, it is the place where an offense (or delict) occurs that governs the laws under which a case is decided. But the personality principle of law causes the law to be applied according to status. The president of the United States is immune from certain kinds of prosecution while in office so as to permit him the time to help govern the country. There are other examples as well. Diplomats have what is known as diplomatic immunity while in a foreign country. If, for example, a diplomat from a foreign country who is serving in Washington, D.C., kills a citizen of the United States while in Washington, D.C., he may not be prosecuted for the homicide. Rather, the U.S. government may declare him a *persona non grata* (unacceptable person) and expel him from the country. The reason for diplomatic immunity is so that a country cannot make false allegations and legal charges against the diplomats of foreign countries as a way of trying to control political relations with the other country.

Another example of the personality principle of law concerns military affairs. The military courts-martial decide cases involving military personnel whether they occur on a military base or not, and whether they involve military matters or not. Further, these courts try legal cases involving military personnel even when the military personnel are on foreign soil. If, while stationed in Germany but not on the U.S. base, a U.S. army private assaults a captain, the case is decided by a U.S. military court rather than by a German court.

The personality principle of law can also be seen at work in the legal system of the former Soviet Union. Under Soviet law, no member of the Communist party could be tried for a crime without permission from the the accused's local party organization. Of course, the other members of the local organization were usually friends or relatives of the accused and would not want to have one of their own tried and punished. Further, the kind of crime in which a Communist party member would most likely be involved was so-called white collar crime involving large amounts of money, often including large bribery payoffs. Other members of the local party organization were also frequently involved, and so by protecting the member who had been apprehended they were protecting themselves.

The personality principle of law was of great importance in Inca law. There, the crucial status difference was between nobles and commoners. The Inca, in fact, had different laws for nobles than they had for commoners. One of the more important differences lay in the sanctions. Inca commoners were usually punished with physical sanctions, and fairly harsh ones at that. Nobles, on the other hand, faced sanctions that were psychological in nature; the Inca believed such sanctions would be more effective in controlling the behavior of the nobles than would physical sanctions.

The Yoruba people of Nigeria traditionally administered the death penalty differently for kings, nobles, and chiefs than they did for commoners. Commoners were put to death either by decapitation or by beating. If decapitated, the head of the commoner was nailed to a tree in a prominent place to admonish others not to commit the crimes that the deceased had committed. If the condemned was put to death by beating, a male corpse was shown to the public, but a female corpse was thrown away in the bush. On the other hand, kings, nobles, and chiefs were given poison and allowed to die at home.

See also INTERNATIONAL LAW; JURISDICTION; TERRITORIAL PRINCIPLE OF LAW.

Ajisafe, A. K. (1946) *The Laws and Customs of the Yoruba People.*

Ioffe, Olympiad S., and Peter B. Maggs. (1983) *Soviet Law in Theory and Practice.*

Means, Philip Ainsworth. (1931) *Ancient Civilizations of the Andes.*

Pospisil, Leopold. (1974 [1971]) *Anthropology of Law: A Comparative Theory.*

PLUTOCRACY

Plutocracy refers to systems in which political power is controlled by the wealthy; the term comes from the Greek words *ploutos* (wealth) and *kratos* (rule). The United States is plutocratic to a degree, in that elected legislative and executive branch officials are often wealthy or dependent upon wealthy donors for funds for their campaigns. In societies headed by big men, wealth is an absolute requirement for political power.

See also BIG MAN; LEADER.

POLITICAL ANTHROPOLOGY

Political anthropology is the scientific study of politics, which may in turn be defined as power relations. Prior to the publication of Henry Maine's *Ancient Law* in 1861, the commonly held belief concerning people generally was that civilized peoples, who had advanced technologies, had governments, whereas the uncivilized, who lacked advanced technologies, lived in a state of anarchy. Maine argued that this was not the case, and that in fact primitive societies were organized by kinship and were patriarchal; the nuclear family was the first stage in the evolution of social organization. Maine believed that societies developed along an evolutionary line that would eventually lead them to what he believed to be the most developed system of political and social organization: modern European society.

Another unilineal evolutionist was Lewis Henry Morgan. Morgan, unlike Maine, had actually done fieldwork in a non-Western society, the Iroquois Indians in New York State. Working primarily with data on kinship and technology, he used these to construct an evolutionary developmental sequence consisting of three main stages: savagery, barbarism, and civilization. The first stage of man's social organization is that of no organization at all, what he called a "promiscuous horde." Later, kinship became a basis for groups, which were exogamous and so became linked to each other through intermarriage. At this and other early stages of social development, there is no political specialization because the technology—hunting, fishing, and gathering or horticulture—does not produce enough surplus food to allow the development of cities or support a specialized political leadership. This can only occur when agriculture takes place, and this requires, as a precondition, private property, which Morgan had supposed did not exist to any large degree in early stages of social evolution. In 1884, Engels used Morgan's findings to support Marx's theory of communism, which involves another similar form of unilineal social evolution.

The idea of a unilineal line of social evolution has been discarded by anthropologists and others for a number of good reasons. First of all, it cannot be shown that all societies are advancing along one line of evolution. Some societies have changed in ways very different from the ways in which European societies have changed. Second, there is no reason to suppose that all societies would, if they had been left alone and not been influenced by Western society, become at all anything like what Western society has become. Third, it is ethnocentric to claim that Western society represents the pinnacle of social evolution and to suppose that all other societies are going to eventually end up like Western societies. Finally, these unilineal evolutionary models are primarily based upon measurements of technology, something that Western societies can with justification claim to have developed to a greater degree than peoples in other parts of the world. However, to measure an entire society's development upon this one criterion alone is meaningless; other criteria may be more important to those who live in other societies, and by these other criteria there is a good chance that Western peoples may not be as advanced.

The next major development in anthropology generally was the work of Franz Boas. Boas attacked grand theorizing supported by insufficient data, as was practiced by the unilineal evolutionists. From the turn of the century and into the 1940s, he influenced American anthropologists, many of whom were his students, to become very mindful of the minute details of the cultures and societies they visited. He felt that if enough data were collected, many of the patterns of society and culture would become evident without the need to impose armchair theories of dubious value and accuracy. The Boasian approach is known as "historical particularism."

Whereas Boas was the major influence on American anthropology in the early twentieth century, in Europe the dominant theoretical influence was provided by Emile Durkheim, a French sociologist. Durkheim championed the idea that the historical development of any particular society is due to invisible internal social forces. This idea was later seen in a slightly altered form in the writings of the British anthropologist Edmund Leach, discussed below. Durkheim's model of organic solidarity, which saw some societies as, by analogy, similar to living organisms, appeared in a not dissimilar form in the writings of A. R. Radcliffe-Brown, a British anthropologist influential in the 1930s and beyond. Radcliffe-Brown introduced the idea that social institutions exist because they have functions, and that their functions are the ways in which they benefit the whole of society, not unlike how organs function in contributing to the welfare of the entire body. Thus, Radcliffe-Brown showed how various institutions, including the political, have functions, and how they fit into an overall structure within the culture; for this reason, Radcliffe-Brown's contribution to anthropological theory is known as structural functionalism, and it is an important part of British social anthropology to this day.

The next major development in political anthropology was the publication in 1940 of the book *African Political Systems,* edited by Meyer Fortes and E. E. Evans-Pritchard. This book, a collection of papers mostly by British anthropologists, began the modern field of political anthropology. The book made two theoretical contributions and provided valuable data for future studies. The first contribution was to make a distinction between societies with a centralized political authority (called primitive states) and those without one (called stateless societies). A second major theoretical contribution was to show how political institutions contribute to political equilibrium. The editors noted that, in the case of so-called primitive states like that of the Zulu people, the genealogical restrictions of succession to kingship, the regimental organization of the society, the power of the king to appoint his kin to chiefships, and the supernatural basis of authority of the king are all things that increase the king's authority; on the other hand, these are balanced by a king's council—officials who have a powerful voice in the king's selection—by the queen mothers' courts, and by other institutions, which all work to control royal authority.

This first major step into modern political anthropology is not without its critics, however. The basic typology of primitive state society and stateless society is too simple to adequately describe the various political systems to be found in Africa. It has also been said that, in their effort to explain how political institutions function to create and maintain political balance, not enough has been said about how political disequilibrium leads to political changes. This second criticism is not wholly justified, since major parts of the book are taken up with discussions of how political systems have changed as a result of the intrusion of colonial powers.

The next significant figures in political anthropology were Edmund Leach and Max Gluckman. Both attempted to elaborate structural functionalism to better describe political change. Leach's perspective is derived from the study of a region of highland Burma, an area in which there were three political systems at work and in which there was no political equilibrium. Leach argued that the people have an ideal conceptual pattern of their political systems in their heads and that this differs from the actual political reality at any moment. Max Gluckman made a significant contribution in saying that political balance in not stable or static, but is the result of ongoing conflicts that are defused by crosscutting sets of social relations and specific cultural practices. For example, kinship and loyalties to other groups in the greater society help to defuse a local feud; witchcraft also helps reduce tension in a way that does not affect actual group cohesion. The epigram "divide and conquer," Gluckman says, should in fact read "divide and cohere." For example, if man A has a dispute with man B, man A may not be able to enlist his brother, man C, to help him fight man B, since both B and C are members of the same athletic team and therefore cannot fight each other; this has the effect of limiting the scope of conflict. The more crosscutting loyalties of this type, the greater the reduction in conflict overall, says Gluckman. Gluckman is also known for bringing the term *process* into the anthropological vocabulary as a focal point for the study of

Franz Boas (1858–1942), American anthropologist, in 1906

sociocultural change. The study of sociocultural processual change is still a lively field of study.

During the 1940s, 1950s, and 1960s, cultural evolution again made an appearance in American anthropology. Notable studies were carried out by Leslie White, Julian Steward, Elman Service, and Morton Fried. White and Steward were interested in the causal factors that led to the large, technologically advanced societies we call modern nation-states. For White, it is technological development that leads to the production of surplus food, which in turn allows social differentiation into many different professions, allowing further cultural elaboration and complexity. Further progress is made by increasing efficiencies in energy use. Steward was a cultural ecologist who stressed the "cultural core" of a society, which largely determined its social structure and ideology. Again, materialism was a central feature of his theory of multilinear evolution.

Elman Service and Morton Fried also tackled the question of the evolution of political systems, but from a different point of view. They did not try to show the factors that may cause political systems to change, but were merely interested in providing a typology of political systems. Both emphasized the varying levels of political centralization and societal integration that are found at different levels in the development of political systems. While there is still an interest among some anthropologists in the subject of political evolution, this interest is primarily dedicated to the subject of state formation.

A main thrust today of political anthropology is that of decision-making processes, a field of inquiry that is also of interest to some legal anthropologists. This particular interest appears to have gotten its start in Max Gluckman's work on the study of individuals in the social process. In fact, the emphasis has moved away from the study of concrete, discrete groups and their composition and structure and moved toward examination of the process of change, of conflict, and

of struggles, victimhood, and other topics that deal not with groups but rather with individuals and categories of people. The latter emphasis has been reinforced by political economy, which deals not primarily with groups, states, and other genuine groups, but instead with economic classes and other categories of people who have similar interests and problems, such as people of a particular ethnicity or racial heritage. Political economy was able to do this by focusing interest on the unequal distribution of wealth in the world, part of which has been created by capitalism and the political influence of the powerful in the world's economic systems. Of course, people who have not benefited, and who indeed have suffered, in the modern era are often the poor of the Third World and the people of the Fourth World (the indigenous peoples of the First World, such as the North American Indians or the Australian Aborigines). The poor of the Third World are not a group, nor are the peoples of the Fourth World. The North American Indians are a case in point. There are a number of very wealthy Indian groups in North America, due in many cases to oil, land claims, or gambling revenues. However, they do not as a rule share their good fortune with other Indian groups who are destitute.

Another trend in political anthropology is world system theory, the concept that nearly all peoples around the world are tied together politically by virtue of their participation in the world capitalist market. Eric Wolf (1982) is certainly the best known of the theorists of this Marxist-oriented school of thought. A major part of world system theory is that the industrially developed nations victimize the less developed ones through the use of capitalist tools; the wealthy peoples continue to enrich themselves while the poor peoples, remaining poor, continue to supply the raw materials that the wealthy need to remain wealthy.

The idea that some peoples experience poverty and suffering as a result of economic and political control by wealthy and powerful people is a common theme in contemporary political anthropology. The so-called "resistance model" is commonly referred to in studies of the relationship between North American Indians and the dominant white society of North America to show that Indians resist the control of the white majority rather than passively accept assimilation. Scott (1985) also portrays the position of the politically weak, although from a closer point of view. He showed that poor peasants work to resist those who dominate them politically and economically by the use of slander, theft, and whatever other tools are available to them.

See also LEGAL ANTHROPOLOGY; MARXISM; POLITICAL ECONOMY; WORLD SYSTEM

Balandier, Georges. (1970) *Political Anthropology.* Translated by A. M. Sheridan Smith.

Fried, Morton H. (1967) *The Evolution of Political Society.*

Lewellen, Ted C. (1992) *Political Anthropology: An Introduction.* 2d ed.

Maine, Henry Sumner. (1963 [1861]) *Ancient Law.*

Morgan, Lewis Henry. (1963 [1877]) *Ancient Society.*

Scott, James C. (1985) *Weapons of the Weak: Everyday Forms of Peasant Resistance.*

Service, Elman R. (1962) *Primitive Social Organization: An Evolutionary Perspective.* 2d ed.

———. (1975) *Origins of the State and Civilization: The Process of Cultural Evolution.*

Steward, Julian. (1955) *Theory of Culture Change: The Methodology of Multilinear Evolution.*

Swartz, Marc, Victor W. Turner, and Arthur Tuden, eds. (1966) *Political Anthropology.*

Wolf, Eric. (1982) *Europe and the People without History.*

POLITICAL CORRUPTION

Political corruption is the practice whereby an official alters the performance of his or her duties for his or her own private gain. Examples of political corruption are all too familiar in the newspapers today; for instance, a congressman who accepts campaign contributions to pass a piece of legislation that will help the contributor, or the police officer who allows illegal drug dealing or gambling to continue without interference in return for payments.

What we in the United States see as political corruption is often considered commonplace or even expected behavior in other parts of the world, however. In Southeast Asia, for example, it is common for government officials to ask people who need a service to pay a little extra so that the work will be expedited; for example, unless such a payment is made, a required license or permit may take months or years to be provided. This pattern goes back hundreds of years, when central governments were reluctant to pay the salaries of rural administrators. The rural administrators were expected to provide their own pay and the money it took to pay for the governmental services to be provided. Those who could not were considered incompetent. The pattern of the central government's paying very little to lower-level government employees continues to this day, as does the bribery that the government employees are expected to engage in to make a living wage.

Another factor also propels political corruption in Southeast Asia. This is that the central governments have for centuries been of little use in protecting the rights of individuals. The individual must rely upon his or her family, extended family, lineage, clan, or other members of his or her economic class, community, or profession for protection and assistance. If an individual then is lucky or skillful enough to get a government post, he or she is expected to assist those who have always stood ready to assist him or her in the past. This means that the new government appointee has to engage in graft to fulfill his or her obligations to all of these people.

During the Vietnam War, Americans sent many different types of consumer goods to Vietnam to be distributed to the rural poor. The idea behind this was that the rural poor would be grateful for American largess and less likely to support the Vietcong. However, the local civil servants who were in charge of distributing the goods would take a significant portion for themselves, and this made many of the Americans who dealt with them angry. The Americans did not understand that the local bureaucrats were simply taking their portion as part payment of their salaries.

In the Philippines in the past, it was known for firemen to ask merchants for money before putting out fires in their stores. When the Philippines legislature was considering the nationalization of the rice industry, the legislators delayed a vote for twenty-four hours so that they could accept cash contributions from rice farmers who would have lost a great deal of money if the bill had passed.

Political corruption in Southeast Asia, as in so many other parts of the world, has the effect of denying basic rights to all but the wealthy who can afford to pay the bribes necessary to get their business done. This pattern of favoring the wealthy has in turn had another effect. The poor are often driven to try to change the system by violent means, as may be seen in the recent history of the region. It has also made the poor far more amenable to the message of Communist movements, and this may still be seen today. The corruption and the much greater advantages of the wealthy have been two reasons for the frequent violent overthrows of central governments in the region.

In the former Soviet Union, however, bribery to avoid minor sanctions was practiced by all sectors of society. Drivers stopped for minor traffic offenses often left a 10-ruble note in their

official papers when these papers were given to a police officer. Of course, avoidance of conviction and sanction for serious offenses was very expensive since judges had to be bribed, and they demanded much larger payments.

One of the more common forms of political corruption is embezzlement, which is the fraudulent use of property belonging to another but that is in one's own care or possession or under one's own control. In the Ottoman Empire, whose capital was in what is now Turkey, the penalties for embezzlement were quite severe by modern Western standards. Following are the statutory rules of the Ottoman Empire regarding embezzlement from the state as they stood in the late eighteenth century (*The Ottoman Penal Code* 1888: 36–40):

POLITICAL CORRUPTION

CHAPTER IV.
Embezzling the Revenue of the State—Peculation.

Art. 82. Whosoever shall embezzle the revenues or property belonging to the State, either in cash or in kind, shall be sentenced to refund the public treasury twice the value of the things embezzled and shall be punished with incarceration for from five to fifteen years. He shall further be declared forever incapable of holding any rank or of occupying any public office.

Art. 83. Every person entrusted with buying, selling or making anything of any kind on account of the Imperial Government, who shall commit any fraud in the buying, or selling, the price, the amount, or the manufacture of such supplies shall be liable, whatever may be the character of the offence proved, to be punished as an embezzler of the public revenues under the preceding article.

Art. 84. Persons guilty of the frauds hereinbefore set forth, who do not hold any rank or public office, shall be liable to the same punishments as in the preceding articles set forth.

Art. 85. Officials who shall receive money from the creditors of the State for the discounting of Treasury bills ("serguis"), or other bonds forming part of the public debt, or who shall accept from the said creditors sums of money and other gratuities in order to secure the payment of their debts, shall be sentenced to surrender the sums or things so received, and punished with incarceration for from three to fifteen years. Persons in the private employment of public officers, or standing in the relation of connections or dependents, who shall discount the "serguis" with their consent, shall be liable to the same punishment, and so shall the officials who connive at such frauds.

Art. 86. Every public servant, whatever be his position, who shall keep back the whole or any part of what is due to any workmen employed by him in the manufacture or in the transport of certain things relating to his office for their wages, or for the price payable in respect of such things as aforesaid, or who shall make the said workmen labor upon State works for nothing, shall be sentenced to pay twice the profit made by him, half of which shall be given to the party to whom it is due, and the other half retained by way of fine. He shall further be punished with incarceration for from three to fifteen years.

. . .

CHAPTER V.
Abuse of Authority—Failure in Duty in a Place of Public Trust.

Art. 88. Public servants and all other persons who shall be guilty of any offence in breach of the law relating to the letting by auction and the allotment of the revenues of the State, or in breach of any other law relating to the letting to farm of the revenues, shall be dismissed from their offices, and punished with imprisonment for from one to two years, or to exile for from two to three years. They shall at the same time be compelled to reimburse to the Treasury the sums which they have caused to be lost to the State.

Art. 89. Every public servant, whatsoever be his position, who in business, whether of greater or less importance, the conduct or the superintendence of which has been entrusted to him, shall speculate either openly or clandestinely, either by the intervention of others or by way of partnership in the buying or selling of supplies for the use of the State; who shall contract for the furnishing of such supplies, or who shall be interested with another in any contract for the furnishing of such things as aforesaid; shall be dismissed from his office and punished with exile for from one to two years.

Where a public servant shall receive any commission on State contracts of this kind, or shall make a profit on the exchange value of money, the punishment shall, besides deprivation of office, be imprisonment for from one to two years, or exile for from two to three years.

Art. 90. Persons employed in the civil service or the financial department, who shall in any way place to their own account the revenues of the State, or connive at a third party doing the same, shall be dismissed from office and punished with imprisonment for from three months to two years, or exile for from six months to three years.

Art. 91. Persons who shall receive an order or undertake a contract for the supply of necessaries for the army or navy, and who by their own act shall fail to carry out their engagement, shall refund what they have received in payment for such supplies, and be subject to a fine equal to one quarter of the amount of such refunding.

Art. 92. Any public servant who shall connive at such failure to furnish such supplied as aforesaid shall be punished with imprisonment for three years.

. . .

Art. 94. Every person without exception, for the purpose of forwarding justice, is justified in supplying to the Courts or Councils, either verbally or in writing, information relating to every pending matter, whatever may be the nature thereof; apart from such communications as aforesaid, which are in all cases only received simply as information, every order, request or petition, addressed by public officers of any description, to a Court or Council, either directly or indirectly, verbally or in writing, whether in favor of or against one of the parties, shall, according to the gravity of the case, entail the attaching of the penalties hereinafter mentioned, both upon the officer who has rendered himself liable thereto, and also on the Court or the Council which has permitted itself to be influenced by these proceedings.

Art. 95. If a public officer has committed such act of interference by means of an order or by exercising pressure in virtue of the authority with which he is clothed, he shall be deprived of his office, upon the employ such full number as aforesaid, or who shall withdraw them entirely from their duties and employ them in the private maintenance of his household, or who shall enter the people employed in his own private service in the registers of the members of the police force, with the object of paying them out of the sums set down for such police force, shall be sentenced to surrender twice the amount so received by him either for the persons who do not truly appear on the role, or for those whom he has employed in the private maintenance of his household, or for the persons in his own employment whom he has entered as members of the police force, and shall be further punished with incarceration for from three to fifteen years.

Bloodworth, Dennis. (1975) *An Eye for the Dragon.*

Ioffe, Olympiad S., and Peter B. Maggs. (1983) *Soviet Law in Theory and Practice.*

The Ottoman Penal Code, 28 Zilhijeh 1274. (1888) Translated by C. G. Walpole.

POLITICAL ECONOMY

Political economy is a type of social analysis in which political and economic data are analyzed together, rather than separately. Both the term and the type of analysis were introduced by Karl Marx and Friedrich Engels in the nineteenth century. Political economy is today one of the most popular forms of political anthropology in terms of research, publication, and student interest.

Political economists assume as a basic foundation of their work that the primary reason for political behavior is economic self-interest. They further assume that middle- and upper-socio-economic classes in capitalist countries express their political behavior largely on the basis of their class; in other words, members of these classes work together with other members of their classes to exploit the working class for their own economic and political gain. Here, the term *exploit*, which is commonly used in the writings of political economists, is used in a new way. The term *exploit* once was synonymous with *utilize*, as in "I wish to exploit the trees in my backyard for firewood." Political economists now use the word to refer to unfair, harmful, and even evil use of workers by their employers or, more generally, the poor by the middle and upper classes. As did Marx and Engels before them, political economists generally assume that the members of the upper and middle classes (collectively the capitalist class, because their members use capital to buy labor and so to reproduce it) are conscious of their class affiliation, and that by benefiting class interests as a whole, they benefit themselves. Working-class people, they assert, are generally not conscious that they belong to a class of people with common interests, and so do not work together very well to advance their common interests. People who replace strikers at factory jobs, for instance, are working against the interests of other members of the working class.

Friedrich Engels (1820–1895) in 1877

This description is of orthodox political economy. It is "orthodox" in that it remains faithful to the style of analysis used by Marx and Engels. More recently, political economists have been studying noncapitalist societies and showing that even here there are upper classes that exploit members of the lower classes, just as Marx found in capitalist and feudal societies.

The term *political economy* is today often used to refer to an actual economic system in which the economy is manipulated politically by the powerful for their own economic benefit and to the economic detriment of other people. The term has often been used to describe the economic relationship between colonial powers (the politically powerful who benefit economically) and the indigenous peoples of the colonies who suffer economically from the colonial relationship.

See also WORLD SYSTEM.

Alverson, Hoyt. (1978) *Mind in the Heart of Darkness*.

Marx, Karl, and Friedrich Engels. (1968) *Karl Marx and Friedrich Engels: Selected Works in One Volume*.

POWER

Power is defined as the ability to influence the behavior of another in a way that is desired. We can see, therefore, that power can come in many forms. There is military power, of course, which can be used to force an entire nation to accede to another nation's demands. There is also the power a child may have over his or her parents when she sheds tears to induce them to behave in the way that he or she wants.

One of the more interesting sorts of power to be found in any society is supernatural power. Many Jews, Christians, and Muslims attribute supernatural power to their God, even though these same people may disdain the concept of magical causation as mere superstition.

The Micmac, although Catholic, have a very strong belief in supernatural power other than that coming from God. They believe that anyone with great ability or skill in one kind of activity, say music, lumberjacking, or even speaking the Micmac language, is acknowledged as a *kinap,* an individual with supernatural power.

See also AUTHORITY; LEADER; POLITICAL ANTHROPOLOGY

Lukes, Steven. (1974) *Power: A Radical View.*

Strouthes, Daniel P. (1994) *Change in the Real Property Law of a Cape Breton Island Micmac Band.*

PROCEDURAL LAW

Procedural law regulates the legal process itself; it determines just how legal actions are adjudicated. Procedural law settles problems of jurisdiction, allocation of authority (who is the legal authority), the sanctions that may be applied in a particular case, court proceedings (such as whether the public is to be admitted to the courtroom), and matters pertaining to the process of appealing verdicts. Procedural law includes the laws determining what is a proper legal hearing, the steps involved in such hearings, what constitutes evidence and what evidence may be admitted, the form of legal arguments in a legal hearing, who may have standing in a legal case, who may be permitted to make arguments in a legal hearing, if and in what form testimony is made, and if and in what form interrogation takes place. In short, procedural law regulates all facets of the conduct of a legal hearing and adjudication, but not the substantive laws themselves.

One of the parts of procedural law in some legal systems is the making of the charge, which outlines the offense on which the accused is to be tried. As shown in the following decision from Rhodesia (now Zimbabwe), the particulars of the charge can be very important (*The Rhodesian Law Reports* 1966: 552–555).

REGINA V. HORNE

Appellate Division, Salisbury
Quénet, J. P., and Macdonald, J. A.
2nd August and 2nd September, 1966

Criminal law-Copper Control Act [Chapter 226]-*s. 6 (2)-contravention of-essentials of offence-not alleged in charge-fatally defective-whether appellant can waive right to complain of irregularity*

Appellant was charged with contravening s. 6 (2) of the Copper Control Act [*Chapter 226*], but the charge omitted to allege that the persons from whom he purchased the copper were neither "dealers nor licensed dealers." It was contended by appellant that this was not an essential element of the offence, or, if it was, it could be implied from the charge. Alternatively, it was contended that appellant had waived his right to complain of the irregularity, and the proceedings were not vitiated.

Held, setting aside the convictions and sentence:

(1) That the words "other than a dealer or licensed dealer" constituted an essential element of the offence, and were not simply words of exception, exemption or excuse.

(2) That to imply an essential element of an offence, from a charge which did not allege it, must mean that an accused is presumed

to know the essential elements of a statutory offence, and, knowing them, be able to supply any words omitted from the charge. This was an untenable argument.

(3) That, if a charge disclosed no offence, any conviction under it was devoid of legal effect, and, even with an appellant's assistance, an appeal court cannot validate such proceedings.

M. R. Tett for the appellant.
J. A. R. Giles for the respondent.

MACDONALD, J. A.: The appellant was convicted of contravening s. 6 (2) of the Copper Control Act [*Chapter 226*], as amended, and sentenced to pay a fine of 30 pounds or, in default of payment, one month's imprisonment with hard labour.

Section 6 (2) of the Act reads:

"No person, including a dealer or a licensed dealer, shall purchase any copper from any person other than a dealer or licensed dealer unless there is produced to him by such last mentioned person such documentary evidence of his title to sell such copper as may be prescribed or a certificate of clearance."

The charge against the appellant reads:

"The accused, at or near Salisbury, did wrongfully and unlawfully purchase from Mishek and Deni, Africans there being, 170 pounds of copper, and the said Mishek and the said Deni not producing at the time of purchase documentary evidence of their title to sell such copper, that is to say that the said Mishek and the said Deni were not at the time of the purchase in possession of a certificate of clearance, and thus the said accused did commit the crime of contravening section 6 (2) of the Copper Control Act [*Chapter 226*]."

In the course of the hearing of the appeal, the Crown submitted that the charge is fatally defective, because it omits to allege that

Mishek and Deni were neither dealers nor licensed dealers.

Mr. *Tett* desires that the appeal be considered on its merits, and submits that the charge is not fatally defective. In support of this submission, he contends that the words "other than a dealer or licensed dealer" and the words "unless there is produced to him by such last mentioned person such documentary evidence of his title to sell such copper as may be prescribed or a certificate of clearance" constitute "exceptions, exemptions, provisos, excuses or qualifications" within the meaning of s. 134 (2) (b) of the Criminal Procedure and Evidence Act [*Chapter 31*]. The latter words unquestionably constitute an "exception, exemption or excuse" within the meaning of that section, but the former words are of the very substance of the offence and, unless it can be said that those words are to be implied in the charge, the Crown's contention that it is fatally defective must be upheld. I am satisfied that the words "other than a dealer or a licensed dealer" constitute an essential element of the offence, for the following reasons: The conduct prohibited by the section is not the purchase of copper but the purchase of copper from a person who is neither a dealer nor licensed dealer. A charge which alleged no more than that the accused had purchased copper would certainly be defective. The words constitute an additional element of the offence, and are not simply words of exception, exemption or excuse.

Mr. *Tett* submits, in the alternative, that, although there is no express allegation that Mishek and Deni are neither dealers nor licensed dealers, this allegation is to be implied from the fact that the charge clearly alleges that the purchase was unlawful by reason of the failure of Mishek and Deni to produce either documentary evidence of their title to sell or a certificate of clearance at the time of the purchase. In effect, he submits that, if the Crown specifically alleges that an accused person has failed to comply with the requirements of an "exception, exemption, proviso, excuse or qualification," the Crown must be taken, by necessary implication, to have alleged all the essential elements of the offense itself. The basis for this submission, although not stated, must necessarily be that an accused person is presumed to know the essential elements of a statutory offence, and, knowing them, be able to supply any words omitted from the charge. Mr. *Tett*'s approach is clearly untenable, and Mr. *Giles* is correct when he submits that there is nothing in the wording of the charge which implies the inclusion of the words "other than a dealer or a licensed dealer."

Mr. *Tett*'s final submission is that, if the omission of these words is a fatal defect, the proceedings are not vitiated thereby, because the appellant, in the course of the hearing of the appeal, has expressly waived his right to complain of the irregularity. In *R. v. Herschel*, 1920 A.D. 575, SIR JAMES ROSE INNES said, at p. 580:

> "I do not think that any court of appeal would be justified in allowing a conviction to stand upon a charge sheet which discloses no offence."

The same view was expressed by VAN DEN HEEVER, J. A., in *R. v. Preller*, 1952 (4) S.A. 452 (A.D.), at 473:

> "A conviction on a charge which discloses no offence is, in itself, a failure of justice and a legal impossibility, and should not be allowed to stand."

In *Roger v. R.*, 1962 R. & N. 385, MAISELS, J., dealing, on appeal, with a charge which disclosed no offence, said, at p. 386:

> "But SCHRIENER, A. C. J., at p. 280, points out what INNES, C. J., says, in effect, in *Herschel's* case, is that, although a defect of the kind now under discussion could have been cured at the trial, it cannot be cured on appeal."

And the learned judge concluded, at p. 388:

> ". . . that, as the indictment discloses no offence, this court is obliged to set aside the conviction."

Since the charge under consideration discloses no offence, the conviction of the appellant was devoid of legal effect, and it must necessarily follow that this court, as an appeal court, even with the appellant's assistance, is powerless to validate the proceedings. If, as Mr. *Tett* has endeavoured to establish in dealing with the merits of the appeal, there are certain facts which the Crown, to its advantage, might have established at the trial but did not, this court, indeed, would possibly assist in bringing about a miscarriage of justice if it were to hold that the appellant at trial was placed in jeopardy on a charge under s. 6 (2) of the Act when, in law, he was not.

The charge discloses no offence, and the conviction and sentence, for this reason, must be set aside.

QUENET, J. P., concurred.

One of the best described examples of the steps taken in a proper legal hearing, an important part of procedural law, is that of the Tibetan legal system as it existed before the Chinese invasion in 1959.

The progression of a civil case is as follows. In order to initiate a proper legal action, a Tibetan litigant had to present his or her case to the court, and the court had to declare it a proper case before accepting it. The petitioner was then called before the court, and the petition presented. Next, the petitioner was questioned by the legal authorities. Following this, the other party to the dispute was called before the court, and he or she made a reply to the petition. The petitioner then made a response to the second party's reply, after which he or she was questioned again. After this took place, the second party had a chance to reply again to the petitioner's statements. It was following this that any evidence pertinent to the hearing was presented. At this point, each party to the case was brought before the court and questioned by the legal authorities. The next stage of the hearing saw witnesses called before the court to give their statements, and this was followed by their questioning. If the court demanded more information, it ordered an investigation, which was presented formally to the court. If the court deemed it necessary, the veracity of the parties to the case could be tested. If the court found either party to be lying, it punished him or her.

The court then made its decision and wrote it down in a special document. Both parties were recalled before the court to hear the decision and they then left to ponder it. After a period of time, both parties were again recalled to the court to give their opinions of the decision. The parties then either signed a clause signifying their agreement to the decision, or refused to sign it, signifying that they were opposed to the decision as an unfair one. Copies of the decision were then exchanged by the litigants.

The case was closed in the following manner. The court accepted the litigants' signatures or refusals to sign the decision. Any payments of court costs were then made. The terms of the decision, usually involving the payment of damages from one party to another or the sanctioning of either or both parties by the court, were then carried out. Following this, the two parties to the case made a formal reconciliation with each other. Finally, as the case concluded, the court had the option to send the case to a higher authority, and either or both of the parties had the option to appeal the case.

The series of steps in the legal hearing involving a crime in Tibet were usually fewer because the identity of the criminal was usually known and the facts of the case were more easily determined. The identity of the alleged criminal was usually known because most Tibetans lived in small towns in which everyone knew everyone else, including those who frequently behaved badly or who held grudges.

Once a crime occurred, the victim or his or her family either made a petition to the legal authorities or informed their local governmental official of the crime. If the alleged criminal was considered likely to try to escape, he or she was arrested immediately, before the official investigation of the crime. The crime was then investigated by a clerk from the district office. The investigation consisted of collecting evidence and interviewing the victim and his or her family. At this point, the identity of the alleged criminal was clearly determined by the investigating officials, and he or she was arrested if he or she had not been previously. From this point until the legal authority made his decision in the case, the criminal was presumed guilty, and any show of remorse he or she made was weighed in his or her favor in determining sanctions.

The criminal was brought before the court and the crime was announced by the governmental official who presided as the legal authority in the case. The criminal was then whipped and placed in jail, and sometimes in stocks and fetters as well. The legal authority then began to review the case and to hear evidence. The criminal, the victim, and the victim's family were interviewed by the judge. If the facts established in the hearing did not conform to the criminal's testimony, the judge had the option of having the criminal whipped.

If the criminal's testimony continued to disagree with the testimony of the victim and the victim's family, as well as the other facts established in the case, the case could be prolonged indefinitely. In most instances, on the other hand, the legal authority was able to devise a written statement of the facts with which all parties could agree. The statement, which also included the sanctions to be imposed upon the criminal, was read to the assembled parties to the case, who in turn were given time to discuss the provisions of the statement privately. Unless the case was to be referred directly to a higher legal authority, all parties to the case then signed their agreement to the statement. If a long-term

punishment, such as laboring for the victim or victim's family or being kept under house arrest, was to be imposed, guarantors for the imposition of these sanctions had to sign the statement as well.

Following the signing, the criminal (or his family, employer, landlord, or the owner of the land on which the crime was committed) paid the monetary fines imposed by the legal authority. Court costs and fees were then paid. Finally, the physical sanctions imposed upon the criminal were carried out, which may have included whippings and fetters.

As mentioned above, the Tibetans made use of various devices, including oaths, to test the veracity of the parties to a dispute. Persons taking an oath would have to loosen their hair and remove amulets, knives, and religious strings. Then, while standing before the portrait of a powerful god or goddess, they would swear that they were telling the truth. The god or goddess was believed to punish those who lied. In one case, a woman who took an oath that she had not committed sorcery began to bleed from her nose shortly after taking the oath, and she later died, her death being attributed to the goddess Lhamo, before whose portrait she had taken the oath. If both parties to a case agreed to an oath, the oath was considered to settle the case because the supernatural sanctions that the gods and goddesses applied in the case of liars were so sure and so severe. However, not all people believed in the efficacy of an oath, and they were allowed to prohibit it from the legal hearing. Also, some people were alleged to employ deception in the taking of oaths, and opposing parties could refuse to accept the use of the oath.

If the established facts of a case were too vague for a clear decision to be made by the authorities, the parties would often agree to allow the case to be decided by the rolling of the dice. Again, the power of the supernatural came into play. Before rolling the dice, shouts were uttered for the Dharma Protector Gods to make the dice roll in such a way as to indicate the truth of the case. Each party rolled, and the one who rolled the highest number won the case. It was believed that if the dice gave the highest score to the party in the wrong, the gods would later punish the party who won unfairly.

The Tibetans also had a device, called a *Bab* or *Ba*, which they employed to ensure that contractual obligations would be honored. It set forth fees that a party who did not perform according to a contract would have to pay.

Finally, the Tibetans at one time made use of ordeals. First, the person who was to give testimony spoke and then was given a test in which supernatural forces would determine if the testimony was true or false. These tests typically consisted of a person coming in contact with some very hot item, such as boiling oil or water or hot stones. In one type of ordeal, the person's tongue was touched to a piece of hot iron. The individuals were then examined the next day, and if blisters were found they were deemed to have lied in giving testimony. The use of ordeals in Tibet had ended decades before the Chinese invasion.

Yet another way of handling a legal case is presented by the Native American people of the Cochiti Pueblo of New Mexico. There, the procedure is much simpler and faster. A person with a complaint brings it to the pueblo's governor. The governor himself investigates the matter. He then makes a decision on the basis of the information he has collected and upon legal precedent. If he cannot make a fair decision on this basis alone, he convenes a court of his lieutenant and members of the council. The court then hears the testimony of the parties to the case and of all of the witnesses. The officers of the court then discuss the matter and render a decision. The governor then announces the decision and the sanction, if the offender warranted one; sanctions in the early 1950s included fines, community service, and whippings.

See also OATH; ORDEAL; SUBSTANTIVE LAW.

Barton, Roy F. (1973 [1949]) *The Kalingas: Their Institutions and Custom Law.*

French, Rebecca. (1990) *The Golden Yoke: A Legal Ethnography of Tibet Pre-1959.*

Lange, Charles H. (1990 [1959]) *Cochiti: A New Mexico Pueblo, Past and Present.*

The Rhodesian Law Reports, 1966. (1966) Edited by H. G. Squires.

PURGE

A purge is the removal of suspected or actual political opponents from any sort of human group, whether they be political, geographic, or commercial in nature. Purges usually refer to the expulsion of relatively large numbers of people at a single time. In commercial groups, purges may be accomplished through firings. In more purely political groups, purges are accomplished through deportations, exiles, imprisonments, and killings.

The most infamous use of purges was in the former Soviet Union, especially under the regimes of Lenin and Stalin. During the Soviet period, direct political action was used to bring about purges far more frequently than was the legal system, although the legal system was not inactive either. Under Stalin, for instance, the legal code was enlarged with a great number of new criminal offenses that were of a political nature.

Most of the truly large-scale purges took place under Lenin's CHEKA (All-Russian Extraordinary Commission for the Suppression of Counterrevolution and Sabotage) and Stalin's NKVD (People's Commissariat for Internal Affairs), political action groups with tremendous powers to kill or imprison in labor camps without legal trials. The activities of the CHEKA

A purge removes political opponents either physically or geographically from any group. Adolf Hitler determined that Jews should be purged as part of his goal of an Aryan nation. Jewish women and children were gathered in Warsaw, Poland, in 1943 to be sent to concentration camps and then killed.

were directed against opponents of communism and the Communist party. The NKVD, on the other hand, attacked huge numbers of ordinary Soviet citizens who were suspected of disloyalty to Stalin, and even political functionaries within the government whom Stalin believed disloyal. However, the victims of the NKVD left behind kin and friends, and often these people wished to avenge these deaths. This led the NKVD to kill or imprison the kin and friends of those whom they had killed or imprisoned in the first place. In turn, the relatives and friends of these people had to be dealt with, and so the killings went on in ever-widening circles, and before Stalin was done with his purges, millions had been killed, the majority of them Soviet citizens who had once been loyal to him. Another reason for the purges was to fill the labor camps; Stalin needed a great deal of cheap labor for his building and industrialization plans, and he believed that the best way to do that was with forced labor.

The legal system was especially decimated by the purges, and it was left with virtually no personnel with legal training.

Ioffe, Olympiad S., and Peter B. Maggs. (1983) *Soviet Law in Theory and Practice.*

Real property refers to property that is not movable, such as land and buildings that are permanently attached to the land. Real property also includes the minerals beneath the surface of the land. The term *real property* was given this name because earlier English speakers believed that land and permanent buildings had more intrinsic worth than moveable items, or "personal property," and thus was more genuine or "real." The term *real property* may also be abbreviated as realty. Real property law is sometimes called *land tenure.* The laws that govern the use and transfer of rights in real property are, in European, U.S., Canadian, and many other legal systems, different from those regulating personal property. In the United States, for example, sale of rights in real property usually requires the use of a deed, whereas the sale of rights in personal property usually does not. Likewise, real property is frequently leased, whereas personal property is not normally leased. The division of property along these lines does not appear in all cultures. In many socie-ties, for example, buildings are personal property.

Among the Ifugao of the Philippines, for example, houses are frequently disassembled and moved by their owners. Houses are sometimes sold and then moved for use by the purchaser. Among the Ifugao, it is the house that has value, not the land upon which it is situated. Likewise, trees such as coconut, coffee, and areca trees also have value and are owned, whereas the land upon which they grow is valueless and therefore cannot be sold or owned.

Under the laws of the United States, Canada, and the countries of Europe, all land that is not owned by individuals or groups of individuals is owned by the state or the crown. This is not so in many societies, including the Ifugao. There, only three kinds of land may be owned. Land that is used for the cultivation of rice and forested land are owned by an individual or family until they are sold or given to another party. Land used for the cultivation of sweet potatoes is owned by the cultivator so long as he cultivates it; when it grows over with weeds and trees, it may be used by anyone who cares to clear the new vegetation and grow another few crops of sweet potatoes. All other land is unowned or free land that may be used by anyone. The types of ownership are linked to the length of time that the land is valuable. Forested lands provide wood in perpetuity unless too many trees are cut. Likewise, rice fields, or *padis,* produce rice as long as there is sufficient water for the rice plants to thrive. Both of these types of land are owned in perpetuity. As well, they may be pawned to another if the owner needs money; the lender has the right to farm the rice fields until the owner pays back the money he has been lent. Sweet potato fields only produce usable amounts of sweet potatoes for a few years, until weeds grow to the point that cultivation becomes more work than it is worth. Thus, sweet potato fields are only owned as long as they are cultivated.

Among the highly mobile Naskapi Indians of Labrador, Canada, there was traditionally no ownership of land. The only rights the Indians had, which could be transferred, were rights of *ususfructus,* or usufruct. Ownership of land, which is a bundle of rights including those of usufruct, made no sense to the Naskapi because they were only interested in using the animals and trees on the land before they moved on to a new place where the animals and trees were in greater abundance. The various bands within the area would give each other usufructuary rights; for instance, one band gave another the right to hunt porcupines on the land it used in exchange for the right to hunt bears on the other band's land. Individuals and families had exclusive hunting rights on specific tracts of land, but this may have been because of competition for fur-bearing animals as a result of the fur trade, which was introduced by white people. These tracts of land have been called hunting territories, and their use is governed by the headman of the band, who must also resolve disputes over hunting territory use. Hunting territory boundaries are made up of natural features of the land, particularly streams and rivers.

The Gusii people of western Kenya actually developed for themselves a new system of real property law in the period from 1925 to 1950. This development occurred as a result of a great increase in population. The Gusii are farmers who raise both crops and livestock. Prior to the 1920s, there was plenty of land for everyone to farm. If one could not get land from one's parents, one simply went into the bush and cleared whatever clan-owned land one wanted (all Gusii lands were owned collectively by clans). By the 1920s, however, there were so many people in Gusii society that land was becoming insufficient in quantity. Land that one man had in mind for his young son's future use often turned out to be land that a neighbor had in mind for his own son's future use. Also, people began to put up fences and hedges to keep their neighbors from encroaching on their own farm lands. Disputes over land became more common, and for the first time people began to take these disputes to legal authorities. Legal authorities weighed the strength of each claim to land and made decisions as to where the proper boundary lines should lie. They also made decisions in cases concerning the future use of land (for the later use of the children of the parties to the dispute). In such cases, they decided the boundary lines of lands that were to become farms years later.

The main purpose of the decisions of the Gusii legal authorities concerning land was not to preserve the rights of those who had strong claims to land ownership, but to provide all Gusii with relatively equal amounts of land. Thus, the goal of the Gusii land tenure system is very different from our own. Our land tenure system strives to protect the ownership rights of valid landowners, no matter how much land one owns. Thus, in our society, there are people who may own real estate worth hundreds of millions of dollars, while other people are homeless. The Gusii system strove to eliminate great differences in the amount of land members of the society could own, at least in its earliest stages.

Various aspects of a society's real property law can tell a great deal about other aspects of the culture. Among the Yoruba of Nigeria, there traditionally was no such thing as tenancy. This was because the land for a community was controlled by the community and owned by individuals. Thus, if one is by descent a member of the community, one thereby has automatic access to land ownership. If one is a stranger to the community, then one either becomes a naturalized member of the community, and thus able to own land within its bounds, or moves on to another place. Naturalization meant, for a man, that he married women within the community and swore loyalty to the community's chief.

See also PERSONAL PROPERTY.

Barton, Roy F. (1969 [1919]) *Ifugao Law.*

Lips, Julius E. (1947) "Naskapi Law." *Transactions of the American Philosophical Society* 37(4): 378–492.

Lloyd, Peter C. (1962) *Yoruba Land Law.*

Mayer, Philip, and Iona Mayer. (1965) "Land Law in the Making." In *African Law: Adaptation and Development,* edited by Hilda Kuper and Leo Kuper, 51–78.

REASONABLE MAN

The term *reasonable man* refers to a society's ideas about what is reasonable behavior by determining what a reasonable man would do in a given situation. These standards are not part of any society's codified law, but rather come into play in judicial proceedings and vary from society to society. The concept of the reasonable man is common to all legal systems, although the people using it may not be able to state it as a distinct concept.

Among the Barotse of Africa the concept of the reasonable man was applied in determining basic legal standards. The Barotse have two standards in their law: (1) the reasonable man and (2) the ideal man. The ideal man is one who behaves in the best possible manner in all conditions. Such a man obviously does not exist. But if one behaves at the minimally correct standards of behavior, one behaves as a reasonable man would and, therefore, in a legal fashion.

In Western legal systems and some other places, the reasonable man is a hypothetical man who is used in the judgment of an accused person. The actions of the accused are compared with what a reasonable, normal person would do in the circumstances in which the accused found himself during or after the commission of a crime or civil offense. Would a reasonable man who had just committed a robbery be running down the street wearing clothes other than athletic clothes? Yes. The shooting of a policeman by Lee Harvey Oswald was consistent with what a reasonable man would have done after shooting the president of the United States and being confronted by the policeman. Acting as a reasonable man would after commission of an offense is taken as a form of proof of guilt.

The concept of the reasonable man comes up in the law in many different guises in different societies. It does not always refer to people who have committed crimes and who are being judged on the basis of their behavior after the crime. For example, an Ifugao man or woman can divorce a spouse if that spouse is unreasonably jealous or unreasonably lazy. If an Ifugao person uses another person's rice field, and the owner wants it back, the owner must pay the one who worked the field for his labor, unless that payment is unreasonable.

Among the Nuer of Africa, if two groups are feuding with each other, and a man from the first group kills a man from the second group, the killing is considered a malicious rather than an accidental killing, since this is reasonable behavior for members of groups that are feuding with each other. The same is true for the Kalingas of the Philippines and there have even been cases there in which accidental woundings between members of feuding groups have been called deliberate by the person who committed the wounding, so that he could claim to be carrying out his obligations in the feud.

Among the Tiv of West Africa, the concept of the reasonable man came into play in determining the degree of behavior that constituted an offense. For example, the Tiv considered it reasonable for a man to beat his wife, but unreasonable and thus illegal for him to beat her to the point that she could not work. It was reasonable for a man to want to sleep with as many women as possible, but unreasonable and therefore illegal to commit incest in doing so. It is reasonable (though wrong) to steal from people to whom one is not related, but unreasonable and thus illegal to steal from one's family.

Also among the Tiv, there were reasonable grounds for divorce, and grounds that were unreasonable, in which cases the legal authorities did not grant divorces. For example, a woman who asked for a divorce from her husband simply because she did not like him was regarded as being unreasonable in her request, and she was denied. On the other hand, a woman who asked for a divorce because her husband failed to give her adequate clothing and fields, and who refused to pay attention to her, was successful. Also successful was the woman who asked for a divorce on the ground that her husband used magic to restrict her social contact with others; she used as proof that her husband had cut some of her hair and fingernails to use in a magical charm. His behavior was regarded as unreasonable.

The concept of *reasonable* is one that obviously can be used flexibly in law and elsewhere. As such, it helps law adapt to new situations.

Barton, Roy F. (1973 [1949]) *The Kalingas: Their Institutions and Custom Law*.

———. (1969 [1919]) *Ifugao Law*.

Bohannan, Paul J. (1957a) *Justice and Judgement among the Tiv*.

Evans-Pritchard, E. E. (1940) *The Nuer*.

Gluckman, Max. (1967 [1955]) *The Judicial Process among the Barotse of Northern Rhodesia*.

———. (1965c) "Reasonableness and Responsibility in the Law of Segmentary Societies." In *African Law: Adaptation and Development*, edited by Hilda Kuper and Leo Kuper.

REBELLION

Rebellion is open and active resistance to the established leadership and authority of a society. Sometimes, the goal of a rebellion is to remove and replace the existing government with another. Successful removal of the existing government is known as a revolution.

An interesting case of rebellion took place in China around 1900. In that example, rebellion broke out not against the official central government, but against the de facto government of China, which was composed of an informal alliance of provincial Chinese leaders and foreign businessmen. At the time, China was economically in poor shape. Much of the reason for China's condition was due to a lack of effective national leadership. For whatever reasons, the emperor and his government (the Ch'ing Dynasty) was initially unable or unwilling to prevent foreign interests from controlling the national economy for their own profit, to the detriment of the well-being of the Chinese people. Foreign businesses brought in many products that were less expensive than Chinese-made products, and so drove Chinese manufacturers out of business, creating widespread unemployment. Foreign interests also imported railways, which put much of the Chinese transportation industry out of business. This, in addition to the behavior of the foreign missionaries, which many Chinese found offensive, led to a wave of xenophobia among much of the Chinese population.

Perhaps no one was more xenophobic than the members of some of the Chinese secret societies. The societies, with names like Society of the Elder Brothers (*Ko-lao-hui*) and Society of the Big Saber (*Ta-tao-hui*), had been dormant for some time previously, but rallied behind the task of ridding China of its foreign influences. Many of the members of these secret societies practiced Chinese martial arts, and so were known as "Boxers" in the West. The Boxers believed that they were invulnerable to danger because of the magic they used.

Their xenophobia translated into physical attacks upon whatever they considered to be

Rebellion is an open and active resistance to established leadership and authority. Chinese citizens urged that their government become more democratic in a rebellion in 1989. During the uprising, one man stood against a column of government tanks in Beijing.

foreign or tainted by foreign influence. They attacked factories, Christian Chinese people, railroads, stores that sold imported goods, and missionaries. Foreigners in China, or those with business interests in China, became worried when the rebellion spread to the large cities of China.

Chinese who supported the Boxers gained control of the official Ch'ing government, and the government in turn declared war on the foreign nations involved in China. But the Ch'ing government controlled China only nominally. Most of the country was controlled by various individuals in the provincial regions of China, people who paid little attention to the central Ch'ing government in Beijing. These provincial leaders favored the continued presence of foreign interests because they profited from it and because the foreigners helped to keep them in power. The foreign powers, including the United States, with the support of the Chinese provincial leaders, used their armies to defeat the Boxer Rebellion, drive the emperor and empress into hiding, and sack Beijing. In 1901, the defeated central Chinese government agreed to pay reparations of $450 million to forbid all hostilities to non-Chinese, to stop importing weapons, to execute some of the governmental leaders of the Rebellion, and to agree to allow foreign troops to safeguard the Tianjin-Beijing railroad.

Though rebellions have occurred, and continue to occur, all over the world, certain places at certain times were the scene of frequent rebellions. For example, the southeastern United States saw many slave rebellions prior to the emancipation of the slaves. Another example of frequent rebellion was seen in what is now the southwestern United States and northern Mexico during the seventeenth and eighteenth centuries, when many of the Indian peoples there rebelled against the Spanish government and the Catholic priests and missions. One of the Indian peoples who came under Spanish and Catholic rule was the Yaquis of northern Mexico. The Spanish began by converting people to Catholicism, and to do this quickly, they moved the Yaqui people from their dispersed settlements to large towns, where the Jesuit missionaries could minister to many Yaquis at once. The Yaquis resented being forced to move. The missionaries taught the Yaquis European farming methods, but then forced them to work in large communal farms, the surplus of which was used to extend the reach of the Jesuit missions in California. The missionaries tried to make the Yaquis give up much of their traditional culture, such as long hair on men, the Yaqui pole dance (which involved dancing around a pole on which were placed parts of the bodies of enemies or lawbreakers), and the use of alcohol, all of which caused further resentment among the Yaquis. The Spanish also forced the Yaquis to pay taxes and to labor uncompensated in the mines. The Spanish punished offenses against Spanish law with corporal punishment (whipping), something the Yaquis had never before experienced. Also, the Spanish encouraged "coyotes" (people of mixed Spanish and Indian blood) to live in the Yaqui towns; the Yaqui people resented this because the coyotes actively supported the Catholic priests. Finally, the Spanish took much of the Yaquis' land and gave it to Spanish set-

tlers. All of these resentments began to come to a boil in 1739. To compound the problem, the annual September harvest was very poor. The Yaquis were hungry, and yet the missionary priests would not let them eat food the Yaquis had grown for the mission; later, one priest sold to the Yaquis some of the corn from the mission farm, the very same corn that the Yaquis themselves had grown.

Thus began the Yaqui rebellion of 1740. To start with, the rebellion began as a series of raids by Yaqui people on Spaniards simply to obtain food. The Spanish responded by sending out the citizen militia. Early fights produced standoffs. The Yaqui rebellion leaders also took an interest in beating and lecturing missionary priests and other Spaniards who had in the past tormented the Yaquis.

The scale of the rebellion grew, and genuine battles ensued in which people were killed. Eventually, the Spanish killed all of the rebel leaders, and indeed all Yaqui leaders. In fact, the Yaquis were to emerge from the rebellion with an inability to produce native leaders for another fifty years. The Yaquis were thoroughly beaten, and the Jesuits were in control.

Gernet, Jacques. (1982) *A History of Chinese Civilization*. Translated by J. R. Foster.

Spicer, Edward H. (1980) *The Yaquis: A Cultural History*.

 **RECIDIVISM**

A recidivist is a person who commits the same legal offense one or more times after having already been convicted of the offense, or who repeatedly commits an offense of similar magnitude or gravity after having already been convicted of one such offense.

Another term for the recidivist is "repeat offender." In many societies, the legal system provides greater sanctions for those who commit legal offenses repeatedly.

Following are some Egyptian statutes, and commentary on those statutes, on the matter of recidivism. These statutes indicate the attention paid to recidivists in many societies, reflecting the widespread belief that those who violate the law are those most likely to so again in the future.

48. A person is said to be a recidivist:—

(1) Who, having been sentenced to a criminal penalty, is found guilty of a crime or misdemeanor committed subsequently to the passing of such sentence; or

(2) Who, having been sentenced to imprisonment for a year or more, is found guilty of a misdemeanor committed subsequently within a period of five years from the expiration of his sentence or from the date at which such sentence is barred by prescription; or

(3) Who, having been sentenced for a crime or misdemeanor to imprisonment for less than a year or to fine, is found guilty of a misdemeanor similar in nature to his former offence and committed within a period of five years from the passing of such sentence.

For the purposes of recidivism, theft, obtaining by false pretenses, and abuse of confidence are deemed to be offences of a similar nature.

49. In the case of recidivism as defined by the preceding article, the Court shall have power to impose a penalty in excess of the maximum prescribed by law for the offence, so nevertheless that such penalty shall not exceed twice such maximum.

Provided always that the duration of a sentence of penal servitude for a term or of detention shall in no case exceed twenty years.

1. The Egyptian articles may be compared with Articles 56-58 of the French Penal Code as modified by the Law of March 26, 1891, and also with Articles 54-57 of the Belgian Penal Code.

2. The interpretation of Article 48 has given rise to certain difficulties, and the following points should be noted:—

(a) It is the existence of a previous sentence and not that of a previous offence which makes a man a recidivist. The idea of the legislator appears to be that the heavier penalty for recidivity is necessary because the previous sentence has not been sufficiently deterrent. Indeed, if a person is prosecuted for an offence committed prior to a previous sentence, he may be entitled to a mitigation of sentence under Article 35. Yet it is clear that it is not necessary that the recidivist should have actually undergone his previous sentence. He may have escaped, but the previous sentence nevertheless counts against him, subject to the provision of paragraph 2 of Article 48. A conditional sentence does not however count for recidivity if the conditions of discharge have been fulfilled. As, however, sentences to imprisonment for less than a year can alone be made conditional under Article 52, and do not count for recidivity under Article 48 (3) after five years from the date of the sentence, this point can but rarely arise under Article 48.

(b) The distinction between sentence to a criminal penalty and being found guilty of a crime must be remarked (*cf.* Articles 25, 27). The Code does not treat as a recidivist under Article 48 (1) a person who, though found guilty of a crime, is punished only with a correctional penalty by application of Article 17, unless he is found guilty of a subsequent misdemeanor within a period of five years. If the subsequent offence was also a crime, he is not a recidivist at all, for the second offence must, under Article 48 (2) and (3), be a misdemeanor. The commission of a crime subsequent to a sentence for a misdemeanor does not make a person a recidivist. This at first strikes one as illogical, but the court has such wide powers in sentencing for crime that it becomes unnecessary in this special case to increase them.

(c) The French jurisprudence favors the view that no sentence can count for recidivity until it is final, and from that date only. This may raise a difficulty in the case of sentences by default which have not been notified, or sentences in contumacy, since these are not final. It has been therefore suggested that the courts should hold that the first sentence must count for recidivity as from the date when it was first pronounced, if it has been subsequently confirmed or made absolute.

(d) The terms of Article 48 (2) are ambiguous. They have been generally interpreted to mean that the period during which the second sentence must have been pronounced begins to run only from the date when the first sentence has either expired, or been prescribed. The more recent French jurisprudence upon the similar terms of F.P.C., Article 57, favors the view that the period begins to run from the date of the first sentence and continues until the end of five from the expiration or prescription of that sentence. This view seems more consonant with the scheme of the article.

(e) Contraventions do not count for recidivity; but there exist outside the Code certain special provisions providing for the enhancement of penalties on repeated commission of breaches of various decrees.

3. The provisions of Article 48 (3) establish a form of "special" recidivity. The infliction of the severer punishment here depends, not upon the habitual criminality of the offender in a general sense, but upon the tendency to commit offences of a particular kind. Compare Article 58 of the French Penal Code.

The offences committed by the recidivist under this paragraph must therefore be similar. The Committee of Judicial Supervision has laid down that "in order that there may be between two offences sufficient analogy or similarity to be a ground for the application of the penalties for recidivity, each offence must be a breach of the same right. Theft is essentially an attack upon the property of another. It cannot consequently count so as to

render an execution liable to the penalties for recidivity, such a misappropriation being an offence *sui generis,* punished as being a disobedience to the orders of the law and authority, not as a breach of rights of property." As I have elsewhere remarked, this Circular of the Committee was issued prior to the Code of 1904, and related to the offence punishable under Article 460 of the Code of Civil and Criminal Procedure. Its reasoning does not appear to me to be applicable to the offence under P.C., Article 180. There is indeed good ground for holding that the offence under this latter article is assimilated in all respects to theft, and is an application of a broader conception of theft than that suggested by the Committee. Other circulars of the Committee have laid down that attempt to commit theft is a similar offence to theft, and that insult is not a similar offence to the infliction of wounds and blows. These conclusions are obvious. Whether the receiving of stolen goods under Article 279 is a similar offence to theft has been disputed. One would have thought that there could have been no doubt as to the similarity, but that M. Grandmoulin adopts the contrary view. In France, receiving stolen goods is a species of complicity and is as such similar in nature to the theft. I can entertain no doubt that extortion is a similar offence to theft, and that the abuse of a signature in blank is similar to forgery, and is also similar to abuse of confidence.

50. If a recidivist, who has previously been sentenced to two penalties restrictive of liberty, each of which was one year or more in duration, or to three such penalties one of which at least was one year or more in duration, for theft, receiving stolen goods, obtaining by false pretenses, abuse of confidence or falsification or for attempt to commit any of such offences, is found guilty of any misdemeanor of theft, receiving stolen goods, obtaining by false pretenses, abuse of confidence or falsification, committed subsequently to the last of the former convictions, the Court may sentence him to penal servitude for a period of not less

than two nor more than five years instead of applying the provisions of the preceding article.

51. The Court shall have the like power in the case of a recidivist who, having been previously sentenced to two penalties restrictive of liberty each of which was one year or more in duration, or to three such penalties one of which at least was one year or more in duration, for any of the offences falling under Articles 310, 311, 321 or 322, is found guilty of an offence falling under Article 310 or Article 321 committed subsequently to the last of the former convictions.

1. These two articles have a view particular cases of *récidive spéciale.*

They deal with: (a) persons who are in the habit of committing theft and other offences involving fraud and dishonesty; (b) persons who are in the habit of injuring animals or property, offences very common in Egypt.

2. To be liable to the increased penalties under these articles the accused must in all cases be a recidivist, that is to say, he must come within the terms of Article 48. "In order that the accused may come under Article 50 he must be a recidivist, that is to say, that the condition of recidivity must have existed at the time when he committed the offence of which he is accused; in other words, there must have been against him a previous conviction, he having been sentenced either to a criminal penalty under Article 48 (1) or to penalties under the conditions specified in Article 48 (2) (3)." Thus it is an essential condition of the application of Articles 50 and 51 that the offence for which the offender is sentenced under that article makes him a recidivist under Article 48 by relation to a sentence previously pronounced.

3. The list of "similar" offences under Article 50 is wider than that under Article 48, for the former expressly includes, besides the offences mentioned in the latter section, the receiving of stolen goods and falsification. I have already mentioned that attempt and participation should be regarded as similar in character to the consummated or principal offences. Article 50 expressly states that attempt is to count as the first or second term for recidivity under it. It is rather odd that it should not be expressly mentioned in the list of offences to count for the third term and the conclusion has been drawn that it would not so count. M. Grandmoulin points out that Articles 50, 51 do not seem to require that each offence counting for recidivity under these articles should be separated from the other by a previous conviction. Only we must note that the last offence of the series must be committed subsequently to the last of the former convictions. Indeed, it seems that the first two sentences counting in the series might have been inflicted simultaneously. This at least is the opinion of the Committee of Judicial Supervision.

4. Note further that, so long as the offender is a recidivist (this condition governing both Arts. 50 and 51), it is not requisite that the sentences counting for recidivity should have been passed within any particular time limits. Thus, suppose A is sentenced to a year's imprisonment for theft and seven years afterwards to six months' imprisonment for obtaining property by false pretenses. If within five years from the second sentence he is found guilty (say) of theft, he will be a recidivist under Article 48 (3) and liable to penal servitude under Article 50.

See also CAPITAL PUNISHMENT; CRIME.

Goadby, Frederic M. (1914) *Commentary on Egyptian Criminal Law, Part I.*

RES JUDICATA

Res judicata (or, originally in Latin, *res iudicata*) can be translated as "the thing that has been decided." It refers to the final decision made by a legal authority in a case, which then cannot be reopened; it signals the end of the legal affair. In the federal law of the United States, a situation of res judicata comes about when the United States Supreme Court makes a decision on a case, or when it refuses to hear a case, thereby allowing the previous decision to stand as the final one. For offenses against the law of a particular state, it is the decision of the state supreme court (or court of appeal in some states) that signifies res judicata. In these situations, res judicata comes about because there are no higher courts to which one can appeal.

It is a commonly held understanding of legal anthropologists that res judicata is found in all societies because it is in the interest of every society that disputes be put to an end at some point or another. Disputes that are allowed to continue over long periods of time are destructive to social unity, order, and peace.

In one society, at least, there is no res judicata in civil cases. Under the law of Tibet (before the 1959 invasion by Communist China), a party to a civil legal proceeding could renew the dispute in the courts at any time, even years after a decision. Far from bemoaning this as a weakness in their legal system, the Tibetans see this feature in a positive light. According to Rebecca French (1990: 406), the Tibetans consider the absence of res judicata as promoting "harmony, catharsis, reconciliation and truth." French (1990: 407) gives the following account by a Tibetan of a case that was reopened years after the courts had made a decision.

> There was a land case in our area which was the basis of a dispute. When the parties went to court, the district official favored one side, it was thought dishonestly. When the new district official came after three years, the man decided to bring the case up again even though there had been a final decision which the parties had signed, a liquidated damages clause

had been assessed and everything else!! Some people do this all the time; it is common. There is even a lama in our area who always brings up new cases like this regardless of the reason.

The Tibetan party to a dispute could choose the court in which he wanted his case heard. If he disliked the verdict given by that court, he could take his case to another. Unlike the United States legal system, if a Tibetan high court produced a verdict that one party disliked, he could take the case to a lower court, prolonging by years the time the case spent before the courts.

The end result of the extensive legal actions that the Tibetan legal system encouraged was that the parties would finally come to some mutual agreement on the facts of the case, then come to an agreement on the resolution of it. A formal ritual was performed when this occurred, involving apologies, the exchange of white scarves and food, and a statement that the conflict had ended. So, in fact, though the Tibetan legal system has no res judicata, it does promote social peace and unity in the end, even though the end may take years to reach.

French, Rebecca. (1990) *The Golden Yoke: A Legal Ethnography of Tibet Pre-1959.*

REVENGE

Revenge is the infliction of harm on another party in return for the harm suffered at the hands of that other party. It is also known as the avenging of, or taking vengeance for, acts of injury by another. Revenge is not law, and it may or may not be permissible under the law, depending upon the circumstances, the society, and the legal system involved. Revenge not infrequently leads to counterrevenge and feud.

The Kaoka people of Guadalcanal, in the Pacific, believe, as do many peoples around the world, that death is always or almost always the product of homicide inflicted by another party. If a child dies within the first five years of life, he or she is believed to have died of ordinary illness. Any other death is believed caused by the actions of another human being and accomplished by the use of sorcery (unless there are obvious physical means at work). In order to punish the murderer, revenge is taken.

The Kaoka wishing to exact revenge is first faced with the problem of identifying the sorcerer. People generally have a good idea of who the sorcerer may be, usually someone belonging to a group that has long been hostile to the group of the deceased. However, to find the individual responsible requires the hiring of a diviner known as a *to'iai*. The diviner is capable of bringing the soul of the deceased into a certain kind of nut, which he holds in his hand. Once there, the diviner asks him or her a number of questions in order to establish the identity of the murderer. The soul in the nut is only capable of answering either "yes" or "no." A "no" answer is signaled by a still nut. A "yes" is given by the nut moving, and sometimes pulling the diviner. So, the diviner asks the soul questions such as "Did your killer come from the north?" or "Did your killer come from the X group?" Finally, the culprit's name is revealed.

Next, those wishing to take revenge must decide upon the manner in which they will do it. The headman of the village will call a general meeting to discuss the matter. In the past, before colonial powers came to Guadalcanal, fighting could be used for the revenge of a murder, but today, only sorcery can be used.

In the past, the villagers who chose to kill the murderer would also select someone to carry out the revenge killing. This would be someone with a good reputation as a fighter, often the headman himself. The person selected would then take several other men and form a troop to do the killing. The troop leader would also make sure that the priests had performed the necessary magical acts to ensure the success of their mission.

The troop leader then assembled his men for the attack. The men would be armed with spears, the points of which were carved from the shinbones of former enemies. They also carried clubs and shields, and a few had bows and arrows. One of the objectives of the raid was to use surprise, and so the raiders would attack at dawn, when members of the enemy's camp began to leave their huts. Though the raiders aimed primarily at killing the sorcerer, they also killed other people if they could. Sometimes, surprise was not possible, and the enemies killed some of the raiders.

The raiders took heads and legs as trophies and then returned home. The raiding had made the raiders spiritually polluted, and so they remained in seclusion from the other members of the village for a few days. After this time, the villagers who had requested the raid gave the raiders a large feast, at which the decaying head of the sorcerer was displayed.

The victims of the raid had scattered in the jungle, and returned only after they were sure that the raiders had completely gone. Then they began plotting their own raid in revenge of the one they had suffered. Their targets were the raiders who had attacked them, never the villagers who had requested the raid in the first place. Raiding turned into feuding, and eventually the two enemies met in a large pitched battle. The losers would then escape into the jungle to live far away.

In the society of the Tiwi, an Aborigine people in northern Australia, revenge was often used as a means of saving face. If, for example, an older man with many wives found that one of his wives was having sexual relations with a young man (who was not married because most of the women were married to older men), his pride was injured. In order to achieve social peace, the two men took part in a highly formalized act of revenge, designed to insult the culprit and restore the other man's pride. In formal Tiwi revenge taking, all of the people in the village would gather around in a circle. There, the older man would face the younger man and begin to insult him. He would loudly proclaim that the young man had acted badly, and that he should not have done so, and then proceed to list all of the good things that he himself had done in the past on behalf of the young man. The point of all this was to shame the young man and to portray him as someone who had repaid the kindness of the old man by seducing one of his wives. It also had the effect of telling the young man that in a peaceful society everyone had to help one another rather than try to hurt one another.

At this point, the old man was quite angry and began to throw spears at the young man. By the established rules of this form of revenge taking, the young man was allowed to jump in the air or to weave and duck so as to avoid being struck by the spears, but was not allowed to run around to do so. This the young man proceeded to do for ten or fifteen minutes, unless one of the spears went wild and struck a bystander, which ended the affair. The young man could easily dodge the spears all day if he wanted to, because the spears were slow and the young man was quite agile. However, to do so would make the old man appear even more foolish than had the seduction of his wife, and this would have been the direct opposite of what the formal revenge taking aimed to achieve. So, after dodging the spears for a while, the young man allowed himself to be struck by the spear in such a way as to make a flesh wound that would appear serious and give a lot of blood, but which would, in fact, heal quickly. This done, the old man had his honor restored, and the matter was finished.

Hart, C. W. M., and Arnold R. Pilling. (1960) *The Tiwi of North Australia.*

Hogbin, Ian. (1964) *A Guadalcanal Society: The Kaoka Speakers.*

REVITALIZATION MOVEMENTS

Anthony F. C. Wallace has defined the revitalization movement as "a deliberate, organized, conscious effort by members of a society to construct a more satisfying culture" (1956: 265). One of the main aspects of culture that is typically involved in revitalization movements is politics. What distinguishes revitalization movements from other types of culture change is that in revitalization movements the members of the society who are changing the culture are conscious of their decisions to change the culture and are also conscious of the direction in which they wish to change the culture. Most culture change occurs without the people affected being very much aware of it, at least until after it occurs. Most culture change comes about as a result of people simply going about their lives while trying to attain their own goals, without thinking much about the effects of their actions on the culture as a whole.

There are several kinds of revitalization movements, which have been called by various names in the past, including nativistic movement, reform movement, religious revival, social movement, mass movement, utopian community, cargo cult, charismatic movement, and others. It is, however, possible to organize revitalization movements by the type of culture change being effected and by the agent by which the members of the society believe the change is to take place.

One important type of revitalization movement is the nativistic movement. This is a conscious effort to return a people culturally and socially to an earlier time when, it is believed, things were better. This is to be done by removing all elements of the culture and environment that are believed to be foreign. A distinguishing feature of this type of movement is the belief that it is culturally alien things that have caused harm. A good example of this is the Ghost Dance Religion, which appeared among American Indians of the Great Basin and the Great Plains of the United States in the late nineteenth century. This religion began with a vision that came to a Paiute man named Wovoka, who lived in Nevada. Wovoka said that in his vision he was instructed that if Indians performed a special dance (the Ghost Dance) and did some other things, all the dead Indians would return to life, thus the name "Ghost Dance." Wovoka's message traveled across the plains, and was especially well received among the Sioux. The Sioux added their own unique touches: they believed that the performance of the Ghost Dance would mean that all the bison would return to provide abundant food for the Indians, and that all of the white people would die. The Sioux Ghost Dance Religion also promised its adherents that they could fight the white man safely if they wore special Ghost Dance shirts, which would protect them from the white man's bullets. The Ghost Dance found a receptive audience among the other Indians of the Great Plains, Great Basin, and parts of the Southwest, who had been dispirited and in social turmoil following the disastrous effects of their contact with the white man, and spread to most of the peoples of these regions. The end of the Ghost Dance Religion came when approximately 200 Sioux Indians, among them some Ghost Dance adherents, were killed by U.S. Army personnel in the Wounded Knee, South Dakota, massacre of 29 December 1890; the effectiveness of the white man's bullets on those who wore the special shirts cast doubt on the Ghost Dance Religion.

The antiwhite message of the Ghost Dance Religion marks it as a nativistic movement. However, because it also involved belief in an apocalyptic world transformation, involving the extermination of whites, the return of the dead Indians, and the return of the bison, the Ghost Dance Religion can also be called a millinerian movement.

Another kind of millenarian movement, found in parts of Melanesia, is the cargo cult. Cargo cult movements also emphasize apocalyptic world transformation, but rather than working for the removal of foreign cultural elements, they actively seek to import foreign cultural elements as a means to cultural revitalization. Such movements are known as vitalization movements.

Cargo cults came about largely because of the great differences in technology between the Melanesian peoples and the explorers, missionaries, and military men from Europe, North America, and Japan. Melanesian groups, from time to time, believed that the European, North American, and Japanese people would eventually, if given proper ritual treatment, let the Melanesians in on the secret of their wealth in goods, which bespoke a much higher technology. The word "cargo" is Melanesian pidgin for trade goods, the central focus of the cargo cults' activities. These activities included the construction of mock radio aerials in some places, such as the westerners and Japanese had, or mock landing strips for airplanes, or mock docking facilities for ships, depending upon the particular cargo cult. The Melanesians had apparently decided that since their foreign visitors had made these things, and following their construction trade goods had arrived, then it must be these things that would likewise bring trade goods to them.

The history of one cargo cult is as follows. In 1946, an Australian patrol entered an

Self-proclaimed messiah David Koresh, leader of the Branch Davidian Sect, an example of a revitalization movement, stands with his wife, Rachel, and son, Cyrus.

unpacified part of central highlands New Guinea. There, the patrol found a group of people who, after seeing the white people, believed that an earlier prophecy was about to be fulfilled. The prophecy was that the arrival of the white people indicated that the end of the world was also about to come. In preparation for the end, they slaughtered their pigs, a major source of food for the group. They did so in the belief that the end of the world would bring with it the "Great Pigs," and that their ordinary pigs would be of no account. They erected mock aerials to receive news of the apocalypse, and many also believed that the apocalypse would turn their dark skins white. The notion of an impending

end of the world was a common feature of cargo cults, and this is why they are termed millenarian movements.

Another type of revivalistic movement is built around a belief in a divine savior who takes human form, a type of movement called "messianic." The religions of Buddhism and Christianity were both originally messianic movements. A more recent example is the Branch Davidians, whose leader, David Koresh, was apparently considered by its members to be a divine savior. Others include Jim Jones of Jonestown, Guyana, and Syoko Asahara of Japan.

An especially famous example of a messianic movement is the Handsome Lake Religion of Iroquois Indians of New York State and Ontario. In the 1700s, the Iroquois, demoralized by military defeat, the loss of land, new diseases, and alcohol, heard a new voice, that of Handsome Lake, a Seneca (one of the Iroquois tribes). Handsome Lake's prophecy stressed a fusion of traditional Iroquois religious beliefs, Christianity, abstention from the consumption of alcohol, and a strengthening of family ties. The Handsome Lake Religion survives today with a substantial following.

A final type of revitalization movement is the revivalistic, a type of movement that emphasizes a return to an earlier form of the culture, in whatever form the movement leaders portray it, whether such a form actually once existed or not. An example of this type of movement is the *Gush Emunin* (bloc of the faithful) movement in Israel. This movement emphasized the revival of Zionist ideology, Zionism being a movement for Jews to settle Palestine, which had been largely dormant since the creation of the state of Israel. Zionist ideology includes the idea that in the past, in biblical times, the Jews were a great and heroic people. The *Gush Emunin* stresses a return to the kind of strict religious observance that, adherents believe, characterized the behavior of the ancient Jews who had been so great. It also has as one of its recurrent themes the land of Palestine, which the ancient Jews controlled and which modern Jews must once again control if they are to return to their former greatness. Thus, movement followers believe that the lands won in the wars of 1967 and 1973 are of crucial importance and must never be surrendered. Members of the *Gush Emunin* were the ones who illegally occupied houses in the Sinai in an effort to prevent its return to Egypt, which the government of Israel had decided to do to promote peace. The *Gush Emunin* has since developed into a bureaucratic organization with specialized arms to pursue its political and religious aims. One of these arms is the *Amana*, which is specifically dedicated toward creating and preserving settlements in Israeli-occupied territories. In short, the *Gush Emunin* was a successful revitalization movement in the respect that it became a standard feature of the Israeli political scene with a constant presence and influence on national politics.

Not all revitalization movements are so successful. The Ghost Dance Religion ended tragically with the deaths of many people, as did the Branch Davidians, the People's Temple of Jonestown, Guyana, and a cargo cult in Melanesia whose members attempted to fight the Japanese navy in World War II and who believed that their magic would protect them against Japanese bullets. Other revitalization movements have simply evaporated as adherents came to realize that their leaders were not messiahs, or that the millennium was not going to come, or that the cargo would never arrive.

Lewellen, Ted C. (1992) *Political Anthropology: An Introduction.* 2d ed.

Wallace, Anthony F. C. (1956) "Revitalization Movements." *American Anthropologist* 58: 264–281.

Worsley, Peter M. (1959) "Cargo Cults." *Scientific American* 200: 117–128.

RIGHTS, CHILDREN'S

The legal rights of children within the family make up an important part of the field of family law. Among the Kuria people of Tanzania, children traditionally belonged to the man who was at the time of birth married to the child's mother; marriage, in this society, was finalized by the payment of a bride-price by the husband. However, it was not unheard of for a child to

A Pakistani boy digs clay with two men to feed brick kilns near Rawalpindi in 1994. The legal rights of children make up a large part of family law as well as laws involving their exploitation as laborers.

have been born into and raised in the house of a man with whom the mother was living, even though she was legally married to another man. Under traditional law, the child still belonged to the man who was married to the mother, even if the child never met him and even if he or she knew only the man with whom her mother lived, the man who was often his or her own natural father. This law is known as the patrilineal principle.

In later times, when the national courts (as opposed to the Kuria legal authorities) established jurisdiction over the Kuria people, the law changed. The national courts considered it cruel and against the interests of the child to remove the child from the only home he or she had ever

known and put him or her into the house of the mother's husband, especially if the man with whom the woman was living was the child's natural father. In other words, the national courts considered the child's rights as well as the rights of the parents. The question for the judges was how to balance the traditional rights of the father under the patrilineal principle with the interests of the children. One early attempt to achieve this balance was to name the husband of the mother the father, but to give custody of the children to the mother. The mother's husband also received the right to arrange his children's marriages and to receive the bride-price paid for his daughters. Still later, the courts said that in cases in which women who deserted their husbands and whose children thus were the product of unions with other men, the children belonged to the mothers and not to the husbands.

The law, in attempting to improve the conditions for children in cases in which their mothers have left their husbands, has given rights over the children to the mothers. This has made it difficult to preserve the bride-price arrangement for two reasons. First, a man might think that he should not pay a bride-price if he is not going to have any rights in the children, because his wife might run away and his children would in later life support the wife, and perhaps her lover, but not him. Secondly, a man might be tempted to forgo marriage altogether. He could live with a woman, have children, and then the children would in later life support their mother and, since he is their mother's lover, support him as well; in this type of arrangement, the man could acquire all of the benefits of marriage without having to pay the bride-price. In short, the change in the rights of children in Kuria society has had far-reaching effects on the law and on the very basis of Kuria society.

Rwezaura, Barthazar Aloys. (1985) *Traditional Family Law and Change in Tanzania: A Study of the Kuria Social System.*

RIGHTS, HUMAN

Interest in the basic rights of individuals goes far back in human history; such rights are mentioned in documents such as the Old Testament, the Magna Carta, and the U.S. Declaration of Independence. However, it is only since the end of World War II that human rights have emerged as a major focus of worldwide concern. The emergence of human rights and its continuation as a major worldwide issue is the result of a number of factors. These include the genocide and other large-scale human rights violations of World War II, the erosion of colonialism, and the demand for rights by indigenous and minority peoples.

The basic definition and framework for the subsequent consideration of human rights is contained in the Universal Declaration of Human Rights, adopted and proclaimed by the United Nations General Assembly as resolution 217 A (III) of 10 December 1948. This document, reprinted in full below, establishes as a moral principle that all human beings are entitled to certain human rights and freedoms. The Universal Declaration has been followed by numerous other documents focusing on specific rights or categories of rights pertaining to genocide, protection of war captives and victims, collective bargaining, prostitution, children, refugees, prisoners, slavery, marriage, forced labor, racial discrimination, cultural rights, political asylum, mental retardation, hunger and malnutrition, disabled persons, religion, and medical care.

Human rights violations involving ethnic groups are purposeful acts intended to harm both individuals who are members of a specific ethnic group and the group itself. Such violations commonly include mass killings, deportations, rapes, denial of food and housing, torture, detention without due process, destruction of dwellings and material possessions, and destruction of cultural, educational, and religious institutions. When the national government is directly involved in ethnic conflict it may be a perpetrator of rights violations while at the same time render itself unavailable as a protector of rights. Similarly, when ethnic groups use terrorism against civilian populations, they too are guilty of human rights violations.

Efforts to apply the concept of human rights to ethnic groups has produced three controversies in the international community. The first is whether the concept of human rights as set forth in the Universal Declaration and subsequent documents applies only to individuals or whether it also applies collectively to groups such as religious groups, ethnic minority groups, indigenous peoples, etc. It is clear from the policy and practice in many nations that, with regard to certain matters, ethnic groups do have a collective, corporate identity. For example, land claims and other rights asserted by Native Americans have been adjudicated in courts or settled by administrative bodies within the framework of the group's rights. Similarly, in New Zealand, the Maori right to political representation is a group right, not an individual right. However, when it comes to rights defined as human rights, the question of whether those rights apply only to individuals or also to groups is not clear. Human rights advocates argue for the latter view as a way of more broadly protecting human rights, while many national governments adhere to the individual rights only position as a means of defining human rights as an internal matter. Efforts at applying rights protection to entire groups has led to many as yet unanswered questions, such as: What is an ethnic minority? Is group size a reasonable criteria for measuring group existence? Does a group need to be localized to be a group? How does one measure group cohesiveness?

The second controversy concerns the issue of differentiation versus discrimination that often arises when one group is afforded some rights denied to other groups. The controversy arises because in many nations ethnic minority groups want to be treated differently, often in order to maintain their cultural integrity or to regain rights lost during times of colonial domination. The question is whether this differential treatment of groups—as in affirmative actions programs for African-Americans in the United States or programs for Untouchables in India—is a form of discrimination, either against individual members of the group or members of other groups who are not eligible for differential treatment. Outsiders sometimes see these special group rights designed to reverse the effects of past discrimination as a form of reverse discrimination. In general, groups that are given collective rights tend to be ones with a clear ethnic identity and membership, who are different from other groups, and who can be awarded rights on the basis of objective criteria that also can be applied to other groups.

The third controversy is over the cross-cultural validity of current conceptions of human rights, which are seen in some non-Western nations as reflecting Western values and therefore as ethnocentric. This ethnocentrism is seen by some experts as a hurdle to the universal adoption and enforcement of human rights protections. From a cross-cultural perspective, much attention has been focused lately on Islam and Islamic nations and the need to balance universal human rights concepts with such Islamic practices as the use of amputation as a punishment for crime.

UNIVERSAL DECLARATION OF HUMAN RIGHTS

PREAMBLE

Whereas recognition of the inherent dignity and of the equal and inalienable rights of all members of the human family is the foundation of freedom, justice and peace in the world,

Whereas disregard and contempt for human rights have resulted in barbarous acts which have outraged the conscience of mankind, and the advent of a world in which human beings shall enjoy freedom of speech and belief and freedom from fear and want has been proclaimed as the highest aspiration of the common people,

ful assembly and association.

2. No one may be compelled to belong to an association.

Article 21

1. Everyone has the right to take part in the government of his country, directly or through freely chosen representatives.

2. Everyone has the right to equal access to public service in his country.

3. The will of the people shall be the basis of the authority of government: this will shall be expressed in periodic and genuine elections which shall be by universal and equal suffrage and shall be held by secret vote or by equivalent free voting procedures.

Article 22

Everyone, as a member of society, has the right to social security and is entitled to realization, through national effort and international cooperation and in accordance with the organization and resources of each State, of the economic, social and cultural rights indispensable for his dignity and the free development of his personality.

Article 23

1. Everyone has the right to work, to free choice of employment, to just and favorable conditions of work and to protection against unemployment.

2. Everyone, without any discrimination, has the right to equal pay for equal work.

3. Everyone who works has the right to just and favorable remuneration ensuring for himself and his family an existence worthy of human dignity, and supplemented, if necessary, by other means of social protection.

4. Everyone has the right to form and to join trade unions for the protection of his interests.

Article 24

Everyone has the right to rest and leisure, including reasonable limitation of working hours and periodic holidays with pay.

Article 25

1. Everyone has the right to a standard of living adequate for the health and well-being of himself and of his family, including food, clothing, housing and medical care and necessary social services, and the right to security in the event of unemployment, sickness, disability, widowhood, old age or other lack of livelihood in circumstances beyond his control.

2. Motherhood and childhood are entitled to special care and assistance. All children, whether born in or out of wedlock, shall enjoy the same social protection.

Article 26

1. Everyone has the right to education. Education shall be free, at least in the elementary and fundamental stages. Elementary education shall be compulsory. Technical and professional education shall be made generally available and higher education shall be equally accessible to all on the basis of merit.

2. Education shall be directed to the full development of the human personality and to the strengthening of respect for human rights and fundamental freedoms. It shall promote understanding, tolerance and friendship among all nations, racial or religious groups, and shall further the activities of the United Nations for the maintenance of peace.

3. Parents have a prior right to choose the kind of education that shall be given to their children.

Article 27

1. Everyone has the right freely to participate in the cultural life of the community, to enjoy the arts and to share in scientific advancement and its benefits.

2. Everyone has the right to the protection of the moral and material interests resulting from any scientific, literary or artistic production of which he is the author.

Article 28

Everyone is entitled to a social and international order in which the rights and freedoms set forth in this Declaration can be fully realized.

Article 29

1. Everyone has duties to the community in which alone the free and full development of his personality is possible.

2. In the exercise of his rights and freedoms, everyone shall be subject only to such limitations as are determined by law solely for the purpose of securing due recognition and respect for the rights and freedoms of others and of meeting the just requirements of morality, public order and the general welfare in a democratic society.

3. These rights and freedoms may in no case be exercised contrary to the purposes and principles of the United Nations.

Article 30

Nothing in this Declaration may be interpreted as implying for any State, group or person any right to engage in any activity or to perform any act aimed at the destruction of any of the rights and freedoms set forth herein.

See also INTERNATIONAL LAW

An-Na'im, Abdullahi A., ed. (1992) *Human Rights in Cross-Cultural Perspective: A Quest for Consensus.*

Brownlie, Ian. (1992) *Basic Documents on Human Rights.*

Felice, William. (1992) *The Emergence of Peoples' Rights in International Relations.*

Heinz, Wolfgang S. (1991) *Indigenous Populations, Ethnic Minorities and Human Rights.*

Lawson, Edward, ed. (1991) *Encyclopedia of Human Rights.*

Ramaga, Philip V. (1993) "The Group Concept in Minority Protection." *Human Rights Quarterly* 15: 575–588.

Stavenhagen, Rodolfo. (1987) "Ethnic Conflict and Human Rights: Their Interrelationship." *Bulletin of Peace Proposals* 18: 507–514.

Van Dyke, Vernon. (1985) *Human Rights, Ethnicity, and Discrimination.*

Whalen, Lucille. (1989) *Human Rights: A Reference Handbook.*

RIVALRY

A rivalry is a state of competition between two individuals or groups, and is usually long-standing. Among the various men's clubs of the Crow Indians, rivalries could become fierce. The clubs were often paired in rivalrous activities and were always trying to best each other. One of these was bravery in battle, in which each side tried to beat the other in counting coup (being the first to be able to go up to an enemy and touch him, often with a special coup stick). Counting coup was very dangerous, because while you were trying to touch the enemy, he and all of his compatriots were usually trying to kill you. If a club was the first to count coup, it could sing the songs of the club with whom it had a rivalry; otherwise, this stealing of songs was not allowed. The rivalry helped to make the clubs competing with each other very brave, as in the following case.

One of the men's societies known as the Fox club was in rivalry with another known as the Lumpwood club. As they were approaching the enemy in battle one day, a Fox man snuck up some distance in the direction of the enemy with the Fox's coup stick, and then stopped. A Lumpwood man went up to him and asked him if he was going to count coup. The Fox man replied that he was afraid to go. The Lumpwood man then took the Fox coup stick, used it to touch an enemy, and then ran back part of the way and put the coup stick in the ground between the two enemy parties. He dared the Fox men to get their own coup stick back, but none would. In order to humiliate the Foxes further, the Lumpwoods claimed the right to sing the Fox's songs that night, and the Foxes had to borrow songs from other clubs so that they would have something to sing.

Crow men's club rivalries were restricted to the warm seasons; the rest of the time the members of the clubs were friendly and helpful toward each other.

Lowie, Robert H. (1956 [1935]) *The Crow Indians*.

seen by the kin of the offender as unjustified, so the killing often brings about a feud.

Barton, Roy F. (1969 [1919]) *Ifugao Law.*

Pospisil, Leopold. (1974 [1971]) *Anthropology of Law: A Comparative Theory.*

SANCTION

Sanction is one of the four attributes of law. That is, sanction must be present for law to exist. A sanction is either a negative device that withdraws rewards or favors that otherwise (if the law had not been violated) would have been granted, or a positive measure that inflicts some painful physical or psychological experience.

The Ifugao people of the Philippines primarily use fines as sanctions, even in cases of murder. However, unlike our own system in which the offender is forced to pay the fine by the court system and by law enforcement personnel, the Ifugao place the burden of forcing payment on the injured party who is to receive the fine (among the Ifugao, fines are paid to the directly injured parties and not to the people of the society as a whole). The party due to receive the payment must vigorously pursue it, not merely ask for it. The offender, on the other hand, has a very good reason to pay the fine; if he does not, he may be lawfully killed by the one due the payment of the fine. However, killing an offender who has not paid a fine is often

SEGMENTARY LINEAGE

The segmentary lineage system is a social and political form of organization in which a person belongs to a number of related descent groups that telescope from an apical ancestor and that have different functions in different social situations. The segmentary lineage system is organized vertically in levels of greater and greater inclusion. The segmentary lineage system is common in parts of Africa and the Middle East. It functions most often in times of conflict, as may be seen in the following common Bedouin (Arab) saying, "Myself against my brother; my brother and I against my cousin; my cousin, my brother, and I against the outsider" (Murphy and Kasdan 1959: 20).

Segmentation occurs within the lineage. Suppose there are three brothers in a patrilineal society, named A, B, and C. Each one has male children, and they in turn have male children themselves, and so on. Suppose that after five generations, the great-great-grandchildren and the great-great-great-grandchildren decide that they wish to be in separate groups from each other, due to conflicts. They might make segments based upon the brothers A, B, and C. For instance, all of the descendants of A make up one segment, all of the descendants of B make up another, and all of the descendants of C make up another. The same thing will happen to the descendants of the great-great-great-grandsons of these descendants in another five generations or so, and this principle will continue to be applied in perpetuity. However, segmentation is not the same as fission. Fission, which often occurs with lineages of hunting and gathering peoples, makes two or more new groups out of one, but the old group ceases to exist. With segmentation, the old group can still come into form and action as a group when circumstances call for it. For example, if a descendant of A got into a fight with a descendant of A's first cousin, then all of the descendants of A's father (all of the descendants of A, B, and C) would unite to support the descendant of A against the other man.

Among societies with segmentary lineages, lineage segments usually only run three or four generations deep. In some segmentary lineage societies such as the Amba of western Uganda, all or nearly all of the members of a lineage segment can be found within one local group. In other societies, such as the Lugbara of the West Nile district of Uganda, the Dinka of the southern Sudan, and the Mandari, also of the southern Sudan, members of lineage segments were frequently dispersed among a number of local settlement groups.

Segments come together to the degree that the interests of the members of each segment are affected. In some societies, it is possible to unite all members of a language group or "tribe," as it may be called. For example, under traditional circumstances, all of the speakers of Dinka could come together into one politically united group for some particular action that affected the entire Dinka tribe. The same is true of the Lugbara, the Nuer of the Sudan, and the Konkomba of Togo. However, among the Mandari, the largest group that could become politically united was the chiefdom. For the Amba, no groups larger than exogamous clusters could unite, and among the Tiv of Nigeria, it is maximally only a lineage of eight or ten generations in depth.

When the lineages are dispersed in many different localities, partial or complete tribal unity is often achieved by the tribe having a dominant or leading lineage. This lineage would provide the leaders of the communities and would also create a core around which the rest of the tribe could be organized. Since the members of this lineage would be found in all communities, they could rally all the members of the tribe behind them in action. Such is the case among the Nuer and the Lugbara. Among the Mandari, the Bora lineage supplies the tribe's several chiefs.

The most important aspect of segmentary systems, from a political perspective, is that societies so organized have no central leadership and authority. They are able to unite all or part of the society to face a common threat, but have no ability to unite under a single leadership and no way to keep the segments permanently united.

There appear to be three major types of social organization in segmentary lineage societies. In societies of the first type, exemplified by societies such as the Nuer and the Lugbara, social unity is created by the belief in a single large genealogy that unites the entire tribe. Despite the fact that there are many segments, Nuer people, for example, still consider themselves and all other Nuer members part of a single lineage descended from one man. Thus, the number of people who can be united for political or military action is larger than can be assembled in societies of the types discussed below.

A second way in which social unity may be created in segmentary lineage societies can be seen in the examples of the Konkomba, Amba, and Tallensi societies. In these societies, there is no large single lineage to which all other members of the tribe belong. Rather, social unity is created by each segment having ritual obligations toward other segments and by intermarrying with them. Typically, lineages are exogamous, thus increasing the ties with other lineages. There are very few examples of chiefs within this type of society, and whatever authorities and leaders there are have relatively little power.

The third means by which a society with segmentary lineages may create social unity is to unite within territorial sections of the tribe's entire region. Thus, there are numerous united small groups, but no unity at the tribal level, even though members of lineages are dispersed over a wide geographic area. An example of this type of social organization is seen in Dinka society. Societies with this type of organization frequently have chiefs as the leaders of each of these territorially based groups.

I will use the example of the Tiv people to illustrate some salient aspects of the segmentary lineage system as found among the members of that society. The members of Tiv society all consider themselves descendants of a man called Tiv because they belong to Tiv's lineage. It is not true that a modern-day Tiv person could trace each link in his or her genealogy to Tiv himself, but he or she could name the segments in the overall Tiv lineage and describe where his or her segment fits into the entire descent group.

Each division in the lineage is known to the Tiv as *nongo* ("line" or "queue"). Thus, the three children of a man, if they have many descendants, may sometime in the future each be the beginner of a *nongo*. A *nongo* typically refers, however, to the living members of a line of descent.

The Tiv make a distinction between lines of descent and actual patrilineal descent groups, which they call *ityô*. In addition to a man's own *ityô*, those of his mother, his father's mother, his father's father's mother, and his mother's mother's were important to him, especially since he was protected when he was among any of these other *ityôs*, which are called *igbas*.

The Tiv lineages are divided into segments, which are known as *ipaven*. Each *ipaven* lives by itself on a *tar*, a particular piece of land on which live no people ouside of the *ipaven*.

The *ipaven* functions in times of war between Tiv groups. A man will be involved in a fight if he belongs to the *ipaven* of a man who has a dispute with a man of another *ipaven*. Every male is involved in the fighting who is a descendant of the two linking sons to the first common ancestor reckoned genealogically from the disputants upward. In other words, let us say that there were three brothers, A, B, and C, sons of D. Four generations later, a great-grandson of A has a serious dispute with a great-grandson of B. If there was to be a war, all of the men descendants of A would be involved in a war with all of the men descendants of B. The men descendants of C would not be involved except possibly as peacemakers. On the other hand, if man descendant of E, D's brother, had a dispute with a man descendant of D, all of the men descendants of D (all of the men descendants of A, B, and C) would be involved in fighting against all of the men descendants of E.

Bohannon, Laura. (1958) "Political Aspects of Tiv Social Organization." In *Tribes without Rulers*, edited by John Middleton and David Tait, 33–66.

Fortes, Meyer. (1953) "The Structure of Unilineal Descent Groups." *American Anthropologist* 55: 17–41.

Middleton, John, and David Tait. (1958) "Introduction." In *Tribes without Rulers*, edited by John Middleton and David Tait, 1–31.

Murphy, Robert F., and Leonard Kasdan. (1959) "The Structure of Parallel Cousin Marriage." *American Anthropologist* 61: 17–29.

SELF-REDRESS

Self-redress, also known as self-help, is the process whereby one who has been wronged rights, or redresses, the wrong through personal action, without making use of the law. For example, if a man steals a shovel, the owner of the shovel may engage in self-redress by simply going to the thief's residence and re-possessing the shovel. Self-redress is extralegal behavior, although a legal authority may determine that a particular act of self-redress is legal after the fact, according to the laws of that society at that particular time. In our legal and political system, certain kinds of self-redress are permitted, although they are discouraged because of the potential for the dispute to become violent; use of the legal system is preferred.

Among the Garia people of New Guinea, there are not many legal institutions, and none that are effective, so many disputes lead to self-redress because there is no other way to resolve them. Unfortunately, self-redress often results in fighting and bloodshed. The way in which the Garia people keep these disputes from erupting into more serious disputes is somewhat complicated. A Garia individual is connected to other members of society through a variety of social relationships, including his or her kindred (close kin on both the father's side or the mother's side), his or her patrilineal descent group, his or her affines (kin by marriage), as well as bush brothers (people whose land borders his), trading partners, and, for men, other men with whom one went through age-grade initiations. These people together are called by the ethnologist Lawrence (1973 [1971]: 76) a security circle. Towards these people, correct behavior must be observed, because their proper behavior in return is very important. People within the security circle have reciprocal obligations to each other, and when one does not fulfill his obligations to others, one does not in turn receive the help one needs from them. Within the security circle, morality shapes one's behavior, and any individual who does not observe morally correct behavior should, if he or she has been properly socialized as a youth, feel shame. Lawrence calls the effect of morality and shame self-regulation (1973 [1971]: 82). Self-regulation applies only to the people in one's own security circle.

It is only in cases involving people outside of one's security circle that self-redress comes into play. Normally, when there is a dispute, there are accepted ways in which one can retaliate, and accepted degrees of severity of retaliation. If someone defrauds another in a pig exchange, the culprit either pays what he owes or, if he attempts to escape without paying, the one defrauded may initiate a fight or a blood feud or use sorcery. The outcome of many cases in which the culprit does not agree to make amends voluntarily is that the culprit and the one seeking self-redress begin a feud as a result of their disagreement. If someone who has been wronged seeks self-redress, and in the process starts a feud with the culprit, he may expect members of his security circle to come to his aid. However, it is often the case that many members of the plaintiff's security circle are also members of the culprit's security circle. Such people cannot take one side or the other, since they are obligated to both sides. Instead, they try to act as peacemakers, because they do not want to see any member of their own security circle injured or killed. Frequently, the number of people who can commit wholeheartedly to one party or the other, that is, people who have one of the parties in their own security circle but not the other, are very few, and so the feud does not become too large. Thus, the security circle of people that surround a Garia individual works not only to protect the individual in case of a fight or a feud but also helps to keep down the level of violence in Garia society as a whole.

Among the Micmac Indians of Nova Scotia, self-redress is the preferred means of handling most types of disputes, even though they have, and have long had, an adequate legal system. The reason for this seemingly strange preference lies in the Micmac's placing a highly positive value on equality and self-reliance. To use a legal authority to solve a dispute requires the use of a person of authority, and the idea of another person having authority over one is not one that appeals to many Micmac. Rather, it is ideal to take care of one's own problems. To call upon a legal authority makes one look weak, as if one is incapable of handling problems. Also, to use a legal authority is considered vindictive. It is as if one wishes to increase the sanction the other party in the dispute will have to bear. It also makes the party asking for legal help appear that he or she is trying to "gang up" on the other party by enlisting the aid of others. The Micmac value people who handle their disputes without involving others.

The use of self-redress almost never leads to a feud or an enlarged or intensified dispute. This is because the culprit is already known and the problem is being discussed throughout the community, which will result in ostracism. Should the culprit resist or attempt to fight the person coming to redress the wrong, it will appear that the culprit is committing a second and more serious offense, which will result in greater ostracism and perhaps violence by other members of the community.

In Micmac society, self-redress is ideally undertaken with cleverness and humor. If one takes self-redress in such a way as to make the other party look foolish, then the other people in the group will always remember what happened, and the effect will be to remind that person of his or her misdeed and thus less likely to continue a pattern of offensive behavior. The following case exemplifies an ideal method of self-redress.

In the 1940s, the federal government was building a great many new houses on a Micmac reserve. It employed many Micmac men in the forest, cutting trees to supply the lumber needed. The men were still using axes in those days. When the men took a break to eat their lunches, they frequently put their gloves down on one stump, buried the blades of their axes on another stump, and sat down on a third stump,

from which they would converse with each other while eating. One fellow had a nasty habit of pretending to approach a colleague to converse with him, then burying his axe blade in a stump nearby so that the two might talk. It just so happened that the stump into which he buried his axe blade was the same stump on which the other fellow had placed his gloves, which the culprit had pretended not to see. The result was that many workers had had their gloves ruined by this man. After this went on for a while, one man decided to stop the culprit through self-redress. He bought some new gloves and some large nails. When the time for the lunch break came, he took his gloves and inserted into each of the fingers one of the nails, and put them down on the stump next to him. The culprit saw the new gloves and could not resist the temptation that they presented. He walked over and swung the axe at the gloves, but to his surprise, the axe bounced back from the gloves. The nails also made a number of deep nicks in the axe's blade, which took the culprit a long time to remove by filing. Needless to say, the glove axing stopped.

The following legal decision, from India, answers the question as to those circumstances under which self-redress is legal in a fight in which both parties come to the fight armed for conflict (*General Index of the Indian Law Reports, Allahabad Series*, 1949: 258–278).

APPELLATE CRIMINAL.

Before Mr. Justice Agarwala
PARASRAM and Another v. REX.
Self-defense—Right of—When obtained and by whom—If both parties come armed with weapons—

Indian Penal Code ss. 323, 304.

Even when both the parties to a conflict come armed with lathis, if there be no evidence to show that they had made any pre-arranged plan of fighting out the dispute by force that day, the party that attempted to strike the first blow must be deemed to be the aggressor, and the other party, if obviously in danger of an injury to the persons of its members, has a right to strike in self-defense.

Case law discussed and certain propositions of law deduced therefrom. *Queen Empress v. Prag Daf (1), King Emperor v. Kaliji (2), Queen Empress v. Narsang Pathabhai (3), Maniruddin v. Emperor (4), Qinn v. Leathem (5), Punjab Co-operative Bank Ltd. v. Commissioner of Income tax (6), Hariram Mahatha v. Emperor (7), Summa Behera v. Emperor (8),* referred to.

Criminal Appeal No. 57 of 1948, from an order of C. B. Lal Mathur, First Additional Sessions Judge of Budaun dated the 27th of January 1948. The facts appear in the judgment.

Roop Kishor Srivastava for the appellants.

J. S. David, holding the brief of the Assistant Government Advocate (*D. P. Uniyal*) for the Crown.

Agarwala, J. Parasram *alis* Har Prasad, and Basant were prosecuted under section 304 Indian Penal Code, read with section 34 Indian Penal Code, for having caused the death of one Munnalal. They have been convicted of the offence with which they were charged and sentenced to ten years rigorous imprisonment. They have come up in appeal to this Court.

The prosecution case was that the accused, who are father and son, were neighbors of Munnalal residing in village Chitora in the district of Budaun. They were relations of each other and had descended from a common ancestor. Their houses were adjacent to each other. There was a cattle trough in front of the house and *baithak* of the deceased Munnalal. This cattle trough adjoined the platform of the house of the accused. There was a long standing dispute as to the ownership of the cattle trough between the accused and the deceased. On the 14th of June, 1947, there was a quarrel over this trough between Munnalal deceased on the one hand and the accused and one Ramdin on the other, which resulted in a fight. The accused and Ramdin gave lathi blows to the deceased as a result of which his skull was fractured and he died.

The defense was that there was a quarrel between Parasram accused and Munnalal over the cattle trough; that Munnalal was the aggressor and gave him a lathi [stick] blow first with the result that he fell down and became unconscious; that when Basant, the second accused, wanted to protect his father and raised his lathi with that object, then Pashpati and Shankar, on the side of Munnalal, and Munnalal himself gave him lathi blows. In self defense Basant struck lathi blows on Munnalal who fell down and became unconscious.

The medical report showed that Munnalal had received five injuries: (1) contused wound on the right side of the head; (2) contusion just above the right ear; (3) contusion, left side of the head near tuft of hair; (4) contusion with abrasion, right upper arm; and (5) swelling on left ankle joint. Cause of death was extensive fracture of skull caused by injury No. 1. Basant accused had received two injuries; (1) contused wound on the top of head—size 1 $\frac{1}{2}$" x $\frac{1}{4}$" x skin deep; and (2) painful defused swelling on back of lower third right forearm.

The prosecution could produce only one eye-witness of the occurrence. He was Tara. Four others were examined in the court of the Committing Magistrate as eye-witnesses but they denied that they had seen the occurrence. They were, therefore, not examined by the prosecution in the Sessions Court. Now Tara said that on hearing a noise he had gone to the place of occurrence; that on reaching there he heard hot words being exchanged between Munnalal on one side and the accused on the other; that it was Munnalal who wielded his lathi first and then the accused used his lathi in return; and that the deceased received a lathi blow from Basant accused. From this statement it is quite clear that it was Munnalal who was the aggressor because he struck the first blow without the accused having assaulted him or having threatened to assault him. The learned Sessions Judge, however, says that Tara appears to have stated about the deceased having used his lathi first only to save the accused from punishment and to give them an opportunity to plead the right of private defense. The learned Sessions Judge did not believe this part of the statement of the witness and held that no occasion for the exercise of the right of self-defense arose. I have no reason to think that the witness was not telling the truth when he stated that Munnalal was the first to strike. The learned Sessions Judge then goes on to say that if this statement be taken to be true, even then the accused had no right of self-defense. According to him "when two parties are armed with lathis for a fight to enforce their supposed ownership over a property it does not matter which party attacks first and right of private defense also does not arise in such cases. It is quite evident that both the accused were armed with lathis from before starting the fight. They must have, therefore, come there with the intention of fighting and cannot be given the benefit of the right of private defense simply because the deceased wielded his lathi first." The learned Sessions Judge is right in saying that both the accused were armed with lathis from before starting the fight, but there is no evidence on the record to show that the parties had made any pre-arranged plan of fighting out the dispute that day or had made any preparations to that end from before the start of the fight. It appears that there was a quarrel as usual over the cattle trough. In the absence of any evidence it cannot be said that the parties came out of their houses with the intention of fighting. It is quite possible that the quarrel started all of a sudden on some hot words or abuse being exchanged. In the absence of evidence to show

that there was a pre-arranged plan or preparation to fight, it could not be said that the intention of the parties was to decide the question of ownership of the cattle trough by an armed fight.

The question, however, is of some importance and I think I should deal with it at length, especially when the view expressed by the learned Sessions Judge finds support from the observations made in some of the reported cases.

In *Queen v. Nawabdee* (1), the facts were that prisoners 93 and 94 having reason to apprehend an attack, stood outside their house. Presently the attacking party came, then words arose, and then blows followed on both sides. Steer, J. held that the accused courted the attack, and instead of sitting within doors when, if their house had been attacked they would have had a right of defense, they went outside, and met the assailants, and that, therefore, they were guilty. With all respect to the learned Judge, I have grave doubts as to the soundness of the decision. It is not only when the property of a person is actually attacked that he is invested with right of self-defense. If there is an attempt or threat to attack the property, then also there is a right of self-defense. There is nothing wrong if the party threatened to try to prevent the threat materializing and to meet the attack by standing in such a position that no harm be inflicted on the property. In the case before Steer, J. the accused were perfectly entitled, to my mind, to stand outside their house to prevent any harm being caused to their house.

In *Queen Empress v. Prag Daf* (1) there was a dispute between the Thakurs and Chaubeys of Madhonagar over a strip of waste-land. The Chaubeys asserted that the land appertained to a grove which admittedly belonged to them, but the Thakurs on the other hand maintained that the disputed land was part of their cultivation, which as a fact did adjoin it. It was found that on the day of occurrence the Thakur party consisted of from 30 to 50 men, and that one of that party had a gun and the others had lathis. On the other side were arrayed the seven accused; one of them carried a gun; others had nothing in their hands except perhaps sticks. The Thakurs gave orders for the demolition of a mud-wall. Upon this the Chaubeys interfered and begged that the matter be referred to court. Words ensued and then blows, and almost immediately Laltu fired at Ajudhia on the Thakur side and shot him dead on the spot. Upon this all ran away. CHIEF JUSTICE KERSHAW and Mr. Justice KNOX observed: "The use of force in defense of property by private individuals is a matter defined by law. The presence of Laltu with his gun, unexplained as it is by any evidence for the defense, proves that the Chaubeys were prepared to defend this mud-wall even to the voluntarily causing of death; and the burden lay heavily upon them of proving that they acted under reasonable apprehension that death or serious hurt would be the consequence if the right of private defense were not exercised. The harm intended was so light that persons of ordinary sense and temper would have and should have refrained from taking the law into their own hands. . . . The fact that 40 or 50 persons began the attack and that after the attack began, Laltu fired a shot which struck Ajudhia is not enough to show that Laltu was justified in firing. Laltu had to prove that he had reason to apprehend that the Brahmins might be killed. He gave no evidence of this, or of facts from which we could hold it proved." As in that case death was caused by firing the action could be justified only if the case fell within the purview of section 103 Indian Penal Code. That section runs as follows:

> "The right of private defense of property extends, under the restrictions mentioned in section 99, to the voluntarily causing of death or of any other harm to the wrong-doer, if the offence the committing of which, or the attempting to commit of which, occasions the exercise of the right, be an offence of any of the descriptions hereinafter enumerated, namely:

> *firstly*—Robbery;

> *secondly*—House breaking by right;

> *thirdly*—Mischief by fire committed on any building, tent, vessel, which building, tent or vessel is used as a human dwelling, or as a place for the custody of property;

> *fourthly*—Theft, mischief or house trespass, under such circumstances as may reasonably cause apprehension that death or grievous hurt will be the consequence, if such right of private defense is not exercised."

The facts of that case did not show that any of the offences mentioned in section 103, Indian Penal Code, were attempted or threatened to be committed by the Thakurs and, therefore, the Chaubeys had no right to cause death. The Chaubeys were rightly held guilty of murder, their case not being covered by exception 2 to section 300 Indian Penal Code, inasmuch as they had intended to do more harm than was necessary for the purpose of defense. Their lordships, however, went on to quote from a passage from the unreported judgment of SIR JOHN EDGE in *Queen-Empress v. Rupa* (1) that "when a body of men are determined to vindicate their rights or supposed rights, by unlawful force, and when they engage in a fight with men who, on the other hand, are equally determined to vindicate by unlawful force their right or supposed rights, no question of self-defense arises. Neither side is trying to protect itself, but each side is trying to get the better of the other." As the case of *Queen-Empress v. Rupa* (1) has not been reported I cannot say what its facts were. The proposition of law, as stated by SIR JOHN EDGE, is of course unquestionable. The important words in that dictum are 'Neither side is trying to protect itself, but each side is trying to get the better of the other.' The enquiry, therefore, in every case has to be whether the accused were trying to protect themselves or their property, or whether they were trying to get the better of the other side and enforce a supposed right by use of force.

General Index of the Indian Law Reports, Allahabad Series. (1949).

Lawrence, Peter. (1973 [1971]) "The Garia of the Madang District." In *Politics in New Guinea*, edited by Ronald Berndt and Peter Lawrence, 74–93.

Strouthes, Daniel P. (1994) *Change in the Real Property Law of a Cape Breton Island Micmac Band.*

SERVITUDE

Servitude is a legal duty to give one's labor to another person, who then has the right to the value of that labor. Servitude may be voluntary or involuntary. In the United States, servitude is prohibited by the thirteenth amendment to the constitution.

An interesting type of servitude was once practiced by the Yoruba people of Nigeria. In that society, a person could pawn himself or herself, that is, use himself or herself as security for a loan. The person pawned was then legally bound in servitude to the creditor. The debtor would have seventeen days after initiating the pawn to deliver himself or herself to the creditor to begin work. The work the debtor performed for the creditor did not reduce the amount of the debt owed, but rather constituted the interest on the loan. For each day that an adult debtor worked for the creditor, he or she was allowed by law one day to work for himself or herself to earn money to repay the debt and to end the period of servitude, which extended until the debt was paid.

People were also able to pawn others within their family. A woman could pawn her child. However, unless her husband had mistreated her, she could only pawn the child with her husband's permission. If her husband had mistreated her, and especially if he had failed to support her materially, a wife could pawn her child without her husband's permission so as to acquire money to support herself. A boy could pawn his younger brother with the consent of both parents and the younger brother to be pawned. Child pawns had no right to work for themselves to end their servitude; the payment of the debt was the responsibility of their parent(s) or sibling. Child pawns generally lived most of the time with the creditor, who had the responsibility of feeding them.

The Yoruba person who pawned him or herself could not do so without providing a surety, a person who promised to pay to the creditor the amount of the debt should the debtor fail to do so. The debtor paid the surety a small sum called *egba*, and by accepting this sum the surety agreed to act as a surety.

A Yoruba creditor who had sexual intercourse with a woman who had pawned herself to him was treated differently by the law depending upon whether she was married or betrothed to another man or was unmarried. If she was married or betrothed, the creditor had to pay the penalties that any man who seduced a married or betrothed woman paid, and in addition was no longer able to collect the debt the woman owed him. If the woman was unmarried, he would not face prosecution, but again was unable to collect the debt under the law. On the other hand, if the unmarried woman was agreeable, the two could marry, in which case the creditor did not have to pay a bride-price.

Another form of servitude was found in the Spanish parts of the Americas, including parts of the United States that were once under Spanish control. This form of servitude is known as peonage. A peon is someone who was legally bound to provide another person with labor in order to pay a debt. In central and southern Mexico, from the time of Mexico's war for independence in 1823 until the Mexican Revolution in 1910, a particularly dark form of peonage was once practiced. In this form, called the hacienda system, an individual would receive ownership of a piece of land from the central government. There were, of course, people already living on the land, often Indians, who had no other place to go, since most of central and southern Mexico was even then densely populated. Under Mexican law, the original inhabitants had no ownership rights to the land. In order to be able to remain on the land, the price of the rent was to labor for the owner of the land in whatever manner the owner determined and under whatever conditions he dictated. Another form of peonage developed later. Whereas the hacienda system allowed people to leave the haciendas legally whenever they chose, the new system of debt peonage kept most bound to the hacienda. The haciendas would operate small stores from which the people who lived there could buy what they needed on credit. As long as there was a debt outstanding, they were bound by law to remain on the hacienda; of course, they had no choice but to work there, since there was no other employment available by which they could pay their debts. Debt peonage was instituted for two reasons. The first was to keep agricultural labor available, since many people were tempted to move to the cities to seek better paying work there. The second reason was to prevent Indians from leaving the haciendas and living together with other Indians, thereby preventing their acculturation and assimilation.

In some nations, peonage obligation is passed on to children. In India alone, there are an estimated 6.5 million people living in debt bondage. In India, the situation was created in part by the absence of bankruptcy laws, which made it necessary for people to place themselves in debt bondage in order to repay their debts. Although debt bondage was banned by law in 1976, the practice continues in many rural regions. Debt bondage is common throughout all of south Asia and is found in Pakistan, Nepal, and Bangladesh as well as India. Most of those in debt bondage perform agricultural work.

Forced labor refers to a situation where individuals are coerced into working, often in conditions that are unsafe and usually for low wages. Recent examples of forced labor include the use of Brazilian Indians in forestry, mining, rubber tapping, and prostitution; forced prostitution in Turkey; Haitian sugarcane workers in the Dominican Republic; prisoner labor in the People's Republic of China; and Peruvian and Salvadorian domestic laborers in the United States. The latter are individuals who are in the United States illegally and thus are sometimes exploited by their employers, who pay them low wages and make them work long hours, knowing that as illegals they have less recourse to judicial and administrative protection than legal immigrants or citizens.

Ajisafe, A. K. (1946) *The Laws and Customs of the Yoruba People.*

Spicer, Edward H. (1980) *The Yaquis: A Cultural History.*

SERVITUS A servitus is a legal restriction, such as a covenant, on the use of land and other real property. It is a burden on the interests of the owner or lessor and is applicable to those who lease the property or subsequently own the property. Some kinds of servitus are known as equitable servitudes. Servitus is a part of the law of real property.

One example of servitus is a covenant that a certain part of a parcel of land will never be logged. Covenants are created by the owner and "run with the land," as attorneys state it. That is, they come with a parcel of land and apply to future owners no matter who they happen to be or when they happen to own the real property. Owners normally do not like to create covenants because they are a burden on the use of the property by future owners and usually reduce the property's value when sold.

Another type of servitus is a right-of-way, which is an easement to travel over the land of another. An example of this is a right-of-way for a railroad track. Under U.S. law, such a right-of-way normally ceases to exist once the railway ceases to use the line.

Among the Yoruba people of Nigeria, the law recognizes a number of types of servitus, though most relate to rights of access. If a man owns a farm in one place, but it is surrounded by the farms of others, the man has a right to cross from the road, across the farm of another, to get to his own farm. Similarly, if a body of water is a source of drinking water, the owners of land adjoining the body of water must allow the public to cross their lands to get to the body of water. Finally, those people who own land adjoining bodies of water that are used as sources of drinking water are prevented by law from clearing vegetation within fifty yards of the water's edge, so as to reduce the likelihood of the body of water running dry.

Ajisafe, A. K. (1946) *The Laws and Customs of the Yoruba People.*

SLAVERY Slavery is the ownership of human beings. All nations presently outlaw slavery, although it is practiced quietly in many parts of the world.

Slavery in its various forms is distinguished from other related institutions such as serfdom, peonage, compulsory military service, pawning, and imprisonment, all of which are forms of servitude.

Slavery has a long history in the human experience and was important in the development of both the Islamic and Western (Greek and Roman) civilizations and the European settle-

ment of the New World. Slavery, primarily in the forms of both domestic and productive slavery, was also common in non-Western, nonindustrialized societies.

From a historical and cross-cultural perspective, slavery comes in two primary forms, domestic and productive. In Islamic societies, slavery took yet another form. And, as discussed below, slavery or related institutions are still common around the world, and the long-term effects of productive slavery are still being experienced by the descendants of slaves.

Domestic Slavery

Domestic slavery (also known as household and patriarchal slavery) was a form of slavery found in small-scale, nonindustrial societies whose economies were based on horticulture or simple agriculture. According to two worldwide surveys of slavery with samples of 186 and 60 nonindustrial societies respectively, domestic slavery occurred in 35 percent of societies. The label *domestic* indicates that slaves in these societies performed mostly household work, including gardening, child care, wood and water fetching, and concubinage. In many societies, however, they also performed chores outside the household including soldiering, trading, and serving as sacrificial victims. It is generally assumed that one key feature of domestic slavery is that the slaves or their offspring were integrated into the families that owned them and, eventually, into society. Most domestic slaves were women or girls who were either purchased from other societies, born into slavery, or taken in slave raids. Women were preferred over men for a number of reasons. First, most of the work performed by domestic slaves is work traditionally performed by women in horticultural societies. Second, women were more easily integrated into these societies because female slaves could produce offspring for their masters. Third, women were more easily controlled than male slaves, who might revolt.

Although domestic slavery is distinguished from productive slavery, in any given society the distinction was often less than clear as slaves might be used for a variety of purposes, their treatment varied widely, and the possibility of integration into society was not always certain. Perhaps the key distinction between domestic and productive slavery was that, in the former, slaves played only a limited economic role, while in the latter, they were a major source of labor in the economic system.

A few examples from around the world indicate the variations found in domestic slavery. The Tlingit of the northwest coast of North America enslaved both Tlingit from other Tlingit subgroups and neighboring peoples such as the Flathead of Oregon. Only wealthy Tlingit owned slaves, who evidently performed domestic chores and helped hunt and fish, freeing their wealthy owners to engage in ceremonial and social activities. Slaves were also sacrificed by the wealthy as a sign of their wealth. Tlingit slaves were ethnic outsiders who were not integrated into Tlingit clans. Although they lived in the same houses as their owners, they were poorly treated and upon death were simply thrown into the ocean without ceremony. Tlingit slavery was ended by the Russians in the nineteenth century.

In pre-Communist China, the Black Lolo enslaved Han Chinese, who occupied the lowest status in Lolo society, beneath both the upper-class Black Lolo and lower-class White Lolo. Han slaves worked in the fields and in households. They might also have been enslaved by the White Lolo, but this was less common. Slaves were acquired by kidnapping Han travelers, raiding Han villages, or stealing slaves from other Black Lolo villages. While children of Han slaves were slaves, over three or four generations they might establish their own households, disavow their Han ancestry, and assimilate into society as White Lolo, in which status they could own Han slaves.

The Somali participated in the slave trade as traders, but they also used domestic slaves. These slaves occupied a social category beneath the outcaste *sab*, who performed most menial economic labor as part of a patron-client relationship. Slaves, on the other hand, were owned by their masters, although they might be paid for their work; those who traveled as traders certainly were. Somali domestic slaves could be integrated into society through marriage or sexual relations. A slave woman who married a *sab* remained a slave, but her children were *sab*. Children of a slave woman and her master were free and looked after by the master. Slaves could also win their freedom through manumission, although as freemen they did not enjoy the same status as Somali and had no clan affiliation.

Productive Slavery

Productive slavery (also called chattel or economic slavery) was an economic arrangement in which slave owners, driven by the profit motive, used slaves as their labor force to produce raw materials for processing. Slavery was governed by laws, with slaves defined as the property of their owners, who could buy, sell, trade, and utilize them in any way they choose that market conditions permitted. However, in no slave society did the legal system afford slave owners total control of all aspects of their slaves lives. In terms of the social stratification system, slaves were in most societies considered to be outside the system and were denied rights afforded citizens or even noncitizens who had a place in the social order of the society.

Productive slavery was justified by a European racist ideology that characterized Africans and other non-Europeans as nonhuman or inferior to Europeans. Productive slavery usually developed in advanced nonindustrialized agricultural societies in which other sources of labor such as hired free labor were not available. While slavery was usually an economic arrangement in

Brazilian landowners used Africans and indigenous peoples as slaves during the 1850s, a practice that continued until 1888.

which slave owners sought to make a profit, the overall enterprise could be quite costly, given the expense of acquiring, transporting, and maintaining slaves. Another cost was frequent slave rebellions, although only one, in Haiti in 1801, actually led to the overthrow of a government and the establishment of a free nation.

Slavery in the New World is the major example of productive slavery in human history. Between 1500 and 1850, from 12 to 15 million African slaves were imported to the New World by the Dutch, Spanish, Portuguese, English, and French. An undetermined number of Native Americans were also enslaved, mainly by the Spanish and Portuguese in South America. The transatlantic slave trade and New World plantation economy was a highly profitable economic arrangement for the European colonists. Slaves

in West Africa were captured mainly by other Africans from different ethnic groups. This activity represented a European-instigated expansion of traditional domestic slavery and made raiding for slaves a major economic activity. It also caused a shift from taking women for domestic slavery to taking men, who were more desirable for New World productive slavery. West Africa was then and remains today a heavily populated region, and even centuries of slave trade had little effect on the overall population or on the ability of West African societies to sustain themselves. In the New World, the majority of slaves went to large plantations in Brazil, northern South America, and the Caribbean, with sugarcane plantations taking the majority of the slaves. In North America, there were relatively few large plantations, and most slaves worked on family farms where cotton and tobacco were the major crops. The slave trade and slavery ended in the 1800s. Britain outlawed slavery in 1808 and freed slaves in its colonies in 1838, and by the 1870s, nearly all slave societies had outlawed slavery. Brazil was the last New World society to do so, in 1888. Under pressure from European nations, slavery was also banned in the Islamic world and Africa by the early twentieth century.

A variety of explanations have been offered for productive slavery. One suggests that slavery is a step in the evolution of human society, an idea now dismissed given that the majority of human societies never had slavery. Another explanation stresses the economic rationality of slavery and suggests that slavery occurs when the costs of keeping slaves are less than the economic benefits reaped from their work. This explanation also suggests that slavery ends when the costs exceed the benefits. The weakness of this explanation is that it ignores the social and political costs and benefits of slavery, which were often beyond the control of the slave owner. The most compelling explanation for productive slavery is the idea that, as in New World societies, when land is free or easily available and can be worked by the landowners, labor will be difficult to acquire for large agricultural enterprises. Therefore, the only way help can be obtained is through subjugation, with slavery being one alternative. This explanation also assumes that a strong centralized government will enact and enforce laws that support slavery and that the economic system is sufficiently developed to support large-scale slave trading. All of these conditions were present in the New World during the slave era.

Islamic Slavery

Distinguished from both domestic and productive slavery is Islamic slavery, which took place throughout the Islamic world from A.D. 650 until the early twentieth century. The rules governing slavery were carefully spelled out in the Qur'an and subsequent interpretations. As in many forms of slavery, enslavement of members of one's own ethnic group (in this case, Muslims) was forbidden. Slavery was of crucial importance in the Ottoman Empire, with Slavic slaves imported from the Balkans and others imported from Africa. Numbering perhaps 20 percent of the population in Istanbul, slaves performed much of the physical labor required to maintain the empire and served as domestic help and concubines until the decline of slavery in the late 1800s. Islamic slavery, particularly in the Middle East, was both domestic and productive in purpose. About 18 million slaves were taken by Islamic nations in the thirteen centuries from 650 to 1900. Many were used as household help, servants, and concubines, and some served as soldiers. Female slaves, because of their value as domestics and concubines, were especially valued. So too were eunuchs as household help, and many boys were castrated for this purpose. Slaves taken or purchased in Africa were widely traded across the Middle East and Southeast Asia, and in some places, such as East Africa, worked in productive roles on plantations in addition to their domestic duties. In Islamic slavery, there was a deep tradition of manumission; allowing slaves to buy their freedom brought honor to their masters.

Contemporary Forms of Slavery

Both domestic and productive slavery are now mainly institutions of the past. Mauritania, the last nation to practice productive slavery, has essentially ended the institution, although former slaves continue to live in poverty. However, slavery or slavery-like practices in different forms are still common around the world, and some experts believe that there are now more individuals living in slavelike circumstances than at any point in human history. The three major forms of slavery today are child labor, debt bondage, and forced labor. Other forms include servile marriage, in which women have no choice in getting married, prostitution, and the sale of human organs.

Perhaps as many as 100 million children worldwide are exploited for their labor. That is, they are forced to work long hours in unhealthy conditions and are paid little or nothing for their labor. Some children are local or from the same nation as the exploiters, while in other cases they may be taken, with or without parental permission, and shipped elsewhere. Children so exploited may be as young as five years of age and most are under twelve. Forms of child labor include child carpet weavers in India, Pakistan, Nepal, and Morocco; child domestic servants in many West African nations, Bangladesh and elsewhere; street beggars in many Third World nations and especially in cities that draw many Western tourists; prostitutes for the tourist trade in the Philippines and Thailand; and camel jockeys in the Middle East. The sale of children—by their parents and middlemen, often with government sanction—from poor families in Third World nations to wealthier people in developed nations is also considered a form of child labor, especially since it is not always clear how much freedom the parents had in choosing to sell their child. Until the end of Communist rule, Romania was a major source of adoptive children for the United States, with Peru now filling that role. Child labor is considered desirable by employers because it is cheap, children are easy to control and replace, they can perform some tasks that require small fingers and dexterity better than adults, and they are less likely to revolt.

See also SERVITUDE.

Centre for Human Rights. (1991) *Contemporary Forms of Slavery*. Fact Sheet No. 14.

Christensen, James. (1954) *Double Descent among the Fanti*.

Gordon, Murray. (1989) *Slavery in the Arab World*.

Jordan, Winthrop. (1974) *The White Man's Burden*.

Klein, Laura F. (1975) *Tlingit Women and Town Politics*.

Lewis, I. M. (1955) *Peoples of the Horn of Africa*.

Lin, Yueh-hwa. (1947) *The Lolo of Liang-shan*. Translated by Ju Shu Pan.

Miers, Suzanne, and Igor Kopytoff, eds. (1977) *Slavery in Africa: Historical and Anthropological Perspectives*.

Nieboer, Herman J. (1900) *Slavery as an Industrial System*.

Patterson, Orlando. (1982) *Slavery and Social Death: A Comparative Study*.

Pryor, Frederic L. (1977) *The Origins of the Economy*.

Rubin, Vera, and Arthur Tuden, eds. (1977) *Comparative Perspectives on Slavery in New World Plantation Societies*.

Sawyer, Roger. (1986) *Slavery in the Twentieth Century*.

Van den Berghe, Pierre. (1981) *The Ethnic Phenomenon*.

SORCERY

Sorcery is the use of magic to cause harm for the purpose of achieving political and other goals. Magic, in turn, may be defined as the manipulative use of supernatural power for the purpose of achieving a goal. Magic is typically used when other means of achieving the desired goal are blocked or impractical. For example, if an individual wished to kill an enemy, he or she might use sorcery to do it because killing the person with physical means might expose the individual to legal action. Sorcery requires the use of a sorcerer who, through his of her knowledge of formulae and rituals, can direct supernatural power.

Sorcery predominates in native cultures in North and South America. Nearly 50 percent of cultures that attribute illness to sorcery are in North or South America. Belief in sorcery as a cause of illness is found mostly in technologically unadvanced societies, those with no indigenous writing system, small communities, and an economy based on foraging or horticulture. This suggests that sorcery is more likely to flourish in cultures where people have relatively equal access to the supernatural world. This is more typical of relatively simple cultures where there is less social inequality in all spheres of life.

Sorcery is found primarily in cultures that rely on coordinate control to maintain social order (that is, where conflict is resolved through the direct action of the persons involved by means such as retaliation, apology, avoidance, etc.) and that do not have agencies of superordinate control (that is, where social order is maintained through the actions of culturally recognized authorities such as a council, a chief, or courts). Sorcery acts as a coordinate control in that it causes individuals to pause before causing harm to others for fear that the other person will retaliate by using sorcery to cause them to become ill, have an accident, or even die.

Among the Pawnee Indians of the Great Plains, much of the sorcery was used to attain political goals, and was practiced by both men and women. Sorcerers never sold their services, but frequently used them on behalf of others, particularly family members.

Such was the case of the Pawnee leader Brave Chief. When Brave Chief was young, he coveted possession of a powerful position in tribal politics. But being from a poor family with a low social status, Brave Chief had far to go. He began by putting himself in the good graces of a famous Pawnee chief, Pahukatawa (Hill Against the Bank), by giving him the prizes that he collected during his raids. He would bring Pahu-katawa the horses he had captured, even though he would bring none to his own father. He also gave Pahukatawa other gifts at various times. When Pahukatawa became sick, Brave Chief was by his side and brought him whatever he wanted. Just before Pahukatawa died, he named Brave Chief as his replacement. But other people in the tribe believed that Brave Chief used sorcery in his quest to become chief. According to them, Brave Chief wanted not only to become chief, but to do it before his own father, Old Man Meat Offering, died himself. So, it was said, Brave Chief and his father plotted to make Pahukatawa ill and die, and that they did so by Old Man Meat Offering using sorcery on him.

See also AUTHORITY; CONTRACT; CRIME; FACTION; HOMICIDE; LEADER; PROCEDURAL LAW; REVENGE; SELF-REDRESS; THEFT.

Murdock, George Peter. (1980) *Theories of Illness: A World Survey.*

Weltfish, Gene. (1965) *The Lost Universe: Pawnee Life and Culture.*

Whiting, Beatrice B. (1950) *Paiute Sorcery.*

Whiting, John W. M. (1967) "Sorcery, Sin and the Superego: A Cross-Cultural Study of Some Mechanisms of Social Control." In *Cross-Cultural Approaches,* edited by Clelland S. Ford, 147–168.

STATE

The state may be defined as a political unit with the following features:

1. It has a single government that has authority over all members of the group.

2. The government is sovereign and is not subject to external control.

3. The government has authority over an area that falls within clearly defined geographical borders.

4. Both the government and societal structure are hierarchical; there are several social levels between the most common people and the elites, and several political levels between the common man and the supreme ruler.

5. The government has a monopoly on the legitimate use of force to implement policy.

6. The government has the power to tax or to draft labor in order to support itself.

The question of the definition of the state has caused anthropologists, political scientists, and historians considerable argument among themselves. For some, the concept was meaningless. Others said that the size of the population was important, but Lowie (1961) correctly saw that population meant nothing of conceptual importance. What would be the line dividing the state from all other forms of political organization? If, for example, we set it at 50,000 people, we would include the Navajo Indian tribe as a state (which it is not because it is not sovereign) and exclude Liechtenstein, a European nation-state. Furthermore, states in the past had truly small populations in many cases, such as the Greek city-states.

Some anthropologists have disputed the idea that there is such a thing as a state, a kind of political and social organization that is different in some important way from other societies. E. Adamson Hoebel (1949) was of this opinion. It is clear, however, that living in a state society is different from living in a society that is not a state. It is, of course, far easier to escape the force of authority in a nonstate society, in which authority may not be centralized. In nonstate societies, small groups are usually able to leave and to form societies of their own. Further, in nonstate societies, it is much easier to

directly challenge the power of the authorities and to take power from them.

One of the questions that has most captured the interest of cultural anthropologists and archeologists is the following: Why have peoples all over the world and for thousands of years chosen to live together in the large groups we call states, which have central authorities of great power, taxes, forced labor (including military drafts), and legalistic forms of social control, when they could have much more freedom living in small groups? This question, which anthropologists usually render as "Under what conditions do states evolve?" has yet to be answered to the full satisfaction of most anthropologists. This entry will describe some of the most widely accepted attempts to answer that question. The interest of anthropologists is directed toward so-called "primitive" or "pristine" states, states that became states due to their own development, not by imitation of states that were already in existence. The United States of America, for example, is not a primitive or pristine state because it is modeled after European states.

One of the earliest attempts to describe the beginnings of the state was made by Karl Marx and Friedrich Engels. The origin of the state, they argued, was ultimately but indirectly the result of improvements in technology. Marxist theory states that societies pass through stages of evolution based upon their level of technological advancement. When technology reached a certain stage, the stage accompanied by the invention of writing and known as "civilization," man had reached the point at which division of labor developed out of a need to operate the ever-more sophisticated devices that technological advances had developed. It made sense, for example, to have someone who knew how to run a loom run that loom all day, and for someone else who knew how to farm run a farm all day. Both were more efficient producers in that way. From this separation of consumer from production came businessmen who traded the goods, accumulated wealth, bought machinery, and employed workers who made them more money. Thus came about, in one set of circumstances, a situation in which socioeconomic classes developed, one rich (the entrepreneurs), the other poor (the workers). The two classes were mutually antagonistic. The poor wanted the wealth that they had mostly created, and the rich wanted to keep it for themselves. The state came into being when governments, through the use of laws, courts, prisons, militia, etc., kept the workers from revolting and destroying the social and economic arrangement that kept them poor and hard at work. One somewhat atypical example of the state was that of ancient Athens, which had a class of slaves kept in check by the threat of the use of violence. And in feudal times, the purpose of the state was to keep the serfs subservient to the nobility. In any event, according to Marx and Engels, the state rests upon what some have called a socially "internal conflict" between classes, in which the privileged class or classes hold down and oppress the unprivileged class or classes through armed force. The problems facing Marx's theories are discussed in the entry on Marxism.

Another early theory, first made public in 1920, was created by Robert Lowie (1961). He argued that states form when two conditions exist in the same society at the same time. The first condition is the "territorial bond," meaning that the society has an attachment to and exclusive control over a specific territory. The second condition is a development of an authority with coercive power over the entire society. This power, in turn, intensifies and brings into consciousness the feeling of neighborliness that has been found a universal trait of human society. Once established and sanctified, the sentiment may flourish well without compulsion, glorified as loyalty to a sovereign king or to a national flag (Lowie, 1961: 116-117).

A third theory of how states come into being is called the hydraulic theory. This theory, first put forth by Steward (1955) and then greatly developed by Wittfogel (1957), places irrigation systems and their management at the center of the forces that push a society toward state status. Wittfogel, whose name is now considered almost synonymous with the hydraulic theory, argued that the first peoples to use irrigation were those who lived in floodplains. They began by using their technology to control natural flooding and later developed true irrigation systems. As the population of an irrigated area grew, the size and complexity of irrigation systems grew as well. Growing at the same time was the number of owners of various small parcels of land that would have to be crossed by irrigation ditches or pipes, thus involving increasingly complex legal and political disputes. To manage the technological, political, and legal matters growing out of a spreading irrigation system, a corps of professional managers was needed. These managers later became an administrative body that governed the society, and thus the society developed into a state with a centralized government.

Unlike other anthropologists, Elman Service (1975) emphasized the evolution of culture and of forms of political leadership and authority in his theory of how states have come into being. He argues that human societies begin as band societies, later turn into tribal societies, then become chiefdoms, and even later evolve into primitive states. At each stage, political power is further centralized and made more enduring and less dependent upon the characteristics of the person or persons holding power. A ruling class develops and works to protect its own advantages, while at the same time the rest of a society's members come to appreciate the benefits of a stable and centralized political power. When centralized political power reaches a truly stable stage, the society is a state.

One of the more famous theories of how states come into being was developed by Robert Carneiro (1970). His theory, known as a theory of circumscription, argues that two types of circumscription, environmental circumscription and social circumscription, cause the formation of states. Environmental circumscription works in the following manner. In agricultural societies with limited available land because they are surrounded by mountains, ocean, deserts, rivers, etc., wars are frequently wars of conquest. In areas not so bounded in which available land is plentiful, wars are for revenge, prestige, to acquire women, and for other reasons, but not for reasons of conquest and subjugation; conquest and subjugation could not easily take place because the defeated would simply escape. But in regions where land is short, wars of conquest and subjugation readily take place because it is through subjugation of another group that one's own group is able to exact from the subjugated group taxes or some other form of tribute. As wars of this sort continue, the size of the territory and the number of people controlled by a single authority increase. As this increase continues, political complexity increases, and political evolution takes place. Eventually, entire regions are controlled by one ruler, who is a chief or, later in the evolutionary process, a king. At this point, the society often becomes a state.

Social circumscription works in much the same way. In some cases, the population of an area is large, but land is freely available. If, however, the population concentrates itself in one area, for example, to better deter attacks from outsiders, land in that area becomes scarce. If the groups in the area fight each other, the same progression toward political complexity becomes possible because the defeated cannot escape, prevented as they are by the presence of groups of other people all around them.

Marvin Harris (1977) believes that states came about in quite another way. He saw that in many societies people did many things to keep their populations at or below the carrying capacity of the land, that is, the number of people the land would support. But, he noted, in agricultural societies, people can work harder or develop a new technology, both of which can increase the production of food and, thus, the carrying capacity of the land. In fact, in many agricultural societies, there is a surplus of food. Harris states that in such circumstances, powerful individuals take control of these surpluses and distribute them among the population. These powerful people become even more powerful by virtue of their control over some of the food supply of the society, and eventually this elite group evolves into the centralized authority that characterizes a state.

See also CIVILIZATION; MARXISM.

Carneiro, Robert. (1970) "A Theory of the Origin of the State." *Science* 169: 733–738.

Fried, Morton H. (1967) *The Evolution of Political Society.*

Harris, Marvin. (1977) *Cannibals and Kings: The Origins of Culture.*

Hoebel, E. Adamson. (1949) *Man in the Primitive World.*

Lowie, Robert H. (1961 [1920]) *Primitive Society.*

Marx, Karl, and Friedrich Engels. (1968) *Karl Marx and Friedrich Engels: Selected Works in One Volume.*

Service, Elman R. (1975) *Origins of the State and Civilization: The Process of Cultural Evolution.*

Steward, Julian. (1955) *Theory of Culture Change: The Methodology of Multilinear Evolution.*

Wittfogel, Karl. (1957) *Oriental Despotism: A Comparative Study of Total Power.*

STATUS AND RANK

Status refers to the relative social position an individual has within a society. The president of the United States has a higher status than does a gas station attendant among the population of the United States. A person's status is often in accordance with his or her political power, prestige, and access to resources, though this is by no means always true, nor is it true in the same ways in all societies.

Status may be either ascribed or achieved. Ascribed status is acquired through birth and not by anything the individual herself or himself has done. The queen or king of England acquires royal status by birth. Achieved status must be acquired by the personal efforts of the individual. The president of the United States has achieved status.

Rank refers to status that is graded. While most people in the United States would agree that a U.S. senator, a winner of the Nobel Prize in chemistry, and the basketball player Michael Jordan are all people of high status, there is no agreement as to which is higher in status than the others. In rank systems, all statuses have well-known grades, and everyone knows which is of higher status and which is of lower status than the others. The U.S. Army's system of military rank is a good example of this. The rank of major is a higher rank than that of captain, but lower than that of lieutenant colonel. That means that all majors enjoy a higher status than all captains but a lower status than all lieutenant colonels. The level of authority and the pay each person at these ranks receives varies relative to those above and below in rank; that is, a person at the rank of major has more authority and receives a higher rate of pay than the person at the rank of captain.

Among the Kwakiutl Indians of the northwest coast of North America, ranking was applied not to categories of people but to individuals. The Kwakiutl, as did other northwest coast Indian tribes, gave large feasts known as potlatches, in which the giver of the potlatch gave away gifts of value, in addition to the food, in an attempt to raise his own position of rank within the group. His guests at the potlatch, those who were to receive the goods, were seated around the giver in a fashion that indicated their rank, as well as the order in which they would receive their gifts and the relative value of those gifts. In other words, the first person to receive gifts would have the highest rank of the guests, would sit closest to the potlatch giver, and would receive gifts of the greatest value. The person with the next highest rank would sit slightly farther away, would receive gifts second, and would receive gifts of a slightly lesser value than those given the first guest, and so on.

Among the traditional Tongans, a Polynesian people, rank was accorded on the basis of one's sex and kinship relations. People of one rank were expected to behave with respect and deference to those of higher ranks. Within the nuclear family, fathers held the highest rank, daughters and their children were next in rank, and sons and their children were of yet lower rank. The oldest daughter and her children had a higher rank than the next oldest daughter and her children. The oldest son and his children all held a lower rank than that of the youngest daughter and her children, but a higher rank than that of the next younger son and his children.

Within the extended family, however, it was the father's sister who held the highest rank. She chose her brother's sons' wives and made the arrangements for their weddings. Also, her children were able to get labor from her brother's sons. People descended from older sons had a higher rank than those descended from younger sons.

Codere, Helen. (1966) *Fighting with Property: A Study of Kwakiutl Potlatching and Warfare, 1792–1930.*

Hogbin, Ian. (1972 [1934]) *Law and Order in Polynesia: A Study of Primitive Legal Institutions.*

Kaeppler, Adrienne L. (1971) "Rank in Tonga." *Ethnology* 10: 174–193.

SUBSTANTIVE LAW

Substantive law is the law that sets limits to behavior, and is the kind of law we usually think of as "law." Substantive law deals with those behaviors that are prohibited for the members of society. Criminal law, civil law, inheritance law, property law, contract law, family law, marriage law, etc., are all types of substantive law.

See also CIVIL LAW; COMMON LAW; CONTRACT; FAMILY LAW; INHERITANCE; MARRIAGE; PERSONAL PROPERTY; PROCEDURAL LAW; REAL PROPERTY.

Pospisil, Leopold. (1974 [1971]) *Anthropology of Law: A Comparative Theory.*

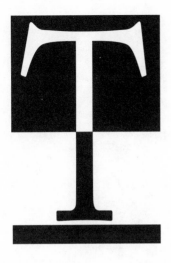

criminate killing of people who are not directly involved in a conflict. We have seen in recent history that terror is a commonly used means to fight a war in which one of the parties has relatively much less power than the other. Terrorists use terror to try to force their more powerful opponent into granting the political ends that they desire. The Irish Republican Army, for example, until recently used terror to try to force Great Britain to end its authority over Northern Ireland. The Palestine Liberation Organization until recently used terror to try to force Israel to end its authority over Palestinian people and the land they occupy.

TERRITORIAL PRINCIPLE OF LAW

The territorial principle of law is the principle that legal jurisdiction is determined by the location of the offender at the time that an offense is committed. If, for example, a man commits a murder in Washington State, he is subject to Washington State's laws and is tried in Washington State (even if he is apprehended in Florida). He will not be subject to the death penalty, because Washington state (as of this writing) does not use capital punishment. If he commits a murder in Florida, he is subject to Florida laws and is tried in Florida even if he is apprehended in Washington State. It is possible that he will be subject to the death penalty, because Florida (as of this writing) does use capital punishment.

See also JURISDICTION; PERSONALITY PRINCIPLE OF LAW.

TERROR

Terror is defined by Leopold Pospisil of Yale University as the indis-

THEFT

Theft is stealing, that is, taking possession of property owned by another with the intent of transferring ownership rights from the owner to the thief without consent of the owner. Different peoples handle theft differently. In some societies, theft of many kinds of property is not considered a crime and is tolerated. In other societies, theft is considered a serious crime worthy of the death penalty (such as Britain at one point in time).

In the society of the Tikopia of Polynesia, owners who lose property to theft rely primarily on self-redress and the morals of the thief. A man who discovers that he has been burglarized will usually begin by repeatedly shouting loudly "*Iefu*," which has the effect of bringing people from all around the area. The people then ask the reason for the call and, when they learn it, give sympathy to the victim and make guesses about the identity of the thief.

If the owner can find out who stole from him, he usually will go directly to the suspect and ask him about the theft. If the thief admits the theft, he or she will return the stolen property or the owner will take some other property from him or her as compensation.

Yale University's Leopold Pospisil defines terror as indiscriminate killing of people not directly involved in a conflict. A young woman, a victim of such terrorism, is carried from the scene of a 1986 car bombing in which thirty people were killed or wounded in Beirut, Lebanon.

However, most thieves will lie about the theft, so the owner must resort to other tactics. One of these is for the owner to try to shame the thief into admitting guilt. The owner does this by composing a song calling attention to his loss and has it sung as a dance song, in which the members of the community, including the thief, dance to the song. The Tikopia believe that hearing the song will make the thief feel shame, and that dancing to it will increase the shame.

The Tikopia save as a last resort their most effective remedy for theft, which is the use of sorcery against the thief. Using sorcery against a thief is called *tautuku,* and is designed to cause the thief to become ill or even to die. The *tautuku,* being the product of the power of the spirit world, is actually administered by specialists, chiefs, elders, and spirit mediums who act as intermediaries with the spirit world. Those who resort to *tautuku* keep their activities secret. One reason for this is that if the thief knows that he is the target of sorcery, he can find supernatural remedies to protect himself. But just as important, the practice of *tautuku* is in itself a morally negative act, and to engage in it is considered bad.

Another way in which Tikopians use supernatural powers to counter theft is to use the power of taboo to guard their crops. To put a taboo on one's crops is to put supernatural guardians there, who will make anyone who steals from the protected garden ill. In fact, most people who steal from gardens do so from gardens that are not protected by taboo. On the other hand, there are those people who do not believe in the power of taboo and steal from protected gardens anyway.

For Tikopian men of high rank, theft presents a somewhat different set of circumstances. First, they had at their disposal the ability to quickly employ *tautuku* themselves, and so were perhaps less of a target for thieves. On the other hand, the threat of *tautuku* never stops all theft in any case. Men of high rank were generally people of high morals, but when one such man decided to be a thief, he could steal virtually with impunity. This is because one whose property is stolen by a high-ranking man could not accuse him, and this is true even for other people of high rank. Nobody has a right to insult a high-ranking person by making accusations of theft, and the high-ranking person has the right to beat anyone who does make such an accusation. In short, the Tikopians do not possess any good means of preventing theft.

Theft was a wrong among the traditional Cheyenne, but punishment of this wrong conflicted with the Cheyenne ideal of generosity. It often happened that someone who had stolen an article was confronted by the owner and told that if the thief had simply asked for the article, it would have been freely given. The idea behind this process was to shame the thief into refraining from theft, not to retrieve the stolen article, since it was considered unseemly to be too concerned about a loss of a personal item.

Firth, Raymond. (1975 [1965]) *Primitive Polynesian Economy*.

Llewellyn, Karl N., and E. Adamson Hoebel. (1961 [1941]) *The Cheyenne Way*.

THEOCRACY
Theocracy refers to a political system in which the political power of a society rests in the hands of priests (the term *priest* refers to all religious practitioners, not simply Roman Catholic ones), people who are professional religious functionaries as well as the intermediaries between ordinary people and a god or gods. The term *theocracy* is derived from the Greek words *theos* (god) and *kratos* (rule).

Examples of modern theocracies are Vatican City, traditional Tibet (though presently the traditional government is in exile from Tibet), and several local areas in which priests hold the majority of political power. An example of the latter is the island of Newfoundland in Canada (which, along with Labrador, constitutes one of the nation's ten provinces). There, Catholic priests, though not controlling the legislature directly, do influence people's votes to the degree that they effectively control a great deal of political power. For example, the theory of human evolution cannot be taught in the grade schools of Newfoundland because of opposition to such teachings by the priests there.

Another example is the British monarch, who is, as the head of the Church of England, a theocratic ruler.

An interesting case of a theocratic government concerns that of the Micmac Indians of Cape Breton Island, Nova Scotia. The Micmac converted to Roman Catholicism in the seventeenth century. When the British drove the French out of Canada in the eighteenth century, most of the Roman Catholic priests in eastern Canada also left. Those who remained could do very little for the Micmac, outside of saying the last rites and conducting funeral and wedding masses once a year. This left the work of giving sermons, saying prayers, and leading the singing of hymns largely undone. On Cape Breton, the Micmac headmen, members of the *Sante: Mawiomi* (Grand Council) took up these functions in their respective bands. They used their sermons as a tool of leadership, referring obliquely to various people and their improper acts in the sermons in order to coordinate public ostracism of them. Being able to say prayers and sing hymns in the Micmac language was a prime requirement to become a headman and member of the Grand Council; therefore, it was necessary to be literate in order to read prayer and hymn books printed in Micmac. Also, as priests (though not recognized as such by the Roman Catholic Church), the members of the Grand Council had an additional claim to legitimate authority as intermediaries between the people and God.

Strouthes, Daniel P. (1994) *Change in the Real Property Law of a Cape Breton Island Micmac Band.*

TOTALITARIAN DICTATORSHIP

See AUTOCRACY.

TREATY

A treaty is an agreement made between two independent political groups (nowadays, usually state societies). There are several kinds of treaties, but most treaties differ largely in the degree to which their provisions are enforced by the authorities that sign them. Most international law is based upon treaty agreements.

In the affairs of modern nation-states, treaties made by leaders or their representatives have no force of law with respect to the people in the signatory countries unless the provisions of the treaty are also approved by the legislatures and the courts. This protects the people from the effects of leaders who may not have the best wishes of the people in mind. For example, if the president of the United States became mentally deranged and made a treaty with the president of Russia that stated that the United States would give Russia all the gold in Fort Knox, it is highly unlikely that the U.S. Congress would approve such a treaty, and thus it would never have the force of law. Of course, even if the legislature approves a treaty, it has no effect unless the legislation is enforced by the courts. Courts in the former Soviet Union, for example, did not prevent the Soviet military from flagrantly breaking the Strategic Arms Limitation Treaties that the former Soviet Union had made with the United States. Similarly, Canadian courts have damaged Canada's observance of the Migratory Birds Act Treaty with the United States by allowing Canadian Indians to kill migratory birds outside of the hunting season as defined by the treaty and enacted by legislation.

One instance of how the absence of legislation affects treaty rights concerns the Jay Treaty of 1794, which was signed by the United States and Great Britain. The terms of the treaty allowed the citizens of the United States and Great Britain, as well as the Indians living here and in Canada (which was part of Great Britain at the time), to cross the boundaries between the two countries freely and without the payment of duties on personal belongings. Great Britain never passed legislation to grant the rights contained in the treaty, and therefore Indians in Canada do not have the right to bring goods from the United States into Canada free of duty payments.

In other societies, such as band and tribal societies, the ability of leaders to make successful treaties is limited by their authority over their own people. In the 1940s, the Canadian government tried an experiment in which Indians living in Nova Scotia in small bands over a large area were to be concentrated in just two communities, where they would be more easily administered; this plan was known as the Centralization Program. The Grand Chief of the

Grand Council was the leader/authority of the Cape Breton Island, Nova Scotia, Micmac people. He concluded a treaty with the Canadian government in which he agreed to lead the other Micmac of Cape Breton to the area chosen as the target point of the Centralization Program on Cape Breton, the Eskasoni reserve. In return, the Micmac people there were to receive employment, new houses, agricultural implements, a priest, electricity, telephone service, and a new school. The Grand Chief, who was to receive a good farm for himself as part of the treaty, saw in the treaty a chance for the Micmac of Cape Breton to advance themselves materially. However, the vast majority of the Cape Breton Micmac did not want to live in one place together and refused to move to Eskasoni. They opposed the Grand Chief so vigorously that he was forced to resign. The Grand Chief was eventually allowed to resume his position as Grand Chief, but under the condition that he would no longer engage in political relations of any kind with foreign powers.

The problems Indian leaders have faced in ensuring that their followers abide by the provisions of a treaty have been common in treaties between Indians and whites. In fact, it was fairly rare that an Indian leader could do so. When Indian groups sold lands to the white people, not all of the people in the group usually agreed with the sale and refused to recognize it. This led to the old epithet "Indian Giver" to refer to someone who had agreed to give something and then wanted it back. Today, Indian treaties constitute a special kind of treaty, in which preference for Indian interests is superior. The Canadian courts have called Indian treaties *sui generis* (of their own kind, or unique), and have given them legal force when they benefit Indians, even if the Indians involved had themselves broken the treaties decades ago. The situation is much the same in the United States.

In addition to ordinary treaties and Indian treaties, there is a third kind of treaty, made today by the executive branches of national governments. This is known as the executive agreement. With respect to the United States, executive agreements do not require approval by the Senate. Typically, their provisions are very narrow in scope and fall within the limits set by legislation, or else the Senate may vote permission for an executive agreement of a particular type to be made at a later date. Trade agreements between nations are usually executive agreements.

The following is an actual treaty that was made by the King of Great Britain and the President of the Chinese Republic in 1928 over a matter of trade (*Treaty between His Majesty and the President of the Chinese Republic,* 1929).

Treaty between his Majesty and
the President of the
Chinese Republic relating to
the Chinese Customs
Tariff, &c.,with Annexes thereto.

Nanking, December 20, 1928
[Ratifications exchanged at London, March 14, 1929.]

His Majesty the King of Great Britain, Ireland and the British Dominions beyond the Seas, Emperor of India, and

His Excellency the President of the National Government of the Republic of China,

Desiring to strengthen the good relations which happily exist between them to facilitate and extend trade and commerce between their respective countries, Have resolved to conclude a treaty for this purpose and have appointed as their plenipotentiaries:

His Majesty the King of Great Britain, Ireland and the British Dominions beyond the Seas, Emperor of India:

For Great Britain and Northern Ireland,

Sir Miles Wedderburn Lampson, K.C.M.G., C.B., M.V.O., His Majesty's Envoy Extraordinary and Minister Plenipotentiary to the Republic of China;

U.S. President Jimmy Carter, left, and Soviet leader Leonid Brezhnev exchange documents after signing the second Strategic Arms Limitation Treaty (SALT II) in Vienna in 1979. A treaty's terms are usually negotiated by representatives of the involved nations until there is mutual agreement, and then, in the case of democratic societies, the treaty is presented to the national legislative body for approval.

His Excellency the President of the National Government of the Republic of China;

His Excellency Dr. Chengting T. Wang, Minister for Foreign Affairs of the National Government of the Republic of China;

who, having communicated their full powers, found in good and due form, have agreed as follows:—

Article 1.

It is agreed that all provisions of the existing treaties between the High Contracting Parties which limit in any way the right of China to settle her national customs tariff in such way as she may think fit are hereby abrogated, and that the principle of complete national tariff autonomy shall apply.

Article 2.

The nationals of either of the High Contracting Parties shall not be compelled under any pretext whatsoever to pay in China and the territories of His Britannic Majesty to which the present treaty applies respectively any duties, internal charges or taxes upon goods imported or exported by them other than or higher than those paid on goods of the same origin by Chinese and British nationals respectively, or by nationals of any other foreign country.

Article 3.

His Britannic Majesty agrees to the abrogation of all provisions of the existing treaties between the High Contracting Parties which limit the right of China to impose tonnage dues at such rates as she may think fit.

In regard to tonnage dues and all matters connected therewith, British ships in China and Chinese ships in those territories of His Britannic Majesty to which the present treaty applies, shall receive treatment not less favourable than that accorded to the ships of any other foreign country.

Article 4.

The present treaty shall be ratified and the ratifications shall be exchanged in London as soon as possible. It shall come into force on the date on which the two Parties shall have notified each other that ratification has been effected.

The English and Chinese texts of the present treaty have been carefully compared and verified; but in the event of there being a difference of meaning between the two the sense as expressed in the English text shall be held to prevail.

In witness whereof, the respective plenipotentiaries have signed the present treaty in duplicate, and have affixed thereunto their seals.

Done at Nanking, the twentieth day of December, nineteen hundred and twenty-eight, corresponding to the twentieth day of the twelfth month of the seventeenth year of the Republic of China.

[Seal] MILES W. LAMPSON.
[Seal] CHENGTING T. WANG.

Cohen, Fay G. (1986) *Treaties on Trial.*

Morse, Bradford W., ed. (1985) *Aboriginal Peoples and the Law.*

Strouthes, Daniel P. (1994) *Change in the Real Property Law of a Cape Breton Island Micmac Band.*

Treaty between His Majesty and the President of the Chinese Republic together with other Documents relating to the Chinese Customs Tariff, &c., Nanking, December 20, 1928. (1929).

TRESPASS

Trespass, as it is applied by the U.S. legal system, refers to entering onto and remaining upon land owned by another without the owner's permission and against his wishes.

This definition of trespass does not apply in all societies. In fact, the entire idea of trespass does not exist in all societies. For the Naskapi Indians of Labrador, the concept has no meaning. The only separately owned parcels of land are hunting territories. One cannot trespass on these territories because anyone may cross another's hunting territory and, along the way, may kill any animal he or she comes across for food. The only thing that a person traveling upon the hunting territory of another may not do is to kill fur-bearing animals to collect the furs for sale. Fur-bearing animals may be killed for their meat, but the skins always belong to the owner of the hunting territory.

Barton, Roy F. (1969 [1919]) *Ifugao Law.*

Lips, Julius E. (1947) "Naskapi Law." *Transactions of the American Philosophical Society* 37(4): 378–492.

TRIBE AND TRIBALISM

A tribe is a collection of small, nonstate societies sharing the same language and overall culture who join together periodically or in times of trouble to form one politically united group. Tribal societies, prior to dramatic cultural change resulting from contact with industrialized societies, numbered several thousand. Anthropologists have attempted to categorize all societies of the world (or at least all known, well-described societies, about 1,500 in all) using a band-tribe-chiedom-state typology. However, in reference to societies today, the typology is difficult to apply because most cultures have changed markedly in the last fifty years. This typology of band-tribe-chiefdom-state also suggests an evolutionary progression throughout human history, for as one moves along the scale, each type of society is larger and more complex and exerts more control over its natural and social environment than the previous type.

The term *tribe* is used in three other ways. First, it is used in efforts to produce a typology of cultural types. Tribe is used in this sense to refer to all so-called "primitive" cultures of the world in contrast to all "civilized" ones. When used objectively, technologically primitive (small-scale, preliterate or nonliterate, and non-industrialized) cultures are ones that are at the low end of the scale of social, political, techno-logical, and economic complexity, while civilized cultures are at the high end. For example, among the cultures of the indigenous New World, most of the hundreds of Native American cultures, at the time of first contact with Europeans, would be considered tribal or primitive, while the Inca, Aztec, and Maya would be considered civilized. When used objectively in this way, such use of the concept of tribe is legitimate, although perhaps not very enlightening. However, the use of tribe or tribal as an equivalent for primitive and in opposition to civilized often opens the door for ethnocentric, simplistic, and sometimes racist interpretations. This view also has nothing to do with the concept of tribe as it has been traditionally used by social scientists.

A second, additional use for the term *tribe* is as a concept to distinguish societies. In this usage, we refer to the Badaga tribe, the Kota tribe, the Kurumba tribe, and the Toda tribe, four neighboring groups of the Nilgiri Hills of south India. The use of the word *tribe* indicates that each is a separate social entity, distinct from the other social entities. Thus, tribe is in some sense an equivalent concept to ethnic group, with tribe used more commonly for small, non-Western societies and ethnic groups than for the present-day descendants of immigrants to new lands. Various attempts have been made to define the basic features of a tribe as it is used in this way, focusing on factors such as common territory, name, language, sense of common identity, religion, technology, and others. In general, however, when tribe has been used in this way a group is usually identified as a distinct group because it speaks a language different than its neighbors, occupies a defined territory, and has a distinct name (although the name may be given by outsiders rather than by the group to itself).

The third additional usage of the term *tribe* involves specific legal and political arrangements that accrue to groups and the members of those groups in various nations. In the United States, the designation of over 300 Native American groups as tribes (or some related term such as communities, towns, nations, bands, reservations, rancherias, colonies, or pueblos) defines the legal and political relationships between the group and federal and state governments. Similarly, the designation of a group in India as a Scheduled Tribe indicates that the government considers it to be disadvantaged and that its members are eligble for special benefits not available to others. Thus, the label *tribe* takes on a clearly defined legal meaning that may have major political and economic consequences for the tribe, its members, and other members of the nation.

Tribalism is sympathy for and political advocacy of tribal interests, including the interests of fellow tribespeople. Tribalism became a particularly important issue in areas in which colonial powers have or had dominance, such as Africa. Max Gluckman observed that, in Africa at least, tribalism manifests itself in two very different and distinct ways.

The first way concerns benefits that an individual derives from membership in his or her tribe within the tribe's own territory. It is the tribe, for example, that grants a person land on which to grow crops. So long as the tribe exists and has sufficient power, the individual has a guarantee that he will have land to use. Therefore, in rural areas, it is important for an individual to support his tribe. Moreover, it is the tribe that gives the individual his or her identity and determines the customs, rules, and laws that influence his or her behavior when he or she is at home.

In urban areas, tribalism works first of all to help a person categorize the people whom he or she meets. But most importantly, tribalism comes into play in political struggles. If there are elections, a tribalist will seek to elect someone of his own tribe, regardless of other issues that may also be important. Generally speaking, however, in an urban environment, workers frequently act in ways that are of direct benefit to themselves, rather than out of purely tribalist motives.

Ghurye, G. S. (1963) *The Scheduled Tribes.* 3d ed.

Gluckman, Max. (1960) "Tribalism in Modern British Central Africa." *Cahiers d'études africaines* 1: 55–70.

Native American Directory. (1982)

Sahlins, Marshall. (1968) *Tribesman.*

Service, Elman R. (1962) *Primitive Social Organization: An Evolutionary Perspective.* 2d ed.

Winthrop, Robert H. (1991) *Dictionary of Concepts in Cultural Anthropology.*

TRIBUTE

Tribute refers to money, goods, or services required of the people of a society by the society's political leaders. In some societies, tributary payments are largely redistributed among the members of the society, while in others, tribute is used largely to provide for the livelihood of the elite. In our society, we pay tribute in the form of taxes. In other societies, tribute is or was paid in the form of goods such as agricultural produce.

Another important form of tribute is known as corvée, or labor required by the political leaders from the people. The Inca Indians of Peru used corvée. Households were required to provide men to work without pay on a parcel of land set aside for religious leaders and on another parcel set aside for civic leaders. Food, primarily maize, was grown on these lands for the support of the leaders, namely the bureaucrats, priests, and royalty. This food also supported the disabled, who could not farm themselves, as well as the military. The state provided for corvée workers all the tools and seed required for the planting, and also gave the workers food and beer when they worked. The people who worked for the state were required only to labor, and bore no responsibility for the crops or their quality. Nevertheless, the amount of work required was such that huge surpluses of food were stored in immense warehouses.

Inca men were not required to supply labor until they had married and had land of their own. But once children became old enough to do so, they helped their fathers with the corvée duties of his household. The *kuraka,* or local district political leader, if he had a large number of households to administer within his district (either more than 100 or more than 500, according to different sources), did not have to perform corvée labor himself. Men were also required to participate in the Inca military corvée. In addition, from time to time, households were required to provide labor for building projects, such as roads and fortresses. People were also sometimes taken by the king to work for the rest of their lives as royal retainers.

Murra, John V. (1967 [1958]) "On Inca Political Structure." In *Comparative Political Systems,* edited by Ronald Cohen and John Middleton, 339–353.

War War is defined as authorized violence between independent groups (Pospisil 1974: 10). We say "authorized" because it is approved by the appropriate social authorities. For example, if a group of men from New York State went to Canada and attacked the Canadian Parliament, it would not be an act of war since the president of the United States and the U.S. Congress had not approved the attack; rather, it might be a case of external self-redress, if the New Yorkers felt themselves wronged by the Canadian government, or feud, if the violence is part of a long-term pattern between subgroups of a society or societies (two families on opposite sides of the Canadian-U.S. border for example); it would also be a violation of Canadian law in any case. In addition, warfare can only exist between independent groups. If the states of North Dakota and Montana decided to engage each other with military violence, it would not be a case of war since both states are subordinate to the federal government in Washington, D.C., which would undoubtedly intercede to end the violence.

Wars take place for many reasons. Some of these are to exterminate an enemy (as in the 1990s war in the former Yugoslavia between Serbs and Muslims); to take wealth (as in the war between Iraq and Kuwait); to acquire land (as in the nineteenth century wars between the whites and Indians in the United States); over ideological differences (the war between Iran and Iraq in the 1980s); self-defense (World War II); to change the leadership of another group (the U.S. war against Panama in 1989); to take women (as among the Yanomamö people); for warriors to gather personal glory in battle (as among the Plains Indians in the eighteenth and nineteenth centuries); to take revenge; and for other reasons.

A number of anthropologists have also looked at some of the less obvious reasons why people go to war. Some anthropologists, for example, believe that man is by nature warlike, that warfare is instinctive. Other anthropologists have pointed to societies in which warfare seems to be a source of entertainment; such seems particularly true of some of the Indian peoples of the Great Plains, who fought raids against each other for horses, prestige, and revenge.

Another theory as to why people go to war is the sociobiological theory. This theory states that men go to war to increase their reproductive success, that is, that they work to increase the proportional representation of their genes in the next generation. According to this theory, successful warriors attract more wives and thus usually have more children. Also, successful warriors kill off other men whose genes dilute the relative proportion of the successful warrior's genes. One who has done much work on this idea is Napoleon Chagnon.

Another idea as to why there is war is that people fight to gain material resources. A cross-cultural study suggests that many nonstate society peoples fight to alleviate short-term food shortages. A well-known variant of this argument was made by Marvin Harris. Harris's idea

Wars between nations involve purposeful use of organized military force. A state of war exists between Bosnian Serbs and Croatians that causes death and disruption among civilian populations. Serb refugees who have fled Croatia enter the Bosnian stronghold of Banja Luka in August 1995.

that it is the material conditions of life that have the greatest effect on the basic culture is known as cultural materialism. For Harris, cultural materialism explains why some nonstate societies frequently engage in war. Some of these societies, it turns out, have very little regular access to high-quality protein in their diet, protein of the kind provided by meat. Harris used the case of the Yanomamö Indians of the rainforests of South America to illustrate his theory.

The Yanomamö Indians of South America practice female infanticide because they feel a strong need to raise as many men, who can be

warriors, as possible. It is not possible to raise all of the children born because there are often food shortages; if all of the children born were raised, some would die, and some of these would be male children. When the men become adults, they search for wives; finding that there are not enough to go around, they decide to steal females from neighboring bands. Of course, the neighboring bands resist, and fighting ensues. Further, the neighboring Yanomamö bands also steal women from their neighbors. Thus, the fighting requires a large number of warriors both for defense and for the taking of women from other bands. The process is therefore circular and repetitive. They need warriors to get women, but must kill female infants to have more warriors, who need more females as mates and who have to go to war to get them. The Yanomamö themselves believe that they go to war simply to acquire women. But according to Harris, the root cause of the warfare is a lack of proper protein in the diet. The warfare that the relative paucity of females causes in turn forces the warring bands to move away from each other, thus enlarging the amount of forest uninhabited by people and increasing the amount of game, and thus protein, available to the Yanomamö. War, therefore, indirectly leads to a better diet and less need for war. But population increase inevitably causes a dearth of protein in the diet, and the whole cycle starts all over again.

Many anthropologists are less concerned with the causes of warfare than with the historical effects of colonial powers on indigenous band and tribal societies. In tribal and band societies in many areas of the world, there are no political leaders or legal authorities with power over all of the individual small groups. This means that the individual groups are independent and no one has the authority to stop wars between them. This state of affairs almost always changes when colonial powers take control of a region and pacify the area, ending all such hostilities. The Cheyenne, Sioux, Arapaho, Crow, and other Plains Indians, for example, no longer practice the raiding of each other's bands and tribes that was common in the eighteenth and nineteenth centuries.

Following is an example of warfare in a tribal society. One of the better-described cases of warfare in a small, non-Western society is that of the Jivaro (also called Jibaro) Indians of eastern Ecuador. The Jivaro, until being largely pacified in recent years, were a fiercely independent people prone to the use of violence with little provocation. So independent were they that each family lived alone rather than with others in a village. So prone to the use of violence were they that boys were raised to be warriors from a young age, and deadly and prolonged blood feuds between families were a frequent occurrence within the Jivaro tribe.

The wars that the Jivaro fought against neighboring tribes were generally fought to avenge some act of aggression against a Jivaro person or group. Once begun, however, the ultimate aim of the Jivaro warriors was to completely erase the other tribe from the face of the earth. So long as the other tribe existed, the Jivaro were in danger of retaliation by its members, and so it is logical that the Jivaro should try to completely annihilate their enemies.

Those groups that decided to wage war would combine and elect an experienced chief to lead them. The warriors and chief drank hallucinogenic drugs that allowed them to see visions of spirits, who then gave omens as to the success of the future military operations. Spies were sent out to find out how many men the enemy had, whether they had fortified their houses, and what types of weapons they had. The chief, before the raid, told the men to have courage and gave them the details of his battle plan. The men also took part in a ceremony that used magic to build courage, the men repeating a memorized dialogue in pairs to each other. The warriors also wore special clothing for the raid, especially a monkey-skin cap and jaguar-tooth necklace. They painted themselves black, believing that this gave them the appearance and some of the supernatural powers of the "iguanchi" (demons). Men often brought their sons along to observe a real war in order to prepare them to become warriors themselves in the future.

The Jivaro tried to surprise their enemies if at all possible. For this reason, raids were usually made at night or just before dawn. The warriors surrounded a house and killed the occupants as they tried to leave it. If they did not leave the house, the Jivaro set fire to it, forcing them out. Then they moved on to the next house. When they couldn't surprise the enemy because the enemy's dogs or chickens gave alarm, resistance was organized through the use of a signal drum.

The Jivaro warriors killed all of the enemy, with some exceptions. Young women were usually kept alive to be wives of the Jivaro men, and children were sometimes spared to be raised as Jivaro. The others were killed, their bodies mutilated, and the heads taken as trophies.

The taking of a head as a trophy was cause for a feast afterward, and the head of a courageous warrior was the most valued of all. A head was later "shrunk" by removing the skull, boiling it, pouring hot sand in it (to remove any remaining flesh), and then forming the skin so that it remained recognizably human.

Like the Jivaro, the Crow Indians of the nineteenth-century North American Plains engaged in warfare with great determination. And, like the Jivaro, the Crow Indians practiced a form of warfare known as raiding. But the usual reason given for Crow raiding, like the raiding of other Plains peoples of the time, was to take horses (and sometimes revenge) from the enemy (usually other Plains peoples). However, this simple reason hides an entire war culture complex with which the Crow people were frequently preoccupied. Men found that their position in society, ability to achieve political leadership, and reputation were based upon their military successes. Ability as a storyteller and medical technique were important, but of little significance in comparison with military skill. Men also found in warfare activities a great source of excitement and for this reason were very interested in pursuing them.

Let us take the acquisition of horses as a reason for warfare. If one wanted only to acquire horses, then why did a warrior gain far more prestige by stealing an enemy's tethered horse than for acquiring several free-roaming horses? Why also did warriors continue to raid for horses even when they had more than enough? One Crow family could not possibly use more than a

dozen horses, yet one man, Gray-Bull, had between 70 and 90 head at one time. Therefore, one must conclude that the Crow men raided for reasons other than simply acquiring horses, and that those were to gain individual prestige and for excitement.

Crow women and children were also involved with the war culture complex. Children, both male and female, acquired their names from the famous battles fought by various warriors. Women, when dacing, wore the scalps that their husbands brought back from raids. They also displayed their husbands' shields and weapons in public with pride. Further, the women, through their cries over the deaths in battle of male members of their families, acted as principal instigators of raiding for revenge.

The men sought and achieved military glory in four accepted manners, the accomplishment of any one of which made one an "araxt–si'wice" (honor-owner). One manner was to be the first person in battle to count coup, that is, to touch the body of any enemy individual, usually during battle, whether the enemy was wounded, dead, or unharmed (while it is obviously dangerous and thus indicative of courage for a soldier to touch an armed enemy soldier in battle, one could count coup on any enemy person at any time, as when one Crow man crept up to a Dakota [a Siouan people, enemies of the Crow] camp, found a woman urinating, and killed her). The second manner was to take from an enemy soldier his bow or gun during a fight. The third was to cut loose and steal a horse tied up at an enemy encampment. The final means to military glory was to act as either the pipe-owner or the raid-planner of a raiding party. Achievement of any one of these feats made a man worthy of respect and earned him a place as a herald, next in rank to chief. Having accomplished each of the four types of deeds made one a chief. And the more times one accomplished each type of deed, the more famous one became.

Boys learned the skills of warfare early. They counted coup on animals, encouraged girls to dance with the fur of animals and pretended that the furs were scalps, and reproduced the military societies of adult men in their Hammer Society. In addition, the boys were made physically fit through athletics. Finally, the boys were prepared for the rigors of warfare by frequently being told by the men that to become old is a disgrace and that it is far better to die young in battle.

A horse-raiding party often went as follows: The men would go on foot, each carrying, or bringing a dog to carry, his moccasins, a small pail, and a rope to tie the captured horses. Most parties started out after sunset and sheltered themselves with rudimentary windbreaks. After they camped for the night, the captain sent the scouts forth to find an enemy camp. The scouts did not eat until they found the enemy. When they found the enemy, they returned to camp holding up their guns as a signal of their success. After they came into camp, they kicked over a pile of specially collected buffalo chips to further signify their success and then they ate.

The members of the war party attached magical objects to their bodies and painted their faces so as to improve their magical "medicine." The leader of the war party then prayed to the Sun, promising to build a sweatlodge or give some other gift in the Sun's honor if the Sun allowed the members of the war party to return safely with many horses.

The men then went on the raid at night. They hoped to be able to take enough horses that they could all ride back to their own encampment. This was not only a matter of comfort; the enemy would be chasing them on horseback, trying both to kill them and to recapture their horses. Thus, if not enough horses were captured, those who had to walk back often were killed.

If the raid was successful, they rode at top speed all night, through the next day, and the next night as well. Finally, on the second day they stopped, killed a buffalo, and ate it. When they arrived home, they fired their guns in the air and paraded the captured horses around the village. It was at this time that the spoils were divided. Under the rules, the captain could claim all of the horses as his own, but he always gave most of them to the other men in the party to avoid charges of greed.

When fighting with the specific intent of killing the enemy, the Crow carried out their raiding differently. The usual reason for raiding to kill an enemy individual was to take revenge for the killing by the enemy of a Crow individual. Often, a revenge raid was precipitated by the request of a woman to a famous warrior to avenge the death of her son at the hands of the enemy. The woman would bring gifts to the warrior in order to induce him to carry out the raid. Before the raid took place, the warriors blackened their faces. When they returned victorious, having killed one or more of the enemy, they were treated to a celebration, where the men who had earned war honors in the raid were honored. Before they entered their home camp, the first man to count coup on an enemy individual and the first person to capture an enemy weapon were celebrated and had their shirts entirely blackened with a mixture of buffalo blood and two kinds of charcoal. Those who did those same deeds second and third had their shirts only half blackened, and those who did these deeds fourth had only the sleeves of their shirts blackened. Then the group of warriors camped just outside their home camp one last night. In the morning, they went to their home camp and fired their rifles into the air. The women came out and led them back into camp in a special dance. Later, there was more dancing, feasting, and the singing of special praise songs. Celebrations would last all of that day and through the night.

The Crow people had greatly different ideas about what makes successful warfare than do the military leaders of modern national armed forces. Whereas modern military leaders seek some strategic or tactical goal, such as the neutralization of an opposing force or the capture of some geographic area, the Crow were interested in horses, revenge, and personal glory. Further, whereas the miliatry leaders of modern nation-states accept that they will likely lose members of their forces in the pursuit of a strategic or tactical objective, the Crow military objective was to carry out their warfare with the goal of losing none of their members to the enemy. In fact, the Crow military leaders who lost none of their raiding parties in military action were considered superior to those military leaders who got more horses or those who killed more of the enemy if they lost men in the process. While it is true that the Crow highly esteemed as brave the individual who attacked large numbers of the enemy in a suicidal rush, the normal ideal was to kill the enemy in such a way as to present the least danger to oneself.

That the Crow sincerely and with great emotion hated their enemies cannot be doubted. The evidence for this may be seen in the way that the Crow treated their captives and the enemy dead. Though it is true that women captives were treated well (they married Crow men and assumed the same life as a Crow woman), captive men were often tortured. This was especially the case when the enemy put up a frustrating defense, thereby inflaming Crow emotions. For example, there is the case of one fight with a Blackfoot group, in which the Blackfoot built a defensive obstacle of logs and stones and held off the Crow for a long while. When the Crow finally prevailed, they tortured their Blackfoot captives for a long time before they slaughtered them. The corpses were then beaten and mangled. In another case, a Blackfoot man was caught by the Crow, hanged from a tree by the neck, shot at by the men, and perforated with sharp sticks by the women. And it was often the case that the bodies of enemy dead were mutilated and dragged along the ground with a rope.

Bohannan, Paul J., ed. (1967) *Law and Warfare: Studies in the Anthropology of Conflict.*

Chagnon, Napoleon. (1989) "Response to Ferguson." *American Ethnologist* 1989: 565–569.

Ember, Carol, and Melvin Ember. (1992) "Resource Unpredictability, Mistrust, and War." *Journal of Conflict Resolution* 36: 242–262.

Haas, J., ed. (1990) *The Anthropology of War.*

Harris, Marvin. (1995) *Cultural Anthropology.* 4th ed.

Karsten, Rafael. (1967 [1923]) "Blood Revenge and War among the Jibaro Indians of Eastern Ecuador." In *Law and Warfare: Studies in the Anthropology of Conflict,* edited by Paul Bohannan, 303–325.

Lowie, Robert H. (1956 [1935]) *The Crow Indians.*

Pospisil, Leopold. (1974 [1971]) *Anthropology of Law: A Comparative Theory.*

WORLD SYSTEM The basic premise of the world system set of theories is that the world has one giant economic system that involves nearly all people on Earth and that is divided up between industrially developed nations (the First World [the United States, Canada, the countries of western Europe, Australia, New Zealand, and Japan] and Second World [the former Soviet Union and the Soviet Bloc countries of eastern Europe]) and the industrially undeveloped nations (the Third World [the rest of the world]). The ideas behind the theory of the world system ultimately grew out of Marxist thought and theories of political economy.

The idea of world system theory depends upon a concept of development and especially a concept of underdevelopment. When the European capitalists began their colonization of the rest of the world, it was in large part to acquire wealth. This wealth has fueled the technological and industrial growth of First World nations since then. The colonies, by and large, have remained technologically and industrially behind in their development; they have not "modernized" and therefore remain "underdeveloped." In many Third World countries that are former colonies of European nations, only the elite of the countries has done well financially, while most of the rest of the population remains poor.

While there was undoubtedly poverty and starvation in what are now Third World nations prior to the coming of the Europeans, the world system theorists say that the continued poverty in those countries after the coming of the Europeans is due to certain basic features of capitalism. The world system theorists explain that the Third World has continued in poverty because the capitalist First World has kept the majority of the world's technology and industry for itself and relegated the Third World to producing cheap raw materials and providing cheap labor. In other words, the Third World countries continue to be treated as colonies, despite the fact that they have won political independence. The analogy to colonies and the relationship between a country and its colonies is frequently used by world system theorists. For example, while the urban centers of most Third World countries are developed, at least for the elite, the rest of these poor countries remain underdeveloped, and these places are often referred to as "internal colonies" of a Third World country, thereby making the analogy that the Third World country's central

elite is like the country in a country-colony relationship.

The ideas of a "core" and a "periphery" in the world economic system were introduced by Immanuel Wallerstein. The core countries are those in the First World, the major capitalist powers in the world economic system. The periphery consists of those countries that supply raw materials and cheap labor. There is also a "semi-periphery" of countries that were underdeveloped but that are presently partially developed, such as South Korea, Taiwan, Argentina, and Brazil.

The core countries benefit from the world economic system, but the peripheral countries remain poor even while supplying the raw materials and cheap labor that make core nations wealthy. The division of labor that is a basic feature of capitalism is manifested in an international division, just as the entire economy is international. While countries can over time go from being core countries to being peripheral countries, and vice versa, the system remains the same.

The major problem with this theory is that it does not take into account the factors within any particular country that keep it a peripheral country or a core country, or especially why any one country in particular, such as Japan, goes from being a peripheral country to being a core country, as Taiwan and South Korea seem likely to do in the future. A second problem is that the theory explains all poverty as a result of underdevelopment. In Peru, for example, the legal and political systems are so inefficient that most people prefer to work and trade in the illegal economy. This has the effect of placing the country's tax burden onto the legal businesses, which cannot produce enough wealth to support adequate development efforts by the government. Further, the illegal economy does not operate efficiently because their contracts cannot be enforced by the legal system, and because the entrepreneurs can be arrested and their businesses closed. So, as a result of these purely internal problems, Peru remains a poor nation, regardless of the world economic system.

---

de Soto, Hernando. (1989) *The Other Path: The Invisible Revolution in the Third World.*

Lewellen, Ted C. (1992) *Political Anthropology: An Introduction.* 2d ed.

O'Brien, Rita Cruise, ed. (1979) *The Political Economy of Underdevelopment: Dependence in Senegal.*

Wallerstein, Immanuel. (1974) *The Modern World-System I: Capitalist Agriculture and the Origins of the European World-Economy in the Sixteenth Century.*

———. (1980) *The Modern World-System II: Mercantilism and the Consolidation of the European World-Economy 1600–1750.*

Wolf, Eric. (1982) *Europe and the People without History.*

BIBLIOGRAPHY

Ajisafe, A. K. (1946) *The Laws and Customs of the Yoruba People.*

Albuquerque, C., and D. Werner. (1985) "Political Patronage in Santa Catarina." *Current Anthropology* 26(1): 117–120.

The All Pakistan Legal Decisions. (1993) Vol. 45. Edited by Malik Muhammad Saeed.

Allen, Martin G. (1972) "A Cross-Cultural Study of Aggression and Crime." *Journal of Cross-Cultural Psychology* 3: 259–271.

Alverson, Hoyt. (1978) *Mind in the Heart of Darkness.*

Amsbury, Clifton. (1979) "Patron-Client Structure in Modern World Organization." In *Political Anthropology: The State of the Art,* edited by S. Lee Seaton and Henri J. M. Claessen, 79–107.

An-Na'im, Abdullahi A., ed. (1992) *Human Rights in Cross-Cultural Perspective: A Quest for Consensus.*

Austin, John. (1954) *The Province of Jurisprudence Determined and the Uses of the Study of Jurisprudence.*

Bacon, Margaret K., Irvin L. Child, and Herbert Barry III. (1963) "A Cross-Cultural Study of the Correlates of Crime." *Journal of Abnormal and Social Psychology* 66: 291–300.

Balandier, Georges. (1970) *Political Anthropology.* Translated by A. M. Sheridan Smith.

Barton, Roy F. (1969 [1919]) *Ifugao Law.*

———. (1973 [1949]) *The Kalingas: Their Institutions and Custom Law.*

Beattie, John. (1960) *Bunyoro: An African Kingdom.*

Bentham, Jeremy. (1876 [1780]) *Introduction to the Principles of Morals and Legislation.*

Bishop, William W., Jr. (1971) *International Law: Cases and Materials.*

Bloodworth, Dennis. (1975) *An Eye for the Dragon.*

Bohannan, Paul J. (1957a) *Justice and Judgement among the Tiv.*

———. (1957b) *Tiv Farm and Settlement.*

Bohannan, Paul J., ed. (1967) *Law and Warfare: Studies in the Anthropology of Conflict.*

Bohannon, Laura. (1958) "Political Aspects of Tiv Social Organization." In *Tribes without Rulers,* edited by John Middleton and David Tait, 33–66.

Boissevain, Jeremy. (1966) "Patronage in Sicily." *Man,* n.s. 1:18–33.

Brownlie, Ian. (1992) *Basic Documents on Human Rights.*

Bukurura, Sufian Hemed. (1994) "The Maintenance of Order in Rural Tanzania: The Case of the Sungusungu." *Journal of Legal Pluralism and Unofficial Law* 34: 1–29.

Burn, A. R. (1974 [1965]) *The Pelican History of Greece.*

Buxton, Jean Carlile. (1967 [1957]) "'Clientship' among the Mandari of the Southern Sudan." In *Comparative Political Systems,* edited by Ronald Cohen and John Middleton, 229–245.

Campbell, J. K. (1964) *Honour, Family, and Patronage: A Study of Institutions and Moral Values in a Greek Mountain Community.*

Carneiro, Robert. (1970) "A Theory of the Origin of the State." *Science* 169: 733–738.

Caudill, Harry M. (1963) *Night Comes to the Cumberlands.*

Centre for Human Rights. (1991) *Contemporary Forms of Slavery.* Fact Sheet No. 14.

Chagnon, Napoleon A. (1968) *Yanomamö: The Fierce People.*

———. (1989) "Response to Ferguson." *American Ethnologist* 1989: 565–569.

Childe, V. Gordon. (1950) "The Urban Revolution." *Town Planning Review* 21(1): 3–17.

The Chinese Government. (1887) *A Chapter of the Chinese Penal Code.*

Christensen, James. (1954) *Double Descent among the Fanti.*

The Civil Code of Japan. (1896).

The Civil Code of the Republic of China. (1931) Book IV, Family. Translated by Ching-lin Hsia, James Chow, Liu Chieh, and Yukon Chang.

Codere, Helen. (1966) *Fighting with Property: A Study of Kwakiutl Potlatching and Warfare, 1792–1930.*

Cohen, Fay G. (1986) *Treaties on Trial.*

Dahl, Robert A. (1971) *Polyarchy.*

Davis, Shelton H. (1977) *Victims of the Miracle: Development and the Indians of Brazil.*

de Soto, Hernando. (1989) *The Other Path: The Invisible Revolution in the Third World.*

Debo, Angie. (1961 [1934]) *The Rise and Fall of the Choctaw Republic.*

Driberg, J. H. (1928) "Primitive Law in East Africa." *Africa* 1: 65.

Durkheim, Emile. (1933 [1893]) *The Division of Labor in Society.*

———. (1953) *Montesquieu et Rousseau.*

Ember, Carol R., and Melvin Ember. (1992) "Resource Unpredictability, Mistrust, and War." *Journal of Conflict Resolution* 36: 242–262.

———. (1992) "Warfare, Aggression, and Resource Problems: Cross-Cultural Codes." *Behavior Science Research* 26: 169–226.

Ember, Carol R., Bruce Russett, and Melvin Ember. (1993) "Political Participation and Peace: Cross-Cultural Codes." *Cross-Cultural Research* 27: 97–145.

Ericksen, Karen Paige, and Heather Horton. (1992) "'Blood Feuds': Cross-Cultural Variations in Kin Group Vengeance." *Behavior Science Research* 26: 57–86.

Escarra, Jean. (1926) *Chinese Law and Comparative Jurisprudence.*

Evans-Pritchard, E. E. (1940) *The Nuer.*

Felice, William. (1992) *The Emergence of Peoples' Rights in International Relations.*

Ferguson, R. Brian. (1990) "Blood of the Leviathan: Western Contact and Warfare in Amazonia." *American Ethnologist* 17: 237–257.

Firth, Raymond. (1975 [1965]) *Primitive Polynesian Economy.*

Forde, Daryll. (1961) "The Governmental Roles of Associations among the Yakö." *Africa* 31(4): 309-323.

Fortes, Meyer. (1953) "The Structure of Unilineal Descent Groups." *American Anthropologist* 55: 17–41.

Fortes, Meyer, and E. E. Evans-Pritchard, eds. (1940) *African Political Systems.*

French, David. (1948) *Factionalism in Isleta Pueblo.*

French, Rebecca. (1990) *The Golden Yoke: A Legal Ethnography of Tibet Pre-1959.*

Fried, Morton H. (1967) *The Evolution of Political Society.*

Friedrich, Paul. (1968) "The Legitimacy of a Cacique." In *Local-Level Politics,* edited by Marc Swartz, 243–269.

Gellner, Ernest, and John Waterbury, eds. (1977) *Patrons and Clients in Mediterranean Societies.*

General Index of the Indian Law Reports, Allahabad Series. (1949) 1949: 258–278.

Gernet, Jacques. (1982) *A History of Chinese Civilization.* Translated by J. R. Foster.

Ghurye, G. S. (1963) *The Scheduled Tribes.* 3d ed.

Gierke, Otto von. (1957 [1934]) *Natural Law and the Theory of Society: 1500 to 1800.*

Gluckman, Max. (1940) "The Kingdom of the Zulu of South Africa." In *African Political Systems,* edited by Meyer Fortes and E. E. Evans-Pritchard, 25–55.

———. (1955) *Custom and Conflict in Africa.*

———. (1960) "Tribalism in Modern British Central Africa." *Cahiers d'études africaines* 1: 55–70.

———. (1965a) *The Ideas in Barotse Jurisprudence.*

———. (1965b) *Politics, Law and Ritual in Tribal Society.*

———. (1965c) "Reasonableness and Responsibility in the Law of Segmentary Societies." In *African Law: Adaptation and Development,* edited by Hilda Kuper and Leo Kuper.

———. (1967) "The Judicial Process among the Barotse." In *Law and Warfare,* edited by Paul J. Bohannan, 59–92.

———. (1967 [1955]) *The Judicial Process among the Barotse of Northern Rhodesia.*

———. (1974) *African Traditional Law in Historical Perspective.*

Gluckman, Max, ed. (1969) *Ideas and Procedures in African Customary Law.*

Goadby, Frederic M. (1914) *Commentary on Egyptian Criminal Law, Part I.*

Gordon, Murray. (1989) *Slavery in the Arab World.*

Greene, Fred. (1970 [1966]) "Toward Understanding Military Coups." In *African Politics and Society,* edited by Irving Markovitz, 242–247.

Griaule, Marcel. (1938) *Dogon Games.* Translated by Michael A. Marcus.

Grotius, Hugo. (1925 [1625]) *De Jure Belli ac Pacis. Libri Tres.* Translated by Francis W. Kelsey.

Gubser, Nicholas J. (1965) *The Nunamiut Eskimos: Hunters of Caribou.*

Haas, J., ed. (1990) *The Anthropology of War.*

Hall, John Carey. (1906) *Japanese Feudal Law: The Institutes of Judicature: Being a Translation of "Go Seibei Shikimoku"; The Magisterial Code of the Hojo Power-Holders.* (A.D. *1232*).

Hamilton, W. D. (1984) *The Julian Tribe.*

Harris, Marvin. (1977) *Cannibals and Kings: The Origins of Culture.*

———. (1995) *Cultural Anthropology.* 4th ed.

Hart, C. W. M., and Arnold Pilling. (1960) *The Tiwi of North Australia.*

Heinz, Wolfgang S. (1991) *Indigenous Populations, Ethnic Minorities and Human Rights.*

Hocart, A. M. (1927) *Kingship.*

Hoebel, E. Adamson. (1949) *Man in the Primitive World.*

———. (1954) *The Law of Primitive Man.*

Hogbin, Ian. (1964) *A Guadalcanal Society: The Kaoka Speakers.*

———. (1972 [1934]) *Law and Order in Polynesia: A Study of Primitive Legal Institutions.*

Hohfeld, W. N. (1923) *Fundamental Legal Conceptions as Applied in Judicial Reasoning and Other Essays.* Edited by Walter Wheeler Cook.

Holleman, J. F. (1952) *Shona Customary Law.*

Howell, P. P. (1970 [1954]) *A Manual of Nuer Law: Being an Account of Customary Law, Its Evolution and Development in the Courts Established by the Sudan Government.*

The Indian Law Reports, Bombay Series. (1925) Vol. XLIX. Edited by K. McI. Kemp.

Ingersoll, Jasper C. (1969) *The Priest and the Path: An Analysis of the Priest Role in a Central Thai Village.*

Ioffe, Olympiad S., and Peter B. Maggs. (1983) *Soviet Law in Theory and Practice.*

Jordan, Winthrop. (1974) *The White Man's Burden.*

Kaeppler, Adrienne L. (1971) "Rank in Tonga." *Ethnology* 10: 174–193.

Karsten, Rafael. (1967 [1923]) "Blood Revenge and War among the Jibaro Indians of Eastern Ecuador." In *Law and Warfare: Studies in the Anthropology of Conflict,* edited by Paul J. Bohannon, 303–325.

Klein, Laura F. (1975) *Tlingit Women and Town Politics.*

Kolakowski, Leszek. (1978) *Main Currents of Marxism: Its Rise, Growth, and Dissolution.* Vol. 1.

Kottak, Conrad. (1983) *Assault on Paradise.*

Kovalevsky, Maxime. (1966 [1891]) "The Modern Russian Family." In *Anthropology and Early Law,* edited by Lawrence Krader, 148–170.

Kratochwil, Friedrich. (1985) "The Role of Domestic Courts as Agencies of the International Legal Order." In *International Law: A Contemporary Perspective,* edited by Richard Falk, Friedrich Kratochwil, and Saul Mendlovitz, 236–263.

Lange, Charles H. (1990 [1959]) *Cochiti: A New Mexico Pueblo, Past and Present.*

The Law Codification Commission. (1919) *The Criminal Code of the Republic of China (Second Revised Draft).*

The Law Reports of Tanzania. (1979).

Lawrence, Peter. (1973 [1971]) "The Garia of the Madang District." In *Politics in New Guinea,* edited by Ronald Berndt and Peter Lawrence, 74–93.

Laws of the Sudan. Vol. II, 1978–1979–1980–1981.

Lawson, Edward, ed. (1991) *Encyclopedia of Human Rights.*

Legum, Colin. (1970 [1966]) "The Tragedy in Nigeria." In *African Politics and Society,* edited by Irving Markovitz, 248–251.

Lenin, Vladimir I. (1976 [1917]) *The State and Revolution.*

Lewellen, Ted C. (1992) *Political Anthropology: An Introduction.* 2d ed.

Lewis, I. M. (1955) *Peoples of the Horn of Africa.*

Lienhardt, Godfrey. (1964) *Social Anthropology.*

Lin, Yueh-hwa. (1947) *The Lolo of Liang-shan.* Translated by Ju Shu Pan.

Linton, Ralph. (1936) *The Study of Man: An Introduction.*

Lips, Julius E. (1947) "Naskapi Law." *Transactions of the American Philosophical Society* 37(4): 378–492.

Llewellyn, Karl N., and E. Adamson Hoebel. (1961 [1941]) *The Cheyenne Way.*

Lloyd, Peter C. (1962) *Yoruba Land Law.*

———. (1967) "The Traditional Political System of the Yoruba." In *Comparative Political Systems,* edited by Ronald Cohen and John Middleton, 269–292.

Lowie, Robert H. (1956 [1935]) *The Crow Indians.*

———. (1961 [1920]) *Primitive Society*.

Lukes, Steven. (1974) *Power: A Radical View*.

Maine, Henry Sumner. (1963 [1861]) *Ancient Law*.

———. (1978 [1888]) *International Law: A Series of Lectures Delivered before the University of Cambridge 1887*.

Maitland, F. W. (1936) *Equity*.

Malinowski, Bronislaw. (1959 [1932]) *Crime and Custom in Savage Society*.

———. (1964) "An Anthropological Analysis of War." In *War: Studies from Psychology, Sociology, Anthropology*, edited by Leon Bramson and George W. Goethals, 245–268.

Markovitz, Irving. (1970 [1966]) "Ghana without Nkrumah: The Winter of Discontent." In *African Politics and Society*, edited by Irving Markovitz, 252–265.

Marshall, Lorna. (1967 [1960]) "!Kung Bushman Bands." In *Comparative Political Systems*, edited by Ronald Cohen and John Middleton, 15–43.

Marx, Karl. (1906 [1883, 1885, 1894]) *Capital: A Critique of Political Economy*, edited by Friedrich Engels. Translated by Samuel Moore and Edward Aveling.

Marx, Karl, and Friedrich Engels. (1968) *Karl Marx and Friedrich Engels: Selected Works in One Volume*.

Mayer, Philip, and Iona Mayer. (1965) "Land Law in the Making." In *African Law: Adaptation and Development*, edited by Hilda Kuper and Leo Kuper, 51–78.

Means, Philip Ainsworth. (1931) *Ancient Civilizations of the Andes*.

Messing, Simon D. (1957) *The Highland-Plateau Amhara of Ethiopia*. Ph.D. dissertation, University of Pennsylvania.

Michels, Robert. (1937) "Authority." In *Encyclopedia of the Social Sciences*. Vol. 2.

Middleton, John, and David Tait. (1958) "Introduction." In *Tribes without Rulers*, edited by John Middleton and David Tait, 1–31.

Miers, Suzanne, and Igor Kopytoff, eds. (1977) *Slavery in Africa: Historical and Anthropological Perspectives*.

Ministry of Justice of the Hungarian People's Republic. (1978) *The Statutes of the Hungarian People's Republic, Act IV of 1978 on Criminal Code*.

Montesquieu, C. L. J. de Secondat, Baron de la Brède et de. (1750) *De l'esprit des lois*. Vols. I, II.

Moore, Sally Falk. (1978) *Law as Process*.

Morgan, Lewis Henry. (1851) *League of the Ho-De'-No-Sau-Nee, or Iroquois*.

———. (1963 [1877]) *Ancient Society*.

Morse, Bradford W., ed. (1985) *Aboriginal Peoples and the Law*.

Mosher, Steven W. (1983) *Broken Earth: The Rural Chinese*.

Murdock, George Peter. (1980) *Theories of Illness: A World Survey*.

Murdock, George Peter, et al. (1987) *Outline of Cultural Materials*. 5th ed.

Murphy, Robert F., and Leonard Kasdan. (1959) "The Structure of Parallel Cousin Marriage." *American Anthropologist* 61: 17–29.

Murra, John V. (1967 [1958]) "On Inca Political Structure." In *Comparative Political Systems*, edited by Ronald Cohen and John Middleton, 339–353.

Nader, Laura. (1964) "An Analysis of Zapotec Law Cases." *Ethnology* 3(4): 404–419.

Nader, Laura, and Duane Metzger. (1963) "Conflict Resolution in Two Mexican Communities." *American Anthropologist* 65(3) part 2: 584–592.

Native American Directory. (1982).

Nieboer, Herman J. (1900) *Slavery as an Industrial System.*

Nisbet, Robert. (1973) "Kinship and Political Power in First Century Rome." In *The Social Organization of Law,* edited by Donald Black and Maureen Mileski, 262–277.

Oberg, K. (1940) "The Kingdom of the Ankole in Uganda." In *Comparative Political Systems,* edited by Ronald Cohen and John Middleton, 121–162.

O'Brien, Rita Cruise, ed. (1979) *The Political Economy of Underdevelopment: Dependence in Senegal.*

Offner, Jerome A. (1983) *Law and Politics in Aztec Texcoco.*

The Ordinances of the Northern Territory of Australia, in Force on 1st January 1961. (1961) Vol. II.

Otterbein, Keith F. (1986) *The Ultimate Coercive Sanction: A Cross-Cultural Study of Capital Punishment.*

Otterbein, Keith F., and Charlotte S. Otterbein. (1965) "An Eye for an Eye, a Tooth for a Tooth: A Cross-Cultural Study of Feuding." *American Anthropologist* 67: 1470–1482.

The Ottoman Penal Code, 28 Zilhijeh 1274. (1888) Translated by C. G. Walpole.

Pagès, G. (1933) *A Hamitic Kingdom in the Center of Africa: In Ruanda on the Shores of Lake Kiva (Belgian Congo).* Translated by Bernard Scholl.

Palmer, Stuart. (1965) "Murder and Suicide in Forty Non-Literate Societies." *The Journal of Criminal Law, Criminology, and Police Science* 56: 320–324.

Parker, Arthur Caswell. (1968) *Parker on the Iroquois: Iroquois Uses of Maize and Other Food Plants, the Code of Handsome Lake, the Seneca Prophet, the Constitution of the Five Nations.* Edited by William N. Fenton.

Patterson, Orlando. (1982) *Slavery and Social Death: A Comparative Study.*

Paulme, Denise. (1940) *Social Organization of the Dogon.* Translated by Frieda Schutze.

Pocket Criminal Code and Miscellaneous Statutes. (1987).

The Political Laws of the South African Republic. (1896) Translated by W. A. Macfadyen.

Pollock, Frederick, and Frederic W. Maitland. (1966 [1899]) "Corporation and Person." In *Anthropology and Early Law,* edited by Lawrence Krader, 300–336.

Pospisil, Leopold. (1958) *Kapauku Papuans and Their Law.*

———. (1963) *The Kapauku Papuans of West New Guinea.*

———. (1964) "Law and Societal Structure among the Nunamiut Eskimo." In *Explorations in Cultural Anthropology: Essays in Honor of George Peter Murdock,* edited by Ward H. Goodenough, 395–431.

———. (1974 [1971]) *Anthropology of Law: A Comparative Theory.*

———. (1978) *The Ethnology of Law.*

Poulet, Dom Charles. (1950) *A History of the Catholic Church.* Vol. I. Translated by Sidney A. Raemers.

Pound, Roscoe. (1942) *Social Control through Law.*

———. (1965) *An Introduction to the Philosophy of Law.*

Powell, H. A. (1967 [1960]) "Competitive Leadership in Trobriand Political Organization." In *Comparative Political Systems,* edited by Ronald Cohen and John Middleton, 155–192.

Prefix to Statutes, 1960. (1960).

Pryor, Frederic L. (1977) *The Origins of the Economy.*

Pufendorf, Samuel von. (1927 [1682]) *De Officio Hominus et Civis Juxta Legem Naturalem Libri Duo.* Translated by Frank Gardener Moore.

Ramaga, Philip V. (1993) "The Group Concept in Minority Protection." *Human Rights Quarterly* 15: 575–588.

Rattray, R. S. (1969 [1911]) *Ashanti Law and Constitution.*

The Rhodesian Law Reports, 1966. (1966) Edited by H. G. Squires.

The Rhodesian Law Reports, 1968. (1968) Part 1.

Roberts, John M. (1967) "Oaths, Autonomic Ordeals, and Power." In *Cross-Cultural Approaches,* edited by Clelland S. Ford, 169–195.

Rodman, Margaret, and Mathew Cooper, eds. (1983) *The Pacification of Melanesia.*

Rodman, William. (1985) "'A law unto Themselves': Legal Innovation in Ambae, Vanuatu." *American Ethnologist* 12(4): 603–624.

Ross, Marc H. (1983) "Political Decision-Making and Conflict: Additional Cross-Cultural Codes." *Ethnology* 22: 169–192.

Rubin, Vera, and Arthur Tuden, eds. (1977) *Comparative Perspectives on Slavery in New World Plantation Societies.*

Russell, Elbert W. (1972) "Factors of Human Aggression: A Cross-Cultural Factor Analysis of Characteristics Related to Warfare and Crime." *Behavior Science Notes* 7: 275–312.

Rwezaura, Barthazar Aloys. (1985) *Traditional Family Law and Change in Tanzania: A Study of the Kuria Social System.*

Sahlins, Marshall. (1968) *Tribesman.*

Savigny, Friedrich Karl von. (1831) *On the Vocation of Our Age for Legislation and Jurisprudence.* Translated by Abraham Hayward.

Sawyer, Roger. (1986) *Slavery in the Twentieth Century.*

Schapera, Isaac. (1970 [1938]) *A Handbook of Tswana Law and Custom.*

Schlesinger, Rudolf B. (1980) *Comparative Law: Cases—Text—Materials.* 4th ed.

Scott, James C. (1985) *Weapons of the Weak: Everyday Forms of Peasant Resistance.*

Seidler, Michael. (1990) *Samuel Pufendorf's On the Natural State of Men.* Translated and annotated by Michael Seidler.

Service, Elman R. (1962) *Primitive Social Organization: An Evolutionary Perspective.* 2d ed.

———. (1975) *Origins of the State and Civilization: The Process of Cultural Evolution.*

Seymour-Smith, Charlotte. (1986) *Dictionary of Anthropology.*

Shepardson, Mary. (1967 [1963]) "The Traditional Authority System of the Navajos." In *Comparative Political Systems,* edited by Ronald Cohen and John Middleton, 143-154.

Spencer, Herbert. (1893) *The Principles of Ethics.* Vol. II.

———. (1899) *The Principles of Sociology.* Vol. II.

Spencer, Robert F. (1959) *The North Alaskan Eskimo.* Smithsonian Institution Bureau of American Ethnology Bulletin 171.

Spicer, Edward H. (1980) *The Yaquis: A Cultural History.*

Spiro, Melford. (1968) "Factionalism and Politics in Village Burma." In *Local-Level Politics,* edited by Marc Swartz, 401-421.

Stark, W. (1960) *Montesquieu: Pioneer of the Sociology of Knowledge.*

Starr, June. (1978) *Dispute and Settlement in Rural Turkey: An Ethnography of Law.*

Stavenhagen, Rodolfo. (1987) "Ethnic Conflict and Human Rights: Their Interrelationship." *Bulletin of Peace Proposals* 18: 507–514.

Steward, Julian. (1955) *Theory of Culture Change: The Methodology of Multilinear Evolution.*

281

Stiefel, Ernst C., Rolf Stürner, and Astrid Stadler. (1991) "The Enforceability of Excessive U.S. Punitive Damage Awards in Germany." *The American Journal of Comparative Law* 39: 779-802.

Stone, Julius. (1950) *The Province and Function of Law.*

Strouthes, Daniel P. (1994) *Change in the Real Property Law of a Cape Breton Island Micmac Band.*

Swartz, Marc, Victor W. Turner, and Arthur Tuden, eds. (1966) *Political Anthropology.*

Swift, Richard. (1969) *International Law: Current and Classic.*

Tanaka, Jiro. (1980) *The San Hinter-Gatherers of the Kalahari.* Translated by David W. Hughes.

Teksbury, William J. (1967) "The Ordeal as a Vehicle for Divine Intervention in Medieval Europe." In *Law and Warfare: Studies in the Anthropology of Conflict,* edited by Paul Bohannan, 267–270.

Territory of Norfolk Island, Consolidated Laws, Being the Norfolk Island Act 1913; the Laws Proclaimed by Proclamation Dated 23rd December, 1913, Which Repealed All Laws Heretofore in Force in Norfolk Island; and Ordinances Made under the Norfolk Island Act 1913, and Rules, Regulations, By-Laws, Proclamations and Notifications Made or Issued under Such Ordinances as in Force on 31st December, 1934 (1934).

Tooker, Elisabeth. (1978) "The League of the Iroquois: Its History, Politics, and Ritual." In *Handbook of North American Indians.* Vol. 15, *Northeast,* edited by Bruce G. Trigger and William Sturtevant, 418–441.

Treaties and Other International Agreements of the United States of America, 1776-1949. (n.d.) Vol. 10, Nepal-Peru. Compiled under the direction of Charles I. Bevans, LL.B.

Treaty between His Majesty and the President of the Chinese Republic Together with Other Documents Relating to the Chinese Customs Tariff, & c., Nanking, December 20, 1928. (1929).

Turnbull, Colin M. (1965) *Wayward Servants: The Two Worlds of the African Pygmies.*

Tyler, Stephen A. (1973) *India: An Anthropological Perspective.*

Van den Berghe, Pierre. (1981) *The Ethnic Phenomenon.*

Van Dyke, Vernon. (1985) *Human Rights, Ethnicity, and Discrimination.*

Van Wolferen, Karel. (1989) *The Enigma of Japanese Power.*

Vincentnathan, S. George. (1992) "The Social Construction of Order and Disorder in Two South Indian Communities." *Journal of Legal Pluralism and Unofficial Law* 32: 65–102.

Vivelo, Frank Robert. (1978) *Cultural Anthropology: A Basic Introduction.*

Voslensky, Michael. (1984) *Nomenklatura: The Soviet Ruling Class.* Translated by Eric Mosbacher.

Wallace, Anthony F. C. (1956) "Revitalization Movements." *American Anthropologist* 58: 264–281.

Wallerstein, Immanuel. (1974) *The Modern World-System I: Capitalist Agriculture and the Origins of the European World-Economy in the Sixteenth Century.*

———. (1980) *The Modern World-System II: Mercantilism and the Consolidation of the European World-Economy 1600–1750.*

Watson, James B. (1973 [1971]) "Tairora: The Politics of Despotism in a Small Society." In *Politics in New Guinea,* edited by Ronald M. Berndt and Peter Lawrence, 224–275.

Weber, Max. (1947) *The Theory of Social and Economic Organization.*

———. (1958) *From Max Weber*, edited and translated by H. H. Gerth and C. Wright Mills.

Weltfish, Gene. (1965) *The Lost Universe: Pawnee Life and Culture.*

Whalen, Lucille. (1989) *Human Rights: A Reference Handbook.*

Whewell, William. (1853) *Grotius on War and Peace.* Vol. I.

Whiting, Beatrice B. (1950) *Paiute Sorcery.*

Whiting, John W. M. (1967) "Sorcery, Sin and the Superego: A Cross-Cultural Study of Some Mechanisms of Social Control." In *Cross-Cultural Approaches*, edited by Clelland S. Ford, 147–168.

Willigen, John van, and V. C. Channa. (1991) "Law, Custom, and Crimes against Women: The Problem of Dowry Death in India." *Human Organization* 50(4): 369–377.

Wilson, Monica. (1967 [1949]) "Nyakyusa Age-Villages." In *Comparative Political Systems*, edited by Ronald Cohen and John Middleton, 217-227.

Winthrop, Robert H. (1991) *Dictionary of Concepts in Cultural Anthropology.*

Wittfogel, Karl. (1957) *Oriental Despotism: A Comparative Study of Total Power.*

Wolf, Eric. (1982) *Europe and the People without History.*

Worsley, Peter M. (1959) "Cargo Cults." *Scientific American* 200: 117–128.

ILLUSTRATION
CREDITS

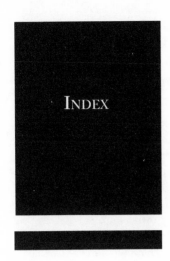

INDEX